The GRE® Test For Dummies, 6th Edition

D0470694

Achieving Success on the Verbal Section

Following are several tips and approaches you can use to increase your chances of success on the GRE's Verbal section. First, we present you with a couple general tips:

- Use roots, prefixes, and suffixes to determine the gist of an unfamiliar word.
- Guess quickly if you're stumped. The computer won't let you go on until you've marked and confirmed an answer, and believe it or not, answering a few questions incorrectly hurts your score less than not finishing a section.

Approach Antonym questions by

- Creating an approximate definition of the word in your mind
- Predicting the obvious opposite
- Remembering that words can have more than one meaning

Avoid getting stuck on a Reading Comprehension question by following these tips:

- Choose positive or neutral answers, not negative ones.
- Guess quickly and move on when you encounter Roman numeral and negative/exception questions, because they're often tricky and time consuming.
- Avoid picking an answer simply because it's true. Always make certain that it answers the question correctly.

When faced with Analogies,

- Create a sentence that shows the relationship between the two words and then use that sentence on each answer choice.
- Beware of answers with inverse relationships (for example, part to whole when the question was whole to part).

For Sentence Completion questions, be sure to

- Read the entire sentence to get its gist before looking at the individual blanks.
- Search for key connector words (such as *because, although,* and *however*) that may change the meaning of the sentence from what you'd expect.
- Predict whether the blanks need positive or negative words.

And last, but most certainly not least, remember:

This test is rated PG — Proctor Guarded.

Proctors have been genetically altered to have eyes in the backs of their heads; they'll catch you if you peek at this cheat sheet during the GRE. Learn it, then burn it.

Reviewing Tips for Computerized GRE Success

You can successfully tackle the computerized GRE by remembering these three tips (and by reviewing the info in Chapter 3):

- The first five or so questions in each section are critical, so take your time to answer them correctly.
- You can't skip and go back to a question, so guess quickly and move on when you're stumped. *Remember:* You benefit from answering every question more than you lose by missing a few.
- Keep an eye on the clock and sprint to the end, being sure to fill in something for every answer before time runs out.

For Dummies: Bestselling Book Series for Beginners

The GRE® Test For Dummies, 6th Edition

Cheat Sheet

Doing Well on the Math Section

Success on the GRE's Math section has a great deal to do with applying logic and common sense. Here are some tips for how to do your best on this section of the test:

Before you start,

- ✔ Lose the calculator (it's not allowed). The proctor will provide scratch paper.
- ✔ Remember that the GRE tests algebra, geometry, and arithmetic, not calculus or trigonometry.
- ✔ Memorize formulas before you take the test. The GRE doesn't provide them.

Following are some tips for those tricky Quantitative Comparison questions:

- ✔ Triple-check your answer before hitting the Confirm button on the computer, because the answers to QC questions often aren't the obvious, first-response answers.
- ✔ Remember that the answer choices are the same for every question. Choose A if Column A is greater; B if Column B is greater; C if the two columns are equal; and D if insufficient information is given. E is never a choice in the QC-question realm.
- ✔ If the columns seem to be equal, do the required calculations to *prove* that they are.
- ✔ Play the "what if" game by plugging in first 1, then 2, 0, –1, –2, and ½. If the answer *depends* on what you plug in for the variable, choose D.

And now for some Problem Solving tips:

- ✔ Note what the question specifically asks you to find: perimeter, area, length, degree, fraction, percentage, and so on.
- ✔ Before you begin working on a problem, read the answer choices. You may be able to estimate and answer without working out the solution.
- ✔ Plug answer choices into the question to see which one works. Do the easy choices first; you may not have to do the hard ones.

Tackling the Analytical Writing Section

When you sit down to begin the Analytical Writing section of the GRE, remember that you must present your perspective on an issue.

- ✔ Answer the question specifically, making your opinion known to the readers in the introductory paragraph.
- ✔ Use all 45 minutes to create a three- to five-paragraph essay, giving supporting reasons and examples for your perspective (and anticipating and addressing counterarguments).
- ✔ Create a final paragraph that summarizes, not merely repeats, the points of your essay.

You also have to analyze an argument.

- ✔ Identify the assumptions the writer is making and discuss how reasonable they are.
- ✔ Provide outside counterexamples or supporting information to strengthen or weaken the argument.
- ✔ Avoid giving your opinion on the topic; the point here is to discuss how well-argued the essay is as written.

For Dummies: Bestselling Book Series for Beginners

The GRE® Test

FOR

DUMMIES®

6TH EDITION

The GRE® Test

FOR

DUMMIES®

6TH EDITION

by Michelle Rose Gilman,
Veronica Saydak, and
Suzee Vlk
Author of *The SAT I For Dummies, The ACT For Dummies,*
The GMAT For Dummies

WILEY

Wiley Publishing, Inc.

The GRE® Test For Dummies,® 6th Edition

Published by
Wiley Publishing, Inc.
909 Third Avenue
New York, NY 10022
www.wiley.com

WILEY

About the Authors

Michelle Rose Gilman

"I get up every morning determined to both change the world and have one heck of a good time. Sometimes this makes planning the day difficult." — E.B. White

Michelle Rose Gilman is proud to be known as Noah's mom (Hi, Noah!). A graduate of the University of South Florida, Michelle found her niche early — at 19 she was already working with emotionally disturbed and learning-disabled students in hospital settings. At 21, she made the trek to California. There she discovered her passion for helping teenage students become more successful in school and life. What started as a small tutoring business in the garage of her California home quickly expanded and grew to the point where traffic control was necessary on her residential street.

Today, Michelle is the Founder and CEO of the Fusion Learning Center/Fusion Academy, a private school and tutoring/test-prep facility in Solana Beach, California, serving more than 2,000 students per year. She has taught tens of thousands of students since 1988. In her spare time, Michelle created the Mentoring Approach to Learning and authored *The ACT For Dummies, Pre-Calculus For Dummies, AP Biology For Dummies, AP Chemistry For Dummies, Chemistry Workbook For Dummies,* and *Pre-Calculus Workbook For Dummies.* She currently specializes in motivating the unmotivatable adolescent, comforting shell-shocked parents, and assisting her staff of 27 teachers.

Michelle lives by the following motto:

"There are people content with longing; I am not one of them."

Veronica Saydak

Veronica graduated from the University of San Diego with a Bachelors Degree in English. She found her real education in travel and seeing the world. She has traveled to more than a dozen countries, studying various cultures through their literature and lifestyles. She has been a highly coveted English teacher, specializing in writing, for more than seven years.

Currently, Veronica is the English Department Head at Fusion Learning Center/Fusion Academy, where she is responsible for overseeing a staff of English teachers and ensuring high educational standards, as well as teaching her students on a one-to-one basis. Her wit and humor might not solve the world's problems, but they definitely make the world feel lighter. She is the coauthor of *The ACT For Dummies.*

Veronica takes the following advice from one of her favorite authors, Goethe:

"Certain defects are necessary for the existence of individuality."

Suzee Vlk

"I'm not a complete idiot. Parts of me are missing."

Although more likely to admit to being a used-car salesperson, Suzee Vlk was a test-prep specialist from 1975 until her death in 2003, working her way through graduate business school and law school teaching courses in ACT, SAT I, GRE, GMAT, and LSAT preparation. By her own description, Suzee found the paranoia and take-no-prisoners mindset required for doing well on the ACT a big help in developing cutthroat tactics to use in the boardroom or courtroom. Eventually, she became president of Suzee Vlk Test Prep and taught thousands of students in dozens of courses at universities and private corporations. She wrote material used in SAT and GRE preparation software and videos, and her prep books for the ACT and other standardized exams have been published worldwide.

Suzee lived by the following motto, which she delighted in sharing with others:

"Madness takes its toll. Please have exact change ready."

Dedication

This book is humbly dedicated to the thousands of students who have, over the years, passed through the Fusion Learning Center/Fusion Academy. When the teacher is ready, the right student appears. You have taught us well. And to the memory of Suzee Vlk, the original author, whose humor, wit, and intelligence live on in these pages.

Author Acknowledgments

We would like to thank agent Bill Gladstone of Waterside Productions in Cardiff, California, for giving us the opportunity to revise this book. Special thanks to Christopher Burger (the Book Fairy) for being a delightful perfectionist and for meticulously reviewing and updating the math sections. Additionally, thanks to Peter Mikulecky, our technical editor, who strived to get us to try to be as smart as him (it didn't work). Much thanks also to Natalie Harris for deciphering the truth amongst the manuscript chaos. Finally, a shoutout to Lindsay Lefevere, our acquisitions editor, who, for reasons unknown, continues to want to work with us.

Publisher's Acknowledgments

We're proud of this book; please send us your comments through our Dummies online registration form located at www.dummies.com/register/.

Some of the people who helped bring this book to market include the following:

Acquisitions, Editorial, and Media Development

Project Editor: Natalie Faye Harris

Acquisitions Editors: Kathy Cox, Lindsay Sandman Lefevere

Copy Editors: Laura Peterson Nussbaum, Jennifer Tebbe

General Reviewers: Don and Diana Garner, Peter Mikulecky

Editorial Supervisor and Reprint Editor: Carmen Krikorian

Editorial Manager: Christine Meloy Beck

Editorial Assistants: Courtney Allen, Nadine Bell, David Lutton

Cartoons: Rich Tennant, www.the5thwave.com

Composition

Project Coordinator: Patrick Redmond

Layout and Graphics: Carrie A. Cesavice, Reuben W. Davis, Ronald Terry, Christine Williams

Proofreaders: Melissa Cossell, Henry Lazarek

Indexer: Broccoli Information Management

Publishing and Editorial for Consumer Dummies

Diane Graves Steele, Vice President and Publisher, Consumer Dummies

Joyce Pepple, Acquisitions Director, Consumer Dummies

Kristin Ferguson-Wagstaffe, Product Development Director, Consumer Dummies

Ensley Eikenburg, Associate Publisher, Travel

Kelly Regan, Editorial Director, Travel

Publishing for Technology Dummies

Andy Cummings, Vice President and Publisher, Dummies Technology/General User

Composition Services

Gerry Fahey, Vice President of Production Services

Debbie Stailey, Director of Composition Services

Contents at a Glance

Introduction 1

Part I: An Aerial View: Putting the GRE into Perspective 7
Chapter 1: Know Your Enemy: What the GRE Looks Like 9
Chapter 2: Knowledge Is Power: Getting the Advantage 17
Chapter 3: Getting Familiar with the Computerized GRE 25
Chapter 4: Starting with the Easy Stuff: Analogies 29
Chapter 5: The Dirty Dozen: Analogy Practice Questions 37

Part II: A Word to the Wise: Verbal Questions 45
Chapter 6: If Opposites Attract, Why Are Antonyms So Repulsive? 47
Chapter 7: Unattractive Opposites: Antonym Practice Questions 53
Chapter 8: Finishing What You Start: Sentence Completions 59
Chapter 9: Reality Check: Sentence Completion Practice Questions 69
Chapter 10: Readings That Can Affect Your Future: Blood Pressure, Astrology, and the GRE 73
Chapter 11: Words to Help You Score: GRE Vocabulary 87
Chapter 12: Practice What We Preach: Reading Comprehension Practice Questions 97

Part III: Two Years of Math in a Handful of Pages: The Dreaded Math Review 103
Chapter 13: More Figures than a Beauty Pageant: Geometry Review 105
Chapter 14: Gotta Catch Some (Xs, Ys, and) Zs: Algebra and Other Sleeping Aids 127
Chapter 15: Miscellaneous Math You Probably Already Know 143

Part IV: Your Number's Up: Math Questions 169
Chapter 16: The Incomparable Quantitative Comparisons 171
Chapter 17: Putting It All Together: QC Practice Questions 183
Chapter 18: Real Math at Last: Problem Solving 189
Chapter 19: A Chance to Show Off: Problem Solving Practice Questions 193

Part V: Getting into Analysis: Analytical Writing 197
Chapter 20: Analytical Writing 199
Chapter 21: Do You Have the Write Stuff? Analytical Writing Practice Questions 209

Part VI: It All Comes Down to This: Full-Length Practice GREs 217
Chapter 22: How to Ruin a Perfectly Good Day, Part I: Practice Exam 1 219
Chapter 23: Practice Exam 1: Answers and Explanations 245
Chapter 24: How to Ruin a Perfectly Good Day, Part II: Practice Exam 2 259
Chapter 25: Practice Exam 2: Answers and Explanations 289

Part VII: The Part of Tens..303

Chapter 26: Ten False Rumors about the GRE..305

Chapter 27: Ten Stupid Ways to Mess Up Your GRE...309

Chapter 28: Ten Relaxation Techniques to Try before and during the GRE.................313

Index..317

Table of Contents

Introduction 1

About This Book...1

Pardon Me for Having a Life: Who Has Time for This?.................................2

    Time required to go through the GRE lectures 3

    Time required to go through the practice GREs 3

How This Book Is Organized...4

    Part I: An Aerial View: Putting the GRE into Perspective 4

    Part II: A Word to the Wise: Verbal Questions 4

    Part III: Two Years of Math in a Handful of Pages: The Dreaded Math Review 4

    Part IV: Your Number's Up: Math Questions 4

    Part V: Getting into Analysis: Analytical Writing 4

    Part VI: It All Comes Down to This: Full-Length Practice GREs.................4

    Part VII: The Part of Tens 5

Icons and Conventions Used in This Book 5

Part 1: An Aerial View: Putting the GRE into Perspective 7

Chapter 1: Know Your Enemy: What the GRE Looks Like 9

Looking at the Breakdown (To Avoid Having One!)..................................10

Scoring 101 11

    Figuring out your scores 11

    Knowing how your scores measure up 12

    Playing the guessing game 12

    Discovering the number of correct answers you need for specific scores 12

Understanding When Your Answers Don't Count: The Possible Unscored Section........13

Gimme a Break! The GRE Intermissions 14

Chapter 2: Knowledge Is Power: Getting the Advantage.....................17

Beating the Clock: Tips on Timing 17

Scratching like a Crazed Chicken 18

Packing Your Bags on Test Day 18

You Can't Take It with You 19

Déjà Vu: Repeating the Test 20

Experience Counts: Using Older Scores 21

Taking Care of Yourself before the Test 21

    Staying active...21

    Eating well 21

    Discovering relaxation 21

    Avoiding artificial study aids (drugs) 22

Approaching a Question with Confidence 22

    Anticipating test questions 22

    Changing your attitude..22

    Remembering that this is only a test 23

Chapter 3: Getting Familiar with the Computerized GRE.................................**25**

Bracing Yourself for the Tutorials...25
Knowing the Rules so You Don't Sink Your Score...26
What You See Is What You Get: On-Screen Icons...26
Blacking In the Bubbles: How to Select Your Answers.................................27

Chapter 4: Starting with the Easy Stuff: Analogies **29**

If Only All Relationships Were This Easy: The Format.................................29
Approaching Analogy-Solving Perfection: A Two-Step Program.................30
They Really Are Out to Get You: Avoiding Traps and Tricks with a Few Good Tips.......31
Turn a verb into an infinitive...31
Determine the part of speech of the question word............................31
Look for the salient features of a word..32
Work backward..33
Identify common relationships...33
Use roots, prefixes, and suffixes..33
The Terminator: Eliminating Idiotic Answers...36
Déjà Vu Review...36

Chapter 5: The Dirty Dozen: Analogy Practice Questions.......................**37**

Part II: A Word to the Wise: Verbal Questions *45*

Chapter 6: If Opposites Attract, Why Are Antonyms So Repulsive?.........**47**

Is That All There Is? The Format..47
Let's Get This Over with Fast: The Approach..48
What to Do When You Ain't Got a Clue..49
Bad Things Come in Small Packages: Tricks, Traps, and Tips.....................49
Ignore the synonym...49
Use roots, prefixes, and suffixes..49
Memorize connotation cards...50
Don't anticipate and misread..50
Peroration (A Summing Up)..51

Chapter 7: Unattractive Opposites: Antonym Practice Questions............**53**

Chapter 8: Finishing What You Start: Sentence Completions **59**

Recognizing Sentence Completion Questions..59
Looking at the Sentence and Drawing a Blank..60
Read the entire sentence..60
If possible, predict words to fit the blanks 60
Insert the answer choices..61
Blowing Sentences Away: Dynamite Traps 'n' Tricks...................................62
Remember that connections count 62
Use your crystal ball...62
Guess and go..63
Getting Back to Your Roots...64
A Sense of Completion: Review...66
Approaches...66
Tricks 66

Chapter 9: Reality Check: Sentence Completion Practice Questions.......**69**

Chapter 10: Readings That Can Affect Your Future: Blood Pressure, Astrology, and the GRE 73

What Do They Look Like? Reading Comprehension Passages and Their Questions 73
Acing the Three Commonly Tested Reading Comprehension Passages.........................74
  Beam me up, Scotty! Biological and physical science passages 74
  It's not a disease: The social sciences passage...75
  Gimme a break, I'm only human: The humanities passages.................................76
All or Nothing: Questions to Take Seriously; Questions to Laugh Off............................77
  It's the attitude, dude: The attitude or tone question 77
  What's the big idea? Main idea or best title questions..79
  Don't pester me with details: The detail or fact question 80
  The power of positive thinking: Negative or exception questions 80
  Toga! Toga! Toga! The Roman numeral question...81
  Journey into the deep: Text-referenced questions 81
  The swing vote: Extending the author's reasoning 82
Something Up Your Sleeve: Tips for Making GRE Life a Little Easier 83
  Be positive or neutral, not negative..83
  Choose answers containing key words 83
  Be wishy-washy, not dramatic 83
The Final Paragraph: Review 84
  Approaches 84
  Tips 85

Chapter 11: Words to Help You Score: GRE Vocabulary 87

The Long but Easy Journey: Studying Vocabulary 87
The Paramount 300: Memorizing the Most Common Words..88

Chapter 12: Practice What We Preach: Reading Comprehension Practice Questions 97

Passage I..97
Passage II..100

Part III: Two Years of Math in a Handful of Pages: The Dreaded Math Review 103

Chapter 13: More Figures than a Beauty Pageant: Geometry Review 105

An Angular Look at Geometry 105
Triangular Tidbits 108
  Working with similar figures 110
  Calculating a triangle's area and perimeter 111
  Understanding the Pythagorean theorem...112
  Recognizing Pythagorean triples...112
Thanks 4 Nothing: Quadrilaterals 114
  Quaint quads: Bizarre quadrilaterals 115
  Leftovers again: Shaded-area problems 115
Missing Parrots and Other Polly-Gones: More Polygons 116
  Determining total interior angle measure 117
  Finding one interior angle 117
Getting the Total Picture: Volume & Total Surface Area 118
  Calculating volume 118
  Figuring out total surface area..119
I'm Too Much of a Klutz for Coordinate Geometry..120
Running Around in Circles 120

Chapter 14: Gotta Catch Some (Xs, Ys, and) Zs: Algebra and Other Sleeping Aids 127

The Powers That Be: Bases and Exponents 127
Keepin' It in Proportion: Ratios 130
Things Aren't What They Seem: Symbolism.............................132
Abracadabra: Algebra 135
    Alphabet soup: Solving for x 136
    Curses! FOILed again 137
    Fact or fiction: Factoring 138
Too Hip to Be Square: Roots and Radicals..............................139
    Adding and subtracting 139
    Multiplying and dividing...139
    Working inside out 140
Probably Probability...140

Chapter 15: Miscellaneous Math You Probably Already Know 143

DIRTy Math: Distance, Rate, and Time....................................143
It All Averages Out: Averages..144
    Solving missing term average problems 145
    Working with weighted averages.....................................147
Percentage Panic..148
    Ignorance is bliss: Converting percentages to decimals or fractions 149
    Life has its ups and downs: Determining percent increase/decrease 149
Ready, Set, Go: Number Sets 151
Prime Time: Prime and Composite Numbers 152
I'm All Mixed Up: Mixture Problems 153
Greed Is Great: Interest Problems 154
All Work and No Play: Work Problems 155
Reading between the Lines: Absolute Value 156
Smooth Operator: Order of Operations 157
Measuring Up: Units of Measurement.....................................157
What's the Point: Decimals..159
    Adding and subtracting decimals 159
    Multiplying decimals 160
    Dividing decimals 160
Broken Hearts, Broken Numbers: Fractions.............................160
    Adding or subtracting fractions 160
    Multiplying fractions 161
    Dividing fractions 162
    Playing with mixed numbers 162
The Stats Don't Lie: Statistics..162
    Median 162
    Mode 163
    Range 163
A Picture Is Worth a Thousand Words: Graphs.........................164
Math Concepts You Absolutely MUST Know.............................166
    Angles 166
    Circles 166
    Common Pythagorean ratios 167
    Exponents..167
    FOIL method of algebra 167
    Graphing..167
    Linear algebraic equations..167
    Ratios 168
    Square roots 168
    Symbolism 168

Part IV: Your Number's Up: Math Questions..............*169*

Chapter 16: The Incomparable Quantitative Comparisons 171
Where Did All the Answers Go? The QC Format.................................171
As Easy as π: Approaching QC Questions..172
Gotchas and Other Groaners: Tips, Traps, and Tricks.......................173
    Remembering that equal appearances can be deceiving 173
    Keeping an eye out for scale...173
    Testing your artistic abilities — or not 175
    Avoiding distraction from a pretty picture 176
    Canceling out identical quantities 177
    Weighing the columns...177
    Plugging in the Sacred Six 178
    Throwing down a hundred 179
    Inserting variety when working with multiple variables..............180
Familiarity Breeds Content(ment): A Review 181
    Approach...181
    Tips 181

Chapter 17: Putting It All Together: QC Practice Questions...................183

Chapter 18: Real Math at Last: Problem Solving.................................189
Strategic Planning: The Attack Strategy..189
Three Common-Sense Suggestions for Problem Solving 190
    Eliminate illogical (read: stupid) answer choices 190
    Don't choose a "close enough" answer 190
    Give your pencil a workout 191
I'm Sure I Know You from Somewhere: A Quick Review 191
    Approach...191
    Tricks 191

Chapter 19: A Chance to Show Off: Problem Solving Practice Questions.............193

Part V: Getting into Analysis: Analytical Writing........................*197*

Chapter 20: Analytical Writing...199
Your Opinion Counts: Present Your Perspective on an Issue 199
Full of Sound and Fury: Analyze an Argument...................................200
Half a Dozen Is Better than None: Scoring..201
    Hunting for the next Hemingway: What evaluators look for 201
    Providing pointless information: What drives evaluators crazy......202
Presenting Your Perspective in a Well-Wrapped Package 203
    Paragraph one...203
    Paragraph two 203
    Paragraphs three and four 204
    Paragraphs five and six 205
    Paragraph seven..205
    Time's up 205
Analyzing an Argument in Six Paragraphs 205
    Paragraph one...206
    Paragraphs two, three, and four...206
    Paragraph five...206
    Paragraph six 207
    Time's up 207

Chapter 21: Do You Have the Write Stuff? Analytical Writing Practice Questions 209

    Present Your Perspective on an Issue 210
        Answer explanations 210
        Sample answer one: Score 6 (outstanding) or 5 (strong) 210
        Reader comments on the 6/5 essay 211
        Sample answer two: Score 4 (adequate) or 3 (limited) 211
        Reader comments on the 4/3 essay 212
        Sample answer three: Score 2 (seriously flawed) or
          1 (fundamentally deficient) 212
        Reader comments on the 2/1 essay 213
    Analyze an Argument 213
        Answer explanations 213
        Sample answer one: Score 6 (outstanding) or 5 (strong) 213
        Reader comments on the 6/5 essay 214
        Sample answer two: Score 4 (adequate) or 3 (limited) 214
        Reader comments on the 4/3 essay 215
        Sample answer three: Score 2 (seriously flawed) or
          1 (fundamentally deficient) 215
        Reader comments on the 2/1 essay 215

Part VI: It All Comes Down to This: Full-Length Practice GREs 217

Chapter 22: How to Ruin a Perfectly Good Day, Part I: Practice Exam 1 219

    Answer Sheet 221
    Analytical Writing: Present Your Perspective on an Issue 223
    Analytical Writing: Analyze an Argument 228
    Verbal Section 233
    Math Section 239
    Answer Key for Practice Exam 1 243

Chapter 23: Practice Exam 1: Answers and Explanations 245

    Verbal Section 245
    Math Section 250
    Analytical Writing Sections 257

Chapter 24: How to Ruin a Perfectly Good Day, Part II: Practice Exam 2 259

    Answer Sheet 261
    Analytical Writing: Present Your Perspective on an Issue 263
    Analytical Writing: Analyze an Argument 270
    Verbal Section 277
    Math Section 283
    Answer Key for Practice Exam 2 287

Chapter 25: Practice Exam 2: Answers and Explanations 289

    Verbal Section 289
    Math Section 294
    Analytical Writing Sections 301

Part VII: The Part of Tens *303*

Chapter 26: Ten False Rumors about the GRE 305
Missing the First Few Questions Gives You an Easier Test and a Better Score 305
The GRE Has a Passing Score 305
Your Score Won't Improve if You Keep Retaking the GRE 306
You Can't Study for the GRE 306
Your GRE Score Will Be about the Same as Your High School SAT Score 306
The GRE Tests IQ 307
You Must Pass Certain Classes to Take the GRE 307
You Can Take the GRE on Your Own Computer at Home 307
You Can Bring Your Own Laptop to the Testing Center 308
Computer Geniuses Have an Unfair Advantage on the GRE 308

Chapter 27: Ten Stupid Ways to Mess Up Your GRE 309
Cheating 309
Losing Concentration 309
Not Taking Advantage of the Breaks 310
Obsessing about the Previous Sections 310
Panicking over Time 310
Rushing through the Confirm Step 310
Scheduling the Test at the Same Time as Your Best Friend 311
Stressing Out over Your Computer Skills (Or Lack Thereof) 311
Trying to Keep Track of the Question Breakdown 311
Worrying about the Hard Problems 312

Chapter 28: Ten Relaxation Techniques to Try before and during the GRE 313
Breathe Deeply 313
Rotate Your Head 313
Rotate Your Scalp 314
Cross and Roll Your Eyes 314
Cup Your Eyes 314
Hunch and Roll Your Shoulders 314
Shake Out Your Hands 314
Extend and Push Out Your Legs 314
Curtail Negative Thoughts 315
Visualize before the Test or during a Break 315

Index *317*

Introduction

Welcome to *The GRE Test For Dummies,* 6th Edition. Don't take the title personally. Being a dummy is good; it just means you're normal. Unfortunately, the GRE is anything *but* normal. As we've discovered in more than two decades of fighting the GRE wars, the GRE has no connection to the Real World. When you were given the dire news that you had to take the GRE to get into graduate school, you probably flashed back to the SAT (lovingly known as Sadists Against Teenagers) that you had to take to get into college. Although the two tests share some similarities (both exams are the leading causes of ulcers, migraines, and decisions to become a Bora Bora beachcomber), they're more dissimilar than similar.

The primary dissimilarity has to do with your familiarity with the material. In high school, instructors often "teach to the test." They know that their students are going to take the SAT, know the kids themselves, and teach them what will be on the test and how to take the exam. In college, you're on your own. Your professors may not have any idea who you are ("The kid in the *I'm only here for the beer* T-shirt who sits in the upper row of the lecture hall? In our mind we call him Bud, but we don't know him at all."), and they almost certainly aren't going to take time away from class to discuss the traps and tricks on the GRE. In addition, you've spent the last few years of college working on the courses specific to your major: invertebrate biology, lifestyles of the upper Botswana natives, or maybe sociological and psychological implications of domestic dissonance. It has been a long, long time since you've taken basic algebra, geometry, and arithmetic (found in the math portions of the GRE) or vocabulary and logic (found in the verbal and analytical portions of the GRE). And what if you're no longer in college? No doubt about it; you need some help. And a specialist is in the best position to provide the skills you need. Think of this book as a SWAT team that you can call in when the situation gets desperate.

Like a SWAT team, this book aims to deal with the crisis efficiently, do the job, save the day, and get you out as quickly as possible. We know that you have a life you want to get back to. The goal of this book is to help you learn what you need and can use on the GRE — period. No extra garbage is thrown in to impress you with esoteric facts; no filler is added to make this book the fattest one on the market. If you need a doorstop, go pick up the New York City telephone directory. If you need a quick 'n' easy guide to surviving the GRE, you're in the right place.

About This Book

It's Us versus Them. Who are They? The creators of the GRE, those gnomes in green eyeshades. The next time you're trying to get away from a *soporific dolt* (sleep-inducing blockhead) at a party, answer the question, "So, what do you do for a living?" with the response, "I create questions for the GRE." That conversation-stopper is guaranteed to send any *paramour manqué* (would-be sweetie) running and screaming into the night.

In *The GRE Test For Dummies,* 6th Edition, we show you how to approach each type of question, recognize the traps that are built into the questions, and master the tricks that help you to avoid those traps. The book is full of Gotchas! we (test-prep tutors since the Dawn of Time) have seen test-takers fall for repeatedly. In this book, you learn to think the GRE way (don't worry; it's not permanent) in order to identify the point behind the various styles and types of questions and to figure out what each style and type is trying to test. This book also gives you a review of the basics (from math formulas and common roots to prefixes and suffixes useful for improving your vocabulary), along with a laugh or two to make absorbing the material as painless as possible.

If you only use this book to prop open a window or serve as a booster seat for a toddler, you won't get the most out of it. We suggest two alternatives:

- ✔ **Fine-tune your skills.** Turn to specific sections for specific information and help. The organization of this book makes it very easy to find the type of math question you always have trouble with, suggestions for answering Reading Comprehension questions without having finished the passage, and tricks for guessing. If you're in college classes or a career in which you use this jazz every day (maybe you're a math major at school or you teach high school English classes) and need just a nudge in one or two areas, you can work through those sections only.

- ✔ **Start from scratch.** Read through the whole book. Actually, we want you to follow this approach. No matter how well you do on a section, you can improve. Believing you should work on your weakest sections only is a mistake. The 50 points you gain in your mediocre section by skimming through the suggestions in this book are just as worthwhile as the 50 points you get by grunting, groaning, and sweating through your most difficult area. If you have the time, do yourself a favor and read the book from cover to cover. Besides, you don't want to miss any of our jokes, now do you?

The GRE Test For Dummies, 6th Edition, is simple and straightforward enough for first-time GRE victims, er, test-takers that they can understand the entire exam and do well right out of the starting gate. But it's also detailed and sophisticated enough that veterans — folks who've taken the exam once or twice before but aren't resting on their laurels (sounds painful, anyway) — can learn the more complicated information necessary to get those truly excellent scores.

Note to nontraditional students: We're aware of the fact that you may not be a 21-year-old college senior taking this exam to go into graduate school right after college. You may have been out of college so long that your *children* are 21-year-old seniors! Maybe you've just decided to go back to grad school after a long career or after raising a family, and you need help getting back into math and verbal stuff that you had in what seems like another lifetime. We sympathize with you; dealing with nonagons, quadratic equations, and analogies again is tough. Don't despair; you can get outside help, especially in math, which is one of the first bits of knowledge to fade when people get away from school. Call a community college or even a high school (the math on this exam doesn't exceed what's taught in upper-division high school math classes, depressing as that may seem to you as you're sweating through it). Ask for help finding a tutor or for suggestions on finding a quick review course in your area. You can also call your local library for assistance.

Pardon Me for Having a Life: Who Has Time for This?

You have school or work, sports or other hobbies, family responsibilities and, oh yes, something that vaguely resembles a social life. How on Earth are you going to fit in studying for the GRE? The following sections break it down for you in a nice, neat little package.

Time required to go through the GRE lectures

Buying this book was brilliant. (Okay, so your roommate, your spouse, or some significant other bought it and tossed it at you with the snide comment, "Hey, you can sure use all the help you can get." Whatever.) How much time should you take to go through this book? We suggest 25 hours.

Each subject (Antonyms, Analogies, Sentence Completions, Reading Comprehension, Quantitative Comparisons, Problem Solving, and Analytical Writing) includes a chapter on the format, approach, and traps and tricks for that particular type of question. Following each lecture, we include a quiz chapter featuring a sampling of questions that tests what you learned in that lecture. The detailed answer explanations point out the traps you may have fallen for and the tips you should've used to avoid the traps. You discover which questions to skip (as either too hard or too time-consuming) and which to double-check. You should spend about two hours per lecture, including the quiz — you're looking at 14 hours total here. The book also includes a three-part math review; each section (geometry, algebra, and arithmetic) should take roughly one hour, for a total of three hours.

Time required to go through the practice GREs

At the end of the book are two full-length GREs. Each exam takes two and a quarter hours to complete and about another hour to review. Our thinking that you should take an hour to review the exam doesn't reflect a lack of confidence in your *erudition* and *sagacity* (knowledge and wisdom). We're not saying that you're so *inept* and *bungling* (unskilled) that you're going to miss a *plethora* (abundance) of questions. Our suggestion is that you review *all* the answer explanations — even those for the questions you answer correctly. You'll learn some good stuff from the explanations; you'll also review formulas, find short-cuts, and see more traps and tricks. We'll exaggerate and say that the whole test and review should take you three and a half hours. The following table gives you what we think is a reasonable timetable.

Activity	Time
7 lectures at 2 hours per lecture	14 hours
2 exams at 3½ hours per exam (including review)	7 hours
3 math review chapters at 1 hour per chapter	3 hours
2 Analytical Writing essays at 45 minutes and 30 minutes	1 hour 15 minutes
Time spent laughing hysterically at the authors' jokes	5 minutes
Time spent composing letter complaining about the authors' crummy jokes	5 minutes
TOTAL	25 hours, 25 minutes

No one expects you to read this book for 25 hours straight. Each unit is self-contained. The answer explanations may remind you of things from other units because repetition aids learning and memorizing, but you can read through each unit separately.

Are you ready? Stupid question. Are you resigned? Have you accepted your fate that you're going to take the GRE no matter what and that you may as well have fun studying for it? Take a deep breath, turn the page, and go for it. Here's hoping that, for you, GRE comes to stand for Genius Rocks Exam!

How This Book Is Organized

This book is divided into seven parts. Each one focuses on a separate aspect of preparing for the GRE, but together they lay the foundation for improving your test scores.

Part I: An Aerial View: Putting the GRE into Perspective

In this part, you get some perspective on the GRE as a whole. We introduce you to what's on the exam, what you need to know to do your best on the test, and what the scores look like.

Part II: A Word to the Wise: Verbal Questions

The Verbal portion of the GRE tests your vocabulary (with Antonyms, Analogies, and Sentence Completion questions) and reading skills (with Reading Comprehension passages and questions). In Part II, we put you through the paces so that these questions (hopefully) become second nature to you.

Part III: Two Years of Math in a Handful of Pages: The Dreaded Math Review

We know that all those geometry formulas, algebra rules, and arithmetic concepts you learned once upon a time still lurk back in the dim, dark recesses of your mind. The job of the three math-review chapters in this part is to force all that info front and center, where you can make good use of it.

Part IV: Your Number's Up: Math Questions

The bits of wisdom imparted to you in Part IV allow you to do your best on the two types of math questions found on the GRE — Quantitative Comparisons and Problem Solving.

Part V: Getting into Analysis: Analytical Writing

The newest portion of the GRE, Analytical Writing, asks you to craft two essays on topics presented to you. This part gives you tips on how to overcome writer's block and get started, as well as what the readers reward you for writing . . . and what causes them to scream in anguish.

Part VI: It All Comes Down to This: Full-Length Practice GREs

What good is all this brilliance if you can't show it off? Part VI lets you take two full-length exams to make sure you can practice what we've preached.

Part VII: The Part of Tens

At last, the good stuff! This part has fun — but useful — information such as ten stupid things you can do to mess up your GRE and ten relaxation techniques you can try before and during the GRE.

Icons and Conventions Used in This Book

To help you get through this book more quickly, we include some icons that flag the particularly important stuff. The icons look like this:

This icon marks sample problems that appear in the lectures.

Be wary of the important stuff that this icon points out to you. If you skip these sections, we accept no responsibility for what may happen to you.

As you stumble through your GRE preparation, these little commandments are tidbits you should never forget.

This icon directs you to tips that make taking the GRE go much more smoothly. These tips alone are worth the price of this book. Trust us.

The test-makers throw in some nasty traps that may get you if you don't think about the questions carefully. Memorize the tricks marked by this icon, and you'll be amazed at how easily you can outsmart the GRE.

In addition to the icons, keep your eyes peeled for words that look *like this.* This special typeface indicates a GRE word that you may not know and is followed directly by its meaning. (Here's a handy tip: Fix these words successfully in your memory by trying to use them in everyday life. Call your roommate or your children *indolent, lethargic,* and *listless* when they don't jump up to do the dishes right after dinner, or promise your professor or boss you'll be *diligent, meticulous,* and *painstaking* in your next assignment.)

You should also know that Web addresses appear in their own font (www.wiley.com) so you can easily pick them out amidst our copious amounts of wit and knowledge.

Part I

An Aerial View: Putting the GRE into Perspective

The 5th Wave
By Rich Tennant

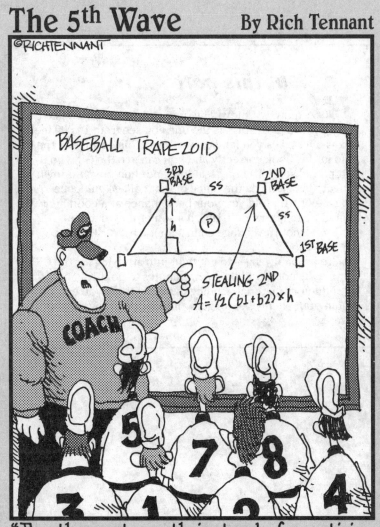

"For the next month, instead of practicing on a baseball diamond, we'll be practicing on a baseball trapezoid. At least until everyone passes the geometry section of the GRE test."

In this part . . .

We know, we know. The only aerial view you'd like to have of the GRE is the one you see from 10,000 feet up as a jet takes you far, far away from this exam. Use the info in this book correctly and you can ace the GRE, go to a top grad school, get a great job, and then buy your own private jet and buzz the office of that college guidance counselor who told you your best chance at a good life would be to marry rich. Hey, it's something to aim for (the goal, not the college counselor).

You're probably eager to get right into studying for the GRE (or maybe not), but take a few minutes to go through this introductory material. Finding out everything you can about your enemy before going into battle is always good strategy.

Chapter 1

Know Your Enemy: What the GRE Looks Like

In This Chapter

▶ Understanding the format of the GRE

▶ Scoring the exam

▶ Preparing to encounter an unscored section

▶ Remembering to stretch during breaks

*U*nlike traditional, standardized paper-and-pencil tests, which feature a roomful of test-takers sweating and fretting together in a lecture hall, the GRE is now totally computer based in the United States. Paper-and-pencil tests are only available in countries with limited access to computers. No, you don't get to take the test on your home computer with a dictionary in one hand and a tropical drink with a paper umbrella in the other (sorry if we got your hopes up only to dash them cruelly).

The GRE is offered at designated technology centers throughout the world on most days of the year, usually during standard business hours. This schedule means that if you're not a morning person, you don't have to worry about getting up at the crack of dawn and trudging across town to attempt to make your lethargic brain cells function at 8 a.m. You can take the test at any hour you personally consider civilized, such as later in the afternoon, or even in the evening. For info on signing up for the GRE, see the current *GRE Information and Registration Bulletin*. (You can pick up this bulletin at a college admissions office, register online for it at www.ets.org, or register via phone by calling 800-473-2255.) To see the GRE test centers nearest you, visit www.ets.org and plug in your state.

For each section of the GRE, the difficulty level of the questions is tailored to your abilities. You thus have a *bespoke* (custom-tailored) exam. Each section begins with a question of average difficulty (500 level). If you answer this question correctly, the computer elevates you to the 580-ish level and gives you a question that's more difficult than the first.

If you answer this second question correctly, the computer places you at about 640, and you receive a question commensurate with that ability level. As long as you keep answering questions correctly, your score goes up, and you get more difficult questions. Later questions don't cause as dramatic a jump in your score as the first few questions. And when you miss a question, your score goes down, and you get an easier question.

Eventually, you reach a level at which you're answering about half the questions correctly. At that point, the computer only adjusts your score by about ten points at a time. (Test-takers scoring at or near 800 may never get to the point at which they're missing half the questions; in contrast, those poor souls scoring at or near 200 may never achieve a level at which half of their answers are correct.)

Looking at the Breakdown (To Avoid Having One!)

The GRE consists of three scored sections: one 30-minute Verbal subtest, one 45-minute Math (Quantitative) subtest, one 45-minute Analytical Writing essay, and one 30-minute Analytical Writing essay. Typically, you get 30 verbal questions, 28 math questions, and 2 essay topics. In the Verbal and Math sections, the number of each question type (such as Analogies and Quantitative Comparisons) is proportional to what appeared on the old paper-and-pencil version of the test.

Table 1-1 provides a quick overview of what the GRE is all about, how many questions it torments and delights you with, and how much time you have to complete each section. The various sections may be arranged in any order. (For the scoop on the unscored section of the test, flip to "Understanding When Your Answers Don't Count: The Possible Unscored Section" later in this chapter.) Note that the sections marked with asterisks in Table 1-1 aren't always given, but you should be prepared for the worst just in case.

Table 1-1	GRE Breakdown by Section	
Section	*Number of Questions*	*Time Allotted*
Verbal	30	30 minutes
Math	28	45 minutes
Analytical Writing	2	75 minutes
*Unidentified unscored	28 to 35	30 to 60 minutes
*Identified unscored	Test-maker's surprise	

On the GRE, the first five questions of the Verbal section and the first five questions of the Math section are the most important. You get a much higher score if you answer the first five questions correctly and miss all the rest than if you miss the first five questions and answer all the others correctly.

Be sure to use your time wisely. Because you can't go back and change your answers, you must be as accurate as possible on each section's first five questions to ensure you'll receive harder questions (that are worth more points!) for the rest of the exam. That sounds bizarre, we know. But you really do want harder questions because the level of difficulty you reach determines your score. If you slip up and miss one early question, you can still reel off a series of correct answers, show that your mistake was a fluke, and get to the harder questions. However, if you miss a handful of early questions, the computer determines that these questions are too difficult for you and gives you easy questions. You may answer all these easy questions correctly, but your test will be over by the time the computer raises the difficulty level to the high-score range.

So exactly what types of questions and how many of each type can you expect to run into on the GRE? Check out Table 1-2 for the answers.

Table 1-2	GRE Breakdown by Question Style (Not Including the Possible Unscored Section)
Type of Question	**Number of Questions**
Antonyms	8–10
Analogies	6–8
Sentence Completions	5–7
Reading Comprehension	6–10
Quantitative Comparisons	14
Problem Solving/Data Interpretation	4
Discreet Quantitative (multiple choice)	10
Perspective on an Issue	1 topic
Analysis of an Argument	1 topic

These different question types are mixed throughout the section in which they belong. For example, you may encounter two Analogies, two Sentence Completions, and two Antonyms to start off your Verbal section. Next, you may see some Reading Comprehension questions, then more Analogies, and so on. The Math section could feature three Quantitative Comparisons, two Problem Solving questions, two Data Interpretation questions, four more Quantitative Comparisons, and so on.

Scoring 101

You don't own the Ferrari yet. (If you do, and you're a single, eligible male, please write to us care of the publisher.) You don't bring in the six-digit paycheck yet. (If you do, please see the previous parenthetical comment.) Being 21 (or 25 or 30) is rough, huh? After all, you need something to boast about. How about your GRE scores? GRE scores are to would-be graduate students what salaries are to people in the Real World. Students brag about them, exaggerate them, and try to impress others with them.

When you finish the test, you have the option of either seeing your Verbal and Math scores or canceling them. If you cancel your scores, you won't get a chance to see how you did. On the other hand, you can't decide to cancel your scores after you see them, so think carefully about how well you feel you've done. Finding out your scores at the end of the testing session is part of what people like about the computerized testing process. Instead of waiting two to four weeks to receive your scores in the mail, you can get the good news immediately! Schools still have to wait a little while though, generally about 15 days.

Figuring out your scores

With the GRE, you receive three separate scores: Verbal, Math, and Analytical Writing. Although you can obtain your unofficial Verbal and Math scores immediately after taking the test (as explained in the preceding section), you must wait 10 to 15 days to get your Analytical Writing score in the mail. Here's the scoring range for each of the three sections:

- **Verbal:** The Verbal score (also called verbal ability) ranges from 200 to 800 in 10-point increments. Yes, you read that right. You automatically get 200 points for showing up at the testing facility and staring at the computer.

- **Math:** The Math score also ranges from 200 to 800 in 10-point increments.

- **Analytical Writing:** The Analytical Writing score ranges from 0 to 6. Two graders each assign you up to 6 points; then anonymous GRE employees average those two scores together. If the two graders don't agree, another grader steps in to settle the discrepancy.

Knowing how your scores measure up

On a recent GRE, the median scores on the Verbal and Math sections (that is, half the people taking the exam were above these scores, half were below these scores) were 480 and 570, respectively. Averages for the Analytical Writing section change according to which GRE you take.

The average of students taking the exam in April may be slightly different from the average of students taking the exam in June. Your individual goals should depend on which grad schools you're applying to and what GPA (grade-point average) you have. There's no such thing as a passing or failing score — only what you need to get accepted to the program that you have your heart set on.

Playing the guessing game

You may have no choice but to guess because the computer won't budge until you choose an answer. Unlike paper-and-pencil tests, on which you can move around and choose questions that are more to your liking, the computer requires you to mark an answer before you go on to the next question.

So if you're completely stuck, don't waste time agonizing. Guess quickly and move on. Which oval should you fill in? Any. Don't listen to the obscenely abusive rumors that the correct answers on the exam more often correspond to the first, second, third, fourth, or fifth ovals. Instead, remember that on the computer screen, the ovals aren't marked A, B, C, D, and E; they're left blank. Every answer has the same probability. Which oval you choose has no bearing.

Be sure to answer all the questions. You're penalized more for unanswered questions than for wrong answers, so make sure that you get to the end, even if that means guessing wildly in the last minute or so.

Discovering the number of correct answers you need for specific scores

Following are rough estimates of how many questions you must answer correctly to achieve certain scores on each section. These numbers change from exam to exam. Also, keep in mind that your individual scores are based upon the difficulty level of the questions, your performance on the questions, and the number of questions that you answer.

Verbal scores

To get a 400, you need to correctly answer 14 out of 30 questions (about 47 percent).

To get a 500, you need to correctly answer 18 out of 30 questions (about 60 percent).

To get a 600, you need to correctly answer 22 out of 30 questions (about 73 percent).

To get a 700, you need to correctly answer 25 out of 30 questions (about 84 percent).

Math scores

To get a 400, you need to correctly answer 11 out of 28 questions (about 39 percent).

To get a 500, you need to correctly answer 15 out of 28 questions (about 54 percent).

To get a 600, you need to correctly answer 19 out of 28 questions (about 68 percent).

To get a 700, you need to correctly answer 23 out of 28 questions (about 82 percent).

Analytical Writing scores

There's no particular "number correct" in this section because you have two essays to write. See Chapter 20 for more info on how the essays are scored.

Understanding When Your Answers Don't Count: The Possible Unscored Section

The GRE test you take may in fact feature an additional Verbal or Math section, and you won't necessarily know which section is the unscored one. So what's the story behind this "unscored" section anyway? (Some people — okay, okay, the GRE powers-that-be — refer to it as an *experimental* or *equating section*.) Why does the GRE often feature a section that doesn't count?

One of the two possible unscored sections isn't identified as such because the test-makers want to use you as a guinea pig, trying out new questions and double-checking that all questions are fair. You're an unwilling — and unwitting — participant. You're obviously unwilling (who'd actually want to prolong this agony?). You're unwitting, because you don't know which section is unscored. The test-makers wouldn't exactly find out much about their new questions if you could sit back and refuse to do your best, knowing that your unwillingness wouldn't hurt your score, now would they?

The unscored section can be Verbal or Math. Either way, you'll have no idea which one isn't counted. Well, you may have *some* idea: If your test has two Verbal sections, you can deduce that one of them is unscored — but which one? Don't try to outsmart the test-makers. The GRE powers-that-be employ rooms full of men and women whose only task in life is to create these mind-warping questions. You, as a normal person, don't stand a chance of outsmarting them, so why even try? Just do your best on every section.

If you want to give your brain a break, you may be able to do so on an identified unscored section. The GRE sometimes tells you about an unscored section, which you don't need to take, at the end of the test. If you feel like playing with the computer and helping out the Educational Testing Service (the organization that creates and administers the GRE), you can go ahead and answer the questions, but you aren't obligated to do so.

I wish it were all Greek to me: A welcome to international students

Students from all over the world take the GRE in order to attend American graduate schools. There are GRE test-prep courses for students from Brazil, Taiwan, the Ivory Coast, Egypt, Japan — all over the globe. Many courses are enriched by the contributions of students from Korea, Hong Kong, Saudi Arabia, the Netherlands, China, and Mexico. To all of you readers from other nations, welcome!

As international students, you have strengths and weaknesses that are different from those of American students; therefore, the focus of your study should be different as well. Here are our suggestions to help you get the most out of this book and do your best on the actual GRE:

✔ **Concentrate on the questions that test vocabulary — Antonyms and Analogies.** You probably have an advantage over American students on these questions, believe it or not — especially if your native tongue is a Romance language, such as Spanish or French. Romance languages are Latin-based and commonly use words that are uncommon in English. Take, for example, *bibliophile*. A Spanish speaker knows *biblio* means book (*bibliotéca* means library) and can figure out this "hard" word pretty easily. (A bibliophile is a book-lover.)

One more thing: Because you've studied English, you're used to memorizing vocabulary (unlike American students who haven't taken vocabulary tests since junior high school). Although you probably can't dramatically change your basic reading comprehension level in a few hours, you *can*

dramatically add to your vocabulary. You, more than American students, need to keep and learn the vocabulary lists suggested throughout this book.

✔ **Forget about the Reading Comprehension section.** The reading passages in the GRE are long, hard, and booooring. They're difficult enough to understand for people who grew up speaking and reading English and are totally demoralizing for people who didn't. Our suggestion is that you not take Reading Comprehension too seriously. Take your time on the first passage, reading it slowly and carefully. Then scroll through the passage thoroughly to answer the questions. Making quick guesses when you get to the other passages is a good idea.

✔ **Concentrate on the math, especially geometry.** Although you do get separate Verbal and Math scores, some colleges concentrate on your *overall*, or combined, score. Doing extremely well on math can compensate for weaker verbal skills. We suggest that you pay particular attention to the geometry problems. Rarely are they *word problems* — questions that require a lot of reading. Geometry problems usually feature figures that you can easily understand and use to answer the questions — regardless of whether you're good at English.

✔ **Go, Go, Go!** We can't say it enough: The GRE penalizes you more for unanswered questions than for wrong answers. Be sure to fill in an answer for every question, even if you have to guess wildly. You absolutely must finish the exam.

Add it all up, and you realize that the part of the test that determines your future takes two and a half hours. (That's right. Two hours and 30 minutes of this test may be roughly as important as four years of college.)

Keep in mind, though, that you'll probably be at the testing center for approximately four and a half hours. You get some breaks (highlighted in the next section), and you walk through some procedures (such as getting comfortable with the computer via a tutorial and receiving scratch paper). In other words, kiss an entire morning or afternoon goodbye.

Gimme a Break! The GRE Intermissions

You have the option of taking a ten-minute break between the second and third sections of the GRE. Depending on whether your bladder is the size of Rhode Island or Texas, you may or may not spend most of your break in the bathroom. Do yourself a favor: Don't drink or eat too much during the break. Nothing's worse than sitting there crossing and uncrossing your legs during the test as your eyeballs slowly turn yellow.

Between other sections of the test, you get a one-minute break — just enough time to stand up and stretch a bit. You don't have time to leave your seat and come back before the test resumes. If you absolutely, positively have to go to the restroom and leave the computer during the test, the clock keeps ticking.

You may want to grab some munchies to eat and water to drink at the big break, but make sure that the snacks are light and nutritious. Sugar makes you high for a few minutes and then brings you way down. You don't need to crash right in the middle of a quadratic equation. Take a handful of peanuts, some trail mix, or anything else light that isn't going to send all the blood from your brain down to your stomach for digestion. Life's hard enough without trying to calculate the interior angles of a nonagon by using your stomach rather than your brain.

Chapter 2

Knowledge Is Power: Getting the Advantage

In This Chapter
▶ Pacing yourself through the test
▶ Doing the Backpack Boogie: What to take with you to the test
▶ Figuring out whether you should repeat the exam
▶ Tackling the GRE with confidence

Question: What do standardized tests really test?

Answer: They test how well you take standardized tests!

The GRE isn't an IQ test. Nor is it a measure of your worth as a human being or a predictor of whether you'll be so successful that you'll make Bill Gates look like a pauper. The GRE tests how well you take a test because test-taking skills determine how well you'll do in grad school. (A logical premise when you think about it, isn't it?) In this chapter, we provide you with some of the general strategies that can help you on the exam as a whole. Wonder whether Bill Gates ever knew these strategies?

Beating the Clock: Tips on Timing

The computer provides you with a stopwatch — an on-screen clock — to time each section. You have the option of removing the clock from the screen. If that ticker makes you nervous, by all means, get it out of sight (the computer tutorial at the beginning of the session tells you how to do so).

Professionally, we definitely recommend that you hide the clock when you begin each section. You should do whatever it takes to get the first five questions right (we cover the importance of those first five questions in Chapter 1). Bring the clock back when you finish the first five questions, or at least check the clock every 15 minutes or so. Because the early questions count more than later ones, if you've answered fewer than half the questions when half of your time has expired, you're still doing okay. *Note:* The clock comes on and stays on during the last five minutes; you can't banish it from that point on. Its nagging presence serves as a reminder that you may have to sprint to the finish soon.

Answer ALL the questions, even if you have to make wild guesses. Your score isn't penalized for wrong answers; in fact, blank answers (as in not finishing the entire test) hurt your score more than wrong answers.

Scratching like a Crazed Chicken

You aren't allowed to bring in a grease pencil and do scratch work on the computer screen! (Don't laugh: We've had more than one student ask us about doing so!) The test proctor gives you blank scratch paper (you can't bring in your own) before the test begins. Sure, you can use this paper for such traditional scratch work as mathematical calculations. But you can also use it in another key way.

Use the general instruction time (a few minutes during which you go through some computer tutorials before the exam officially starts) to write down any key strategies and formulas you want to help you get through the exam. You aren't allowed to bring any memory aids into the testing center, but you can create your own just before you start tackling the questions.

Packing Your Bags on Test Day

Take your brain down from the shelf, dust it off, and take it to the exam with you. In addition, take along a few more items:

- **Authorization voucher from ETS:** You need to bring proof that you've signed up for the test. This evidence can take the form of an *authorization voucher,* which is proof directly from ETS that you've registered for the test. It contains your confirmation number, reporting time, and the test center's address. You can request that ETS mail, fax, or e-mail a voucher to you when you register for the test.

- **Map or directions:** Be sure that you know in advance how to get to the testing center. Drive there a few days prior to your test and check out how long the drive takes you, where to park, and so on. One of our students had to take the test at a center in the middle of a downtown area. On the day of the test, she couldn't find any parking and became totally stressed out before she even got to the testing center. The last thing you need the day of the test is something more to worry about.

- **Photo ID:** You must have identification with three key elements:

  - A recognizable photo (one that shows you as the haggard, sleep-deprived person you are after studying for this test, not as the perky, cheerful person you vaguely remember having been a month or so ago)

  - The name you registered under (if your driver's license lists you as Steven Boyd Brown, don't sign up under your nickname of "Boatman" or "Bubbles" or whatever your friends call you)

  - Your signature

  Usually, a driver's license, passport, employee ID, or military ID is acceptable. A student ID alone often isn't enough, although it's acceptable as a second form of ID in case you encounter some confusion with the first form. Note that a Social Security card or a credit card isn't acceptable identification.

- **Clothes:** You signed up for the special Nude GRE, you say? Well, everyone else should remember to take a few extra layers. Testing centers may be boiling hot or freezing cold. Sitting there for hours either shivering with hands so cold they can't hit the computer keys or sweating all over your keyboard from the heat is the pits. Dress in layers and be prepared for anything.

You Can't Take It with You

Besides your dreams, hopes, goals, and aspirations, leave these other items at the door of the GRE testing center:

- ✔ **Books and notes:** Forget about last-minute studying. You aren't allowed to take books or notes into the testing center. If you don't know the material by that time, you never will. (One student asked us whether he could take in a dictionary. You gotta give the guy credit for hope, but somehow we think he missed the point of the verbal questions.)

- ✔ **Scratch paper:** You aren't allowed to bring in your own scratch paper (with handy notes prepared ahead of time). The proctor gives you scratch paper when you arrive at the testing center. If you run low during the test, request some more from the proctor during the one-minute breaks between sections. Although you have plenty of room to do calculations and scribbling, we understand that ETS owns the copyright to all last wills and testaments written during the exam.

- ✔ **Calculator:** You aren't allowed to use a calculator during the exam. Don't think that because your watch has a calculator, you can bend this rule — absolutely no mechanical or digital calculating devices are allowed.

- ✔ **Friends as cheerleaders:** Leave your friends at home. The ETS frowns on visitors.

- ✔ **Test aids:** You may not bring in a radio, cassette, or CD player with headphones; a cellphone; or a personal computer (either a laptop or a hand-held device). In other words, leave the electronics at home. The most you can bring is that good old-fashioned #2 pencil.

Isn't that special? Unique circumstances

Dare to be different. If you have a special circumstance, the GRE powers-that-be are usually willing to accommodate you. For example, if you have a learning disability (no, that doesn't include being bored and frustrated), you may be able to get additional testing time. Following is a brief list of special circumstances and what to do about them.

- ✔ **Learning disabilities:** These circumstances can range from Attention Deficit Disorder to dyslexia and all sorts of other conditions. To find out whether you qualify for a disabilities waiver of any sort, contact the ETS Disability Services, Educational Testing Service, P.O. Box 6054, Princeton, NJ 08541-6054; phone 866-387-8602 (toll free) or 609-771-7780 United States, U.S. territories, and Canada (Monday–Friday 8:30 a.m. to 5:00 p.m. Eastern Time), TTY 609-771-7714, fax 609-771-7165; Web site www.ets.org, e-mail stassd@ets.org.

- ✔ **Physical disabilities:** Pay attention: We're about to say something nice about ETS here, a once-in-a-googolplex occurrence for us. ETS tries very hard to accommodate everyone. Those folks who need special arrangements can get Braille or large-print exams, have test readers or recorders, work with interpreters, and so on. You can get the scoop about what the ETS considers to be disabilities and how the disabilities can change the way you take the GRE

in the *Supplement for Test Takers with Disabilities*. This brochure contains information, registration procedures, and other useful forms for individuals with disabilities. Use the supplement in conjunction with the information and registration forms in the appropriate program bulletin. To get this supplement and the program bulletin, send a request to ETS Disability Services, P.O. Box 6054, Princeton, NJ 08541-6054. Or better yet, log onto www.ets.org, click the GRE link, and then click the Test Takers with Disabilities link. Voilà! All the info you need to know. We thank you, ETS!

- ✔ **Financial difficulties:** Until you ace the GRE, get into a top-notch graduate school, and come out with a smokin' brain ready to make your first million before your 30th (40th? 50th?) birthday, you may have a rough time paying the GRE fees. Fee waivers are available. Note that this waiver applies only to the actual GRE fee, not to miscellaneous fees such as the test-disclosure service, hand-grading service, and so on. Your college counselor can help you obtain and fill out the appropriate request forms. (If you're not currently in college, a counselor or financial aid specialist at the closest college or university may still be glad to help you. Just call for an appointment.) The GRE is inflicted upon rich and poor alike.

Déjà Vu: Repeating the Test

Should you repeat the test? Before you make that decision, ask yourself the following questions:

- ✔ **Am I repeating the test to get a certain minimum qualifying score or just to satisfy my ego?** If you have your heart set on a particular graduate school that requires a minimum GRE score, you may want to take the test again and again and again until you get that score. If you're taking the test only because your ego was demolished when you didn't score as well as your friends, you should probably think twice before putting yourself through all that trauma again.

- ✔ **Am I willing to study twice as hard, or am I already burned out?** If you put your heart and soul into studying for the exam the first time, you may be too pooped (or *enervated,* as we didactic dames like to say) to pop for the second exam. After all, scores don't magically go up on their own; you have to put in a lot of effort.

- ✔ **What types of mistakes did I make on the first test?** If you made mistakes because of a lack of familiarity with either the test format (you didn't understand what to do when faced with a Quantitative Comparison question) or substance (you didn't know the vocabulary words or were baffled by the geometry problems), you're a good candidate for repeating the test. If you know what you did wrong, you can fix it and improve your score.

  However, if your mistakes were due to carelessness or a lack of concentration, you're very likely to make those same types of mistakes again. If you truly, honestly, sincerely, and without *dissembling* (lying) feel that you can sit in the test room and stay focused this time and not make the same stupid mistakes, go for it. But chances are, if you're the type of test-taker who either always makes a lot of careless mistakes or rarely makes them, you're not going to change your whole test-taking style overnight.

- ✔ **Were there extenuating circumstances beyond my control?** Maybe your nerves were acting up on the first exam, you were feeling ill, or you didn't get enough sleep the night before. In that case, by all means repeat the exam. You're bound to feel better the next time.

- ✔ **Did I not finish?** If you didn't reach a lot of questions, take the test again. (You may take the test only once during each calendar month, but a smart test-taker can schedule her testing so that she takes the exam on, say, October 31 and then again on November 1.) You can only take it a total of five times per GRE calendar year, which runs from July 1 to June 30. This time, fill in something for every question. *Remember:* You lose more points for not reaching a question than you do for answering the question incorrectly.

Can repeating the exam hurt you? Not really. Most schools look only at your highest score. Find out from the individual schools you're interested in whether that's their policy; it isn't the case for every school. If you're on the borderline, or if several students are vying for one spot, sometimes having taken the exam repeatedly can hurt you (especially if your most recent score took a nosedive). On the other hand, an admissions counselor who sees several exams with ascending scores may be impressed that you stuck to it and kept trying, even if your score went up just a little bit. In general, if you're willing to take the time to study and take the repeat seriously, go for it.

GRE score reporting is cumulative. That is, all the scores you obtain for five years are sent to the schools you designate. You can't, we repeat, *you can't* send scores from only one exam date. For example, if you do great in October, take the exam again in April, and blow it big time, you can't tell ETS to ignore the April *debacle* (a sudden collapse, a rout) and send just the October scores. All scores are part of your permanent record.

Experience Counts: Using Older Scores

What if you took the GRE five to ten years ago when you thought you were going to go to grad school, and then elected to take a job or start a family instead? Well, if it was five years ago or less, you're in luck. The GRE folks make the scores reportable for up to five years. That means that if you were pleased with your five-year-old score, you can send it right along to the university and say adios to us right here and now. However, if you took the test more than five years ago, you have to take it again. Don't worry though, we'll stick around until the end and see you through the studying process.

Taking Care of Yourself before the Test

Just like the long-distance swimmer, you're in training for a long period of time. Also like the swimmer, who doesn't just swim in order to prepare for the race, you need to take care of your body by practicing what we recommend in the following sections.

Staying active

You can't just be a bookworm for the year before the exam. You need to use other body parts, too. Exercise helps all parts of the body, including the brain. More exercise, more oxygen to the brain. More oxygen to the brain, clearer thinking. So get moving!

Eating well

Just like exercising, the right food contributes to sustained attention and clear thought. You want to avoid sugar highs that eventually result in a crash. Forget those energy drinks that combine huge amounts of caffeine and sugar to get you to a state of heightened paranoia. The ads may tell you that you focus better when you drink those, but you'll only be reading and writing at a superhuman speed, and your recall will be nada after you come down. Your mom was right: Eat your veggies, fruits, and well-balanced meals. Your brain will be nourished and in turn will thank you with a better score.

Discovering relaxation

We've seen students who are so overextended and overachieving that they don't have any time for pleasant relaxation. They stress out, take anti-anxiety pills, have trouble sleeping and concentrating, get panic attacks, and generally exhaust themselves and get sick. Stop for a minute, get in a comfy position, and read this next sentence carefully and slowly.

Relaxation isn't a luxury — it's a requirement for a well-balanced life. You're a multifaceted human. You aren't a work-and-study robot.

Relaxation comes in many different forms for all kinds of people. Some folks are relaxed when they're with friends; some read books for enjoyment and play music they like; and some do yoga, meditate, or paint. The only requirement when choosing what relaxation tool to use is making sure your brain isn't running 100 miles an hour. The whole purpose of relaxation is to give your brain a rest. Your poor brain needs that to function properly when called to duty. So find a relaxing activity you enjoy, thank your brain by telling it to take some time off, and whether you choose to "oooomm" or paint tulips, make it peaceful.

Avoiding artificial study aids (drugs)

We're gonna come clean right here: We've pulled all-nighters with the assistance of either a keg of coffee or some over-the-counter caffeine pills, and it wasn't pleasant. The only thing that uppers, stimulants, and amphetamines do is make you feel like you can clean every kitchen in your neighborhood. And you probably can, except these drugs backfire when it comes to studying. Although they aid you in staying awake for longer periods of time, stimulants make it hard to retain and recall information. They leave you jittery, anxious, agitated, and restless. In some situations, taking stimulants is necessary, like if you've been diagnosed with ADHD and require them in order to concentrate. But for everyone else, these drugs do just the opposite. They make you think you're concentrating and studying really hard, but the reality is that you won't remember too much of what you studied. Just say no!

Approaching a Question with Confidence

You've put the time into studying and preparing for this test. You know more than you think you do. Even if you fail to remember every detail of every concept, you know at least something about it. If you come to the test feeling completely insecure and doubting yourself, take a moment to remember that we told you that you know more than you think. If you find a question that makes your heart stop with dread, turn that immediately around and say, "I can do this, I will do this, and I feel good about this question." Following are a few confidence-building strategies for you to use.

Anticipating test questions

The GRE focuses on core concepts and material. There are no surprises. After you've successfully studied this book, you'll be ready to anticipate the types of questions the GRE powers-that-be will throw at you.

Changing your attitude

Tell yourself repeatedly that you've studied very hard and that you're beyond ready for this test. If you need help developing a more confident attitude and staying positive and centered, check out the relaxation techniques presented in Chapter 28. Either way, going into the GRE feeling inadequate isn't an option for you. YOU have done the work. YOU know this material. You ROCK!

Remembering that this is only a test

The GRE isn't an all-or-nothing situation. The success of the rest of your life most definitely isn't tied up in this test. Realizing that you're taking just another test (you've taken hundreds in your life, right?) and understanding that this test isn't a measure of your worth as a person provide you with a level of confidence that's unmatchable.

This is only a test. You don't know these GRE folks. They aren't going to snicker as you walk by and mutter, "There goes the one that didn't know what a variable was." You've come this far, you've studied, you've already triumphed. Approach every question with confidence.

Chapter 3

Getting Familiar with the Computerized GRE

In This Chapter

▶ Sitting through some basic computer tutorials

▶ Knowing a few general rules about the computerized GRE

▶ Reviewing the six on-screen icons

▶ Selecting your final answers on the computer

The GRE test is now completely computerized, which is fortunate if you've been living in the computer age for quite some time. But even if you're a computer whiz, we highly recommend that you review this chapter.

After all, every computer is different, and because you're spending so much time studying for this test, you don't want to risk a silly computer error that messes up your entire score — like hitting a button that deletes your entire essay midway through. This chapter presents the basic rules of the computer-based test, clues you in to the icons you'll see on every page, and explains how to appropriately select your answers.

Bracing Yourself for the Tutorials

Before taking the GRE, you must work through four tutorials. And no, you can't get out of 'em, even if you have a degree in computer science. ETS (the organization that creates and administers the GRE) doesn't allow anyone exposure to its GRE software prior to the test. Consequently, these tutorials are important so that you get comfy with the screen and the way the material looks. We really wanted to show you the screen ourselves, but ETS keeps it under lock and key.

The tutorials occur at the very beginning of the test, and you have 30 minutes to work through them. *Note:* This time is separate from the testing time. Here's what each of the four tutorials explains:

✔ How to use a mouse

✔ How to select an answer (although it doesn't tell you how to pick the *right* answer — the nerve of these people!)

✔ How to use the testing tools

✔ How to scroll

A quick note on scrolling: On the Reading Comprehension passages, you may occasionally need to scroll through the text. The questions will be on the right-hand side while the text remains on the left. To move the text, simply click the up or down arrows located on the scroll bar. Although the answers to your questions may not be flexible, the reading passages always will be.

Knowing the Rules so You Don't Sink Your Score

Before you ever set foot inside a testing center, you need to be familiar with the following rules that rule your GRE experience:

- ✔ **Forget about skipping ahead to the next screen and then trying to return to the previous screen.** You absolutely must answer the question on the screen. We know, we know. You're used to the old paper-and-pencil tests, where you could skip around to your heart's desire. Unfortunately, the GRE folks have taken that luxury away from you.

- ✔ **Don't waste time trying to change a confirmed answer.** Answer each question with confidence because after you click the Confirm Answer button, there's no going back.

- ✔ **Keep an eye on the clock.** The running clock is located on the upper left-hand side of your screen. The Time icon, however, is located on the bottom left-hand side. We recommend that you avoid hitting the Time icon because you'll turn off the running clock if you do — and that's never a good idea on a timed test! (Except of course when you're trying to answer the first five questions in the Math or Verbal sections, as we explain in Chapter 2.)

  If you accidently click the Time icon and the running clock goes away, don't fret. All you have to do is click the Time icon again for the running clock to reappear.

- ✔ **Stick with the test, no matter what.** Although you have the option of exiting the whole test or a particular section at any time (see the next section for the scoop on the icons that allow you to do just that), tucking your tail between your legs and slinking out of the testing center does you no good. Even if you decide halfway through that you aren't going to send these scores to your graduate school of choice, wait to act on that decision until after you finish taking the test. *Remember:* You paid for this great experience, so you may as well make the best of it and use the time as practice for your next go-round.

What You See Is What You Get: On-Screen Icons

The desktop of a testing-center computer isn't going to look like your home computer's desktop. That means no instant-messaging programs or computerized card games. Instead, you get up close and personal with six GRE on-screen icons: the wicked left-hand ones and the benevolent right-hand ones. You must be able to identify these different icons so that you don't accidently delete your test, or worse, lose the greatest GRE test score on the planet.

In general, we recommend you steer clear of the bottom left-hand side of the screen. But because the enemy you know is always better than the one you don't, allow us to introduce you to the wicked, left-hand GRE icons:

✔ **Quit Test:** Avoid this icon at all costs. Clicking Quit Test ends your testing experience immediately. You don't pass go, you don't collect 200 bucks. You go to jail, or worse, go home with shame. So why would the GRE powers-that-be give you this icon? Well, you're not their slave. If for some reason you can't continue with the GRE, you have the option to get up and leave. However, being sick and tired of this darn exam isn't a good reason to click Quit Test.

✔ **Exit Section:** The Exit Section icon isn't as dangerous as the Quit Test one because you only choose to quit the section you're currently working on. The computer then takes you to the next section, and you abandon your score on the previous section. Still, exiting a section really isn't worth it. At the very least, you can probably use the practice. Personally, we can't understand why the GRE folks even give you this option — unless of course you get a sudden case of Montezuma's revenge in the middle of the Math section.

✔ **Time:** The Time icon is another hidden danger. Clicking it can cause the running clock (which lets you know how much time you have left for the test — a rather important program, don't you think?) to disappear.

The bottom right-hand side is home to the following better-intentioned icons:

✔ **Help:** Clicking the Help icon won't give you the answer to a question. In fact, it won't give you any hints at all! So why do they even bother calling it the Help icon? Because clicking this button gives you a rehash of the original directions for the section you're working on. Quite frankly, the Help icon isn't all that helpful — unless of course you managed not to read the directions in the first place.

✔ **Next:** The Next icon tells the computer that you're ready to move on. You're confident that you have the right answer, and you're ready to tackle the next question. Right? Fortunately, the computer is a bit compassionate; clicking Next after answering a question takes you to the Confirm Answer icon, which then puts your wisdom in stone.

✔ **Confirm Answer:** The Confirm Answer icon is your friend. It's the only button that allows you to move forward and get this darn test over with. After you're certain of your answer, you have no choice but to click this icon. Just remember that after you confirm your answer, you can't go back and change it. Your choice — wrong or right — is a done deal.

Blacking In the Bubbles: How to Select Your Answers

Although our practice tests and sample questions are set up with answer choices from A to E, the actual computer-based test uses bubbles that you must click to select your answer. Use your mouse to move the cursor on the screen until it's hovering over the bubble you want to choose as your answer.

Clicking the wrong bubble with your mouse is very easy to do, so pay special attention to which bubble you select. Also, know that you can always change your blacked-in bubble before you click the Next icon. If you change your mind after that point, we're afraid you're stuck with your first guess.

Chapter 4

Starting with the Easy Stuff: Analogies

• •

In This Chapter

▶ Understanding the format of an analogy

▶ Answering an analogy question with a simple two-step approach

▶ Recognizing the nasty and vile traps built into analogies

▶ Building your vocabulary with prefixes and suffixes

▶ Identifying and avoiding stupid (trap) answers

• •

Answer: The shiny red bike you got for your tenth birthday. Your first kiss from someone who wasn't related to you. Analogies.

Question: Name three of the best gifts you've ever received.

Analogies are a gift. Manna from heaven. Freebies. For most test-takers, Analogy sections are places to rack up the points big time. The number of Analogy questions on the computer-based GRE can vary, but you'll almost certainly have at least seven.

The great thing about analogies is that they're doable. Some of the Reading Comprehension passages are ridiculously hard. Some of the Sentence Completion questions are so long you may be tempted to take a snooze in the middle of them. But analogies are great. You read 12 words, apply a few tricks, and you're outta there.

If Only All Relationships Were This Easy: The Format

Some people look at analogies and wonder, "Where's the question?" Even though analogies can be quite simple (with practice), we admit the format is bizarre. Here's an example of what an analogy looks like:

PIG : STY ::

(A) teenager : rubble

(B) roommate : bathroom

(C) bird : nest

(D) swine : house

(E) barnacle : barn

(*Note:* On the actual test, the answer choices are accompanied by ovals to click and aren't labeled with the letters A, B, C, D, and E.)

You see two words in uppercase letters. The five answer choices each consist of two words in lowercase letters. Not a lot of reading here. When you get good at analogies, you can zoom through them faster than you can finish a pint of ice cream.

Your job when faced with an Analogy question? Identify the *relationship* between the question words and then choose a pair of answer words that expresses the *same* relationship.

Approaching Analogy-Solving Perfection: A Two-Step Program

When you see an Analogy question, you should take this very straightforward, two-step approach:

1. Use both words in a *descriptive* sentence.

Make a sentence using the words. Avoid something vague and useless such as "has." For example, don't just say, "A pig *has* a sty." That sentence tells you nothing — you have no idea what the relationship between a pig and a sty is. Pretend that a Bulgarian exchange student comes up to you and says, "Excuse me, please. What is the connection between a pig and a sty?" If you answer that a pig *has* a sty, the Bulgarian may go away thinking that a sty is a curly tail, a snout, or a big stink. But if you say, "A pig *lives in* a sty," your Bulgarian buddy now understands the relationship. A good sentence paints a mental picture: You can actually see the scene in your mind.

2. Apply the *exact* same sentence to each answer choice.

Go through each of the answer choices using your sentence.

(A) A teenager *lives in* rubble.

Maybe you flash back to your teenage years and recall having to wade through the ***detritus*** (trash, rubble) of your bedroom to get to the door, but this is the GRE. The test-makers assume you were a sweet little kid who obeyed your parents, respected traffic signals, and didn't ever use the middle finger of your hand for pointing or otherwise gesticulating. By the way, ***rubble*** is the ruined remains of a building, such as knocked-down bricks and junk. If you forget this word, think of Barney Rubble from the *Flintstones*. He's short, like a knocked-down pile.

(B) A roommate *lives in* the bathroom.

It may seem like it sometimes, but it ain't so. Any answer that's funny, witty, or charming is almost certainly the wrong answer. (The GRE has nooooo sense of humor; you can count on that.) If you think an answer is funny — or desperately *trying* to be funny — you can be sure that it's wrong.

(C) A bird *lives in* a nest.

Sounds pretty good, but you still need to go through all the answer choices, just in case. Just like not marrying the first person you kiss, don't immediately choose the first answer that looks good. Something may come along later that makes you happier.

(D) A swine *lives in* a house.

If you like this answer, remind us not to come to your home! The trap here is that a pig (from the question) and a swine are much the same. Be careful: Just because words are connected in *meaning* doesn't mean the answer is right. What's being tested is the *relationship* between the words. For example, the question may be about perfume, and the correct answer may involve sweat socks. No connection.

(E) A barnacle *lives in* a barn.

If you don't know what a barnacle is, you may be tempted to pick Choice E, but Choice C is the right answer. A **barnacle** is a creature that lives in the water (not in a barn) and often attaches itself to the bottoms of ships. You scrape the barnacles off the ship periodically to clean the ship's hull. *Correct Answer:* Choice C.

They Really Are Out to Get You: Avoiding Traps and Tricks with a Few Good Tips

Face it — discovering traps, tricks, and tips is why you really bought this book. You want to know about those little built-in traps that are just sitting there, waiting to pounce on unsuspecting victims. What time bombs have the test-makers created, ready to go off in your face? The following sections present a few, along with suggestions for how to deal with 'em.

Turn a verb into an infinitive

No, an infinitive isn't the latest Japanese import car. An *infinitive* is the "to" form of any verb: to drink, to burp, to party. When an analogy features a verb, turn it into an infinitive, and the sentence practically writes itself.

GIGGLE : LAUGH ::

To giggle is *to laugh* a little bit.

YELL : TALK ::

To yell is *to talk* loudly.

RUN : WALK ::

To run is *to walk* rapidly.

Notice that we're adding another word on the end. Usually this word is an adverb to answer the "How?" question. How do you laugh when you giggle? A little bit. How do you talk when you yell? Loudly. How do you walk when you run? Rapidly. Saying "To giggle is to laugh" isn't enough. You want to fine-tune the sentence; tweak it a little bit to clarify the relationship between the words.

Determine the part of speech of the question word

Sometimes your sentence is easier to write if you know which part of speech — noun, verb, or adjective — a difficult word is. You find out by looking at the word's counterparts in the answer choices. That is, if you want to know which part of speech the first word in the question is, look at the first words in the answers. If you want to know which part of speech the second word in the question is, look at the second words in the answer choices.

DASHIKI : TAILOR ::

(A) shovel : professor

(B) table : singer

(C) garment : jock

(D) cake : baker

(E) book : poseur

Don't know what the word *dashiki* means? You're not alone; it's a pretty hard word. Not to worry. You know by looking at the first words in the answer choices — shovel, table, garment, cake, and book — that *dashiki* must be a noun and is a thing. (Remember that nouns are persons, places, or things.) Your very simple sentence should be: "A dashiki is a thing of a tailor." That's all you can do for now. Go through each answer choice:

(A) shovel : professor — Although it can get deep in the classroom sometimes, a shovel isn't standard equipment for a professor.

(B) table : singer — A singer may stretch herself out on a table during a Las Vegas lounge act while doing a sexy, sultry number, but a table isn't normally associated with a singer.

(C) garment : jock — This is a trap answer. You may be tempted to choose it because a tailor (from the question) deals with garments. However, you're well aware that the *meanings* of the question words aren't necessarily related to the answer; the *relationship* between the pairs of words is what's important. Had the question said GARMENT : SEAMSTRESS or even GARMENT : MODEL, this would've been a good choice. But a garment isn't necessarily a thing of a jock.

(D) cake : baker — A cake is a thing of a baker. Yeah, this answer sounds pretty good because a logical connection exists. Try the next one to be sure, knowing that Choice D is probably right.

(E) book : poseur — This answer is put here to trap people who immediately assume that the hardest word in a question, or any word they themselves don't know, must be the correct answer. A *poseur* is someone with an attitude, a person who adopts an affected style. People who go around using words like poseur are often poseurs themselves.

The right answer is Choice D. A *dashiki,* by the way, is a type of shirt, and a tailor creates a dashiki just as a baker creates a cake. See? You *can* get the question right without knowing what the word means. *Correct Answer:* Choice D.

Look for the salient features of a word

The *salient* feature is what makes something stand out. The salient feature of a basketball player is his or her height. The salient feature of a genius is his or her intelligence. So when we say you should look for the salient features of a word, we want you to determine what's significant about that word.

MINNOW : FISH ::

(A) elephant : animal

(B) recluse : shy

(C) gnat : insect

(D) giraffe : quadruped

(E) votary : peremptory

The salient feature of a minnow is that it's a *small* fish. Although most of the answers are or may be synonyms (an elephant *is* an animal; a recluse *may* be shy), only Choice C gives the salient or outstanding feature. A gnat is a *small* insect. Choice E features antonyms. A *votary* is a devoted follower (think of a votary as an elegant, grown-up groupie). *Peremptory* means absolute, imperative, allowing no disagreement. The boss may be peremptory; the votary would more likely be *docile* (easily swayed, compliant). *Correct Answer:* Choice C.

Work backward

Question: Is it okay to make the sentence by using the words backward?

Answer: Sure, as long as you remember to use the answer choices backward as well. That is, don't say, "A tailor makes a dashiki," and then say, "A cake makes a baker."

Identify common relationships

Certain standard relationships are often found in analogies. A *plethora* (a lot) of them exist, but here are ten of the more useful ones.

1. **Opposites**
   BIG : LITTLE
   PULCHRITUDINOUS : UGLY

2. **Synonyms**
   HAPPY : GLAD
   PUSILLANIMOUS : COWARDLY

3. **Cause and effect**
   TICKLE : LAUGHTER
   OSSIFY : BONE

4. **Part to whole**
   TOES : FOOT
   TALON : EAGLE

5. **Position**
   FRAME : PICTURE (a frame goes around a picture)
   SHOULDER : ROAD (a shoulder is to the side of a road)

6. **Greater to lesser**
   OVERJOYED : HAPPY
   CATACLYSMIC : UNFORTUNATE

7. **Location**
   PIG : STY
   RABBIT : WARREN

8. **Purpose or function**
   PILOT : FLY
   PUGILIST : BOX

9. **Characteristic**
   BLEAT : SHEEP (a bleat is the sound a sheep makes)
   POD : WHALES (a pod is a group of whales)

10. **Member to group (or specific to general)**
    FORK : UTENSIL
    ISLANDS : ARCHIPELAGO
    (an archipelago is a group of islands)

Use roots, prefixes, and suffixes

Other women like "I love you," but we live for "roots, prefixes, suffixes." These three words can bump up your score significantly. If you know just a few basic roots, prefixes, and suffixes, you can write magnificent analogy sentences and avoid falling into traps.

Suppose you encounter this question: IMPECUNIOUS : MONEY ::

If you don't know *impecunious,* you may be tempted to make the words synonyms and simply say, "Impecunious *is* money." A tempting and logical answer may be reservoir : water, for example. Alas, once again you pay the price for giving in to temptation.

If you know that *-ous* means full of and *im-* means not, you can make a good sentence: "Impecunious is *not full of* money." That changes the whole picture. Now the right answer may be, for example, vacuum : air. A *vacuum* is *not full of* air. Note that a *reservoir* in fact *is* full of water — the opposite of your relationship sentence.

Although you can memorize hundreds of prefixes and suffixes, we realize that you have a limited number of brain cells that you're willing to devote to this subject. So here's a list of ten commonly used prefixes and eight commonly used suffixes, with examples of each. Memorize them. Burn them into your brain. (We get to some of the more common roots in Chapter 8. After all, we don't want you to get overexcited by this stuff all at once.)

Prefixes

1. *a-* = **not or without:** Someone *amoral* is without morals, like the sadist who designed the GRE. Someone *atypical* isn't typical, like the students who wear pocket protectors and love to take tests. Someone *apathetic* is uncaring or without feeling, like most test-takers by the time they finish the GRE and are leaving the exam room. ("The world is going to end tomorrow? Fine. That means I can get some sleep tonight.")

2. *an-* = **not or without:** An *anaerobic* environment is without oxygen (like the test room feels when a killer question leaves you gasping for air). *Anarchy* is without rule or government (like a classroom when a substitute teacher is in for the day).

3. *eu-* = **good:** A *eulogy* is a good speech, usually given for the dearly departed at a funeral. A *euphemism* is a good way of saying something or a polite expression, like saying that someone has passed away rather than calling her worm meat.

4. *ben-/bon-* = **good:** A *benefit* is something that has a good result, an advantage. Someone *benevolent* is good and kind; when you have a date, a benevolent father lets you take his new car rather than your old junker. *Bon voyage* means "have a good voyage;" a *bon vivant* is a person who lives the good life.

5. *caco-* = **bad:** Something *cacophonous* is bad sounding, such as nails on a chalkboard.

6. *ne-/mal-* = **bad:** Something *negative* is bad, like a negative attitude. Someone *nefarious* is "full of bad," or wicked and evil, such as a nefarious wizard in a fantasy novel. Something *malicious* also is "full of bad," or wicked and harmful, such as a malicious rumor that you're really a 30-year-old undercover narc.

7. *im-* = **not:** Something *impossible* isn't possible — it just can't happen. Someone *immortal* isn't going to die but will live forever. Someone *implacable* isn't able to be calmed down; she's stubborn. Notice that *im-* can also mean inside (*immerse* means to put into), but that meaning isn't as common on the GRE. First, think of *im-* as meaning not; if that doesn't seem appropriate, switch to Plan B and see whether *im-* can mean inside in the context of the question.

8. *in-* = **not:** Something *inappropriate* isn't appropriate, such as the language people may use in front of small children when studying for the GRE. Someone *inept* isn't adept, meaning she's not skillful. (Can you sue an inept surgeon who amputates the wrong leg? Nah, you wouldn't have a leg to stand on!) Someone *insolvent* has no money and is bankrupt, like most students after four years of college. *In-* can also mean inside (*innate* means something born inside of you) or beginning (the *initial* letters of your name are the beginning letters). However, the most common meaning of *in-* is not. Think of that one first; if it doesn't seem to work in a particular question, try the other meanings.

9. *ante-* = **before:** When the clock tells you that it's 5 a.m., the a.m. stands for *ante meridiem,* which means before the middle or first half of the day. *Antebellum* means before the war. Tara in *Gone with the Wind* was an antebellum mansion, built before the Civil War. *Antediluvian* literally means before the flood, before Noah's deluge. Figuratively, it means very old; if you call your mother antediluvian, you mean that she's been around since before the flood. (It's a great word to use as an insult because almost no one knows what it means and you can get away with it.)

10. *post-* = **after:** When the clock tells you that it's 5 p.m., the p.m. stands for *post meridiem.* It means after the middle or second half of the day. Something *postmortem* occurs after death. A postmortem exam is an autopsy.

Flash your friends: How to use flashcards

Go out and buy three packages of the largest index cards you can find. One package should be white cards; the other two should each be a different color. Put all the roots, prefixes, and suffixes you learn that have negative connotations on cards of one color. For example, *ne-* means bad or not; put it on a brown card. *Ben-* means good; put it on a pink card. Because *-ous* means full of, it doesn't feel good or bad; it's neutral. Put it on a white card.

When you get to the exam, you may encounter the word *nefarious*. You know you've seen it before, but you can't for the life of you remember what it means. Then a little picture unfolds in front of your eyes: You see *ne-* on a brown card. Aha! If it's on a brown card, it must be something negative. Just knowing that much often helps you get the right answer.

Say the analogy is NEFARIOUS : SAINT. Normally, you assume that the words are synonyms and say, "A saint *is* nefarious." However, remembering that *ne-* is on a brown card, which means that it's negative, makes you change the sentence to "A saint is *not* nefarious," because saints are generally considered pretty good.

There's no right or wrong way to classify the roots. If you think that a root is positive, fine, it's positive. If you think that a root is negative, fine, it's negative. The whole purpose of flashcards is to help you associate the words. Go with whatever works for *you*.

Bonus! When you come across a word that incorporates the root, put that word on the card as an example. That way, you learn both the root *and* the vocabulary word: two for the price of one. If you're reading a newspaper article about a program that will have a *salubrious* effect on the economy, note that *sal* means health and *-ous* means full of. You know immediately that the word means healthful. Put it on both the *sal* card and the *-ous* card. You'll learn the vocabulary without even realizing it!

Suffixes

1. *-ette* = **little:** A *cigarette* is a little cigar. A *dinette* table is a little dining table. A *coquette* is a little flirt (literally, a little chicken, but that doesn't sound as pretty).

2. *-illo* = **little:** An *armadillo* is a little armored animal. A *peccadillo* is a little sin. (Do you speak Spanish? Then you probably know that *pecar* translates as "to sin" in English.)

3. *-ous* = **full of (very):** Someone *joyous* is full of joy. Someone *amorous* is full of *amour*, or love. Someone *pulchritudinous* is full of beauty, and therefore beautiful.

4. *-ist* = **a person:** A *typist* is a person who types. A *pugilist* is a person who fights (*pug* means war or fight), a boxer. A *pacifist* is a person who believes in peace, a noncombatant (*pac* means peace or calm).

5. *-ify (-efy)* = **to make:** To *beautify* is to make beautiful. To *ossify* is to make bone. (If you break your wrist, it takes weeks to ossify again, or for the bone to regenerate.) To *deify* is to make into a deity, a god.

6. *-ize* = **to make:** To *alphabetize* is to make alphabetical. To *immunize* is to make immune. To *ostracize* is to make separate from the group, or to shun.

7. *-ate* = **to make:** To *duplicate* is to make double. To *renovate* is to make new again (*nov* means new). To *placate* is to make peaceful or calm (*plac* means peace or calm).

8. *-ity* = **a noun suffix that doesn't actually mean anything; it just turns a word into a noun:** *Jollity* is the noun form of jolly. *Serenity* is the noun form of serene. *Timidity* is the noun form of timid.

The Terminator: Eliminating Idiotic Answers

The first answer to eliminate is the backward one. Putting answers in reverse order is a common trap. If the question goes from greater to lesser (OVERJOYED : CONTENT), the possible answers almost certainly contain a trap that goes from lesser to greater (displeased : furious). Look for it and then throw it out the window.

Another good answer to eliminate is one that duplicates the *meaning* rather than the *relationship* between the words. The question may be PROFESSOR : EDUCATED. The words are synonyms. A good answer to eliminate is teacher : moronic. Even though a professor is a teacher and those words have the same meaning, the *relationship* between the trap answer words is antonymous, not synonymous.

Finally, forget about humor. Anything that's funny or trying to be funny is outta there. Correct answers are almost always dull and boring.

Déjà Vu Review

Before going on to the practice questions, review what you've discovered about Analogy questions. Don't forget to use this simple two-step approach to answering them:

1. **Use both words in a *descriptive* sentence.**

2. **Apply the *exact* same sentence to each answer choice.**

Even if you don't have a clue what the words in an analogy mean, you can often get the correct answer by using the following six tips, which help you to identify the relationship between the words well enough to make a reasonable guess:

- Turn a verb into an infinitive.
- Determine the part of speech of the question word — noun, verb, or adjective.
- Look for the salient features of a word.
- Work backward.
- Identify common relationships.
- Use roots, prefixes, and suffixes.

Ten words that Angelina Jolie never hears

obese	rotund
corpulent	fleshy
flaccid	homely
drab	frowzy
unkempt	slovenly

Chapter 5

The Dirty Dozen: Analogy Practice Questions

● ●

Ready to practice what we've been preaching? Here are Analogy practice questions to get you into the swing of things. This chapter is loaded with good vocabulary words. Don't forget to pay extra-careful attention to the words in this font: *vocabulary word.*

1. PEANUT : SHELL ::

   (A) atom : proton

   (B) clock : dial

   (C) corn : husk

   (D) emollient : solid

   (E) enamel : tooth

Make a simple sentence defining the relationship between the words: "A *peanut* is surrounded by a *shell.*" *Corn* is surrounded by a *husk. Correct Answer:* Choice C.

Choice E is backward. *Enamel* isn't surrounded by a *tooth* but vice versa. Keep your eyes open for a backward answer among the answer choices; those evil test-makers frequently put one there to getcha.

2. HYMN : SONG ::

   (A) screech : whisper

   (B) waltz : dance

   (C) misnomer : correction

   (D) discussion : altercation

   (E) smile : reproof

A simple sentence is "A *hymn* is a type of *song.*" A *waltz* is a type of *dance.* A *screech* is a loud noise, just the opposite of a *whisper.* Your tires screech when you take the corner wide in your rush to get to the GRE after oversleeping. (We know — we shouldn't even joke about such a thing!) In Choice C, a *misnomer* is the wrong name — calling someone Tracy rather than Stacy, for example. Thus, it's not a *correction* but a mistake. An *altercation* is a disagreement. Although an altercation may involve a *discussion,* Choice D isn't as good an answer as Choice B. In Choice E, a *reproof* is a condemnation, a criticism. *Correct Answer:* Choice B.

3. CHUCKLE : MERRIMENT ::

   (A) goose bumps : denial

   (B) blush : glee

   (C) scowl : perfidy

   (D) wince : discomfort

   (E) shout : fury

Make your sentence: "A *chuckle* indicates *merriment*" or "A *chuckle* is the result of *merriment*." *Merriment* is just what it looks like: happiness. The suffix *-ment* doesn't mean anything; it just turns a word into a noun, as you can see with *content* and *contentment,* or *argue* and *argument*. A **wince** (an involuntary shrinking back or flinching) indicates *discomfort*. You wince when your dearly beloved says to you, "We have to talk." In Choice A, *goose bumps* indicate cold or fright, not *denial*. Choice B can trap a careless reader who thinks that this answer fits because *glee* means happiness or merriment. In Choice C, **perfidy** means disloyalty. Choice E is a "maybe so, maybe not" answer. A *shout* may indicate *fury* (you shout at the ATM when it gobbles up and shreds your debit card), but the connection isn't absolute. *Correct Answer:* Choice D.

Choose an answer based on the relationship between the words, not on the meanings of the words. The question can be about houses and the answer about cantaloupes; the meanings of the words in the question and the correct answer don't need to have any connection whatsoever.

4. COW : TERRIFY ::

   (A) praise : denounce

   (B) interest : fascinate

   (C) invigorate : exhaust

   (D) soothe : agitate

   (E) diminish : lessen

Okay, suppose you have no idea what the word *cow* as a verb means. You can still get this question right by the process of elimination. The relationships between the answers in Choices A, C, and D are all that of antonyms. Because they can't all be correct, they must all be wrong. You now know that *cow* and *terrify* aren't antonyms. As quickly as that, you've narrowed the answers down to two, but can you narrow the answers down even further? The relationship between the words in Choice B is lesser to greater; that is, interesting someone is less intense than fascinating that person. Because *terrify*, in the question, is such a strong word, it's unlikely that the first word, *cow*, is something even stronger. Just so you know, to **cow** means to intimidate, to browbeat. *Correct Answer:* Choice B.

Words often possess more than one meaning — a fact that a test question may key into. If your first response seems to make no sense in the context of the question ("Why would a cow terrify anyone?"), think of alternate meanings of the word or words.

5. XENOPHOBIC : STRANGERS ::

   (A) claustrophobic : Christmas

   (B) hydrophobic : fires

   (C) agoraphobic : open spaces

   (D) pyromaniac : animals

   (E) romantic : love

You may not know the word xenophobic, but you can deduce that *phobic* means fearful of because you know such relatively easy words as **hydrophobia** (fear of water) and **claustrophobia** (fear of closed spaces). Go ahead and make the sentence: "*Xenophobic* is fearful of *strangers*." **Agoraphobic** means fearful of open spaces. An agoraphobe is often afraid to leave the house at all. When it's your turn to shovel the snow off the front walk, you may suddenly turn into an agoraphobe.

Choice A is a lame attempt at humor (and won't be found on the actual GRE, which contains no humor at all, lame or otherwise). *Claustrophobic* doesn't mean fearing Santa Claus and Christmas. *Hydrophobic* means fearing water, not *fires.* A *pyromaniac* has a love of fire. Someone *romantic* has a love of *love,* not a fear of love. *Correct Answer:* Choice C.

6. ELEGIAC : JOY ::

  (A) innocuous : harm

  (B) phlegmatic : peace

  (C) implacable : tranquility

  (D) dynamic : energy

  (E) disparaging : insults

Something elegiac isn't full of joy. An *elegy* is a sad or mournful poem. Something *innocuous* isn't full of *harm.* (Figure this one out by using your roots, prefixes, and suffixes: *In-* usually means not; *noc* means harm; *-ous* means full of. Put that all together and you get this: not full of harm.)

Often, if you don't know a word, you can make the "is" sentence: *Elegiac is joy.* But, in this case, we made the question an opposite to make you miss it and, therefore, to help you remember the word *elegiac* (sad or mournful). But you can still get this question correct because Choice D, *dynamic,* does mean full of *energy,* and Choice E, *disparaging,* does mean full of *insults.* Because two answers can't both be correct, they must both be wrong. Figuring that out should send you back to the drawing board to change your line of thinking from an "is" to an "is not" sentence.

Choice B, *phlegmatic,* means calm, composed. Now that you know this word, you can remain phlegmatic when you encounter it on the GRE and not panic. Choice C, *implacable,* means unable to be calmed. An implacable toddler yells, "NO!" no matter what the harassed parents suggest. (Do you see the roots, prefixes, and suffixes? *Im-* means not; *plac* means peace or calm; *-able* means able to be. Someone implacable is "unable to be calmed down," or just plain stubborn.) *Correct Answer:* Choice A.

7. PECCADILLO : TRANSGRESSION ::

  (A) felony : crime

  (B) nibble : bite

  (C) alias : name

  (D) cacophony : noise

  (E) eructation : volcano

You know the suffix *-illo* means small or little. Make the sentence: "A *peccadillo* is a small *transgression.*" You don't even need to know what the words mean to get a good sentence. (A *peccadillo* is a small wrong or fault. A *transgression* is a trespass or sin, a wrong.) A *nibble* is a small *bite.* In Choice C, an *alias* is a different *name,* not a small name. In Choice D, *cacophony* is a bad or harsh sound, such as our singing voices or the sounds of an orchestra warming up. Roots, prefixes, and suffixes help you to define this word; *caco-* means bad, *phon* means sound. Put them together and you get "bad sound." Choice E is our gift to you, a little comic relief. An *eructation* is a belch. Although a *volcano* may eructate, an eructation itself isn't a volcano. *Correct Answer:* Choice B.

8. PROGNOSTICATION : SOOTHSAYER ::

   (A) tumult : arbitrator

   (B) duplicity : idiot

   (C) fanaticism : zealot

   (D) adulation : adult

   (E) retrospection : prophet

Whoa! Suddenly these words have gotten terribly hard. Try saying: "Prognostication *is* sooth-sayer." Okay. Apparently you're looking for two answer words that are synonyms, or that (at the very least) mean *nearly* the same thing.

Fanaticism is the state of being a fanatic (did you know that the word *fan*, like a rock star's groupie, comes from the word *fanatic?*), or being really into something. *Zealous* also means very into something, enthusiastic, or involved. The words are synonyms. A *zealot* is one who is zealous.

You may have known the words for Choice C but not for the other answers. Here's a quick review. Perhaps you're familiar with *tumult* in another form, **tumultuous,** which means wild, chaotic, or disorganized. An **arbitrator** is a mediator, a go-between in a fight or controversy. An arbitrator's job is to stop tumult, to calm matters down and bring about a rational discussion. The words are closer to antonyms than synonyms.

By the way, a favorite trick of the GRE powers-that-be is to give you a common word in an uncommon form, just to confuse you and make your life miserable. For example, do you know this word?

   RUTH

Seeing it all by itself like that, you may swear you've never seen the word before. But you probably know it in another form:

   RUTHLESS

Ah, you know that **ruthless** means cruel, without pity or compassion. Work backward. If ruth-less means *without* pity, ruth must mean *with* pity. **Ruth** is pity or compassion, kindness, and mercy. (By the way, Ruth also used to be a very popular girl's name.)

The moral of the story? When you see a word that looks slightly familiar, knock it around a little bit. Change its form to see whether you can discover its meaning more easily. *Tumult* is just the noun form of the more common word tumultuous.

In Choice B, **duplicity** is the quality of being *dup*, or double, as in double-dealing, double-crossing, and double-talking. Benedict Arnold was noted for his duplicity. The word has nothing to do with being an *idiot*. However, there's a trick here. A **dupe**, a person who has been double-crossed or swindled, is in fact rather idiotic. That's an easy trap to fall for.

Choice D is silly. *Adulation* has nothing to do with being an *adult*. **Adulation** is hero worship, extreme admiration. You may have adulation for a war hero or for the person who discovers the cure for cancer.

The words in Choice E are also closer to antonyms than to synonyms. **Retrospection** is a look back, a review. A **prophet** is supposed to prophesy or predict the future, not look back at the past. *Correct Answer:* Choice C.

9. EXCULPATE : BLAME ::

    (A) demean : average

    (B) compromise : peril

    (C) proliferate : abundance

    (D) perturb : exasperation

    (E) exonerate : guilt

Just to keep you on your toes, we put in a question in which the right answer actually does have the same meaning as the question words. This situation is rare, but we always want to emphasize to you that our suggestions are tips, not rules. Never shut off your own brain in favor of ours. To *exculpate* is to remove *blame*. Again, think of your roots, prefixes, and suffixes: *ex-* means out of or away from; *culp* means guilt or blame; *-ate* means to make. Together they mean "to make away from guilt or blame." When your roommate comes in breathing fire because someone has borrowed his car and put a big dent in it, you thank your lucky stars that you went to class with friends in their car that day and have witnesses to exculpate you. To *exonerate* is the same thing — to remove the *guilt,* or blame. A defense attorney sends his or her investigators out looking for evidence to exonerate a client.

To *compromise* means to imperil, to put into danger. For example, a young girl who stays out all night long with her date — even though they're just talking — compromises her reputation. A government official seen fraternizing with lobbyists may be compromising her integrity, putting it into some question or doubt. As you learned with *cow* in Question 4, words may possess more than one meaning. The first definition most people provide for *compromise* is to come to terms by mutual concession, to meet in the middle and agree. Because that meaning has no connection with *peril,* you need to wrack your brains for another, less common meaning.

In Choice C, to *proliferate* is to grow in number or size, to become more abundant. The most common meaning of *pro-* on the GRE is big or much; a proliferation is an *abundance,* or very much. In Choice D, to *perturb* is to exasperate, to annoy, or to harass. If you missed this question, you're probably perturbed and exasperated with yourself. *Correct Answer:* Choice E.

10. DESICCATE : MOISTURE ::

    (A) sanction : restrictions

    (B) enervate : energy

    (C) swindle : chicanery

    (D) attenuate : attention

    (E) derogate : epithets

To *desiccate* is to dry out, to remove *moisture.* (Ever hear of desiccated liver tablets? Some health-food stores sell them for people who want the health benefits of liver but prefer to ingest it in dehydrated or pill form.) You can figure out this relationship by knowing that *de* means out of or away from: A desiccant moves moisture out of or away from something. To *enervate* is to devitalize, to remove *energy* from, to weaken.

Choice A, to *sanction* is to restrict. You probably know about economic sanctions, in which a government prohibits businesses from working with companies in other countries. To sanction, therefore, is to add *restrictions* rather than take them away. In Choice C, to *swindle* is to cheat or trick, as in swindling someone out of his money. *Chicanery* is trickery in matters of law. Thus, to swindle isn't to take away chicanery but to add to it. In Choice D, to **attenuate** isn't to take away *attention* (you didn't fall for such a cheesy trick, did you?) but to make slender, thin, or diluted. An **emaciated** person looks attenuated. In Choice E, to **derogate** is to denounce or be critical of. An **epithet** is a descriptive term often used derogatorily or critically. *Correct Answer:* Choice B.

11. TOADY : SYCOPHANT ::

   (A) recluse : pedant

   (B) heretic : leader

   (C) malingerer : prodigy

   (D) bluestocking : gymnast

   (E) miser : penny-pincher

If you don't know the words in the question, you're not alone. They're very difficult words put there in the hopes that you remember what to do when you don't have a clue: First, try making the words synonyms. Make the simple sentence: A *toady* is a *sycophant*. As it turns out, that's correct. Both a **toady** and a **sycophant** are over-flatterers, kiss-ups, and yes-men. A groupie to a rock star is both a toady and a sycophant. A student trying to get the professor to turn a borderline A–/B+ into the A is a toady and a sycophant. In the correct answer, Choice E, a **miser** (a cheapskate, someone stingy) is in fact a *penny-pincher*. A penny-pincher is a cheap person, one who "pinches" pennies and holds them securely, not letting them go or spending them.

Here are the definitions for the other words. A **recluse** is a hermit, a solitary person. You may have heard this word in another form: reclusive. A **pedant** is a teacher, especially one who is overly precise and didactic. A **heretic** is a rebel, particularly one who doesn't agree with the orthodox religion. Joan of Arc was burned at the stake as a heretic. A **malingerer** is one who pretends to be sick in order to get out of work. Perhaps you yourself have been a malingerer on the morning of a big exam at school, swearing to a variety of symptoms that would kill an ox. A **prodigy** is a highly talented person (Mozart was a child prodigy). A **bluestocking** is a learned woman, especially one in literary circles. She has nothing to do with gymnastics. *Correct Answer:* Choice E.

12. PUGILIST : BELLICOSE ::

   (A) benefactor : beguiling

   (B) chatterbox : taciturn

   (C) narcissist : charismatic

   (D) scholar : erudite

   (E) imbecile : obsequious

A **pugilist** is a boxer, one who fights (the root *pug* means war or fight, and *-ist* is a person). **Bellicose** is like belligerent: hostile, argumentative, and fighting. The test sentence is: "A *pugilist* is *bellicose*." If you don't know the words and assume that they're synonyms, you're right. A *scholar* is in fact **erudite,** which means well-educated or scholarly. In Choice A, a **benefactor** is a person who does good, one who brings *benefits* (to use a more common form of the word). He or she probably isn't **beguiling,** which means tricking or confusing. In Choice B, a **chatterbox** is just what it looks like — one who chatters or talks a lot. **Taciturn** means not talkative, or "of few words." A chatterbox isn't taciturn.

Ever hear of a tacit agreement? It's an unspoken agreement. Try to think of more common or familiar forms of a word you're not familiar with. If you can remember how you use those words in context, you can often get a "good enough" definition for a difficult word.

In Choice C, a *narcissist* is a person overflowing with self-love, someone who thinks he or she is just the most wonderful thing around. Although the narcissist may think that he or she is *charismatic* (inspiring loyalty), that's not necessarily so. In Choice E, an *imbecile* is a feeble-minded person; a fool (what most folks feel like when they don't know all these words). An imbecile may or may not be *obsequious,* which means excessively flattering. Remember the toady and sycophant from Question 11? Now *they* would be obsequious. *Correct Answer:* Choice D.

Part II
A Word to the Wise: Verbal Questions

The 5th Wave   By Rich Tennant

THOUGH HIS "CALL" TO THE SCHOOL NEVER WENT THROUGH, GARY WAS PLEASED TO LATER FIND THAT AN ANALYTICAL ABILITY SCORE WASN'T REQUIRED AS PART OF THE ADMISSION REQUIREMENTS.

©RICHTENNANT

Hmm—still no dial tone.

In this part . . .

One of the sections on the GRE is the Verbal section. The questions in this section come in four styles: Antonyms (finding words that are opposites), Analogies (far and away the easiest for most people), Sentence Completions (good ol' fill-in-the-blanks, the same stuff you've been doing since kindergarten), and Reading Comprehension (dull and deadly). Each question style has a chapter of its own. You learn the format of the question (what it looks like), an approach to the question (where to begin and an organized plan of attack), and the various tricks and traps built into the questions (with, of course, suggestions for recognizing and avoiding 'em). Vocabulary-building material features roots, prefixes, and suffixes. Following each lecture chapter is a chapter that includes particularly wicked practice questions as well as detailed answer explanations that show you what you should've done, how to make the best use of your time, and what you should've guessed at random.

Chapter 6

If Opposites Attract, Why Are Antonyms So Repulsive?

· ·

In This Chapter

▶ Getting the format down cold

▶ Cruising through Antonym questions with the right approach

▶ Using the inexact sciences of guessing and dissecting

▶ Watching out for tricks, traps, and tips

· ·

Think of antonyms as the terrible twos of the vocabulary world. Just like a *cantankerous* (grumpy) kid who answers your "Good morning!" with "No, it's not; it's a bad morning!" the GRE's Antonym questions look to contradict everything.

Is That All There Is? The Format

Antonyms are fish out of water, words out of context (clichés out of a *For Dummies* book). Antonym questions feature one word in capital letters followed by five lowercase answer choices. The prima donna antonym stands alone. You have no context to help you define the vocabulary. It's you against the word. For example:

LOQUACIOUS:

(A) quotidian

(B) taciturn

(C) contentious

(D) guileless

(E) perfunctory

Just so you don't have to go running for your dictionary, we'll tell you that the answer is Choice B. *Loquacious* means talkative. (*Loq* means speech or talk; *-ous* means full of. Someone loquacious is full of talk.) *Taciturn* means not talkative, quiet, saying little.

Your task is to define the question word and then choose the answer with the most nearly opposite meaning. The good news is that doing so takes almost no time. These questions are over with faster than your last relationship. The bad news is that some of this vocabulary is so difficult you may think you've wandered into the Greek GRE by mistake.

Let's Get This Over with Fast: The Approach

Antonyms are the least complicated questions on the GRE. Take a simple two-step approach:

1. **Define the question word.**
2. **Choose the opposite.**

Sounds simple, right? It is . . . if you know what the question word means. If the question word is *happy*, choose *sad*. If the question word is *tall*, choose *short*. So far, so good. But what happens when you don't know what the question word means?

All in a day's work, labor, toil, pursuit, grind . . .

Having an extensive vocabulary will help you with the Verbal and Analytical Writing sections of the GRE. One way you can improve your vocabulary quickly is to group words with similar meanings — to remember five or ten for the price of one. If you can remember *harbinger*, you can remember *prescient*.

✔ I'm *looking forward* to this:

auguries	presage
bode	prescient
harbinger	prognosis
portent	prognosticate

✔ You have to keep your sense of *humor:*

badinage	mirth
japing	puckish
jocose	ribald
jocular	risible
jollity	twit
levity	wag

✔ It's a *sad* day when you don't know your vocabulary:

bereft	lachrymose
contrite	lugubrious
doleful	maudlin
dour	saturnine
jeremiad	Weltschmerz

✔ That's easy for you to *say:*

declaim	prolix
exhort	raconteur
persiflage	stentorian
philippic	tergiversate
pontificate	voluble

✔ Just how *boring* is this vocabulary?

banal	prosaic
bromide	somniferous
ennui	soporific
hackneyed	tedious
listless	trite
platitude	vapid

✔ It takes a lot of *guts* to know these words:

audacity	intrepid
doughty	redoubtable
effrontery	uncowed
impudent	undaunted

✔ Hip, hip, hooray! Words of *praise:*

accolade	obsequious
encomium	paean
eulogy	panegyric
extol	plaudits
kudos	sycophant
laud	toady

✔ Are you sick to *death* of vocabulary?

cadaver	morbid
demise	noxious
dirge	obsequies
elegy	valetudinarian
insalubrious	wan

What to Do When You Ain't Got a Clue

Suppose you look at a word and think it looks more like an inkblot test than any vocabulary word you've ever seen. The word may be *cadging*. Not a clue, right? (And no, it's not a typo or a misspelling of *cage*.) What do you do next? You have three options:

1. **Dissect and define the term using roots, prefixes, and suffixes.**

   As we point out in Chapter 4, roots, prefixes, and suffixes are the real key to vocabulary on the GRE. Unfortunately, you haven't learned a root, prefix, or suffix for *cadging*. Proceed to Step 2.

2. **Eliminate answer choices that are synonyms of each other.**

   Suppose that Choice A is **bubbly** and Choice D is **effervescent**. Both words mean exuberant or joyful. Because two answer choices can't both be correct, they must both be wrong.

3. **Bail out! Choose an answer and leave the scene as quickly as possible.**

   Say you have no idea what the word means. It has no identifiable root, prefix, or suffix. No two of the answer choices mean the same thing. You have no way to narrow the answers down. What happens now? Guess and go. Choose something, anything, and go on to the next question.

The biggest mistake you can make on an Antonym question is to waste time. The longer you sit there, staring at the word, scratching your head, and waiting for heavenly revelation, the more the test-makers in their dark cubbyholes chortle with glee at your struggling in the **quagmire** (bog) they designed for you. Get through an Antonym question quickly: You either know it or you don't, and then you're outta there. Think of an Antonym question as a blind date. You can tell in the first few minutes whether something is happening or not. (By the way, **cadging** means begging or scrounging. GRE students often cadge class notes from friends.)

Bad Things Come in Small Packages: Tricks, Traps, and Tips

How, you wonder, can there be tricks and traps in a one-word question? Read 'em and weep.

Ignore the synonym

You may be lucky enough to encounter a very difficult word that you just happen to remember. Pretend that the question word is *pulchritudinous* and that, having gone through the Analogies portion of this book, you remember that **pulchritudinous** means beautiful. Choice A is *beautiful*. You're so pleased with yourself for remembering this hard word that you take Choice A ("Ah, there it is!") and go on your merry way. It isn't until you're boasting to your friend later that afternoon about having remembered *pulchritudinous* that your mistake dawns on you: You were supposed to choose the *antonym*, not the synonym. In short: If you see a word in the answer choices whose meaning is the same, or nearly the same, as the question word, ignore it. The test-writing gnomes put it there just to ruin your day.

Use roots, prefixes, and suffixes

As we mention throughout this material, roots, prefixes, and suffixes (RPS) can save you when you have to wade through this polysyllabic pit. If you haven't memorized the prefixes and suffixes in Chapter 4, we strongly suggest you do so. You can analyze even the most difficult word by using roots (check out Chapter 8). Even if you can't get the exact definition, you can get a general idea of the word well enough to choose it or lose it.

Suppose that the question word is *abjure.* You don't know what it means, but you recall that the prefix *ab-* means away from. A queen abdicates a throne, or goes away from it. One of the answer choices is *embrace.* To embrace something is to take it as your own, to accept it, as in embracing the principles of democracy. If you trust your roots-sense and choose this answer, you can get a hard question correct in just a few seconds. (To *abjure* is to renounce or reject.)

Memorize connotation cards

In Chapter 4, we suggest you create flashcards for the roots, prefixes, and suffixes. After you have those cards completed, you're ready to move on to a more sophisticated type of flashing: *connotation cards.*

Notice that we're not wasting your time or ours by giving you a list of a thousand words. It'd be useless for you to sit down and try to memorize so many. You'd get to a point where each new word would *supplant* (displace, push out) a previous word. So how can you cram the most vocabulary into the least brain space? Memorize groups of words by their connotation.

A *connotation* is an association or idea, an implication. It's what the word means to you — how you remember it. Use index cards to cluster words by their connotations. For example, on one side of a card write *fat,* and on the other side write *thin.* Every time you encounter a word that has one of these meanings, put it on the card. On the fat side, you may have *corpulent, fleshy, rotund,* and *obese.* On the thin side, you may have *emaciated, attenuated, svelte,* and *lanky.*

Suppose you get to the exam and see the word *svelte* but can't for the life of you remember what it means. In your mind's eye, you see the word on the *fat/thin* card. Voilà! Or on second thought: Ooops! Wait a minute: Does *svelte* mean fat, or does it mean thin?

Write words with positive meanings in red ink and words with negative meanings in black ink. Maybe you consider being thin better than being fat. Write all the *thin* words in bright red ink to make them stand out. Write all the *fat* words in black ink. During the exam, you can remember that *svelte* is a red word on the *fat/thin* card, so it must mean thin. You'll be surprised how many questions you can get correct without knowing precise definitions, just hazy general concepts.

You may also benefit from drawing a picture of the definition of the words on each side of the card. Brains like visuals. You may not be able to remember the precise definition of the word, but your brain should be able to conjure up the picture on the card.

Don't anticipate and misread

The GRE often features some pretty bizarre-looking words. Our favorite is *froward* (stubborn). At least once a year, some student calls us, overjoyed at having "conquered" the GRE: "You won't believe it. The GRE had a typo. One of the antonyms said *froward* instead of *forward.* However, the answer choice *backward* was there, so I had no trouble figuring it out." No, no, a thousand times, no! The GRE has no typos. The GRE has no spelling errors. The GRE has no heart. It's very easy to see what you want to see rather than read what's actually shown on the screen. Double-check that you've read the word correctly, not rewritten the test to match your preconceptions.

Peroration (A Summing Up)

An Antonym question requires a simple, two-step approach:

1. **Define the question word.**
2. **Choose the opposite.**

Antonyms are small but deadly. Remembering the following can help you get through these questions efficiently:

✔ Use roots, prefixes, and suffixes.

✔ Eliminate answer choices that are synonyms of each other or the question word.

✔ Learn vocabulary words in clusters by using connotation cards and visuals.

✔ Don't anticipate and misread unusual words (such as *froward*).

Chapter 7

Unattractive Opposites: Antonym Practice Questions

• •

You say you've been using a dictionary for a pillow the last six weeks, believing some of the words and their definitions would penetrate your skull via osmosis? Here's a chance to test your theory. (Consider this chapter to be one big vocabulary list.)

1. CHANGING

    (A) lightweight

    (B) cautious

    (C) immutable

    (D) delicious

    (E) soft

You can get this question correct by the process of elimination. The opposite of *changing* is unchanging or not changing. You know that *lightweight, cautious, delicious,* and *soft* don't mean not changing, which quickly narrows the answers down to the correct one. Use your roots to define **immutable**. *Im-* means not; *mut* means change. *Im-mut-able* literally means not changeable, or unchanging. *Correct Answer:* Choice C.

2. RECUPERATE

    (A) sicken

    (B) invent

    (C) operate

    (D) elongate

    (E) balance

To **recuperate** is to regain your health. The opposite is to *sicken.* Choice C has a small trap in it. A person recuperating may have been operated on, but just because an answer choice seems connected to the question word doesn't mean the choice is correct.

Did you use your common sense to eliminate Choice B? What word could possibly be the opposite of *invent?* As far as we know, no word means "uninvent." If you can't think of a logical opposite for a word, it's probably not an antonym of the question. *Correct Answer:* Choice A.

3. OPAQUE

    (A) old-fashioned

    (B) angry

    (C) improper

    (D) outdated

    (E) transparent

Something *opaque* isn't clear or see-through. It blocks the light (*op* means block or against). Something *transparent* is clear; it doesn't block the light. Did you notice that you can eliminate Choices A and D because they're synonyms of each other? If two words mean the same (or nearly the same) thing, they can't both be correct and therefore must both be wrong. *Correct Answer:* Choice E.

4. LOQUACIOUS

    (A) elegant

    (B) quiet

    (C) overweight

    (D) excited

    (E) incapable

Loq means speech or talk; *-ous* means full of or very. Someone *loquacious* is full of talk, or very talkative. The opposite is *quiet*. *Correct Answer:* Choice B.

Most of our students are quite loquacious in telling us that their biggest problem is vocabulary. They just plain can't remember pages and pages and pages of words. Our suggestion is always the same: Concentrate on learning roots, prefixes, and suffixes, which can expand your vocabulary exponentially. You can find a list of roots in Chapter 8 and lists of prefixes and suffixes in Chapter 4.

5. SKEPTICAL

    (A) fast-acting

    (B) punctual

    (C) depressed

    (D) credulous

    (E) effervescent

If you're *skeptical,* you're dubious or doubtful. So you're looking for a word that means not doubtful. Eliminate the words you know — Choices A, B, and C. You can define *credulous* by using roots and suffixes: *cred* means trust or belief; *-ous* means full of or very. Someone credulous is full of trust, and is therefore naive or gullible — just the opposite of skeptical. *Effervescent* means bubbly. When an *Effer*dent (a brand-name denture-cleaning tablet) is put into a glass of water, it bubbles. *Correct Answer:* Choice D.

6. VIABLE

    (A) solid

    (B) moribund

    (C) vital

    (D) integral

    (E) irreplaceable

If you picked Choice C, you fell for the trap. *Vital* means essential, critical. Sure, vital has a *vi* like the question word, but that doesn't mean vital is the right answer (and anyway, you're looking for antonyms, not synonyms). Choices C, D, and E are similar enough in meaning that selecting one over the others would be hard. You can't have three right answers, so eliminate them all.

Viable means livable, capable of working or developing adequately. A plan for learning several roots like *vi* (meaning life) daily is viable (it can be done). *Moribund* means near death or extinction. A company that's bankrupt and firing employees may be described as moribund. *Correct Answer:* Choice B.

7. SALUBRIOUS

    (A) unhealthy

    (B) serendipitous

    (C) dour

    (D) rapid

    (E) monumental

Salubrious means healthful, wholesome, or salutary (*sal* means health, *-ous* means full of). *Unhealthy* is as logical an opposite as you're ever going to find. Choice B, *serendipitous,* means fortuitous and can be used to describe a happy, lucky occurrence. Walking out your front door to find a hundred-dollar bill on your stoop would be serendipitous. Choice C, *dour,* means gloomy. Finding out that the hundred-dollar bill you so serendipitously found on the sidewalk features a picture not of Ben Franklin but of Alfred E. Neuman will leave you dour. *Correct Answer:* Choice A.

8. IRASCIBLE

    (A) mendacious

    (B) serpentine

    (C) phlegmatic

    (D) fatigued

    (E) tepid

Irascible means hot-tempered, easily angered. Choice C, *phlegmatic,* means slow, having a stolid temperament, not easily excited to action. Choice A, *mendacious,* means lying, dishonest, or untruthful. Don't confuse the adjective mendacious, meaning dishonest, with the noun *mendicant,* a beggar. A mendicant may be mendacious when he tells you how he's going to spend the quarter you just gave him. Choice B, *serpentine,* means like a snake, twisting or turning. The road to Pike's Peak is a serpentine road. Choice E, *tepid,* means lukewarm. A tepid response to a marriage proposal should send you to your lawyer's office to get a prenuptial agreement. *Correct Answer:* Choice C.

9. FRANGIBLE

   (A) refulgent

   (B) histrionic

   (C) unbreakable

   (D) unfriendly

   (E) masculine

Frangible means breakable. The opposite, amazingly enough, is *unbreakable*. Choice A, *refulgent,* means shining, radiant, gleaming. Choice B, *histrionic,* means theatrical, hysterical, and dramatic. *Correct Answer:* Choice C.

10. PALLIATE

   (A) laud

   (B) appraise

   (C) exacerbate

   (D) befriend

   (E) mitigate

To *palliate* is to soften, lessen, or assuage. You can palliate an insult by smiling to take the sting out. Choice C, to *exacerbate,* is to make more severe, to aggravate. You exacerbate a fight when you slam the door in your opponent's face. Choice A, to *laud,* is to praise. (Think of app*laud.*) Choice D, to *befriend,* is to make a friend of. (*Be-* is a prefix meaning completely; however, you can basically ignore this prefix. To befriend someone is simply to "friend" him.) Choice E, *mitigate,* is the same as palliate. To mitigate is to lessen or decrease, to make less severe. You may have heard of "mitigating circumstances." Hot-wiring and stealing a car is a felony that can land you in prison; if your wife is in labor and you have to get to the hospital pronto, that's a mitigating circumstance (but if you take one of our cars, you have *unmitigated* gall!). *Correct Answer:* Choice C.

11. CONDIGN

   (A) incapable

   (B) inevitable

   (C) inconsistent

   (D) unremitting

   (E) undeserved

Condign means deserved or appropriate; the opposite (logically enough) is *undeserved.* A condign punishment if you don't laugh at our jokes is to spend eternity listening to your parents' old record albums. By the way, because *inevitable* and *unremitting* have closely related meanings, neither is the likely answer. *Correct Answer:* Choice E.

12. SALACIOUS

   (A) wholesome

   (B) rustic

   (C) noxious

   (D) merry

   (E) puissant

Salacious means lustful, lecherous, lewd — the opposite of *wholesome*. Choice B, *rustic,* means rural, appropriate for the country. Plus fours and a shooting stick make for a rustic outfit. Choice E, *puissant,* means strong, influential, powerful. *Correct Answer:* Choice A.

Did you fall for the trap answer, Choice C? *Sal* means health; *-ous* means full of. No one can fault you if you thought salacious meant "full of health." However, the word for that is salubrious. Choice C, *noxious,* means poisonous. It's an antonym for salubrious, but not for salacious.

Chapter 8

Finishing What You Start: Sentence Completions

In This Chapter

▶ Identifying Sentence Completion questions

▶ Dissecting and simplifying the sentences

▶ Eliminating wrong answers

▶ Recognizing roots

Sentence Completion questions are the blind dates of the GRE. What you see isn't necessarily what you get . . . or what you want. Looks can be deceiving. Don't judge a book by its cover. Beauty is only skin deep. Have we left out any other trite, banal, hackneyed clichés? The point of all this babbling is that Sentence Completion questions can be sneaky, tricky, duplicitous, and worse than they look. Fortunately, you can beat 'em at their own game.

Recognizing Sentence Completion Questions

A Sentence Completion question consists of one sentence with one or two blanks. Your job, should you choose to accept it, is to fill in those blanks. Usually only one word goes in each blank; occasionally, however, the blank requires a few words or a short phrase instead. Here's an example:

Disgusted at having to spend the entire weekend studying for the GRE instead of going hang gliding, Faye - - - - her book across the room with such - - - - that it soared high into the sky, causing three of her neighbors to call the UFO hot line.

(A) tossed . . . gentleness

(B) hurled . . . ferocity

(C) pitched . . . glee

(D) carried . . . gloom

(E) conveyed . . . reluctance

The key word in this example is *disgusted*, which indicates strong negative emotions. Although Choice D arguably meets the requirement of negative emotion, *carried* books don't soar high into the sky; *hurled* books do. Only Choice B offers two words that match the tone of *disgusted* — and soared high into the air. *Correct Answer:* Choice B.

Looking at the Sentence and Drawing a Blank

Do you look at Sentence Completion questions and draw a blank? (Sorry, we couldn't resist.) Knowing where to start is a great confidence builder and time saver. Try the following steps:

1. **Read the entire sentence for its gist.**
2. **If possible, predict words to fit into the blanks.**
3. **Insert *every* answer choice into the blanks and reread the resulting sentences.**

The following sections explain these steps in detail.

Read the entire sentence

Although this advice may seem obvious, many people read until they get to the first blank and then head for the answers. The problem is that the sentence may change in midstream, messing everything up. Note, for example, the big difference between these two sentences:

> Having been coerced by her mother into accepting a blind date, Mitzi was - - - - *because* Marty turned out to be - - - -.

> — and —

> Having been coerced by her mother into accepting a blind date, Mitzi was - - - - *although* Marty turned out to be - - - -.

In the first example, you may want to say something like this:

> Having been coerced by her mother into accepting a blind date, Mitzi was *ecstatic* because Marty turned out to be *gorgeous.*

In the second example, you can say the following:

> Having been coerced by her mother into accepting a blind date, Mitzi was *content* although Marty turned out to be *mediocre.*

How you fill in the blanks depends on the middle term — in this case, the conjunction *because* or *although.*

Keep in mind that the purpose of Sentence Completion questions is to measure your ability to recognize words and phrases that logically complete the meanings of the sentences.

If possible, predict words to fit the blanks

Notice the careful hedge "if possible." You can't *always* predict words. But you can usually get pretty close. Consider the following example:

> Hal was - - - - when his new computer arrived because he realized he'd have no excuses now for not finishing his homework.

You can predict that the word should be something negative such as *depressed, sad,* or *unhappy.* (If your vocabulary is up to the task, you can also predict negative words such as *lachrymose, dolorous,* and *lugubrious.*) Predicting words in advance helps you eliminate obvious wrong choices.

Did you predict something positive such as *happy* or *glad?* If you did, you probably headed for the answers before you read the entire sentence. What did we just tell you in the preceding section? Tsk, tsk.

Insert the answer choices

Occasionally, you can eliminate answers because you know the word must be positive and the answer choice is negative. After you eliminate all the choices you can, insert the remaining answers into the blanks and read through the resulting sentences.

You need to plug and chug. Don't try to save time by hurrying through Sentence Completion questions. Plug in every answer choice and chug through the whole darn sentence again.

Try the following example:

As a public relations specialist, Susan realizes the importance of - - - - and - - - - when dealing with even the most exasperating tourists.

(A) dignity . . . etiquette

(B) fantasy . . . realism

(C) kindness . . . patience

(D) courtesy . . . compassion

(E) truth . . . honesty

Because the two blanks are connected by *and,* the words in those blanks should be synonyms (or almost synonyms). They may not need to mean exactly the same thing, but they certainly shouldn't be opposites. They should be on the same wavelength. That means you can eliminate Choice B because *fantasy* and *realism* are opposites. That's the only answer, however, that you can eliminate immediately. The others are all close enough in meaning to fit together.

This quandary leaves you with no choice but to plug and chug. Insert every answer and see which one makes the most sense. The right answer here is Choice C. Choice A looks pretty good, but you don't "treat someone with etiquette." ***Etiquette*** is a system of rules for manners. Choice D also looks pretty good, but a public relations specialist is expected to be businesslike, so *compassion* is a less likely attribute than *patience.* Also, treating with compassion someone who is *exasperating* isn't as logical as treating the person with patience. Choice E is very tempting until you plug it into the sentence. *Truth* and *honesty* are synonyms, but they don't fit as well in the context of the sentence as do *kindness* and *patience.* *Correct Answer:* Choice C.

Forget about taking a lot of shortcuts. After you eliminate the obviously incorrect answers, take your sweet time going back and inserting every remaining answer into the sentence. Sentence Completion answers aren't right or wrong so much as good, better, or best. Sometimes all the answers seem to sorta fit; your job is to choose the one that fits best.

Blowing Sentences Away: Dynamite Traps 'n' Tricks

Let us introduce you to the nasty little gremlins lurking in the Sentence Completion questions and give you some suggestions for dealing with them. Your basic course of action is as follows:

1. **Look for key connecting words that may change the meaning of the sentence.**

2. **Predict positive or negative words to fit in the blanks.**

3. **Don't waste time scratching your head over questions with vocabulary that's totally unfamiliar to you — make a guess and go on to the next question.**

The following sections delve further into these steps.

Remember that connections count

Changing *and* to *or* or *because* to *however* can change everything, as this example shows:

> Buzz was content to - - - - *and* - - - - on his weekend, answering to no one but himself, doing exactly as he liked.

Perhaps you'd fill the blanks with *rest . . . relax.* You know that the concepts are synonyms. Now check this version out:

> Buzz was content to - - - - *or* - - - - on his weekend, answering to no one but himself, doing exactly as he liked.

The *or* changes everything. You no longer know for sure that the concepts must not be opposites; you only know that they might be opposites. You may fill the blanks with *sleep . . . party* or perhaps *work . . . play.* However, you can just as easily say that "Buzz was content to fish or hunt on his weekend, answering to no one but himself, doing exactly as he liked." Be careful on these *and* and *or* questions, because they can be tricky.

Some common connecting words are

although	and	because
but	but for	despite
either/or	however	in spite of
moreover	nonetheless	or
therefore		

Whenever you see the preceding words, your antennae should go up, putting you on the alert for a plot twist — a trap of some sort.

Use your crystal ball

Sometimes the sentences are so long and **convoluted** (twisting or turning) that you can't make heads or tails of them. In that case, dissect the sentence. (A sentence so confusing probably makes you **sanguinary**, or bloodthirsty, enough to want to dismember something right about then.) Isolate just a bit of the sentence around the blank and try to predict whether that blank requires a positive or negative word. Consider the following:

"Blah blah blah blah blah blah blah blah blah blah blah," Frances cursed - - - -.

Because people rarely curse or swear nicely, you can predict that the blank must be filled with a negative word. Maybe Frances curses *harshly, rudely,* or *viciously* (or *stridently, stentorianly,* or *fulminatingly*). You can eliminate answer choices such as *sweetly, kindly,* or *courteously* (as well as *benignly, amiably,* or *decorously*).

Guess and go

Many times you can get the right answer in Sentence Completion questions by the process of elimination. You may have a hazy idea what type of word (positive or negative) or words (antonyms or synonyms) go into the blank or blanks. But what happens if you can't eliminate any answers because you don't know what any of the words mean? Hit the road, Jack. Get outta there fast. If you're making a wild guess anyway, why spend time deliberating over it? Guess and go!

Although she usually was of a cheerful nature, Patty was - - - - when she heard the history professor assign a paper that would be due the first day back after spring break.

(A) ebullient

(B) indolent

(C) supercilious

(D) enigmatic

(E) lugubrious

Okay. You know that the blank needs to be filled with a word that means sad, gloomy, or glum. So far so good. But then you get to the answer choices, and life as you know it ceases to exist. You don't know *any* of those words. You can't get this one right except by randomly guessing. Fill in something, anything, and zoom on to the next question.

A vocabulary-helper bonus

You're no doubt delighted to know that roots, prefixes, and suffixes (RPS) help you immensely on the Sentence Completion vocabulary, just as they do on the Analogies and Antonyms sections. If you don't know what the words mean, use your RPS to figure them out (see Chapter 4 and this chapter's "Getting Back to Your Roots" section for more on RPS). For example, consider the following sentence:

> Jane refused to eulogize Donald, saying that she thought he was a - - - - fellow.

Obviously, the entire sentence depends on the meaning of *eulogize.* If it means something bad, Jane refused to bad-mouth Donald and thought that he was a swell fellow. If it means something good, Jane refused to say anything good about Donald, thinking he was a bad fellow. Which is it? As you may recall, *eu-* (along with

ben- and *bon-*) means good. You also probably picked up the suffix *-ize,* which means to make. And *log* means speech or talk. You can therefore reason that *to eulogize* means to make good speech or talk. If she refused "to make good speech or talk" about Donald, she didn't like him. Fill the blank with a bad word, such as *rotten, terrible,* or *disgusting.*

Try this one:

> Ashamed of his obvious trembling and - - - - when confronted by the farmer's wife, Blind Mickey told his two good friends, "I thought I was a man, but I'm just a mouse."

Here, you need a word that means fear. The right answer may be *trepidation.* You can figure out the word if you know that the root *trep* means fear.

Leaving you hanging on this sentence would be too vicious, even for us. After all, we're only *unofficial* test-makers, tyrants-in-training as it were. The correct answer is Choice E. *Lugubrious* means sad. As for the other words, *ebullient* means happy, overjoyed. *Indolent* means lazy, laid back. *Supercilious* means stuck-up, conceited. *Enigmatic* means mysterious, difficult to figure out. An *enigma* is a puzzle or a mystery, such as the enigma of how you ever got yourself into something as soul-leeching as this exam. *Correct Answer:* Choice E.

Getting Back to Your Roots

This section is where you get to increase your vast storehouse of knowledge by adding some of the important roots (see Chapter 4 for a rundown of basic prefixes and suffixes). The following is just a short list, but it's representative of what can greatly help you in figuring out GRE *sesquipedalian* (foot and a half long!) vocabulary words.

If English isn't your first language, vocabulary may be the hardest part of the exam for you. Using roots, prefixes, and suffixes can help you greatly.

- *ambu* = **walk, move:** In a hospital, patients are either bedridden (they can't move) or *ambu*latory (they can walk and move about). A somn*ambu*list is a sleepwalker. *Somn-* means sleep; *-ist* is a person; *ambu* is to walk or move. A *somnambulist,* therefore, is a person who walks or moves in his or her sleep.

- *andro* = **man:** Commander Data on *Star Trek: The Next Generation* is an *andro*id; he's a robot shaped like a man. Someone *andro*gynous exhibits both male *(andro)* and female *(gyn)* characteristics (literally, he/she is full of man and woman). Disturbingly, Marilyn Manson comes to mind. . . .

- *anthro* = **human or mankind:** *Anthro*pology is the study of humans (not just a particular gender but humans in general). A mis*anthro*pe hates humans. (An equal-opportunity hater: He or she hates both men and women alike.)

- *bellu, belli* = **war, fight:** If you're *belli*gerent, you're ready to fight — in fact, you're downright hostile. An ante*bellu*m mansion is one that was created before the Civil War. (Remember that *ante-* means *before.* You can find this word in Chapter 4's list of prefixes.)

- *cred* = **trust or belief:** Something in*cred*ible is unbelievable, such as the excuse, "I would've picked you up on time, sweetheart, but there was a 75-car pile-up on the freeway." If you're *cred*ulous, you're trusting and *naive* (literally, full of trust). In fact, if you're credulous, you probably actually feel sorry for your honey being stuck in traffic.

Be careful not to confuse the words *credible* and *credulous.* Something *credible* is trustable or believable. A credible excuse can get you out of trouble if you turn a paper in late. *Credulous,* on the other hand, means full of trust, naive, or gullible. The more credulous your professor is, the less credible that excuse needs to be.

- *de* = **down from, away from (to put down):** To *de*scend or *de*part is to go down from or away from. To *de*nounce is to put down or to speak badly of, as in *de*nouncing those hogs who chow down all the pizza before you get to the party.

Many unknown words on the GRE that start with *de* mean to put down in the sense of to criticize or bad-mouth. Here are just a few: demean, denounce, denigrate, derogate, deprecate, decry.

- *ex* = **out of, away from:** An *ex*it is literally out of or away from *it* — *ex*-it. (This is probably one of the most logical words around.) To *ex*tricate is to get out of something. You can extricate yourself from an argument by pretending to faint, basking in all the sympathy as you're carried away. To *ex*culpate is to get off the hook — literally to make away from guilt. *Culp* means guilt. When the president of the Hellenic Council wants to know who TP'ed the dean's house, you can claim that you and your sorority sisters aren't *culpable.*

✔ *gnos* = **knowledge:** A doctor shows his or her knowledge by making a dia*gnos*is (analysis of the situation) or a pro*gnos*is (prediction about the future of the illness). An a*gnos*tic is a person who doesn't know whether a god exists. Differentiate an *agnostic* from an *atheist:* An atheist is literally without god, a person who believes there's no god. An agnostic is without knowledge, believing a god may or may not exist.

✔ *greg* = **group, herd:** A congre*greg*ation is a group or herd of people. A *greg*arious person likes to be part of a group — he or she is sociable. To se*greg*ate is literally to make away from the group. *Se-* means apart or away from, as in *separate, sever, sequester,* and *seclusion.*

✔ *gyn* = **woman:** A *gyn*ecologist is a physician who treats women. A miso*gyn*ist is a person who hates women.

✔ *loq, log, loc, lix* = **speech or talk:** Someone *loq*uacious talks a lot. (That person is literally full of talk.) A dia*log*ue is talk or conversation between two people. E*loc*ution is proper speech. A pro*lix* person is very talkative. (Literally, he or she engages in big, or much, talk.)

✔ *luc, lum, lus* = **light, clear:** Something *lum*inous is shiny and full of light. Ask the teacher to e*luc*idate something you don't understand (literally, to make clear). *Lus*trous hair reflects the light and is sleek and glossy.

✔ *meta* = **beyond, after:** A *meta*morphosis is a change of shape beyond the present shape.

✔ *morph* = **shape:** Something a*morph*ous is without shape. *Morph*ology is the study of shape. ("Yes, of course, I take my studies seriously. I spend all weekend on *morph*ology at the beach.")

✔ *mut* = **change:** The Teenage *Mut*ant Ninja Turtles *mut*ated, or changed, from mild-mannered turtles to pizza-gobbling crime fighters. Something im*mut*able isn't changeable; it remains constant. Don't confuse *mut* (change) with *mute* (silent).

✔ *pac* = **peace, calm:** Why do you give a baby a *pac*ifier? To calm him or her down. To get its name, the *Pac*ific Ocean must have appeared calm at the time it was discovered.

✔ *path* = **feeling:** Something *path*etic arouses feeling or pity. To sym*path*ize is to share the feelings (literally, to make the same feeling). Anti*path*y is a dislike — literally, a feeling against. For example, no matter how much the moron apologizes, you still may harbor antipathy toward the jerk who parked right behind you and blocked you in, making you late for a date and causing all sorts of unfortunate romantic repercussions.

✔ *phon* = **sound:** *Phon*ics helps you to sound out words. Caco*phon*y is bad sound; eu*phon*y is good sound. Homo*phon*es are words that sound the same, such as *red* and *read.*

✔ *plac* = **peace, calm:** To *plac*ate someone is to calm him or her down or to make peace with that person. You placate your irate sweetheart, for example, by sending a dozen roses (hint, hint). Someone im*plac*able is someone you aren't able to calm down — or someone really stubborn. If those roses don't do the trick, for example, your sweetheart is too implacable to placate.

✔ *pro* = **big, much:** *Pro*fuse apologies are big, or much — in essence, a *lot* of apologies. A *pro*lific writer produces a great deal of written material.

Pro has two additional meanings less commonly used on the GRE. It can mean *before,* as in "A *pro*logue comes before a play." Similarly, to *pro*gnosticate is to make knowledge before or to predict. A *pro*gnosticator is a fortune-teller. *Pro* can also mean for. Someone who is *pro* freedom of speech is in favor of freedom of speech. Someone with a *pro*clivity toward a certain activity is for that activity, or has a natural tendency toward it.

A fun word: Antepenultimate

Most people know that *ultimate* means the last of something — *Z* is the ultimate letter of the alphabet. But which letter is the antepenultimate? Give up? It's *X*. The ultimate is the last; the *penultimate* is the second to last; the *antepenultimate* is the third to last (literally, before the second to last). Therefore, if you have three younger brothers, you can introduce them as your antepenultimate, penultimate, and ultimate siblings.

- **✔ pug = war, fight:** Someone *pug*nacious is ready to fight. A *pug*ilist is a person who likes to fight — such as a professional boxer. (Did you ever see those big sticks that marines train with in hand-to-hand combat — the ones that look like cotton swabs with a thyroid condition? Those are called *pug*il sticks.)

- **✔ scien = knowledge:** A *scien*tist is a person with knowledge. Someone pre*scien*t has forethought or knowledge ahead of time — for example, a prognosticator (a fortune-teller, remember?). After you study these roots, you'll be closer to being omni*scien*t — all knowing.

- **✔ som = sleep:** Take *Som*inex to get to sleep. If you have in*som*nia, you can't sleep. (The prefix *in-* means not.)

- **✔ son = sound:** A *son*ic boom breaks the sound barrier. Dis*son*ance is clashing sounds. A *son*orous voice has a good sound.

- **✔ sop = sleep:** A glass of warm milk is a *sop*orific. So is a boring professor.

Enough for now. You'll find no **paucity** (lack or scarcity) of roots to learn, but the preceding ones should provide you with a good foundation.

A Sense of Completion: Review

Before you go on to the practice questions in Chapter 9, take some time to review the following approaches and tricks presented earlier in this chapter.

Approaches

1. **Read the entire sentence for its gist.**

2. **If possible, predict words to fit into the blanks.**

3. **Insert *every* answer choice into the blanks and reread the resulting sentences.**

Tricks

- ✔ Look for key connecting words that may change the meaning of the sentence.

- ✔ Predict positive or negative words to fit in the blanks.

- ✔ Guess quickly on questions with answers that depend entirely on unknown vocabulary.

And, of course, you want to remember that using a few basic RPS (roots, prefixes, and suffixes) can help you figure out killer vocabulary.

A whale of an exam

Question: What do the GRE and *Moby-Dick* have in common?

Answer: They both feature the following vocabulary.*

prodigious	fathom	ruefully
blunder	fastidious	tyro
antediluvian	wretched	omnipotent
voracious	incensed	cadge
heinous	precipice	descry
effulgent	inert	leviathan
floundering	disparaging	sagacious
depict	incredulous	superficial
conflagration	dogged	indiscriminate

* Oh sure, you can probably think of other commonalties, such as (1) no one ever finishes either one, and (2) they're leading causes of migraine headaches, and so on. But honestly, this is the real answer: All these GRE words are found in *Moby-Dick*.

Chapter 9

Reality Check: Sentence Completion Practice Questions

*I*t's that time again — when you use it or lose it. Answering the following questions should reinforce what you learned in the preceding chapter about Sentence Completion questions. We made these sentences much more amusing, in our opinion, than the deadly dull ones on the actual GRE, but the difficulty level and the vocabulary are the same.

1. Although dismayed by the pejorative comments made about her inappropriate dress at the diplomatic function, Judy ---- her tears and showed only the most calm and ---- visage to her critics.

   (A) obviated . . . agitated

   (B) suppressed . . . placid

   (C) exacerbated . . . unfazed

   (D) monitored . . . incensed

   (E) curtailed . . . articulate

If Judy had a calm *and* (something) *visage* (a *visage* is a countenance, a facial expression), the (something) must go hand in hand with calm. Although it doesn't have to be an exact synonym, the second word can't be an antonym either. Look for a word that means calm. *Placid* means calm and tranquil, as you know from the root *plac,* meaning peace. Check the rest of the second words. *Agitated* means upset or worried, just the opposite of what you're looking for. *Unfazed* may be good because it means not bothered by. (Erudite types are unfazed by seeing how that word is spelled, knowing that *unphased* is a trap often found on grammar exams.) *Incensed* means upset, burning mad (think of burning incense). *Articulate* means well-spoken. Her visage, or facial expression, wouldn't be well-spoken, although Judy herself may be. So, you've narrowed the answers down to Choices B and C based on the second words alone. Now check out the first words.

To *exacerbate* is to make worse. Words as hard as this one can exacerbate your headache. But if you chose this answer, you let your insecurity complex get the better of you. It's normal to think, "Oooh, big hard word; it must be the right answer." We're not saying that these questions don't feature hard words, but the difficult words may be the trap answers, not the correct answers. *Suppress* means to hold back and fits the sentence perfectly. *Correct Answer:* Choice B.

Take a quick look at some of the other vocabulary. To *obviate* is to prevent, as in your learning these words now obviates your falling for traps and choosing them later. To *curtail* is to shorten. (Think of cutting off the tail of a word when you cur*tail* it.)

Did you take note of the word *although?* A key word like that can change the meaning of the entire sentence. If it weren't there, you may think that Judy in fact burst out crying from the criticism instead of holding back.

2. Although there are those writers who carp and ---- about the current depressed state of our economy, many people insist that such writers don't speak for the common man (or woman) who believes in the ---- of the nation and the security of its future.

   (A) lampoon . . . uniformity

   (B) grouse . . . resilience

   (C) complain . . . morbidity

   (D) laud . . . strength

   (E) ridicule . . . chaos

As we advise in Chapter 8, try to predict the words that fit into the blank or, failing that, predict the sense (positive or negative) of the words. Here, you can predict that the first word must be something bad (because the writers are *carping,* or griping, about a depressed economy) and that the second word must be something good (because the average man or woman believes in the future of the country). Eliminate all second words that aren't good: *morbidity* (meaning the presence of disease) and *chaos* (meaning confusion and disorganization). Eliminate all first words that aren't negative: *laud* (meaning to praise, as in to ap*plaud*). Now you've narrowed the choices down to just two.

To *lampoon* is to ridicule (think of the satirical magazine *National Lampoon*). That may fit, but the second blank doesn't make much sense. Sure, it's good to believe in the *uniformity,* or unity, of a country, but that's not related to worrying about the depressed state of its economy. Choice B, *grouse,* is to complain or grumble. (The poet Dorothy Parker wrote a great stanza that says, "Cavil, quarrel, grumble, grouse/I ponder on the narrow house/I shudder at the thought of men/I'm due to fall in love again!") And *resilience* is elasticity, the state of springing back. The average person thinks the economy will stage a comeback. *Correct Answer:* Choice B.

3. The speaker, ironically, ---- the very point he had stood up to make, and hurriedly sat down, hoping no one had caught his ----.

   (A) prognosticated . . . summation

   (B) divulged . . . information

   (C) refuted . . . solecism

   (D) duplicated . . . duplicity

   (E) ferreted out . . . mistake

Predict that the second blank must be something negative, as the speaker hoped no one had noticed it. That eliminates Choice A (a *summation* is just what it looks like, a summary, and isn't necessarily bad) and Choice B (*information* is also neutral). Now try the sentence with the remaining answer choices inserted.

To *refute* is to disprove or show to be false. It'd be *ironic* (the opposite of what's expected) if the speaker were to disprove the very point he stood up to make. A *solecism* is an inconsistency, a mistake. *Correct Answer:* Choice C.

Take a moment to go through the other words to increase your vocabulary. (As you realize by now, you can narrow down many of the Sentence Completion questions to just two or three answers through the process of elimination. But to get the one right answer, you have to know the words.) To *prognosticate* is to predict. *Pro-* means before; *gnos* means knowledge; *-ate* means to make. To prognosticate is to "make knowledge before," to predict.

If you picked Choice A, you probably fell for the trap of looking only at the answer choices and not reinserting them into the sentence. Yes, something ironic is the opposite of what's expected, and a prognostication is the opposite of a summation, but that answer doesn't fit when reinserted into the sentence. Be sure to take your time and go back to the sentence with each answer choice. The Sentence Completion section isn't a place to try to save seconds.

In Choice B, to *divulge* is to reveal. That first word works, but the second one doesn't. It's not ironic to divulge the very information you stand up to say; it's normal.

In Choice D, *duplicity* is an interesting word. The root *dup* means double, but duplicity isn't "doubleness" in the sense of two of something. **Duplicity** is deception, being two-faced. A traitor is noted for his or her duplicity. And in Choice E, to *ferret out* is to search diligently, as a detective ferrets out clues to help his client. You ferret out the tips and traps scattered throughout these explanations to help you remember them.

4. Although often writing of - - - - activities, Emily Dickinson possessed the faculty of creating an eclectic group of characters ranging from the reticent to the epitome of - - - -.

    (A) questionable . . . taciturnity

    (B) mundane . . . effrontery

    (C) egregious . . . discretion

    (D) horrific . . . stoicism

    (E) commensurate . . . composure

If you know that *reticent* means shy and holding back, you can predict that the second blank must be the opposite of that, something bold and forward. **Effrontery** is shameless boldness and audacity. You have effrontery when you ask your boss for a raise right after he or she chews you out for bungling a project and costing the company money. Effrontery is the only second blank that fits. **Taciturnity** is the noun form of the word *taciturn*, meaning quiet, not talkative, not forward. **Stoicism** is not showing feelings or pain. Only a stoic can look at words such as these without shrieking or ripping out her hair.

Turning to the first blanks, **mundane** means common, worldly. Mundane activities are day-to-day tasks, nothing exciting like winning a lottery or visiting Antarctica. **Egregious** means terrible or flagrant. An egregious mistake is right out there for the world to see. **Commensurate** means equivalent to or proportionate. Your score on this section will be commensurate with your vocabulary. *Correct Answer:* Choice B.

5. Dismayed by the - - - - evidence available to her, the defense attorney spent her own money (even though that would leave her nearly - - - -) to hire a private investigator to acquire additional evidence.

    (A) dearth of . . . affluent

    (B) scanty . . . insolvent

    (C) vestigial . . . pecuniary

    (D) immense . . . bankrupt

    (E) impartial . . . penurious

Predict words to fit into the blanks. If the attorney is dismayed by evidence and hires an investigator to get *more* evidence, she must not have had much evidence to begin with. You can predict that the first word means not very much. *Scanty* means barely sufficient. A *dearth of* is a lack of. Those are the only two words that fit for the first blank. *Vestigial* means functionless, after much of the original has disappeared; for example, the tailbone of humans is a vestigial tail. *Immense* means large, just the opposite of what you want.

The words *even though* tell you that spending her own money to gather the extra evidence would have a negative effect on the attorney. She was nearly *insolvent,* or bankrupt. Choice A, *affluent,* means rich, wealthy, or — as a smart-aleck friend of ours says — financially oversupplied. That doesn't work — eliminate Choice A.

In Choice C, *pecuniary* means consisting of or pertaining to money matters. This can be a tempting answer, because you know that the costs have to do with money as well. However, the first word definitely doesn't fit in this sentence. In Choice E, *penurious* means poor, needy, or destitute. It fits the second blank, but the first blank doesn't work with this answer. *Impartial* evidence is neutral, neither good nor bad. *Correct Answer:* Choice B.

6. Unwilling to be labeled ----, Gwenette slowly and ---- double-checked each fact before expounding upon her theory to her colleagues at the convention.

   (A) precipitate . . . meticulously

   (B) hasty . . . swiftly

   (C) rash . . . desultorily

   (D) efficacious . . . haphazardly

   (E) painstaking . . . heedlessly

The key here is pure vocabulary. You can probably predict the types of words you need, knowing that the first word must mean too fast and careless and the second word slow and careful. But if you don't have a clue what any of the words mean, don't waste time scratching your head over this one. Just guess and go.

Precipitate, hasty, and *rash* all mean overly quick, leaping before looking. Those words fit the first blank. *Efficacious* means efficient and effective, something Gwenette wants to be. *Painstaking* means meticulous, careful, and attentive to detail, another good thing to be. Dump Choices D and E.

You know the second blank must be something good. *Meticulous* means careful with detail, paying careful attention. It's pretty much the opposite of *swiftly* (quickly), *desultorily* (aimlessly, not methodically), *haphazardly* (unsystematically, not methodically), and *heedlessly* (not paying attention). *Correct Answer:* Choice A.

 Even if you don't know the exact meanings of the words, you often have an idea whether they're positive or negative — whether they have good or bad connotations. If you sense that a word is bad when you need a good word, eliminate that answer choice. You'll be pleasantly surprised at how often your subconscious leads you to the correct answer.

 If you didn't grow up in the U.S., you may not be able to sense the meanings (good or bad) of words. In that case, it's even more important for you to make a quick guess and go on.

Chapter 10

Readings That Can Affect Your Future: Blood Pressure, Astrology, and the GRE

● ●

In This Chapter

▶ Covering the most common reading passages

▶ Figuring out whether the questions are worth your time

▶ Checking out some tips designed to save your sanity

● ●

More feared by students than Monday's mystery meat in the college cafeteria, Reading Comprehension questions on the GRE comprise 8 out of the 30 Verbal questions. The number can vary slightly, but in general, approximately 27 percent of your Verbal score is determined by Reading Comprehension questions.

If you're used to taking paper-and-pencil tests, the reading passages on the computer can be quite a challenge. On a paper test, you have the option of skipping around and finding a passage you like (for instance, maybe you prefer a science passage to a humanities passage). You also have the option of skipping a question and coming back to it later. Those options are gone with the computerized GRE. You get only one reading passage at a time, which means you can't preview several and choose your favorite. Also, you must choose and confirm an answer before the computer will allow you to go on to the next question.

What Do They Look Like? Reading Comprehension Passages and Their Questions

The origin of the *misnomer* (wrong name) "Reading Comprehension" is a great topic for a *deipnosophist*. (A deipnosophist is one who converses eruditely at the dinner table. Don't worry; you don't have to know this word for the GRE. We just threw it in so you can sound smart to your friends.)

For now, you don't care so much what the section is called; you just want to get through it. The following information presents an overview of the types of passages you may encounter, the best approach to each distinct type of passage, and tips and traps for answering the questions based on those passages.

Start by taking a look at what a Reading Comprehension question looks like:

Which of the following best describes the tone of the passage?

(A) sarcastic

(B) ebullient

(C) objective

(D) saddened

(E) mendacious

All questions can be answered from information stated or implied in the passage. You aren't expected to answer questions based on your own knowledge, and you don't need to know anything special about science or humanities to answer these questions.

Acing the Three Commonly Tested Reading Comprehension Passages

In their torture chambers over the years (would someone please call Amnesty International?), the test-makers have decided to write passages based on biological or physical sciences, social sciences, and humanities. The following sections offer a preview of the passages to help you separate the devastating from the merely intolerable.

Beam me up, Scotty! Biological and physical science passages

A biological or physical science passage is straightforward, giving you the scoop on how laser beams work, how to build a suspension bridge, how molecular theory applies, and so on. Although the passage itself may be very booooooooring to read (because it's full of just facts, facts, and more facts), this type of passage is often the easiest passage for people because it has so few traps and tricks.

Reading tip

Time to talk reality here: You're not going to remember — and maybe not even understand — what you read in a biological or physical science passage. It's all just statistics and dry details. No matter how carefully and slowly you read through it the first time, you're almost certain to need to go back through the passage a second time to find specific facts. You thus end up reading the passage twice. Why waste time? Zip through the passage to get a general idea of what it's about and where the info is. (The first paragraph tells how molecules combine; the second tells how scientists are working to split the atom; the third tells. . . .)

You may want to jot down a one- or two-word note on your scratch paper to summarize each paragraph in a biological or physical science passage: Molecules. Atoms. Research. No need to waste time understanding every nuance if you can get the answer right by going back and finding the specific fact quickly.

If you're a slow reader, these types of passages can work in your favor because you're not really *reading* them — you're skimming them. You don't have to understand what you read. You merely have to identify some key words.

Bonus: What happens if you swallow a molecule of uranium? You get atomic ache!

Question tip

You can often answer biological or physical science questions directly from the facts provided in the passage itself. They're rarely the inference type that requires you to read between the lines and really think about what the author is saying, what point he or she is trying to make, how he or she feels about the subject, and so on. Here's an example of a typical question for a biological or physical science passage (flip to the later section "Toga, Toga, Toga! The Roman numeral question" for more on this format):

The author states that spices were used

   I. to improve the taste of food.

  II. for medicinal purposes.

 III. to preserve food before refrigeration.

 IV. as a substitute for cash.

  (A) I and III only

  (B) I, II, and IV only

  (C) I, II, and III only

  (D) II and III only

  (E) I, II, III, and IV

To answer the question, return to the passage and look for the specific answers —— which should be easy to locate if you made those handy little notes during your first run-through (in this case, you may have made a notation stating *purposes,* which leads you straight to the right answer).

It's not a disease: The social sciences passage

The GRE usually includes one social sciences passage. It may be about history, psychology, business, or a variety of other topics. In other words, the term *social sciences* is broad enough to include whatever the test-makers want it to include. The social sciences passage is often the most interesting passage you encounter. It may give you a perspective on history that you didn't know or provide insight into psychology or sociology that you can use to manipulate your friends. (Who says the GRE is useless?)

Reading tip

In many ways, the social sciences passage is nearly the opposite of a biological or physical science passage. The questions here deal more with inferences and less with explicitly stated facts. Therefore, you must read the passage slowly and carefully, trying to understand not only what's said but also what's implied. Take some time to think about what you're reading.

Question tip

The questions that follow a social sciences passage may not be as straightforward as those for a biological or physical science passage. You may not be able to go back to a specific line and pick out a specific fact. Instead, these questions ask you to understand the big picture, or to comprehend what the author meant but didn't come right out and say. You may be asked why an author included a particular example or explanation. In other words, you're expected to be a mind reader. Whip out that crystal ball. Here's an example of a typical social sciences question:

The author's primary motive in discussing Dr. Buttinski's theory was to

(A) impress the reader with Dr. Buttinski's importance.

(B) show that Dr. Buttinski overcame great odds to become a psychologist.

(C) ridicule Dr. Buttinski's adversaries who disagreed with the theory.

(D) predict great things for Dr. Buttinski's future.

(E) evaluate the effect Dr. Buttinski's theory has had on our everyday lives.

Determining the author's motive involves reasoning, not just reading. No sentence specifically says: "Okay, listen up, troops. I'm going to tell you something, and my motive for doing so is blah, blah, blah." You need to read the passage slowly enough to develop an idea of why the author is telling you something and what exactly he or she wants you to take from this passage. Going back and rereading the passage doesn't do you much good; thinking about what you read does.

In this particular sample question, every answer given is probably a true statement based on the passage. That is, the author probably thought Dr. Buttinski was important, probably believed that Dr. Buttinski had to overcome great odds to be a psychologist, and so on. Keep in mind, however, what the question is asking: *Why* did the author mention this specific thing? You must probe the author's mind.

Gimme a break, I'm only human: The humanities passages

Humanities passages may be about humans (well, duh!) or about art, music, philosophy, drama, or literature. The passages are usually positive, especially if they talk about a person who was a pioneer in his or her field, such as the first African American astronaut or the first female doctor. Think about this statement logically: If the GRE bothers with writing about someone, that someone must have been pretty darn great or done something noteworthy. Keep this sense of admiration, even awe, in mind as you answer the questions related to the passage.

Reading tip

Have fun with the humanities passages because they're the only ones you may actually enjoy reading. You don't need to zoom through 'em to finish before you fall asleep like you have to with the biological or physical science passages. Nor do you need to read 'em carefully for between-the-lines understanding as you have to with the social sciences passage. You can read this type of passage normally. Pretend that you're reading an article in *People* magazine, for example.

Question tip

Although the humanities passages don't require meticulous, between-the-lines reading, the questions are another matter. The questions following a humanities passage often require you to get into the mind of the author in order to read between the lines and make inferences. While you're reading a passage about a particular person, for example, you're supposed to ascertain not just what the person accomplished but why she worked toward her goals and what mark she hoped to leave on the world. Here's an example of a typical humanities question:

It can be inferred from the passage that Ms. Whitecloud would be most likely to agree with which of the following statements?

(A) A good divorce attorney must take the broader view and in effect represent the marriage itself rather than either of the spouses.

(B) The job of a divorce attorney is similar to that of a psychologist, attempting to ascertain why the marriage failed and address that issue rather than just the legal issues.

(C) The most important function of a divorce attorney is to protect the interests of the children of the marriage.

(D) A divorce attorney's job is merely to represent the legal interests of his or her client and does not include becoming a "friend" to the spouses.

(E) A divorce attorney measures his or her success by how quickly the divorce is accomplished.

All or Nothing: Questions to Take Seriously; Questions to Laugh Off

Knowing how to approach the GRE Reading Comprehension passages is extremely important. Even more important than the passages themselves, however, are the questions following them. After all, the admissions officer at Harvard isn't going to say to you, "Hey, tell me about that GRE passage you read about the curative properties of heavy metal music." The admissions officer is far more likely to ask, "How many questions did you answer correctly on the Reading Comprehension portion?" No matter how carefully you read a passage, no matter how well you understand it, you must be able to put that knowledge to work to answer the questions that follow it.

So just what kinds of questions are you most likely to encounter in the Reading Comprehension portion of the test? The following sections describe the several basic Reading Comprehension question types you may face in the dark alleys of the GRE.

It's the attitude, dude: The attitude or tone question

The author's attitude may be described as . . .

The tone of the passage is . . .

These two questions are variations on a single theme. What's the tone of the passage or the attitude of the author? Nothing in the passage answers this type of question directly. You can't find any one line reading: "In my opinion, which, by the way, is sardonic, the importance of. . . ." You simply must reason this one out.

Table 10-1 lists the tone or attitude likely found in each type of Reading Comprehension passage.

Table 10-1   Predominant Tones or Attitudes Found in GRE Reading Passages

Passage Type	Tone or Attitude	Explanation
Biological or physical sciences	Neutral or positive	A biological or physical science passage gives you just the facts. The author rarely evaluates the facts one way or the other and rarely expresses an opinion. (After all, how opinionated can someone be about a color spectrum?)
Social sciences	Positive or neutral	A social sciences passage may be about how some event unfolded or how some theory was developed. For example, a passage may talk about history, presenting the good events and downplaying the bad ones. Think positive, or at the very worst, neutral.
Humanities	Positive or neutral	If the passage is about an individual, it's probably positive, saying good and respectful things about that person and his or her accomplishments. If it's about the other topics of humanities, such as art, music, philosophy, drama, and literature, it may be either positive or neutral. Very rarely does a humanities passage have a negative tone.

Do you notice a pattern here? Everything is either neutral or positive, positive or neutral. Because so many of the tones or attitudes of the Reading Comprehension passages are positive or neutral, certain words are often good to choose as answers to attitude or tone questions. With neutral passages, the term *objective* (which means neutral, not taking one side or the other, not subjective or opinionated) is often a correct answer. Don't simply turn off your own brain and choose *objective* automatically, of course, but it's a good guess if you're stumped for an answer. Think of a passage as neutral until proven otherwise.

Following are several common positive words. Each word is followed by a more unfamiliar term that has the same meaning:

Common Positive-Attitude Word	More Difficult Word with the Same Meaning
Optimistic	Sanguine
Praising	Laudatory
Admiring	Reverential

You get the idea. Wrong answers — that is, negative answers — may include the following words. **Remember:** These are words that you usually don't want to choose.

Common Negative-Attitude Word	More Difficult Word with the Same Meaning
Ridiculing	Lampooning
Sarcastic	Sardonic
Belittling	Denigrating

The answer choices to an attitude or tone question often use quite difficult vocabulary. If you know from reading the passage that the author is delighted with something, which of the following would you choose to describe his attitude: *phlegmatic, dogmatic, ebullient, cantankerous,* or *lethargic?* The right answer is **ebullient,** which means bubbling over with enthusiasm or excitement — but how many people know that word? It's not as if your best friend asks you, "So, how are you today?" and your immediate response is, "I'm ebullient, thanks. And you?" If you don't know the vocabulary in the answer choices, *quickly* make a wild guess and go on. Doing so can be very frustrating, because you know what kind of word you're looking for, but when you can't define the answer choices, all you're doing is wasting time. Guess and go.

What's the big idea? Main idea or best title questions

You can bet the farm (but, of course, only in states with legalized gambling) that you'll see a few main idea or best title questions; each Reading Comprehension passage usually has one. This type of question can assume any of the following forms:

> The main idea of the passage is . . .
>
> The primary purpose of the author is . . .
>
> The best title for the passage is . . .

The best place to find the main idea of the passage is in its topic sentence, which is usually the first or second sentence of the first paragraph. The topic sentence *may* be the last sentence of the passage, but such a structure is rare. Your game plan upon encountering one of these questions should be to head right back to the first sentence to locate a main idea.

Suppose that a passage begins as follows:

> The uses to which latex has been applied have exceeded the wildest fantasies of its creators.

What's the main idea of the passage: The uses of latex? The applications of latex? The many products made of latex?

If you read the first sentence again, you notice that the writer is planning on writing more about the uses of latex. If you're still unclear after reading the first sentence, check the entire paragraph to make sure that the author continues to write more about specific examples of the uses of latex.

After you've read the entire passage, all the darn answers in the main idea question may look pretty good. That's because they usually consist of facts stated in the passage. Just because something is true and just because it's covered in the passage doesn't mean it's necessarily the main idea. *Remember:* The main idea is what the *entire* passage is about. It's the overall concept and the purpose of the whole essay, not just one true fact contained somewhere within the passage.

As for whether you should really try to answer main idea or best title questions, or whether you should just fly right by 'em, trust us, they're definitely worth a few minutes of your time. Go back and reread the first few sentences. Even if you don't have time to read the entire passage — or even get started on it — you can often hustle up an answer to this question by glancing at one sentence.

Because Reading Comprehension passages are almost always positive or neutral, the main idea/best title is almost always positive or neutral, too. Eliminate any negative answer choices right away.

The main idea of this passage is

(A) the submission and shame of the Native Americans.

(B) the unfair treatment of Native Americans.

(C) how Native Americans are taking charge of their own destinies.

(D) why Native Americans fail.

(E) the causes behind Native American problems.

Because all the answers but Choice C are negative, pick Choice C. Humanities passages are often about people who've beaten the odds — inspirational pioneers and leaders. The passage is certain to be very admiring of those people. *Correct Answer:* Choice C.

Don't pester me with details: The detail or fact question

One type of question very straightforwardly asks you about information that's explicitly stated in the passage. If a question begins with the phrase "According to the passage," you've hit a detail or fact question — which is usually a very easy question to answer correctly. All you need to do is identify the key words in the question, return to the passage, and skim for those words. The answer is usually within a few sentences of those key words. Take a look at a few detail or fact question examples:

According to the passage, what two elements make up Drake's Elixir?

The key words are *Drake's Elixir.* Go back to the passage and find the exact answer.

According to the passage, why did Mr. Sanchez win a medal during the war?

The key words in this question are *Mr. Sanchez, medal,* and *war.* Go back to the passage and find the exact answer.

"According to the author" isn't the same as "According to the passage." The two phrases may look the same, but author questions are often more difficult than passage questions and aren't as straightforward. A question that asks you about the author may be more of a read-between-the-lines question — one you can answer only if you truly understand what you read. An "according to the passage" question, on the other hand, can often be answered by skimming for the key words even without reading the whole passage.

The power of positive thinking: Negative or exception questions

One type of GRE question is a trained killer: the negative or exception question. Here are a few ways this question may be worded:

Which of the following is *not* true?

Which of the following is *least* likely?

With which of the following would the author *disagree?*

All of the following are true *except* . . .

The questions are phrased in the negative, which makes them very tricky. You're actually looking for four correct answers. Then, by the process of elimination, you're supposed to choose the one that isn't correct. It's easy to get confused and even easier to waste a lot of time in this situation. That's why negative or exception questions are good ones to laugh off and just guess at randomly.

Toga! Toga! Toga! The Roman numeral question

A Roman numeral question looks like this:

The author mentions which of the following as support for her argument against unilateral intervention?

    I. Economic considerations

   II. Moral obligations

  III. Popular opinion

(A) I only

(B) II only

(C) III only

(D) I and II only

(E) I, II, and III

Roman numeral questions are usually time-wasters. In effect, you must go back and reread almost the whole passage to find whether I, II, or III was mentioned anywhere. A common trap is to find I and II mentioned close together and then have III mentioned far down the passage. Most people find I and II and then when III doesn't appear to be hanging around, they choose I and II only, going down the tubes. (Hey, maybe the test-makers get bonus points for every test-taker they snare with a trick, rather like a cop writing speeding tickets to meet his quota in a speed trap. Just a thought.) With a Roman numeral question, you have to make a commitment to rereading most of the passage just in case one of the concepts is floating around where you least expect it. If you aren't willing (or able) to commit the time, forget about the question. Just make a random guess and go on.

Bonus: What do you call a pig that won't make a commitment? A hedge hog!

Journey into the deep: Text-referenced questions

The GRE powers-that-be are about to do something nice for you. Consider the text-referenced questions as a guided journey back into the passage. On these types of questions, the test asks you to return to a specific part of the passage to define what the author meant in that section. This scenario can occur in two different ways. The first is by making direct reference to the line numbers to guide you to where you'll find your information. The second is to highlight a specific portion of the passage for you to return to. Be prepared to get all line-referenced test questions or a combination of both line-referenced and high-lighted sections. Following is an example of a text-referenced question with a line reference:

The author refers to conditions in the ghetto (line 79) in order to

(A) highlight the poverty and destitution that people live in.

(B) demonstrate the failure of the government to recognize lower-class living situations.

(C) illustrate an example of gentrification (renovate as to conform to middle-class aspirations) in the U.S.

(D) offer solutions to classification in the U.S.

(E) broaden the application of the term "ghetto."

If you had this question in the highlighted section, it'd read the exact same way, except the "conditions in the ghetto" would be highlighted and not referred to by line number. Whatever the case may be, you need to journey back into the text and read the sentence before the reference, as well as the referenced section.

The swing vote: Extending the author's reasoning

Although this last type of Reading Comprehension question has become increasingly rare, you need to be prepared to meet it. This type of question asks you to extend the author's reasoning to another situation. The GRE may give you a situation that's *analogous,* or similar, to the one described in the Reading Comprehension passage and then ask you to determine how the author's reasoning would or wouldn't work in the new situation. The tone or attitude of this type of passage may be positive, neutral, or negative. Here's an example:

Which of the following would the author most likely feel would be a valid issue to appear on a referendum, based on his argument in the preceding passage?

(A) The right to die

(B) Term limits for members of Congress

(C) Expansion of the powers of the judiciary

(D) Increased student involvement in college application processes

(E) Tax rate increases

This type of question may be ridiculously easy or annoyingly difficult. If you understand the passage well and understand the author's reasoning, this question is simple. Sometimes you can answer this question without understanding the entire passage, as long as you have some general idea of the author's purpose in writing the passage.

Reading passages you'll never see on the GRE

✔ **Biological Science:** Cannibalism and You: The Science of Pigging Out at a Barbecue

✔ **Social Science (Psychology):** The End of Political Correctness: An Analysis of Howard Stern and Rush Limbaugh

✔ **Social Science (Behaviorism):** An excerpt from *Confessions from the Funny Farm,* Chapter Two: How the GRE Pushed Me over the Edge

✔ **Humanities:** The Developer of the Prefrontal Lobotomy: "Inspiration Struck While I Was Studying for the GRE," Says Famous Surgeon

Don't immediately choose an answer just because it refers to the topic covered in the passage. For example, the passage may be about education. The trap answer in the previous question would be Choice D. However, you're asked to extend the author's reasoning to an *analogous* situation. The situation can be about the right to die, congressional term limits, or just about anything else.

Something Up Your Sleeve: Tips for Making GRE Life a Little Easier

Now that you know about the types of passages and the primary types of questions, it's time for the fun stuff — a few tips you can use to beat the test-makers!

Be positive or neutral, not negative

We'll say this tip over and over until you're exasperated enough to cut off our air supply: Because most of the Reading Comprehension passages are positive or neutral, most of the correct answers are positive or neutral. Because the test-makers don't want to get sued for saying mean and vicious things about anyone, these men and women are generally sweet and charming (and probably go home, kick the dog, and evict a few widows and orphans just to get pent-up frustrations out of their systems after having to be so nice at work all day long). Be sweet and charming right back at 'em; pick the positive, goody-goody answer choices.

Choose answers containing key words

The key words, often found in the topic sentence, are what the whole passage is about. The right answers usually feature those words. If the passage is about Chicano history, the right answer often has the words *Chicano history* in it. Don't immediately choose an answer *only* because it has the key words in it, but if you can narrow the answers down to two, choose the one with the key words.

Be wishy-washy, not dramatic

The test-makers realize that people have different points of view. They don't want to be *dogmatic* (narrow-minded), saying, "This is the right way, the only way. Zip your lip and don't argue." They want to hedge their bets and leave some space for personal interpretation. And, of course, they don't want to get sued. If you have two answers, choose the more moderate or wishy-washy of the two. Wimp out big time.

Suppose you've narrowed the answer choices down to two:

(A) The author hates discrimination.

(B) The author is saddened by the discrimination and tries to understand its causes.

Choice B is the kinder, gentler, wimpier answer; it's also likely the correct one.

Eponymous words

An *eponym* is a word derived from the name of a person. For example, the cardigan sweater got its name from the Earl of Cardigan (who'd probably much rather be remembered for the garment than for his other claim to fame — he was the leader of the Light Brigade). Here are a few eponyms to add to your GRE vocabulary:

✔ *bowdlerize:* To omit indecent words or phrases in a book or piece of writing (you bowdlerize a love letter before you let your roommate read it). In 1818, Dr. Thomas Bowdler, an English physician, published a ten-volume edition of Shakespeare's plays called *The Family Shakespeare.* He left out all the dirty parts. For example, instead of "Out, damn'd spot!" the line reads, "Out, crimson spot!"

✔ *boycott:* You'd think that Mr. Boycott started the practice of boycotting, wouldn't you? Just the opposite: He was the victim of the first boycott. Charles Boycott was a retired English army captain who refused to lower rents to his farmer tenants after a few bad harvests and was accused of exploiting the poor. The locals harassed him, stealing his crops and refusing to sell his products in their stores, until he was hounded out of the county. Today, when you refuse to have anything to do with someone, you're said to boycott him or her.

✔ *Draconian:* Extremely harsh and severe. When you tell your professor that dropping your grade one whole letter just because you turned in a report one day late is truly Draconian, you're harking all the way back to about 620 B.C. Draco was an Athenian who wrote a code of laws that made nearly every crime punishable by death, even laziness and, uh, urinating in public. The word Draconian came to apply to any laws that were just too darn cruel or strict.

✔ *maverick:* An individualist, an unconventional person. Samuel Maverick, who lived during the 1800s, was a Texas rancher whose unbranded cattle roamed free. Maverick's neighbors refused to hand back his strays, claiming that because they were unbranded, there was no proof they were his. The word eventually evolved into meaning anything "without a brand," or unusual or unique.

✔ *Quisling:* A traitor. Vidkun Quisling was a Norwegian politician who turned traitor in World War II, siding with Hitler. He was shot by a firing squad at the end of the war, but his name lives on to torment GRE-takers.

✔ *simony:* The buying or selling of religious or sacred objects or privileges. Simon Magus (who's often described as a "reformed wizard" — great job description!) offered St. Peter and St. John money to give him their religious abilities. The word simony was especially popular in the Middle Ages, when people sold pardons, indulgences, and the like.

Bonus! You probably already know these words, but did you know they're also eponyms?

✔ *diesel:* A type of engine, named for Rudolf Diesel, a German engineer.

✔ *mausoleum:* A large tomb or memorial, named for King Mausolus, King of Calia in ancient Greece about 370 B.C.

✔ *nicotine:* The addictive stuff in tobacco, named for French diplomat Jean Nicot.

✔ *saxophone:* A musical instrument, invented by and named after Adolphe Sax, a Belgian musician of the early to mid-1800s.

✔ *shrapnel:* Fragments thrown out by a shell or a bomb, invented in 1802 by Lieutenant General Henry Shrapnel, an English army officer.

✔ *silhouette:* Profile or shadow of a face, named after Étienne de Silhouette (1709–1767), a French finance minister.

The Final Paragraph: Review

Take a moment to review the key points of this chapter before jumping into the practice questions in Chapter 12.

Approaches

▌ ✔ Identify the type of Reading Comprehension passage: biological or physical science, social sciences, humanities.

✔ Identify the type of question (for example, attitude or tone; main idea or best title; detail or fact; negative or exception; Roman numeral; text-referenced; or extending the author's reasoning) and decide how much time to invest in it.

Tips

✔ Be positive or neutral, not negative.

✔ Choose answers containing key words.

✔ Be wishy-washy, not dramatic.

Chapter 11

Words to Help You Score: GRE Vocabulary

In This Chapter

▶ Preparing to study vocabulary

▶ Reviewing the top 300 vocab words found on the GRE

You can't get around it — you absolutely must know vocabulary to do well on the GRE. No matter how good your streetwise lingo is, the GRE is more concerned that you can speak with scholars, dude. Many of the words used on the GRE probably aren't words you use on a daily basis, but you've probably heard them somewhere before. We can't know for certain what words are going to appear on the test, but the odds are good that you'll see some of the ones presented in this chapter.

The Long but Easy Journey: Studying Vocabulary

Sure, you can stay up all night trying to cram 300 vocabulary words into your brain. But we bet you won't remember even a quarter of 'em by the time you sit down at the GRE computer. The best approach to studying vocab is the turtle approach, slow and steady. To begin the studying process, write each vocabulary word on a flashcard. Put the word on one side and the definition on the other. At this juncture, you have options. If you picked up this book one month before the test, memorize ten words a day for the next 30 days. If you were smart enough to buy this book one full year before the GRE test, then (lucky you!) you only need to study about one word a day.

Another helpful suggestion when studying vocabulary is to draw pictures on your flashcards. Visual cues are very helpful to the brain and often aid in the retention of definitions, especially if, unlike us, you have some artistic talent. Never fear if you're not an artist! Just draw a picture of what the word means, coupled with the word's definition, on the same side of the card. Stimulating your brain in as many ways as possible will help you remember the material faster and more accurately.

You can also sing your way to a great Verbal GRE score. No, we don't want you singing at the test site, but you might consider putting the definitions to music. You know how easily your brain remembers songs? Sometimes getting the darn song *out* of your brain is harder then getting it in! In fact, you probably can remember song lyrics and tunes going all the way back to your childhood. Now that's retention!

Just like creating visual images in your brain helps it retain info, the same is true for music. Pick a word and put the word and the definition to any melody you already know well, such as twinkle, twinkle little star, or row, row, row your boat.

If you have the gift of music, you can create your own songs and plug the vocab words and their definitions right into the lyrics. You can sing your songs anywhere! So what if Joe Nextdoor thinks you've lost it as you sing while washing your car? You're the one going to grad school and leaving Joe Nextdoor . . . well . . . next door!

Regardless of when you begin studying, make sure to do it every day. Revisit the words you think you already know. Knowing as much vocabulary as possible will help you immensely with the Verbal section.

The Paramount 300: Memorizing the Most Common Words

This section features the 300 most commonly occurring words on the GRE. Of course, you need to know way more than 300 words for this test. However, for space considerations, we've included only the most popular words here. We recommend that you scour the Internet for additional GRE vocabulary words (they're everywhere!) and then use your findings to supplement our list.

With that said, get ready to dive in and start studying!

1. *Aberrant:* Abnormal; different from the accepted norm

2. *Abeyance:* State of suspension; temporary inaction

3. *Abstemious:* Characterized by a state of self-denial, particularly in the area of food or drink

4. *Acrid:* Bitter; harsh

5. *Acumen:* Keen; quickness of intellectual insight

6. *Admonition:* A gentle reproof

7. *Amalgamate:* To mix or blend together in a homogenous body

8. *Ameliorate:* To relieve, as from pain or hardship

9. *Ascetic:* Given to severe self-denial; practicing excessive abstinence

10. *Assiduous:* Persistent, unceasing

11. *Astute:* Keen; wise

12. *Audacious:* Fearless

13. *Austere:* Unadorned; severely simple

14. *Aver:* To avouch, justify, or prove

15. *Banal:* Trite; commonplace

16. *Blatant:* Offensively loud

17. *Bolster:* To support; to reinforce

18. *Bombastic:* Using inflated language; pompous

19. *Burgeon:* To grow forth; to send out buds

20. *Cacophony:* A disagreeable, harsh, or discordant sound or tone

21. *Chicanery:* Use of trickery to deceive

22. *Coda:* Concluding section of a musical or literary piece; something that summarizes

23. *Cognizant:* Aware; taking notice

24. *Colloquial:* Pertaining to common speech

25. *Consternation:* Panic

26. *Contentious:* Quarrelsome

27. *Contrite:* Penitent

28. *Contumacious:* Rebellious

29. *Craven:* Cowardly

30. *Decorum:* Orderliness and good taste in manners

31. *Deleterious:* Hurtful, morally or physically

32. *Delineate:* To represent by sketch or diagram

33. *Deride:* To ridicule; to make fun of

34. *Derision:* Ridicule

35. *Desultory:* Aimless; haphazard

36. *Diatribe:* Bitter or malicious criticism

37. *Didactic:* Pertaining to teaching

38. *Dilatory:* Causing delay

39. *Disconcert:* To disturb the composure of

40. *Dissemble:* To disguise or pretend

41. *Dissolution:* Breaking up of a union of persons

42. *Divest:* To strip; to deprive

43. *Divulge:* To tell or make known, generally of something secret or private

44. *Dubious:* Doubtful

45. *Dupe:* Someone easily fooled

46. *Ebullient:* Showing great enthusiasm or exhilaration

47. *Efficacy:* Power to produce an intended effect

48. *Effrontery:* Shameless boldness; impudence

49. *Egress:* Exit

50. *Elegy:* A poem lamenting the dead

51. *Elicit:* To extract without violence; to learn through discussion

52. *Embellish:* To add attractive and ornamental features

53. *Emulate:* Imitate

54. *Engender:* To produce

55. *Enervate:* To weaken

56. *Ennui:* Boredom

57. *Ephemeral:* Short-lived; fleeting

58. *Equanimity:* Evenness of mind or temper

59. *Equivocal:* Ambiguous

60. *Eradicate:* To destroy completely

61. *Erudite:* Very learned

62. *Eschew:* To keep clear of

63. *Esoteric:* Hard to understand; known only by a few

64. *Exacerbate:* To make more sharp or severe; to make worse

65. *Exculpate:* To free from blame

66. *Exigency:* Urgent situation

67. *Expatiate:* To speak or write at some length

68. *Extirpate:* To root out; to eradicate

69. *Facetious:* Amusing

70. *Fallacious:* Illogical

71. *Fatuous:* Idiotic

72. *Fervor:* Ardor or intensity of feeling

73. *Fledgling:* Inexperienced

74. *Foment:* To nurse to life; to encourage

75. *Forestall:* To prevent by taking action in advance

76. *Frugal:* Economical

77. *Fulminate:* To cause to explode

78. *Gainsay:* To contradict; to deny

79. *Garrulous:* Trivial talking

80. *Germane:* Relevant

81. *Goad:* To urge on

82. *Grandiloquent:* Pompous; bombastic

83. *Gregarious:* Sociable; outgoing

84. *Guileless:* Without deceit

85. *Gullible:* Easily deceived

86. *Halcyon:* Calm

87. *Harangue:* A tirade

88. *Harbinger:* One who foreruns and announces the coming of a person or thing

89. *Heresy:* Opinion or doctrine subversive of settled or accepted beliefs

90. *Homogeneous:* Of the same kind

91. *Hyperbole:* Exaggeration or overstatement

92. *Iconoclast:* An image-breaker

93. *Ignominious:* Shameful

94. *Impecunious:* Having no money; broke

95. *Impede:* To hinder; to block

96. *Imperious:* Insisting on obedience

97. *Imperturbable:* Calm

98. *Impervious:* Impenetrable

99. *Implicit:* Implied

100. *Importune:* To harass with persistent demands

101. *Impugn:* To assail with arguments or accusations

102. *Inadvertently:* Unintentionally

103. *Inane:* Silly

104. *Inchoate:* Recently begun

105. *Indolence:* Laziness

106. *Ineffable:* Unutterable

107. *Inert:* Inactive; lacking power to move

108. *Inexorable:* Unrelenting

109. *Innocuous:* Harmless

110. *Insouciant:* Nonchalant

111. *Intrepid:* Fearless and bold

112. *Inure:* To harden or toughen by use, exercise, or exposure

113. *Invidious:* Showing or feeling envy

114. *Irascible:* Easily angered

115. *Itinerant:* Wandering

116. *Laconic:* Brief and to the point

117. *Latent:* Dormant

118. *Laudable:* Praiseworthy

119. *Licentious:* Wanton

120. *Loquacious:* Talkative

121. *Lucid:* Easily understood; clear

122. *Magnanimity:* Generosity

123. *Malingerer:* One who feigns illness to escape duty

124. *Malleable:* Pliant

125. *Maverick:* Rebel; nonconformist

126. *Mendacious:* Untrue

127. *Metamorphosis:* Change of form

128. *Meticulous:* Overcautious

129. *Misanthrope:* One who hates mankind

130. *Mitigate:* To lessen in intensity; to appease

131. *Modicum:* A small amount

132. *Mollify:* To soothe

133. *Mordant:* Biting

134. *Morose:* Ill-humored; sullen

135. *Mundane:* Worldly

136. *Nefarious:* Extremely wicked

137. *Negate:* To cancel out; to nullify

138. *Neophyte:* Beginner

139. *Obdurate:* Stubborn

140. *Obfuscate:* To darken

141. *Obsequious:* Servile; ready to serve

142. *Obviate:* To make unnecessary

143. *Odious:* Hateful

144. *Officious:* Meddlesome

145. *Onus:* Burden

146. *Opprobrium:* Infamy; vilification

147. *Oscillate:* To waver

148. *Ostentation:* A display of vanity; showy

149. *Palpable:* Perceptible by feeling or touch

150. *Paragon:* Model of perfection

151. *Parsimonious:* Sparing in spending of money

152. *Partisan:* One-sided; committed to one party

153. *Pathos:* Having a quality that rouses emotion or sympathy

154. *Paucity:* Few

155. *Penchant:* Strong inclination

156. *Penurious:* Excessively sparing in the use of money; frugal

157. *Perennial:* Something long-lasting

158. *Perfidy:* Treachery

159. *Permeable:* Penetrable; porous

160. *Pernicious:* Tending to kill or hurt

161. *Pervasive:* Spread throughout

162. *Phlegmatic:* Not easily roused to feeling or emotion

163. *Pious:* Religious

164. *Placate:* To soothe; to bring from a hostile state to a calm one

165. *Platitude:* Trite or commonplace statement

166. *Plethora:* Excess; superabundance

167. *Porous:* Full of pores

168. *Portend:* Foretell

169. *Pragmatic:* Practical

170. *Precarious:* Perilous

171. *Precipitate:* Rash; premature

172. *Precocious:* Mature at a young age

173. *Prescience:* Knowledge of events before they happen

174. *Prevaricate:* To use ambiguous language for the purpose of deceiving
175. *Proclivity:* Natural inclination
176. *Prodigious:* Immense
177. *Profound:* Deep; not superficial
178. *Proliferate:* To grow rapidly
179. *Propensity:* Natural inclination
180. *Prudence:* Caution
181. *Puerile:* Childish
182. *Pugnacious:* Quarrelsome
183. *Pungent:* Stinging; sharp in taste or smell
184. *Pusillanimous:* Cowardly; fainthearted
185. *Qualm:* Misgivings; uneasy fears
186. *Quibble:* Minor objection or complaint
187. *Quiescence:* Being quiet or still; inactive
188. *Quixotic:* Idealistic; romantic to a ridiculous degree
189. *Recant:* To formally withdraw one's belief
190. *Recondite:* Incomprehensible to one of ordinary understanding; profound
191. *Redress:* To set right by compensation or punishment
192. *Reprobate:* A sinful and depraved person
193. *Repudiate:* To refuse to have anything to do with
194. *Rescind:* To void by enacting authority
195. *Respite:* Interval of rest
196. *Reticent:* Reserved; inclined to silence
197. *Reverent:* Respectful
198. *Rhetoric:* The art of effective communication
199. *Rout:* To drive out; to stampede
200. *Ruminate:* To chew over again; to think over
201. *Sagacious:* Wise
202. *Salacious:* Having strong sexual desires
203. *Salubrious:* Healthful
204. *Sanction:* To approve
205. *Sanguine:* Cheerfully confident; optimistic
206. *Satiate:* To satisfy or fulfill the appetite or desire of
207. *Savor:* To satisfy fully
208. *Secrete:* To hide away
209. *Sedulous:* Persevering in effort or endeavor
210. *Seethe:* To be disturbed
211. *Seminal:* Influencing future developments

212. *Shard:* Fragment

213. *Shirk:* To avoid

214. *Shoddy:* Not genuine; inferior

215. *Sinuous:* Curving in and out

216. *Skeptic:* Doubter

217. *Skittish:* Lively; frisky

218. *Slander:* Defamation

219. *Sloth:* Slow-moving

220. *Solicitous:* Worried; concerned

221. *Sonorous:* Resonant

222. *Soporific:* Causing sleep

223. *Specious:* Seemingly reasonable but incorrect

224. *Spendthrift:* Someone who wastes money

225. *Spurious:* Not genuine

226. *Stentorian:* Extremely loud

227. *Stigma:* A token of disgrace

228. *Stint:* To be thrifty

229. *Stipulate:* To make express conditions

230. *Stolid:* Dull; impassive

231. *Striated:* Marked with parallel bands

232. *Strut:* A pompous walk

233. *Subterfuge:* Evasion

234. *Supercilious:* Careless contempt

235. *Superfluous:* More than what is needed

236. *Supersede:* To cause to be set back

237. *Supine:* Lying on the back

238. *Tacit:* Understood

239. *Taciturn:* Stern; silent

240. *Tangential:* Digressing

241. *Tantamount:* Equivalent in effect or value

242. *Tawdry:* Cheap

243. *Temerity:* A foolish disregard of danger

244. *Tempestuous:* Stormy; impassioned

245. *Tenacious:* Holding fast

246. *Tenuous:* Thin; slim

247. *Tepid:* Lukewarm

248. *Thrall:* Slave; bondage

249. *Thwart:* To frustrate

250. *Titillate:* To tickle

251. *Torpid:* Dull; sluggish; inactive

252. *Tortuous:* Abounding in irregular bends or turns

253. *Tractable:* Docile

254. *Transgression:* Violation; sin

255. *Transmute:* To change

256. *Transparent:* Easily detected

257. *Transpire:* To happen, to be revealed

258. *Trepidation:* Nervous feeling; fear

259. *Truculence:* Ferocity

260. *Tutelage:* The act of training or being under instruction

261. *Tyro:* Beginner

262. *Ubiquitous:* Being present everywhere

263. *Umbrage:* Sense of injury

264. *Unassuaged:* Unsatisfied; not soothed

265. *Uncouth:* Clumsy; dumb

266. *Undermine:* To weaken; to sap

267. *Unerringly:* Infallibility

268. *Ungainly:* Awkward; clumsy

269. *Unison:* Complete accord

270. *Unruly:* Disobedient

271. *Untenable:* Indefensible

272. *Upbraid:* To reproach as deserving blame

273. *Vacillate:* To waver; to fluctuate

274. *Vagabond:* Wanderer

275. *Vainglory:* Excessive; pretentious

276. *Valorous:* Courageous

277. *Vantage:* Position giving advantage

278. *Vapid:* Having lost quality and flavor; dull; lifeless

279. *Variegated:* Many colored

280. *Vehement:* Forceful

281. *Venerate:* To look upon with deep respect

282. *Veracious:* Truthful

283. *Verbiage:* Use of many words

284. *Verbose:* Wordy

285. *Vicissitude:* Change of condition or circumstances, generally of fortune

286. *Viscous:* Sticky; gluey

287. *Vituperate:* Overwhelm with wordy abuse

288. *Vociferous:* Making a loud outcry
289. *Volatile:* Changeable
290. *Warranted:* Justified
291. *Wary:* Very cautious
292. *Welter:* Turmoil
293. *Whimsical:* Fanciful
294. *Whorl:* Ring
295. *Winsome:* Attractive
296. *Wreak:* Inflict
297. *Writhe:* Twist in coils
298. *Yore:* Time past
299. *Zealot:* Fanatic
300. *Zeitgeist:* Intellectual and moral tendencies of any age

Chapter 12

Practice What We Preach: Reading Comprehension Practice Questions

• •

*T*his chapter features two reading passages and nine questions. For now, don't worry about timing yourself. Try to identify each selection as one of the types of Reading Comprehension passages described in Chapter 10 (biological or physical science, social sciences, or humanities) and use the tips we gave you for reading that type of passage. As you answer the questions, try to identify whether each question is attitude/tone, main idea/best title, Roman numeral, and so on, and then try to recall any traps inherent to that type of question.

Passage 1

Line   Microbiological activity clearly affects the mechanical strength of leaves. Although it cannot be denied that with most species the loss of mechanical strength is the result of both invertebrate feeding and microbiological breakdown, the example of *Fagus sylvatica* illustrates loss without any sign of invertebrate attack being evident. *Fagus* shows little sign of
(05) invertebrate attack even after being exposed for eight months in either a lake or stream environment, but results of the rolling fragmentation experiment show that loss of mechanical strength, even in this apparently resistant species, is considerable.

    Most species appear to exhibit a higher rate of degradation in the stream environment than in the lake. This is perhaps most clearly shown in the case of *Alnus.* Examination of the
(10) type of destruction suggests that the cause for the greater loss of material in the stream-processed leaves is a combination of both biological and mechanical degradation. The leaves exhibit an angular fragmentation, which is characteristic of mechanical damage, rather than the rounded holes typical of the attack by large particle feeders or the skeletal vein pattern produced by microbial degradation and small particle feeders. As the leaves become less
(15) strong, the fluid forces acting on the stream nylon cages caused successively greater fragmentation.

    Mechanical fragmentation, like biological breakdown, is to some extent influenced by leaf structure and form. In some leaves with a strong midrib, the lamina break up, but the pieces remain attached by means of the midrib. One type of leaf may break cleanly whereas
(20) another tears off and is easily destroyed after the tissues are weakened by microbial attack.

    In most species, the mechanical breakdown will take the form of gradual attrition at the margins. If the energy of the environment is sufficiently high, brittle species may be broken across the midrib, something that rarely happens with more pliable leaves. The result of attrition is that where the areas of the whole leaves follow a normal distribution, a bimodal
(25) distribution is produced; one peak is composed mainly of the fragmented pieces, the other of the larger remains.

To test the theory that a thin leaf has only half the chance of a thick one for entering the fossil record, all other things being equal, Ferguson (1971) cut discs of fresh leaves from 11 species of leaves, each with a different thickness, and rotated them with sand and water in a
(30) revolving drum. Each run lasted 100 hours and was repeated three times, but even after this treatment, all species showed little sign of wear. It therefore seems unlikely that leaf thickness alone, without substantial microbial preconditioning, contributes much to the probability that a leaf will enter a depositional environment in a recognizable form. The results of experiments with whole fresh leaves show that they are more resistant to fragmentation than
(35) leaves exposed to microbiological attack. Unless the leaf is exceptionally large or small, leaf size and thickness are not likely to be as critical in determining the preservation potential of a leaf type as the rate of microbiological degradation.

1. Which of the following would be the best title for the passage?

   (A) Why Leaves Disintegrate

   (B) An Analysis of Leaf Structure and Composition

   (C) Comparing Lakes and Streams

   (D) The Purpose of Particle Feeders

   (E) How Leaves' Mechanical Strength Is Affected by Microbiological Activity

   Note that because the passage is talking primarily about leaves, that word needs to be in the title, which eliminates Choices C and D right off. Choice A is too broad; there may be other causes of disintegration that the passage doesn't mention. Choice B is too specific. The passage mentions leaf structure, but that topic isn't its primary focus. *Correct Answer:* Choice E.

2. Which of the following is mentioned as a reason for leaf degradation in streams?

   I.   Mechanical damage

   II. Biological degradation

   III. Large particle feeders

   (A) II only

   (B) I and II only

   (C) I and III only

   (D) II and III only

   (E) I, II, and III

   The second paragraph of the passage tells you that ". . . loss of material in stream-processed leaves is a combination of biological and mechanical degradation." Statement III is incorrect, because the passage specifically states that the pattern of holes is contrary to that of large particle feeders. *Correct Answer:* Choice B.

3. The conclusion the author reached from Ferguson's revolving drum experiment was that

   (A) leaf thickness is only a contributing factor to leaf fragmentation.

   (B) leaves submersed in water degrade more rapidly than leaves deposited in mud or silt.

   (C) leaves with a strong midrib deteriorate less than leaves without such a midrib.

   (D) microbial attack is exacerbated by high temperatures.

   (E) bimodal distribution reduces leaf attrition.

Lines 31–33 tell you that it's unlikely that leaf thickness *alone* affects the final form of the leaf. You probably need to reread that sentence a few times to understand it, but this is the type of question you should take the time to be sure you answer correctly — a detail or fact question. Choice B introduces facts not discussed in the passage; there was no talk of leaves in mud or silt. Choice C is mentioned in the passage but not in Ferguson's experiments.

Be careful to answer *only* what the question is asking; the mere fact that a statement is true or is mentioned in the passage means nothing if the question isn't asking about that point. Nothing appears in the passage about high temperatures, which eliminates Choice D. (Did you know the word *exacerbated?* It means made worse — like the fact that this passage probably exacerbated your headache.) Choice E sounds pretentious and pompous — and nice and scientific — but again has nothing to do with Ferguson. To answer this question correctly, you need to return to the passage to look up Ferguson specifically, not merely rely on your memory of the passage as a whole. *Correct Answer:* Choice A.

4. The tone of the passage is

    (A) mesmerizing.

    (B) biased.

    (C) objective.

    (D) argumentative.

    (E) disparaging.

You *had* to get this question correct. If you missed this question, please consider yourself totally humiliated. *Correct Answer:* Choice C.

If you picked Choices A or E, you let your insecurities get the better of you: "Oooh, big hard word. I don't know it. It must be the right answer!" *Mesmerizing* means hypnotic or captivating. You probably weren't held spellbound by this passage (if you were, hey, get a life!). By the way, do you know who Franz Mesmer was? He was called "the father of hypnotism." What we now know as hypnotism used to be called mesmerism, after Franz. (No extra charge for the fascinating facts.) Choice E, *disparaging,* means in a degrading manner, speaking slightingly of. Disparaging is a negative answer, and as Chapter 10 explains, GRE passages are rarely negative in tone.

5. The author most likely is addressing this passage to

    (A) gardeners.

    (B) botanists.

    (C) hikers.

    (D) mechanical engineers.

    (E) Adam and Eve.

The passage is talking about microbiological activity affecting the strength of leaves. (You know this fact because you already answered a best title question on the topic — Question 1.) Although selecting Choice D is tempting, given the technical topic of the passage, mechanical engineers are usually more interested in machines than leaves. Botanists are the folks most likely to read this passage. The advice is probably too technical for gardeners, Choice A, and is waaaay too specific for hikers, Choice C. Choice E was added for comic relief. (If anyone needed to know how and why leaves disintegrate, especially fig leaves, it'd be Adam and Eve.) *Correct Answer:* Choice B.

Passage 11

Line   Multinational corporations frequently encounter impediments in their attempts to explain to politicians, human rights groups, and (perhaps most importantly) their consumer base why they do business with, and even seek closer business ties to, countries whose human rights records are considered heinous by United States standards. The CEOs pro-
(05) pound that in the business trenches the issue of human rights must effectively be detached from the wider spectrum of free trade. Discussion of the uneasy alliance between trade and human rights has trickled down from the boardrooms of large multinational corporations to the consumer on the street who, given the wide variety of products available to him, is eager to show support for human rights by boycotting the products of a company he feels does not
(10) do enough to help its overseas workers. International human rights organizations also are pressuring the multinationals to push for more humane working conditions in other countries and to, in effect, develop a code of business conduct that must be adhered to if the American company is to continue working with the overseas partner.

     The president, in drawing up a plan for what he calls the "economic architecture of our
(15) times," wants economists, business leaders, and human rights groups to work together to develop a set of principles that the foreign partners of United States corporations will voluntarily embrace. Human rights activists, incensed at the nebulous plans for implementing such rules, charge that their agenda is being given low priority by the State Department. The president vociferously denies their charges, arguing that each situation is approached on its merits
(20) without prejudice, and hopes that all the groups can work together to develop principles based on empirical research rather than political fiat, emphasizing that the businesses with experience in the field must initiate the process of developing such guidelines. Business leaders, while paying lip service to the concept of these principles, fight stealthily against their formal endorsement because they fear such "voluntary" concepts may someday be given the
(25) force of law. Few business leaders have forgotten the Sullivan Principles, in which a set of voluntary rules regarding business conduct with South Africa (giving benefits to workers and banning apartheid in the companies that worked with U.S. partners) became legislation.

6. Which of the following best states the central idea of the passage?

(A) Politicians are quixotic in their assessment of the priorities of the State Department.

(B) Multinational corporations have little if any influence on the domestic policies of their overseas partners.

(C) Voluntary principles that are turned into law are unconstitutional.

(D) Disagreement exists between the desires of human rights activists to improve the working conditions of overseas workers and the pragmatic approach taken by the corporations.

(E) It is inappropriate to expect foreign corporations to adhere to American standards.

The main idea of the passage is usually stated in the first sentence or two. The first sentence of this passage touches on the difficulties that corporations have explaining their business ties with certain countries to politicians, human rights groups, and consumers. From this statement, you may infer that those groups disagree with the policies of the corporations. *Correct Answer:* Choice D.

In Choice A, do you know the word *quixotic?* It means idealistic or impractical (think of the fictional character Don Quixote tilting at windmills). Although the president in this passage may not be realistic in his assessment of State Department policies, his belief isn't the main idea of the passage.

Just because a statement is (or may be) true doesn't necessarily mean it's the correct answer to a question. The answer choices to a main idea question in particular often are correct statements, or at least plausible-looking ones, but this appearance doesn't mean they're the main idea.

Choice E is a moral value, a judgment call. An answer that passes judgment, one that says something is morally right or morally wrong, is almost never the correct answer.

7. According to the passage, the president wants the voluntary principles to be initiated by businesses rather than by politicians or human rights activists because

   (A) businesses have empirical experience in the field and thus know what the conditions are and how they may/should be remedied.

   (B) businesses make profits from the labor of the workers and thus have a moral obligation to improve their employees' working conditions.

   (C) workers will not accept principles drawn up by politicians whom they distrust but may agree to principles created by the corporations that pay them.

   (D) foreign nations are distrustful of U.S. political intervention and are more likely to accept suggestions from multinational corporations.

   (E) political activist groups have concerns that are too dramatically different from those of the corporations for the groups to be able to work together.

When a question begins with the words "according to the passage," you need to go back to the passage and find the exact answer. You're told that ". . . businesses with experience in the field must initiate the process of developing such guidelines." Great — but what if you don't know the word *empirical*, which means based on experiment or experience rather than on theory? Keep reading. The rest of the sentence divulges the right answer. Don't tune out as soon as you encounter a difficult word.

Choices B, C, D, and E are all judgment calls. You're assuming facts not in evidence, as the lawyers say. Although you personally may believe the statements in these answer choices to be true, they don't answer the specific question. *Correct Answer:* Choice A.

8. Which of the following best describes the reason the author mentions the boycott of a corporation's products by its customers?

   (A) To show the difficulties that arise when corporations attempt to become involved in politics

   (B) To predict the inevitability of failure of any plan that does not involve customer input

   (C) To disagree with the president's contention that big business is the best qualified to draw up the voluntary principles of workplace conduct

   (D) To indicate the pressures that are on the multinational corporations

   (E) To ridicule the consumers for believing that their small boycott would significantly affect the sales of a multinational corporation

This question is one of those mind-reading ones that we warn you about in Chapter 10. You're expected to get into the author's mind and understand why he or she said what he or she did. That consumers may choose to boycott follows closely the main idea of the passage, which is that the corporations have difficulty trying to explain themselves and their actions to all sorts of groups, including their customers. From that, you may infer that the point of the statement is to indicate the pressures placed on the corporations.

Choice B seems logical; common sense tells you that a company that ignores its customers will probably fail. However, a strong, dramatic word like *inevitably* is rarely correct. Few things in life are inevitable, as we've said before: just death, taxes, and the GRE. *Correct Answer:* Choice D.

9. Which of the following statements about the Sullivan Principles can best be inferred from the passage?

   (A) They had a detrimental effect on the profits of those corporations doing business with South Africa.

   (B) They represented an improper alliance between political and business groups.

   (C) They placed the needs of the foreign workers over those of the domestic workers whose jobs would therefore be in jeopardy.

   (D) They will be used as a model to create future voluntary business guidelines.

   (E) They will have a chilling effect on future adoption of voluntary guidelines.

Choice A is the major trap here. Perhaps you assumed that because the companies seem to dislike the Sullivan Principles, they hurt company profits. However, nothing was said in the passage about profits. Maybe the companies still made good profits but objected to the Sullivan Principles, well, on principle. The companies just may not have wanted such governmental intervention, even if profits weren't decreased. If you picked Choice A, you read too much into the question and probably didn't read the rest of the answer choices.

In Choice E, the words *chilling effect* mean negative effect, or discouraging effect. Think of something with a chilling effect as leaving you cold. If your friend asks you to taste some soup because the dog loved it when she lapped up a few swallows, the statement about canine cuisine can have a chilling effect on your desire to taste the soup. Because few corporations have forgotten the Sullivan Principles, you may infer that these principles may discourage the companies from agreeing to voluntary principles in the future. *Correct Answer:* Choice E.

In order to get this question correct, you really need to understand the whole passage. If you didn't know what was going on here, you'd be better off just guessing and going. An inference question usually means you have to read between the lines; you can't just go back to one specific portion of the passage and get the answer quickly.

Part III

Two Years of Math in a Handful of Pages: The Dreaded Math Review

The 5th Wave   By Rich Tennant

"The image is getting clearer now...I can almost see it...Yes! There it is. The answer is $3ab^2 \times 7d^3 - \sqrt{19L} + U\frac{9}{m4} \div \pm 100.(15) 7\frac{9}{5} \Phi Q69$."

In this part . . .

No, no, please don't go get your pillow and PJs. We promise that this math review won't put you to sleep. We're not going to start at 1 + 1 = 2 and take you through every math concept you've learned since kindergarten; we have more respect for you than that. This math review neither insults you nor wastes your time. Here, we keep the instruction down to what you really need for the GRE.

If you've been out of school for a while, don't despair. After you go through the math review, do as many of the math problems as you can. The answer explanations review the formulas and concepts again and again and again; some of them are bound to come back to you.

Chapter 13

More Figures than a Beauty Pageant: Geometry Review

- -

In This Chapter

▶ Checking out some angle-related tips and traps

▶ Knowing how to handle triangle, quadrilateral, and polygon problems

▶ Playing with points in coordinate geometry

▶ Conquering common circle questions

- -

Question: How can you learn geometry?

Answer: Do it by degrees!

This chapter takes a "just the facts, ma'am" approach to geometry, telling you everything you need to know about angles, triangles, quadrilaterals, and circles.

An Angular Look at Geometry

Angles are a big part of GRE geometry problems. Fortunately, understanding angles is easy after you memorize a few basic concepts. Oh, and here's the best news: You don't have to do proofs. Finding an angle is usually a matter of simple addition or subtraction. These three rules generally apply to the GRE:

✔ You aren't going to see negative angles.

✔ You aren't going to see zero angles.

✔ It's extremely unlikely that you'll see any fractional angles. (For example, an angle won't measure 45½ degrees or 32¾ degrees.) On the GRE, angles are whole numbers. If you're plugging in a number for an angle, plug in a whole number, such as 30, 45, or 90.

In addition to these rules, here are a few more facts you need to know:

1. **Angles greater than 0 degrees but less than 90 degrees are called *acute*.**

45°

Acute

Think of an acute angle as being a cute little angle.

2. Angles equal to 90 degrees are called *right angles;* they're formed by perpendicular lines and indicated by a box in the corner of the two intersecting lines.

Right

A typical GRE trap is to have two lines appear to be perpendicular and look as if they form a right angle. Don't assume that's the way it is. An angle is a right angle *only* if (A) you're expressly told, "This is a right angle;" (B) you see the perpendicular symbol $(\perp)$ indicating that the lines form a 90-degree angle; or (C) you see the box in the angle. Otherwise, you may be headed for a trap.

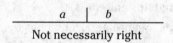

Not necessarily right

3. Angles that sum up to 90 degrees are called *complementary angles.*

Complementary

Think of *c* for *corner* (the lines form a 90-degree corner angle) and c for *complementary.*

4. An angle that's greater than 90 degrees but less than 180 degrees is called *obtuse.*

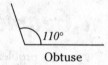

Obtuse

Think of obtuse as obese; an *obese* (fat) angle is an obtuse angle.

5. An angle that measures exactly 180 degrees is called a *straight angle.*

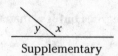

Straight

6. Angles that sum up to 180 degrees are called *supplementary angles.*

Supplementary

Think of *s* for *straight* angles and *s* for *supplementary* angles. Be careful not to confuse complementary angles (c for complementary; c for corner) with supplementary angles (s for supplementary; s for straight). If you're likely to get these types of angles confused, just think alphabetically. In the alphabet, c comes before s; likewise, 90 comes before 180 when you count.

7. An angle that's greater than 180 degrees but less than 360 degrees is called a *reflex angle*.

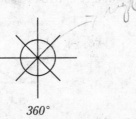

Reflex angle

 Reflex angles are rarely tested on the GRE, but just in case you encounter one, think of a reflex angle as what's left of a circular cake from which one slice (the acute angle) has been removed. The reflex angle makes up the rest of the circle when an acute angle is shown.

8. Angles around a point total 360 degrees.

360°

9. When lines cross, the angles that are opposite each other have equal measures and are called *vertical angles*.

Note that vertical angles may actually be horizontal. Just remember that vertical angles are across the vertex from each other, whether they're up and down (vertical) or side by side (horizontal).

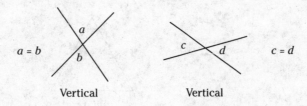

Vertical   Vertical

10. Angles in the same position (*corresponding angles*) formed by two parallel lines and a *transversal* (a line that cuts through the two lines) have the same measures.

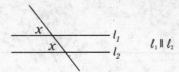

$\ell_1 \parallel \ell_2$

 When you see two parallel lines and a transversal, number the angles. Start in the upper-right corner with 1 and go clockwise. For the second batch of angles, start in the upper-right corner with 5 and go clockwise:

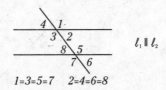

$\ell_1 \parallel \ell_2$

$1=3=5=7 \quad 2=4=6=8$

Note that all the odd-numbered angles are equal, as are all the even-numbered angles.

Be careful not to zigzag back and forth when numbering, like this:

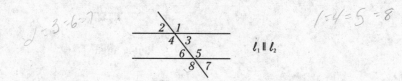

$\ell_1 \parallel \ell_2$

If you zig when you should've zagged, the fact that all even-numbered angles are equal to one another and all odd-numbered angles are equal to one another no longer holds true.

11. **The exterior angles of any figure are supplementary to the interior angles and total 360 degrees.**

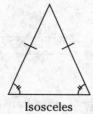

Exterior

Triangular Tidbits

Yes, triangles have three sides. Here are the *other* tidbits you need to know about triangles:

1. **A triangle with three equal sides and three equal angles is called *equilateral* and *equiangular*.**

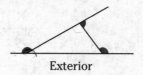

Equilateral

2. **A triangle with two equal sides and two equal angles is called *isosceles*.**

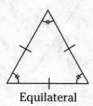

Isosceles

3. **Angles opposite equal sides in an isosceles triangle are also equal.**

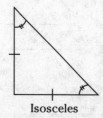

Isosceles

4. A triangle with no equal sides and no equal angles is called *scalene*.

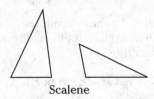

Scalene

5. In any triangle, the largest angle is opposite the longest side.

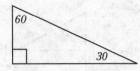

6. In any triangle, the sum of the lengths of two sides must be greater than the length of the third side.

This fact is often written as $a + b > c$ where a, b, and c are the sides of the triangle.

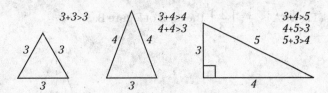

7. In any type of triangle, the sum of the interior angles is 180 degrees.

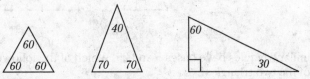

Often a trap question wants you to assume that different-sized triangles have different angle measures. Wrong! A triangle can be seven stories high and have 180 degrees or be microscopic and have 180 degrees. The size of the triangle is irrelevant. Every triangle's internal angles sum up to 180 degrees.

8. The measure of an exterior angle of a triangle is equal to the sum of the two remote interior angles.

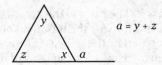

When you think about this rule logically, it makes sense. The sum of supplementary angles is 180, and x (inside the triangle) and a (outside) are supplementary, so $x + a = 180$. The sum of the angles in a triangle is 180, and x, y, and z are inside the triangle, so $x + y + z = 180$. Substitution then gives you $x + a = x + y + z$. Then you subtract the x from both sides to get $a = y + z$.

Working with similar figures

Similar figures are figures that have congruent angles and proportional sides. Two triangles may be radically different in size, but the degrees of their angles are the exact same, and their sides create equal ratios.

1. **The sides of similar figures are in proportion.**

   For example, if the heights of two similar triangles are in a ratio of 2:3, then the bases of those triangles are in a ratio of 2:3 as well.

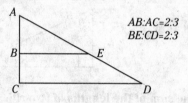

AB:AC=2:3
BE:CD=2:3

2. **The ratio of the areas of similar figures is equal to the square of the ratio of their sides.**

   For example, if each side of Figure A is ⅓ the length of each side of similar Figure B, then the area of Figure A is $\frac{1}{9} = \left(\frac{1}{3}\right)^2$ the area of Figure B.

  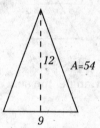

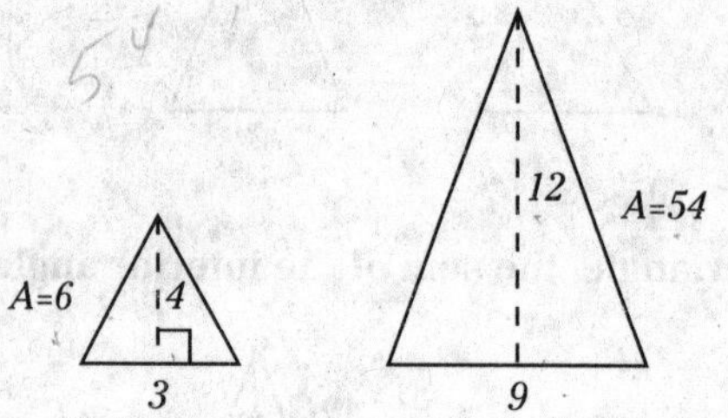

A=6 ... 3 ... 12 ... A=54 ... 9

EXAMPLE

Two similar triangles have bases 5 and 25. Which of the following expresses the ratio of the areas of the two triangles?

(A) 1:5

(B) 1:15

(C) 1:25

(D) 2:15

(E) It cannot be determined from the information given.

The ratio of the sides is ⅕. The ratio of the areas is the square of the ratio of the sides: ⅕ × ⅕ = ¹⁄₂₅. Note that Choice E is a trap for the unwary. You can't figure out the exact area of either figure because you don't know the height. (The area of a triangle is ½ *base* × *height*.) However, you aren't asked for an area, only for the ratio of the areas, which you can deduce from the formula we presented to you. *Correct Answer:* Choice C.

Bonus: What do you suppose is the ratio of the volumes of two similar figures? Because volume is found in cubic units, the ratio of the volumes of two similar figures is the cube of the ratio of their sides. If Figure A has a base of 5 and similar Figure B has a base of 10, then the ratio of their volumes is 1:8 ($[1:2]^3$), which is $\frac{1}{2} \times \frac{1}{2} \times \frac{1}{2} = \frac{1}{8}$.

Don't assume that figures are similar. Wait to be told that they are.

Calculating a triangle's area and perimeter

You must remember one formula for a triangle's area and one for its perimeter.

1. The area of a triangle is ½ *base* × *height*.

The height is always a line perpendicular to the base. The height may be a side of the triangle, as in a right triangle.

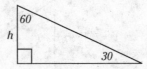

Then again, the height may be inside the triangle. A dashed line and a small 90-degree box often represent the height.

The height may even be outside the triangle. This fact is very confusing and is sometimes used to create trick questions. The good news is that you can always drop an altitude. That is, put your pencil on the tallest point of the triangle and draw a line straight from that point to the base or the extension of the base. The line you draw is the height, and it can be outside the triangle.

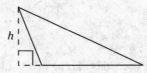

2. The perimeter of a triangle is the sum of the lengths of the sides.

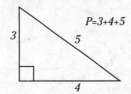

Understanding the Pythagorean theorem

You've probably studied the Pythagorean theorem (known colloquially as PT). Keep in mind that it works only on *right* triangles. If a triangle doesn't have a right (90-degree) angle, you can't use any of the following information.

In any right triangle, you can find the lengths of the sides with this formula:

$$a^2 + b^2 = c^2$$

where a and b are the sides of the triangle, and c is the hypotenuse. The hypotenuse is always opposite the 90-degree angle and is always the longest side of the triangle. Why? Because if one angle in a triangle is 90 degrees, no other angle can be more than 90 degrees. All the angles must total 180 degrees, and negative or 0 angles aren't possible. Because the longest side is opposite the largest angle, the hypotenuse is the longest side.

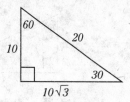

Recognizing Pythagorean triples

Doing the whole PT formula every time you want to find the length of a side is a real pain in the posterior. That's why we're clueing you in to four very common PT ratios in triangles:

1. **Ratio 3:4:5 means that if one side of the triangle is 3, the other side is 4, and the hypotenuse is 5.**

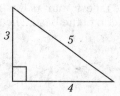

Because this is a ratio, the sides can be in any multiple of these numbers, such as 6:8:10 (twice 3:4:5), 9:12:15 (three times 3:4:5), or 27:36:45 (nine times 3:4:5).

2. **Ratio 5:12:13 means that if one side of the triangle is 5, the other side is 12, and the hypotenuse is 13.**

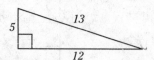

Because you're dealing with a ratio, the sides can be in any multiple of these numbers, such as 10:24:26 (twice 5:12:13), 15:36:39 (three times 5:12:13), or 50:120:130 (ten times 5:12:13).

3. Ratio $s:s:s\sqrt{2}$ where s stands for the side of the figure. Because two sides are the same, this formula applies to an isosceles right triangle — also known as a 45:45:90 triangle. If one side is 2, then the other side is also 2, and the hypotenuse is $2\sqrt{2}$.

This formula is great to know for working with squares. If a question tells you that the side of a square is 5 and wants to know the diagonal of the square, you know immediately that it's $5\sqrt{2}$. Why? A square's diagonal cuts the square into two isosceles right triangles (*isosceles* because all sides of the square are equal; *right* because all angles in a square are right angles). What's the diagonal of a square of side 64? $64\sqrt{2}$. What's the diagonal of a square of side 12,984? $12,984\sqrt{2}$.

You can also write this ratio another way. Instead of writing $s:s:s\sqrt{2}$, you can write it as $\frac{s}{\sqrt{2}}:\frac{s}{\sqrt{2}}:s$. Of course, the s still stands for the side of the triangle, but now you've divided everything through by $\sqrt{2}$. Why do you need this complicated formula? Suppose you're told that the diagonal of a square is 5. What's the area of the square? What's the perimeter of the square? Chances are good that one of the trap answers is "It cannot be determined from the information given." Chances are even better that you may fall for that trap answer.

However, if you know this formula, $\frac{s}{\sqrt{2}}:\frac{s}{\sqrt{2}}:s$, you also know that s stands for the hypotenuse of the triangle, which is the same as the diagonal of the square. If $s = 5$, then the side of the square is $\frac{5}{\sqrt{2}}$, and you can figure out the area or the perimeter. (Actually, after you know the side of a square, you can figure out just about anything.)

4. Ratio $s:s\sqrt{3}:2s$ is a special formula for the sides of a 30:60:90 triangle.

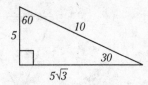

This type of triangle is a favorite of the test-makers. The important fact to keep in mind here is that the hypotenuse is twice the length of the side opposite the 30-degree angle. If you encounter a word problem that says, "Given a 30:60:90 triangle of hypotenuse 20, find the area," or "Given a 30:60:90 triangle of hypotenuse 100, find the perimeter," you can do so because you can find the lengths of the other sides.

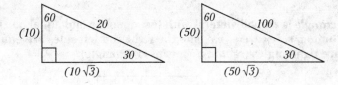

Thanks 4 Nothing: Quadrilaterals

The most famous quadrilateral is the square, but there are plenty of other quads you should get familiar with.

1. Any four-sided figure is called a *quadrilateral*.

Quadrilateral

The interior angles of any quadrilateral total 360 degrees. Additionally, any quadrilateral can be cut into two 180-degree triangles.

2. A *square* is a quadrilateral with four equal sides and four right angles.

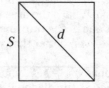

Square

The area of a square is *side*² (also called *base × height*), or ½ *diagonal*².

3. A *rhombus* is a quadrilateral with four equal sides and four angles that aren't necessarily right angles.

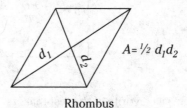

Rhombus

A rhombus often looks like a drunken square — tipsy and wobbly. The area of a rhombus is ½ d_1d_2 (½ *diagonal*₁ × *diagonal*₂).

Any square is a rhombus, but not all rhombuses are squares.

4. A *rectangle* is a quadrilateral with two opposite and equal pairs of sides. That is, the top and bottom sides are equal, and the right and left sides are equal. All angles in a rectangle are right angles (*rectangle* means right angle).

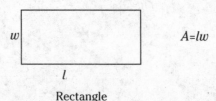

Rectangle

The area of a rectangle is *length × width* (which is the same as *base × height*).

5. A *parallelogram* is a quadrilateral with two opposite and equal pairs of sides. The top and bottom sides are equal, and the right and left sides are equal. Opposite angles are equal but not necessarily right (or 90 degrees).

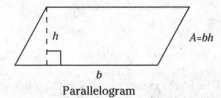

Parallelogram

The area of a parallelogram is *base × height*. Remember that the height is always a perpendicular line from the tallest point of the figure down to the base. Diagonals of a parallelogram bisect each other.

All rectangles are parallelograms, but not all parallelograms are rectangles.

6. A *trapezoid* is a quadrilateral with two parallel sides and two nonparallel sides.

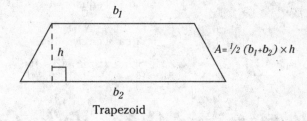

Trapezoid

The area of a trapezoid is ½(*base₁* + *base₂*) × *height*. It makes no difference which base you label *base 1* and which you label *base 2*, because you're adding them together anyway. Just be sure to add them *before* you multiply by ½.

Quaint quads: Bizarre quadrilaterals

Some quadrilaterals don't have nice, neat shapes or special names.

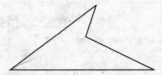

Don't immediately see a strange shape and say that you have no way to find its area. You may be able to divide the quadrilateral into two triangles and find the area of each triangle. You may also see a strange quadrilateral in a shaded-area problem; we tell you more about those problems in the next section.

Leftovers again: Shaded-area problems

Think of a shaded area as a leftover. It's "left over" after you subtract the unshaded area from the total area.

Shaded areas are often rather unusual shapes. Your first reaction may be that you can't possibly find the area of that shape. Generally, you're right, but you don't have to find the area directly. Instead, be sly, devious, and sneaky; in other words, think the GRE way! Find the area of the total figure, find the area of the unshaded portion, and subtract.

1. $s = 8$
Area of square = 64

2. $r = 4$
Area of circle = 16π

3. Shaded area = $64 - 16\pi$

Missing Parrots and Other Polly-Gones: More Polygons

Triangles and quadrilaterals are probably the most common *polygons* (closed figures consisting of straight lines, such as squares, rectangles, decagons, and so on) tested on this exam. Here are a few other polygons you may see:

Number of Sides	Name
5	Pentagon
6	Hexagon (think of x in six and x in hex)
7	Heptagon
8	Octagon
9	Nonagon
10	Decagon

1. A polygon with all equal sides and all equal angles is known as a *regular polygon*.

For example, an equilateral triangle is a regular triangle, and a square is a regular quadrilateral.

The GRE usually doesn't ask you to find the areas of any polygons with more than four sides. It may, however, ask you to find the *perimeter,* which is just the sum of the lengths of all the sides.

2. The sum of the measures of the exterior angles of *any* polygon is 360.

Determining total interior angle measure

Because you may be asked to find the total interior angle measure of a particular polygon, keep this formula in mind:

$(n - 2)180$, where n stands for the number of sides

For example, the interior angles of the following polygons are:

- ✔ **Triangle:** $(3 - 2)180 = 1 \times 180 = 180°$
- ✔ **Quadrilateral:** $(4 - 2)180 = 2 \times 180 = 360°$
- ✔ **Pentagon:** $(5 - 2)180 = 3 \times 180 = 540°$
- ✔ **Hexagon:** $(6 - 2)180 = 4 \times 180 = 720°$
- ✔ **Heptagon:** $(7 - 2)180 = 5 \times 180 = 900°$
- ✔ **Octagon:** $(8 - 2)180 = 6 \times 180 = 1,080°$
- ✔ **Nonagon:** $(9 - 2)180 = 7 \times 180 = 1,260°$
- ✔ **Decagon:** $(10 - 2)180 = 8 \times 180 = 1,440°$

Have you discovered that proportional multiplication is a great timesaving trick? Numbers are in proportion, and you can fiddle with them to make multiplication easier. Suppose you're going to multiply 5×180. Most people need to write down the problem and then work through it. But because the numbers are in proportion, you can double one and halve the other: Double 5 to make it 10. Halve 180 to make it 90. Now your problem is 10×90, which you can multiply to 900 in your head.

Try another one: $3 \times 180 = ?$ Double the first number: $3 \times 2 = 6$. Halve the second number: $^{180}/_2 = 90$. Then multiply: $6 \times 90 = 540$. You can do this shortcut multiplication in your head very quickly and impress your friends.

Finding one interior angle

If you're asked to find the average measure of one angle in a polygon, the formula is

$$\frac{(n-2)180}{n}$$

where n stands for the number of sides (which is the same as the number of angles).

Pentagon: $\dfrac{(5-2)\times180}{5} = \dfrac{3 \times 180}{5} = \dfrac{540}{5} = 108°$

Because all angles are equal in a regular polygon, the same formula applies to one angle in a regular polygon.

If you're given a polygon and *aren't* told that it's regular, you can't solve for just one angle.

What's the measure of Angle *x?* It cannot be determined. You can't assume that it's

$$\frac{(7-2)\times180}{7} = \frac{900}{7} = 128.57° .$$

Getting the Total Picture: Volume & Total Surface Area

You can calculate volume and total surface area for any three-dimensional shape. In this section, we give you the information you need in order to do so, and in order to persevere in this section of the GRE.

Calculating volume

TIP

1. **The volume of any polygon is *(area of the base)* × *height*.**

   If you can remember this formula, you don't need to memorize any of the following more specific formulas.

2. **Volume of a cube:** e^3

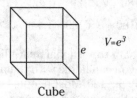

$V = e^3$

Cube

A cube is a three-dimensional square. Think of a die (one of a pair of dice). All of a cube's dimensions are the same; that is, *length = width = height*. In a cube, these dimensions are called *edges*. The volume of a cube is thus *edge × edge × edge = edge³ = e^3*.

3. **Volume of a rectangular solid:** $l \times w \times h$

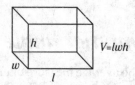

$V = lwh$

Rectangular solid

A rectangular solid is a box. The base of a box is a rectangle, which has an area of *length × width*. Multiply that by height to fit the original formula: *Volume = (area of the base) × height*, or $V = l \times w \times h$.

4. **Volume of a cylinder:** $(\pi r^2)height$

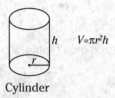

$V = \pi r^2 h$

Cylinder

Think of a cylinder as a can of soup. The base of a cylinder is a circle. The area of a circle is πr^2. Multiply that by the height of the cylinder to get *(area of the base) × height = (πr^2) × height*. Note that the top and bottom of a cylinder are identical circles. If you know the radius of either the top base or the bottom base, you can find the area of the circle.

Figuring out total surface area

1. **The total surface area (TSA), logically enough, is the sum of the areas of all the surfaces of the figure.**

2. **TSA of a cube: $6e^2$**

Cube

A cube has six identical faces, and each face is a square. The area of a square is *side*^{2}. Here, that's called *edge*^{2}. If one face is *edge*^{2}, then the total surface area is $6 \times edge^2$, or $6e^2$.

3. **TSA of a rectangular solid: $2(lw) + 2(wh) + 2(hl)$**

Rectangular solid

A rectangular solid is a box. You need to find the area of each of the six surfaces. The bottom and top each have the area of *(length × width)*. The area of the left side and right side each are equal to *(width × height)*. The front side and the back side each have the area of *(height × length)*. Together, they total $2(lw) + 2(wh) + 2(hl)$, or $2(lw + wh + hl)$.

4. **TSA of a cylinder: $(circumference \times height) + 2(\pi r^2)$**

Cylinder

The TSA of a cylinder is definitely the most difficult TSA to figure out. Think of it as pulling the label off a can, flattening it out, finding its area, and then adding that to the area of the top and bottom lids.

The label is a rectangle. Its length is the length of the circumference of the circle.

Its height is the height of the cylinder. Multiply *length × height* to find the area of the label.

You also need to find the area of the top and bottom of the cylinder. Because both the top and bottom are circles, their TSA is $2(\pi r^2)$. Finally, add everything together.

I'm Too Much of a Klutz for Coordinate Geometry

The horizontal axis is the *x*-axis. The vertical axis is the *y*-axis. Points are labeled (*x*,*y*) with the first number in the parentheses indicating how far to the right or left of the vertical line the point is and the second number indicating how far above or below the horizontal line the point is.

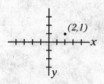

The intersection of the *x*- and *y*-axes is called the *point of origin,* and its coordinates are (0,0). A line connecting points whose *x*- and *y*-coordinates are the same forms a 45-degree angle with each axis.

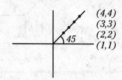

If you're asked to find the distance between two points, you can use the distance formula (which is based on the Pythagorean theorem):

$$\sqrt{\left(x_2 - x_1\right)^2 + \left(y_2 - y_1\right)^2}$$

Find the distance from (9,4) to (8,6).

$9 = x_1$

$8 = x_2$

$4 = y_1$

$6 = y_2$

$(8 - 9)^2 = -1^2 = 1$

$(6 - 4)^2 = 2^2 = 4$

$1 + 4 = 5$

$\sqrt{5}$ is the distance between the two points.

Running Around in Circles

Did you hear about the guy who pulled his son out of college, claiming that the school was filling his son's head with nonsense? As the guy said, "Joe Bob told me that he learned πr^2. But any fool knows that pie are round; *cornbread* are square!"

Circles are among the less-complicated geometry concepts. You just need to remember the vocabulary and be able to distinguish an arc from a sector and an inscribed angle from an intercepted arc. Here's a quick review of the basics:

1. A _radius_ goes from the center of a circle to its circumference (perimeter).

Radius

2. A circle is named by its center.

M _Circle M_

Center

3. A _diameter_ connects two points on the circumference of the circle, going through the center, and is equal to two radii.

Diameter

4. A _chord_ connects any two points on a circle. The longest chord in a circle is the diameter.

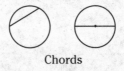

Chords

Here's a lovely question you may see on the GRE. Choose

A if the quantity in Column A is greater.

B if the quantity in Column B is greater.

C if the two quantities are equal.

D if the relationship cannot be determined from the information given.

Column A	_Column B_
Area of a circle of radius 6	Area of a circle of radius 6 of longest chord 12

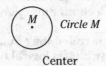

Many people choose D for this question. Although typically in QCs (Quantitative Comparisons, this type of problem) the right answer to a geometry question with no figure is D because the answer _de_pends on how you draw the picture, a circle is frequently an exception to this tip. A circle is a circle is a circle; it rarely depends on how you draw it. The key here is to know that the _longest chord_ is a fancy-schmancy way of saying the _diameter_. Because the diameter is twice the radius, a circle of diameter (or longest chord) 12 has a radius of 6. Two circles with radii of 6 have the same area. (Don't waste even a nanosecond figuring out what that area actually is. It's irrelevant to comparing the quantities in the two columns.) *Correct Answer:* C.

Column A	**Column B**
Area of a circle of radius 10	Area of a circle of chord 20

If you chose C, you fell for the trap. A chord connects any two points on a circle. The *longest* chord is the diameter, but a chord can be any ol' thing. *Correct Answer:* D.

5. **The perimeter of a circle is called the *circumference*. The formula for the length of a circumference is 2πr, or πd (which is logical because 2 *radii* = 1 *diameter*).**

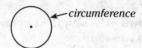

circumference

Bonus: You may encounter a wheel question in which you're asked how much distance a wheel covers, or how many times a wheel revolves. The key to solving this type of question is to know that one rotation of a wheel equals one circumference of that wheel.

A child's wagon has a wheel of radius 6 inches. If the wagon wheel travels 100 revolutions, approximately how many feet has the wagon rolled?

(A) 325

(B) 314

(C) 255

(D) 201

(E) It cannot be determined from the information given.

One revolution is equal to one circumference: $C = 2\pi r = 2\pi 6 = 12\pi = approximately$ 37.68 inches. Multiply that by 100 = 3,768 *inches* = 314 *feet*. Choice E is definitely the worst guess you can make. If you have a radius, you can solve for nearly anything having to do with circles. Remember that there's a difference between "It cannot be determined" and "*I* cannot determine it." Just because you personally may not know what to do doesn't mean the problem isn't doable. If you're guessing, guess something else. *Correct Answer:* Choice B.

6. **The area of a circle is π*radius*².**

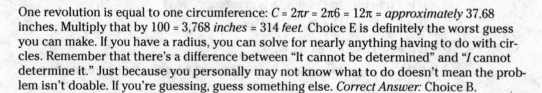

4   A=16π

7. A *central angle* has its endpoints on the circumference of the circle and its vertex at the center of the circle. The degree measure of a central angle is the same as the degree measure of its intercepted arc.

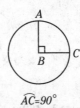

$\overarc{AC}=90°$

8. An *inscribed angle* has both its endpoints and its vertex on the circumference of the circle. The degree measure of an inscribed angle is half the degree measure of its intercepted arc.

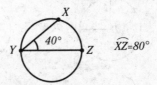

$\overarc{XZ}=80°$

You may see a figure that looks like a string picture you made at summer camp back in the day, with lines running every which way. Take the time to identify the endpoints of the angles and the vertex. You may be surprised at how easy the question suddenly becomes.

In this figure, find the sum of the degree measures of Angles $a + b + c + d + e$.

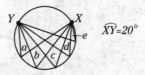

$\overarc{XY}=20°$

Note: Figure not drawn to scale.

(A) 65

(B) 60

(C) 55

(D) 50

(E) 45

Each angle is an inscribed angle. That means the angle has half the degree measure of the central angle, or half the degree measure of its intercepted arc. If you look carefully at the endpoints of these angles, they're all the same: *XY*. Arc *XY* has a measure of 20°. Therefore, each angle is 10°, for a total of 50. *Correct Answer:* Choice D.

9. When a central angle and an inscribed angle have the same endpoints, the degree measure of the central angle is twice that of the inscribed angle.

10. The degree measure of a circle is 360.

11. An *arc* is a portion of the circumference of a circle. The degree measure of an arc is the same as its central angle and twice its inscribed angle.

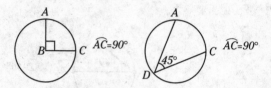

To find the length of an arc, follow these steps:

1. **Find the circumference of the entire circle.**

2. **Put the degree measure of the arc over 360 and then reduce the fraction.**

3. **Multiply the circumference by the fraction.**

Find the length of Arc *AC*.

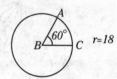

(A) 36π

(B) 27π

(C) 18π

(D) 12π

(E) 6π

Take the steps one at a time. First, find the circumference of the entire circle: $C = 2\pi r = 36\pi$. Don't multiply π out; problems usually leave it in that form. Next, put the degree measure of the arc over 360. The degree measure of the arc is the same as its central angle, 60°, so $^{60}/_{360} = ^{1}/_{6}$. The arc is $^{1}/_{6}$ of the circumference of the circle. Multiply the circumference by the fraction: $36\pi \times ^{1}/_{6} = 6\pi$. *Correct Answer:* Choice E.

Try another one. After you get the hang of arc problems, they're actually kinda fun.

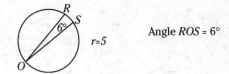

Angle *ROS* = 6°

Find the length of Arc *RS* in this figure.

(A) ⅓π

(B) π

(C) 3π

(D) 4π

(E) 12

First, find the circumference of the entire circle: $C = 2\pi r = 10\pi$. Second, put the degree measure of the arc over 360. Here, the inscribed angle is 6°. Because an inscribed angle is ½ of the central angle and ½ of its intercepted arc, the arc is 12°: ¹²⁄₃₆₀ = ¹⁄₃₀. The arc is ¹⁄₃₀ of the circle. Finally, multiply the circumference by the fraction: $10\pi \times \frac{1}{30} = \frac{10}{30}\pi = \frac{1}{3}\pi$. The length of the arc is ⅓π. *Correct Answer:* Choice A.

Be very careful not to confuse the *degree measure* of the arc with the *length* of the arc. The length is always a portion of the circumference, always has a π in it, and always is in linear units. If you picked Choice E in this example, you found the degree measure of the arc rather than its length.

12. **A *sector* is a portion of the area of a circle. The degree measure of a sector is the same as its central angle and twice its inscribed angle.**

To find the area of a sector, do the following:

1. **Find the area of the entire circle.**

2. **Put the degree measure of the sector over 360 and then reduce the fraction.**

3. **Multiply the area by the fraction.**

Finding the area of a sector is very similar to finding the length of an arc. The only difference is in the first step. Whereas an arc is a part of the *circumference* of a circle, a sector is a part of the *area* of a circle. With that in mind, try your hand at a few sample sector problems:

Find the area of Sector *ABC*.

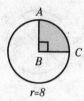

(A) 64π

(B) 36π

(C) 16π

(D) 12π

(E) 6π

First, find the area of the entire circle: $A = \pi r^2 = 64\pi$. Second, put the degree measure of the sector over 360. The sector is 90°, the same as its central angle: $^{90}\!/_{360} = \frac{1}{4}$. Third, multiply the area by the fraction: $64\pi \times \frac{1}{4} = 16\pi$. *Correct Answer:* Choice C.

Find the area of Sector *XYZ* in this figure.

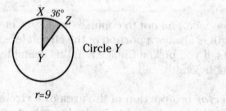

(A) 9.7π

(B) 8.1π

(C) 7.2π

(D) 6.3π

(E) 6π

First, find the area of the entire circle: $A = \pi r^2 = 81\pi$. Second, put the degree measure of the sector over 360. A sector has the same degree measure as its intercepted arc, in this case 36°: $^{36}\!/_{360} = \frac{1}{10}$. Third, multiply the area by the fraction: $81\pi \times \frac{1}{10} = 8.1\pi$. *Correct Answer:* Choice B.

Chapter 14

Gotta Catch Some (Xs, Ys, and) Zs: Algebra and Other Sleeping Aids

• •

In This Chapter

▶ Understanding bases, exponents, and ratios

▶ Knowing what to do with symbolism

▶ Reviewing algebra basics and the FOIL method

▶ Digging deep into roots, radicals, and probability

• •

Question: Where was algebra supposedly invented?

Answer: Algebra was invented in Zabid, Yemen, by Muslim scholars. You can't blame the Greeks for everything!

The Powers That Be: Bases and Exponents

Many GRE questions require you to know how to work with bases and exponents. That's why this section explains some of the most important concepts in the world of bases and exponents.

1. **The *base* is the big number (or letter) on the bottom. The *exponent* is the little number (or letter) in the upper-right corner.**

   In x^5, x is the base; 5 is the exponent.

   In 3^y, 3 is the base; y is the exponent.

2. **A base to the zero power equals 1.**

   $x^0 = 1$

   $5^0 = 1$

   $129^0 = 1$

   There's a long explanation as to why a number to the zero power equals 1, but you don't really care, do you? For now, just memorize the rule.

3. **A base to the second power is *base* × *base*.**

   $x^2 = x \times x$

   $5^2 = 5 \times 5$

   $129^2 = 129 \times 129$

Pretty familiar stuff, right? Well, the same is true for bigger exponents. The exponent tells you how many times the number is repeated. For example, 5^6 means that you write down six 5s and then multiply them all together.

$$3^9 = 3 \times 3 \times 3 \times 3 \times 3 \times 3 \times 3 \times 3 \times 3$$

4. **A base to a negative exponent is the reciprocal of something.**

This concept is a little more confusing. A reciprocal is the upside-down version of something. When you have a negative exponent, put the base and exponent under a 1 and make the exponent positive again.

$$x^{-4} = \frac{1}{(x^4)}$$
$$5^{-3} = \frac{1}{(5^3)}$$
$$129^{-1} = \frac{1}{(129^1)}$$

The *number* isn't negative. When you flip it, you get the reciprocal — the negative just sort of fades away. *Don't* fall for the trap of saying that $5^{-3} = (\frac{1}{5})^3$ or $-\frac{1}{125}$.

5. **When you take a base of 10 to some power, the number of the power equals the number of zeros in the number.**

$10^1 = 10$ (one zero)

$10^4 = 10,000$ (four zeros)

$10^0 = 1$ (zero zeros)

6. **To multiply like bases, add the exponents.**

You can multiply two bases that are the same; just add the exponents.

$$x^3 \times x^2 = x^{(3+2)} = x^5$$
$$5^4 \times 5^9 = 5^{(4+9)} = 5^{13}$$
$$129^3 \times 129^0 = 129^{(3+0)} = 129^3$$

You can't multiply *unlike* bases. That's like trying to make dogs multiply with cats — it doesn't work. All you end up with is a miffed meower and a damaged dog.

$x^2 \times y^3 = x^2 \times y^3$ (Nope, no shortcuts.)

$5^2 \times 129^3 = 5^2 \times 129^3$ (Yes, you actually have to work it out.)

7. **To divide like bases, subtract the exponents.**

You can divide two bases that are the same by subtracting the exponents.

$$x^5 \div x^2 = x^{(5-2)} = x^3$$
$$5^9 \div 5^3 = 5^{(9-3)} = 5^6$$
$$129^4 \div 129^0 = 129^{(4-0)} = 129^4$$

Did we get you on that last one? It should make sense. Any base to the zero power is 1, whereas any number divided by 1 is itself.

Did you look at the second example, $5^9 \div 5^3$, and think that it was 5^3? Falling into the trap of dividing rather than subtracting is pretty easy, especially when you see numbers that just beg to be divided, like 9 and 3. Keep your guard up.

8. Multiply the exponents of a base inside and outside of parentheses.

That's quite a mouthful. Here's what it means:

$$\left(x^2\right)^3 = x^{(2\times3)} = x^6$$

$$\left(5^3\right)^3 = 5^{(3\times3)} = 5^9$$

$$\left(129^0\right)^3 = 129^{(0\times3)} = 129^0$$

Time to try out a few Quantitative Comparison (QC) questions testing this concept! (In QC questions, you compare two columns. We explain all about QC questions in Chapter 16.)

In the following QC questions, your answer choices are

A if the quantity in Column A is greater.

B if the quantity in Column B is greater.

C if the two quantities are equal.

D if the relationship cannot be determined from the information given.

Column A	*Column B*
x^3	$\dfrac{x^7}{x^4}$

$x^{(7-4)} = x^3$, no matter what the value of x is. *Correct Answer:* C.

Column A	*Column B*
$\left(x^3\right)^4$	x^{12}

No matter what value x has, the two columns are the same: $x^{12} = x^{12}$. *Correct Answer:* C.

Column A	*Column B*
$\left(x^3\right)^4$	12

Everything *de*pends on the value of x. Boy, this trap is really easy to fall for. Because you're so busy thinking of $3 \times 4 = 12$, you may be tempted to pick C. But the automatic shutdown valve in the back of your brain should alert you to the fact that *when two columns appear to be equal, it's usually a trap.* (See Chapter 16 for the scoop on this QC trick.) *Correct Answer:* D.

9. To add or subtract like bases to like powers, add or subtract the numerical coefficients of the bases.

The *numerical coefficient* (a great name for a rock band, don't you think?) is simply the number in front of the base. Notice that it isn't the little exponent in the right-hand corner but the full-sized number to the left of the base.

In $31x^3$, 31 is the numerical coefficient.

In $-8y^2$, -8 is the numerical coefficient.

In x^3, the numerical coefficient is 1, because any number is itself times 1. The 1 isn't always written out. Good trap, eh?

In $37x^3 + 10x^3 = 47x^3$, just add the numerical coefficients: $37 + 10 = 47$. The answer is $47x^3$.

In $15y^2 - 10y^2 = 5y^2$, just subtract the numerical coefficients: $15 - 10 = 5$. The answer is $5y^2$.

You can't add or subtract like bases with *different exponents.* For example, $13x^3 - 9x^2$ isn't equal to $4x^3$, $4x^2$, or $4x$. The only thing it's equal to is $13x^3 - 9x^2$. The bases *and* exponents must be the same for you to add or subtract the terms.

Column A	**Column B**
$16x^4 - 4x^3$	$12x$

The answer *de*pends on the value of *x.* If you selected C, you fell for the trap we just covered. *Correct Answer:* D.

10. **You can't simply add or subtract the numerical coefficients of unlike bases.**

Again, doing so is like working with cats and dogs — they don't mingle.

$$16x^2 - 4y^2 = 16x^2 - 4y^2$$

It's *not* $12x^2$, $12y^2$, or $12xy^2$.

Column A	**Column B**
$10x^3 - 2y^3$	$8xy$

The answer *de*pends on the values of *x* and *y.* C is the trap answer. *Correct Answer:* D.

Keepin' It in Proportion: Ratios

After you know the tricks, ratios are some of the easiest problems to answer quickly. We call them "heartbeat" problems, because you can solve them in a heartbeat. Of course, if someone drop-dead gorgeous sits next to you and makes your heart beat a little faster, it may actually take you two heartbeats to solve a ratio problem. So sue us.

1. **A ratio is written as either $\frac{of}{to}$ or of:to.**

   The ratio *of* sunflowers *to* roses = sunflowers:roses.

   The ratio *of* umbrellas *to* heads = $\frac{umbrellas}{heads}$.

2. **A possible total is a multiple of the sum of the numbers in the ratio.**

   You may encounter a problem like this: At a party, the ratio of blondes to redheads is 4:5. Which of the following can be the total number of blondes and redheads at the party?

This one's mega-easy. Add the numbers in the ratio: 4 + 5 = 9. Now you know that the total must be a multiple of 9: 9, 18, 27, 36, and so on. If this "multiple of" stuff is confusing, think of it another way: The sum must divide evenly into the total. That is, the total must be divisible by 9. Can the total, for example, be 54? Yes, because 9 goes evenly into 54. Can it be 64? No, because 9 doesn't go evenly into 64.

After a rough hockey game, Bernie checks his body and finds that he has three bruises for every five cuts. Which of the following can be the total number of bruises and cuts on poor ol' Bernie's body?

(A) 53

(B) 45

(C) 35

(D) 33

(E) 32

Add the numbers in the ratio: 3 + 5 = 8. The total must be a multiple of 8 (or, looking at it another way, the total must be evenly divisible by 8). Only Choice E is a multiple of 8 (8 × 4 = 32). *Correct Answer:* Choice E.

Did you notice the trap answers? Choice A, 53, is a good trap because it features both 5 and 3, the numbers in the ratio. Choice B, 45, is also a trap. If you multiply 3 × 5 = 15, you may think that the total has to be a multiple of 15. Nope! The total is actually a multiple of the *sum,* not of the product. *Add* the numbers in the ratio; don't multiply them. Choice C, 35, again, has both terms of the ratio. Choice D, 33, is a multiple of 3. Only Choice E, 32, is a multiple of the *sum* of the terms in the ratio.

Here's one more, because you should always get this type of problem correct:

When trying to get Willie to turn down his stereo, his downstairs neighbor pounds on the ceiling and shouts up to his bedroom. If she pounds 7 times for every 5 times she shouts, which of the following can be the total number of poundings and shouts?

(A) 75

(B) 57

(C) 48

(D) 35

(E) 30

Add the numbers in the ratio: 7 + 5 = 12. The total must be a multiple of 12 (meaning it must be evenly divisible by 12). Only Choice C, 48, is evenly divisible by 12. Of course, Choice A, 75, and Choice B, 57, try to trick you by using the numbers 7 and 5 from the ratio. Choice D is the product of 7 × 5. *Correct Answer:* Choice C.

Notice how carefully we've been asking which answer can be the possible total. The total can be any multiple of the sum. If a ratio question of this type asks you "which of the following *is* the total," you have to answer, "It cannot be determined." You know only which *can* be true.

Column A	*Column B*
Ratio of CDs to tapes = 2:9	

Total of CDs and tapes	11

You know the total must be a multiple of 11, but it can be an infinite number of terms: 11, 22, 33, 44, 55, and so on. This trap has destroyed many overly confident test-takers over the years. *Correct Answer:* D.

When you're given a ratio and a total and asked to find a specific term, do the following in order:

1. **Add the numbers in the ratio.**

2. **Divide that sum into the total.**

3. **Multiply that quotient by each term in the ratio.**

4. **Add the answers to double-check that they sum up to the total.**

Altogether, that's pretty confusing stuff. Take it one step at a time.

Yelling at the members of his team, which had just lost 21–0, the irate coach pointed his finger at each member of the squad, calling everyone either a wimp or a slacker. If there were 3 wimps for every 4 slackers, and every member of the 28-man squad was either a wimp or a slacker, how many wimps were there?

1. **Add the numbers in the ratio:** 3 + 4 = 7.

2. **Divide that sum into the total:** $^{28}\!/_7$ = 4.

3. **Multiply that quotient by each term in the ratio:** 4 × 3 = 12; 4 × 4 = 16.

4. **Add the answers to double-check that they sum up to the total:** 12 + 16 = 28.

Be sure that you actually do Step 4 because you can catch any careless mistakes you may have made.

Now you have all the info you need to answer a variety of questions: How many wimps were there? 12. How many slackers were there? 16. How many more slackers than wimps were there? 4. How many slackers would have to be kicked off the team for the number of wimps and slackers to be equal? 4. The math-mogul test creators can ask all sorts of questions, but if you have this information, you're ready for anything they throw at you!

It takes longer to talk through these steps than it does to do them. After you understand this technique, it makes a lot of sense. Think of ratios as cliques. If there are 3 girls for every 5 boys, then one clique is made up of 8 kids. If there are 48 kids at a party, there must be 6 cliques (8 divided into 48 = 6). If there are 6 cliques at 3 girls per clique, there are 6 × 3 = 18 girls. If there are 6 cliques at 5 boys each, there are 6 × 5 = 30 boys.

Things Aren't What They Seem: Symbolism

You may encounter two basic types of symbolism problems. Depending on the type of problem, do one of the following (which we explain in greater detail throughout the section):

- Substitute the number given for the variable in the explanation.

- Talk through the explanation to see which constraint fits and then do the indicated operations.

1. Substitute for the variable in the explanation.

You see a problem with a strange symbol. It may be a variable inside a circle, a triangle, a star, or a tic-tac-toe sign. That symbol has no connection to the real world at all. Don't panic, thinking that your teachers forgot to teach you something. Symbols are made up for each problem.

The symbol is included in a short explanation that may look like this:

$$a\#b\#c = \frac{(a+b)^c}{(b+c)}$$

$$x*y*z = \frac{z}{x} + \left(\frac{y}{z}\right)^x$$

$$m@n@o = mn + no - om$$

Again, the symbols don't have any meaning in reality. They mean only what the problem tells you they mean, and that meaning holds true only for this problem.

Below the explanation is the question itself:

3#2#1 =

4 * 6 * 8 =

2@5@10 =

Your job is one of substitution. Plug in a number for the variable in the equation. Which number do you plug in? The one that's in the same position as that variable. For example:

$$a\#b\#c = \frac{(a+b)^c}{(b+c)}$$

$$3\#2\#1 = \frac{(3+2)^1}{(2+1)} = \frac{5}{3}$$

Because *a* was in the first position and 3 was also in the first position, substitute 3 for *a* throughout the equation. Because *b* was in the second position and 2 was also in the second position, substitute 2 for *b* throughout the equation. Because *c* was in the third position and 1 was also in the third position, substitute 1 for *c* throughout the equation.

Do the same for the other problems:

$$x*y*z = \frac{z}{x} + \left(\frac{y}{z}\right)^x$$

$$4*6*8 = \frac{8}{4} + \left(\frac{6}{8}\right)^4 = 2 + \left(\frac{6}{8}\right)^4 = 2 + .316 = 2.316$$

$$m@n@o = mn + no - om$$

$$2@5@10 = (2\times5) + (5\times10) - (10\times2) = 10 + 50 - 20 = 40$$

The problems we just gave you are the simpler of the two types of symbolism problems because all you have to do is substitute the number for the variable and work through the equation.

2. Talk through the explanation and do the operations.

This type of symbolism problem may seem more confusing until you've done a few. Then it becomes so easy that you wonder why you ever struggled with one. Here's an example:

$$\left(x\right) = 3x \text{ if } x \text{ is odd.}$$
$$\left(x\right) = {}^{x}/_{2} \text{ if } x \text{ is even.}$$

Solve for $\left(5\right) + \left(8\right)$.

First, talk through the explanation. You have something in a circle. If that something in the circle is odd, you multiply it by 3. If that something in the circle is even, you divide it by 2.

In the question, a 5 is in a circle. Because 5 is odd, you multiply it by 3 to get $5 \times 3 = 15$. In the second half of the question, an 8 is in a circle. Because 8 is even, you divide it by 2 to get $\frac{8}{2} = 4$. Now add to get $15 + 4 = 19$.

Don't keep going. Do *not* say, "Well, 19 is odd, so I have to multiply it by 3, getting 57." You can bet that 57 is one of the trap multiple-choice answers.

You may still think of this second type of problem as a plug-in or substitution problem because you're plugging the number into the equation for x and working it through. However, you first have to figure out which equation to plug it into. That requires talking things through. You have to understand what you're doing in this type of problem. Try another:

$$\triangle{x} = 3x + {}^{1}/_{3}x \text{ if } x \text{ is prime.}$$
$$\triangle{x} = x^2 + \sqrt{x} \text{ if } x \text{ is composite.}$$

$$\triangle{16} + \triangle{3} =$$

Aha! Now you have to know some math vocabulary. *Prime numbers* are numbers greater than 1; they can't be divided other than by 1 and themselves. Examples are 2, 3, 5, 7, 11, and 13. *Composite numbers* (such as 4, 6, 8, 9, 10, and 12) are numbers that *can* be divided by numbers other than just 1 and themselves. First, decide whether the term in the triangle is a composite number or a prime number.

In $\triangle{16}$, because 16 is a composite number, use the second equation. Square 16: $16 \times 16 = 256$. Take the square root of 16: $\sqrt{16} = 4$. Then add the numbers together: $256 + 4 = 260$.

In $\triangle{3}$, because 3 is a prime number, use the first equation: $3^2 + \frac{1}{3}(3) = 9 + 1 = 10$.

Add the two solutions: $260 + 10 = 270$.

Sometimes the solutions have symbols in them as well. Check out the following:

$$\left(x\right) = {}^{1}/_{2}x \text{ if } x \text{ is composite.}$$
$$\left(x\right) = 2x \text{ if } x \text{ is prime.}$$

Solve for $\left(5\right) \times \left(10\right)$.

(A) $\left(15\right)$

(B) $\left(25\right)$

(C) $\left(50\right)$

(D) $\left(100\right)$

(E) It cannot be determined from the information given.

First, you know to eliminate Choice E. This is the sucker's answer — the one for people who've no idea what that cute little circle means and are clueless as to where to begin. You know by now that you *can* solve a symbolism problem — and pretty quickly, too.

Because 5 is prime, you multiply it by 2: $5 \times 2 = 10$.

Because 10 is composite, you multiply it by ½: $10 \times ½ = 5$.

Multiply: $10 \times 5 = 50$.

Noooo! Don't pick Choice C; that's the trap answer. Choice C doesn't say 50; it says ⓼⓪. That means that you have to solve the answer choice to see what it really is. Think of it as a choice in disguise, with a false beard and glasses to boot. Because 50 is even, you take half of it: $50 \div 2 = 25$. That's not the answer you want. Now go through the rest of the choices:

⑮: Because 15 is composite, multiply it by ½: $15 \times ½ = 7.5$.

㉕: Because 25 is composite, multiply it by ½: $25 \times ½ = 12.5$.

⑩⓪ : Because 100 is composite, multiply it by ½: $100 \times ½ = 50$. You have a winner!

Whenever you see a symbol, get to work. That symbol may be in the question or in the answer choices. Either way, you still need to follow the explanation. But remember the trap we already explained: Be super careful not to keep on going. That is, when you come up with 50 as your answer, don't say, "Well, 50 is composite, so I have to multiply it by ½, getting 25." Stop when you don't see any more symbols. *Correct Answer:* Choice D.

Have you studied functions? Maybe not in school, but if you read the preceding material on symbolism, you just studied functions. A function is very much like symbolism. You may see a problem like this:

$f(x) = (2x)^3$. Solve for $f(2)$.

The f stands for function. Take the same actions you did before: Talk through the problem. Say, "I have something in parentheses. My job is to multiply that something by two and then cube the whole disgusting mess." In other words, just plug in the 2 where you see an x in the explanation.

$f(2) = (2 \times 2)^3 = 4^3 = 64$

Try another one:

$f(x) = x + x^2 + x^3$. Solve for $f(10)$.

Just plug the 10 in for the x: $f(10) = 10 + 10^2 + 10^3 = 10 + 100 + 1{,}000 = 1{,}110$.

Now that you've acquired this skill, you can call yourself fully functional. Yes, we know. We're hilarious.

Abracadabra: Algebra

To correctly answer algebra questions on the GRE, you must be able to

✔ Solve for x in an equation.

✔ Use the FOIL method (first, outer, inner, last — the order in which you multiply the variables in parentheses).

✔ Factor down a quadratic equation and take an algebraic expression from its final form back to its original form of two sets of parentheses.

Alphabet soup: Solving for x

To solve for x, follow these steps:

1. **Isolate the variable, which means getting all the x's on one side and all the non-x's on the other side.**

2. **Add all the x's on one side; add all the non-x's on the other side.**

3. **Divide both sides of the equation by the number in front of the x.**

Now you try it: $3x + 7 = 9x - 5$

1. **Isolate the variable. Move the $3x$ to the right, *changing the sign* to make it $-3x$.**

   Forgetting to change the sign is one of the most common careless mistakes people make. The test-makers realize that and often include trap answer choices to catch this mistake.

2. **Move the -5 to the left, *changing the sign* to make it $+5$. You now have $7 + 5 = 9x - 3x$.**

3. **Add the x's on one side; add the non-x's on the other side.**

   $12 = 6x$

4. **Divide both sides through by what's next to the x.**

   $$\frac{12}{6} = \frac{6x}{6}$$
   $$2 = x$$

If you're weak on algebra, or if know you often make careless mistakes, plug the 2 back into the equation to make sure it works.

$$3(2) + 7 = 9(2) - 5$$
$$6 + 7 = 18 - 5$$
$$13 = 13$$

If you absolutely hate algebra, see whether you can simply plug in the answer choices. If this were a Problem Solving question with multiple-choice answers, you could plug 'n' chug to your heart's content.

$3x + 7 = 9x - 5$. Solve for x.

(A) 5

(B) 3½

(C) 2

(D) 0

(E) −2

Don't ask for trouble. Keep life simple by starting with the simple answers first. That is, try plugging in 5. When it doesn't work, don't bother plugging in 3½. That's too much work. Go right down to 2. If none of the easy answers work, then you can go back to the hard answer of 3½. After all, why fuss with it unless you absolutely have to? *Correct Answer:* Choice C.

Curses! FOILed again

The second trick you need to know to do algebra correctly is the FOIL method. FOIL stands for *First, Outer, Inner, Last* and refers to the order in which you multiply the variables in parentheses. With the equation $(a + b)(a - b) =$, you'd do the following:

1. **Multiply the *First* variables:** $a \times a = a^2$.

2. **Multiply the *Outer* variables:** $a \times (-b) = -ab$.

3. **Multiply the *Inner* variables:** $b \times a = ba$ **(which is the same as *ab*).**

4. **Multiply the *Last* variables:** $b \times (-b) = -b^2$.

5. **Combine like terms:** $-ab + ab = 0ab$.

You can multiply numbers forward or backward, such that $ab = ba$. The positive and negative ab cancel each other out, so you're left with only $a^2 - b^2$.

Try another one: $(3a + b)(a - 2b)$.

1. **Multiply the *First* terms:** $3a \times a = 3a^2$.

2. **Multiply the *Outer* terms:** $3a \times (-2b) = -6ab$.

3. **Multiply the *Inner* terms:** $b \times a = ba$ **(which is the same as *ab*).**

4. **Multiply the *Last* terms:** $b \times (-2b) = -2b^2$.

5. **Combine like terms ($-6ab + ab = -5ab$) to get the final answer:** $3a^2 - 5ab - 2b^2$.

Memorize the following three FOIL problems so that you don't have to bother working them out every time. Knowing these problems by heart will save you time, careless mistakes, and acute misery on the actual exam.

1. $(a + b)^2 = a^2 + 2ab + b^2$

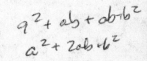

You can prove this equation by using FOIL: $(a + b)(a + b)$.

  a. **Multiply the *First* terms:** $a \times a = a^2$.

  b. **Multiply the *Outer* terms:** $a \times b = ab$.

  c. **Multiply the *Inner* terms:** $b \times a = ba$ **(which is the same as *ab*).**

  d. **Multiply the *Last* terms:** $b \times b = b^2$.

  e. **Combine like terms:** $ab + ab = 2ab$.

Your final solution? $a^2 + 2ab + b^2$.

2. $(a - b)^2 = a^2 - 2ab + b^2$

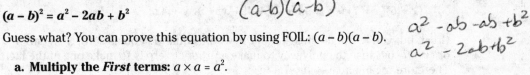

Guess what? You can prove this equation by using FOIL: $(a - b)(a - b)$.

  a. **Multiply the *First* terms:** $a \times a = a^2$.

  b. **Multiply the *Outer* terms:** $a \times (-b) = -ab$.

  c. **Multiply the *Inner* terms:** $-b \times a = -ba$ **(which is the same as *-ab*).**

  d. **Multiply the *Last* terms:** $-b \times (-b) = +b^2$.

  e. **Combine like terms:** $-ab + (-ab) = -2ab$.

Your final solution is $a^2 - 2ab + b^2$.

Be careful to note that the b^2 at the end is *positive,* not negative, because multiplying a negative times a negative produces a positive.

3. $(a - b)(a + b) = a^2 - b^2$

Would you believe you can also prove this equation by using FOIL? $(a - b)(a + b)$.

   a. Multiply the *First* terms: $a \times a = a^2$.

   b. Multiply the *Outer* terms: $a \times b = ab$.

   c. Multiply the *Inner* terms: $-b \times a = -ba$ **(which is the same as $-ab$).**

   d. Multiply the *Last* terms: $-b \times b = -b^2$.

   e. Combine like terms: $ab + (-ab) = 0ab$.

Here's your final solution: $a^2 - b^2$. Note that the middle term drops out because $+ab$ cancels out $-ab$.

Fact or fiction: Factoring

Now that you know how to do algebra forward, are you ready to do it backward? The third trick you need to know is how to factor down a quadratic equation and take an algebraic expression from its final form back to its original form of two sets of parentheses.

Given $x^2 + 13x + 42 = 0$, solve for x. (Our advice? Take this problem one step at a time.)

   1. Draw two sets of parentheses.

      $(\ )(\ ) = 0$

   2. To get x^2, the *First* terms have to be x and x. Fill those in.

      $(x)(x) = 0$

   3. Look now at the *Last* terms.

      You need two numbers that equal $+42$ when multiplied together. You have several possibilities: 42×1, 21×2, or 6×7. You can even have two negative numbers: -42×-1, -21×-2, or -6×-7. Because you aren't sure which one to choose yet, go on to the next step.

   4. Look at the *Inner* terms.

      You have to add two values to get $+13$. Now you know that you need two *positive* values to get $+13$. What's the first one that springs to mind? Probably $6 + 7$. Hey, that's one of the possibilities in the preceding step! Plug it in and try it.

      $(x + 6)(x + 7) = x^2 + 7x + 6x + 42 = x^2 + 13x + 42$

Great, but you're not finished yet. If the whole equation equals zero, then either $(x + 6) = 0$ or $(x + 7)$ because the only way to make a product zero is to make one of the factors zero. Therefore, x can equal -6 or -7.

Again, if you have a multiple-choice problem, you can simply try the answer choices. Never start doing a lot of work until you absolutely have to.

Too Hip to Be Square: Roots and Radicals

To simplify working with square roots (or cube roots or any radicals), think of them as variables. You work the same way with the square root of 7 as you do with x, y, or z.

Adding and subtracting

1. **To add or subtract *like* radicals, add or subtract the number in front of the radical (your old friend, the numerical coefficient).**

$$2\sqrt{7} + 5\sqrt{7} = 7\sqrt{7} \qquad 2x + 5x = 7x$$
$$9\sqrt{13} - 4\sqrt{13} = 5\sqrt{13} \quad 9x - 4x = 5x$$

2. **You *can't* add or subtract unlike radicals (just as you can't add or subtract unlike variables).**

$6\sqrt{5} + 4\sqrt{3} = 6\sqrt{5} + 4\sqrt{3}$ (You can't add the two and get $10\sqrt{8}$.)

$6x + 4y = 6x + 4y$ (You can't add the two and get $10xy$.)

Don't glance at a problem, see that the radicals aren't the same, and immediately assume that you can't add the two terms. You may be able to simplify one radical to make it match the radical in the other term.

$$\sqrt{52} + \sqrt{13} = 2\sqrt{13} + \sqrt{13} = 3\sqrt{13}$$

To simplify: Take out a perfect square from the term. $\sqrt{52} = \sqrt{4} \times \sqrt{13}$. Because $\sqrt{4} = 2$, $\sqrt{52} = 2\sqrt{13}$.

$$\sqrt{20} + \sqrt{45} = \left(\sqrt{4} \times \sqrt{5}\right) + \left(\sqrt{9} \times \sqrt{5}\right) = 2\sqrt{5} + 3\sqrt{5} = 5\sqrt{5}$$

Beware! You must simplify *first*. You can't say that $\sqrt{20} + \sqrt{45} = \sqrt{65} = 8.06$. When you work out the correct answer, $5\sqrt{5}$, you see that it's not 8.06, but 11.18.

Multiplying and dividing

1. **When you multiply or divide radicals, you multiply or divide the numbers and then pop the radical sign back onto the finished product.**

$$\sqrt{5} \times \sqrt{6} = \sqrt{30}$$
$$\sqrt{15} \div \sqrt{5} = \sqrt{3}$$

2. **If you have a number in front of the radical, multiply it as well. Let everyone in on the fun.**

$6\sqrt{3} \times 4\sqrt{2} =$

$6 \times 4 = 24$

$\sqrt{3} \times \sqrt{2} = \sqrt{6}$

$24\sqrt{6}$

Try this example: $37\sqrt{5} \times 3\sqrt{6}$

(A) $40\sqrt{11}$

(B) $40\sqrt{30}$

(C) $111\sqrt{11}$

(D) $111\sqrt{30}$

(E) $1,221$

You know that $37 \times 3 = 111$ and that $\sqrt{5} \times \sqrt{6} = \sqrt{30}$, so the answer is $111\sqrt{30}$. That's just straightforward multiplication. *Correct Answer:* Choice D.

Working inside out

When you see an operation under the radical, do it first and then take the square root.

$$\sqrt{\frac{x^2}{40} + \frac{x^2}{9}}$$

First, solve for $\frac{x^2}{40} + \frac{x^2}{9}$. You get the common denominator of 360 (40×9) and then find the numerators: $9x^2$ and $40x^2$, which make $\frac{49x^2}{360}$. *Now* take the square roots: $49x^2 = 7x$ (because $7x \times 7x = 49x^2$). The answer is $\sqrt{360} = 18.97$. Gotcha, we bet! Did you say that $\sqrt{360} = 6$? Wrong! Although $\sqrt{36} = 6$, $\sqrt{360}$ = approximately 18.97. Beware of assuming too much; you can be led down the path of temptation.

Your final answer is $\frac{7x}{18.97}$. Of course, you can bet that the answer choices will include $\frac{7x}{6}$.

Probably Probability

Probability questions are usually word problems. They may look intimidating, because all those words can make you lose sight of where to begin. Fortunately, two simple rules can help you solve nearly every probability problem tossed your way.

1. **Create a fraction.**

   To find a probability, use this formula:

   $$P = \frac{\text{Number of possible desired outcomes}}{\text{Number of total possible outcomes}}$$

   Make a probability into a fraction. The denominator is the easier of the two parts to begin with. The *denominator* is the total possible number of outcomes. For example, when you're flipping a coin, two possible outcomes exist, giving you a denominator of 2. When you're tossing a die (one of a pair of dice), six possible outcomes exist, giving you a denominator of 6. When you're pulling a card out of a deck of cards, 52 possible outcomes exist (because a deck has 52 cards), giving you a denominator of 52. When 25 marbles are in a jar and you're going to pull out one of them, 25 possibilities exist, giving you a denominator of 25. Very simply, the denominator is the whole shebang — everything that's possible.

The *numerator* is the total possible number of the things you want. If you want to get a head when you toss a coin, there's exactly one head, giving you a numerator of 1. The chances of tossing a head, therefore, are ½ — one possible head, two possible outcomes altogether. If you want to get a 5 when you toss a die, there's exactly one 5 on the die, giving you a numerator of 1. Notice that your numerator isn't 5. The number you want happens to be a 5, but there's only *one* 5 on the die. The probability of tossing a 5 is ⅙. One 5 and six possible outcomes exist altogether.

If you want to draw a jack in a deck of cards, there are four jacks: hearts, diamonds, clubs, and spades. Therefore, the numerator is 4. The probability of drawing a jack out of a deck of cards is ⁴⁄₅₂ (which reduces to ¹⁄₁₃). If you want to draw a jack of hearts, the probability is ¹⁄₅₂, because there's only one jack of hearts.

A jar of marbles has 8 yellow marbles, 6 black marbles, and 12 white marbles. What is the probability of drawing out a black marble?

Use the formula. Begin with the denominator, which is all the possible outcomes: 8 + 6 + 12 = 26. The numerator is how many there are of what you want: 6 black marbles. The probability is ⁶⁄₂₆, which can be reduced or (as is more customary) changed to a percentage. What's the probability of drawing out a yellow marble? ⁸⁄₂₆. A white marble? ¹²⁄₂₆. *Correct Answer:* ⁶⁄₂₆, or ³⁄₁₃, or 23%.

A drawer has 5 pairs of white socks, 8 pairs of black socks, and 12 pairs of brown socks. In a hurry to get to school, Austin pulls out a pair at a time and tosses them on the floor if they are not the color he wants. Looking for a brown pair, Austin pulls out and discards a white pair, a black pair, a black pair, and a white pair. What is the probability that on his next reach into the drawer he will pull out a brown pair of socks?

This problem is slightly more complicated than the preceding one, although it uses the same formula. You began with 25 pairs of socks. However, Austin, that slob, has thrown 4 pairs onto the floor. That means that there are only 21 pairs left. The probability of his pulling out a brown pair is ¹²⁄₂₁, or ⁴⁄₇, or about 57%. *Correct Answer:* 57%.

A cookie jar contains chocolate, vanilla, and strawberry wafer cookies. There are 30 of each type. Bess reaches in, pulls out a chocolate, and eats it. Then, in quick succession, she pulls out and eats a vanilla, chocolate, strawberry, strawberry, chocolate, and vanilla. Assuming that she doesn't get sick or get caught, what is the probability that the next cookie she pulls out will be a chocolate one?

Originally, there were 90 cookies. Bess has scarfed down 7 of them, leaving 83. Careful! If you're about to put ³⁰⁄₈₃, you're headed for a trap. There are no longer 30 chocolate cookies; there are only 27 because Bess has eaten 3. The probability is now ²⁷⁄₈₃, or about 33%. *Correct Answer:* 33%.

Probability must always be between zero and 1. You can't have a negative probability, and you can't have a probability greater than 1, or 100%.

2. Multiply consecutive probabilities.

What's the probability that you'll get two heads when you toss a coin twice? Find each probability separately and then multiply the two. The chance of tossing a coin the first time and getting a head is ½. The chance of tossing a coin the second time and getting a head is ½. Multiply those consecutive probabilities: ½ × ½ = ¼. The chances of getting two heads are one out of four.

What's the probability of tossing a die twice and getting a 5 on the first toss and a 6 on the second toss? Treat each toss separately. The probability of getting a 5 is ⅙. The probability of getting a 6 is ⅙. Multiply consecutive probabilities: ⅙ × ⅙ = 1/36.

Here's a good trick question:

<table>
<tr><td align="center">**Column A**</td><td align="center">**Column B**</td></tr>
</table>

A fair die is tossed twice.

Chances of getting a 5 on the first toss and a 2 on the second toss	Chances of getting a 6 on both tosses

If you chose A, you fell for the trap. You may think that rolling the same number twice is harder, but the probability is the same as rolling two specific, different numbers. Treat each roll separately. The probability of rolling a 5 is ⅙. The probability of rolling a 2 is ⅙. Multiply consecutive probabilities: ⅙ × ⅙ = 1/36. For Column B, treat each toss separately. The probability of rolling a 6 is ⅙. The probability of rolling a second 6 is ⅙. Multiply consecutive probabilities: ⅙ × ⅙ = 1/36. *Correct Answer:* C.

If you've had a course in statistics, you may have learned about independent events, mutually exclusive events, and interdependent events. Forget about them; they're not on the GRE. The material we just covered is about as complicated as probability gets.

Chapter 15

Miscellaneous Math You Probably Already Know

· ·

In This Chapter

▶ Unlocking the mysteries of averages, percentages, absolute values, decimals, and fractions

▶ Setting you straight on the order of operations

▶ Soothing your statistics-related stress

▶ Painting an informational picture with graphs

· ·

You probably already know the material in this chapter, but a quick review can't hurt you. (The humor — now that's another story!)

DIRTy Math: Distance, Rate, and Time

When you have a distance, rate, and time problem, always use the DIRT formula: Distance Is Rate × Time, which is often shown as $D = RT$. Make a chart with the formula across the top and fill in the spaces on the chart.

Jennifer drives 40 miles an hour for two and a half hours. Her friend Ashley goes the same distance but drives at one and a half times Jennifer's speed. How many *minutes* longer does Jennifer drive than Ashley?

Don't start making big, hairy formulas with x's and y's. Jennifer has no desire to be known as Madame x; Ashley refuses to be y. Make the DIRT chart instead.

Distance	=	Rate	×	Time

When you fill in the 40 mph and 2½ hours for Jennifer, you can calculate that she went 100 miles. Think of it this simple way: If she goes 40 mph for one hour, that's 40 miles. For a second hour, she goes another 40 miles. In a half-hour, she goes ½ of 40, or 20 miles. (See? You don't have to write down 40 × 2½ and do all that pencil pushing; use your brain, not your yellow #2.) Add them together: 40 + 40 + 20 = 100. Jennifer has gone 100 miles.

Distance	=	Rate	×	Time
100 (Jennifer)		40 mph		2½ hours

Because Ashley drives the same distance, fill in 100 under distance for her. She goes one and a half times as fast. Uh-uh, put down that pencil. Use your brain: 1 × 40 is 40; ½ × 40 is 20. Add 40 + 20 = 60. Ashley drives 60 mph. Now this problem gets really easy. If Ashley drives at 60 mph, she drives 1 mile a minute. (Think about it: 60 minutes in an hour, 60 miles in an hour.)

Therefore, to go 100 miles takes her 100 minutes. Because the question asks for your final answer in minutes, don't bother converting it to hours; leave it the way it is.

Distance	=	Rate	×	Time
100 (Ashley)		60 mph		100 minutes

Here's the last step. Jennifer drives 2½ hours. How many minutes is that? Solve this problem the easy way — in your brain. One hour is 60 minutes. A second hour is another 60 minutes. A half-hour is 30 minutes. Add them together: 60 + 60 + 30 = 150 minutes. If Jennifer drives for 150 minutes and Ashley drives for 100 minutes, Jennifer drives 50 minutes more than Ashley. However, Ashley gets a speeding ticket, has her driving privileges taken away by an irate father, and doesn't get to go to this weekend's party. Jennifer goes and gets her pick of the hunks, ending up with Tyrone's ring and frat pin. The moral of the story: Slow . . . but steady!

Distance	=	Rate	×	Time
100 (Jennifer)		40 mph		150 minutes
100 (Ashley)		60 mph		100 minutes

Be careful to note whether the people are traveling in the *same* direction or *opposite* directions. Suppose you're asked how far apart drivers are at the end of their trips. If Jordan travels 40 mph east for 2 hours and Connor travels 60 mph west for 3 hours, they're going in opposite directions. If they start from the same point at the same time, Jordan has gone 80 miles one way, and Connor has gone 180 miles the opposite way. They're actually 260 miles apart. The trap answer is 100, because careless people (not *you!*) simply subtract 80 from 180.

It All Averages Out: Averages

When it comes to averages, you can always do them the way Ms. Jones taught you in the third grade: Add all the terms and then divide by the number of terms.

$$5 + 11 + 17 + 23 + 29 = 85$$
$$\tfrac{85}{5} = 17$$

Or you can save wear and tear on your brain cells and know the following rule:

1. The average of evenly spaced terms is the middle term.

First, check that the terms are evenly spaced. If they are, an equal number of units is between each term. In this case, the terms are six units apart. Second, circle the middle term, which is 17. Third, go home, make popcorn, and watch the late-night movie with all the time you've saved.

Try another one. Find the average of these numbers:

32, 41, 50, 59, 68, 77, 86, 95, 104

Don't reach for your pencil. Instead, look and see that the terms are all nine units apart. Because they're evenly spaced, the middle term is the average: 68.

This is an easy trick to love, but don't march down the aisle with it yet. This tip works only for *evenly spaced* terms. If you have just any old batch of numbers, such as 4, 21, 97, 98, and 199, you can't look at the middle term for the average. You have to find the average of those numbers the old-fashioned way.

Find the average of these numbers:

> 3, 10, 17, 24, 31, 38, 45, 52

First, double-check that they're evenly spaced. Here, the numbers are spaced by sevens. Next, look for the middle number . . . but wait! It doesn't exist. You can, of course, identify the two central terms, 24 and 31, and find the middle between them. That works, but what a pain. Now suppose that you have 38 numbers. Making a mistake as to which terms are the central ones is easy with this many numbers. If you're off just a little bit, you miss the question. Instead, use this next rule:

2. **The average of evenly spaced terms is $\frac{(\text{first} + \text{last})}{2}$.**

Just add the first and the last terms, which you can see at a glance, and divide that sum by 2. Here, $3 + 52 = 55$ and $\frac{55}{2} = 27.5$.

Note: Double-check your answer by using your common sense. Perhaps you made a silly mistake and got 45 for your answer. A quick glance at the numbers tells you that 45 isn't in the middle and therefore can't be the average.

This tip works for *all* evenly spaced terms. It doesn't matter whether there's a middle number, as in the first example, or no middle number, as in the second example. Go back to the first example:

> 32, 41, 50, 59, 68, 77, 86, 95, 104

Instead of finding the middle term, add the first and last terms and divide by 2, like this: $32 + 104 = 136$; $\frac{136}{2} = 68$. Either way works.

Solving missing term average problems

You're likely to find a missing term average problem like this one on the GRE:

A student takes seven exams. Her scores on the first six are 91, 89, 85, 92, 90, and 88. If her average on all *seven* exams is 90, what did she get on the seventh exam?

This is called a *missing term average problem* because you're given an average and asked to find a missing term. Duh.

1. **You can solve this type of problem the basic algebraic way.**

$$\text{Average} = \frac{\text{Sum}}{\text{Number of terms}}$$

$$90 = \frac{\text{Sum}}{7}$$

Because you don't know the seventh term, call it x. Add the first six terms (and get 535) and x.

$$90 = \frac{(535 + x)}{7} \text{ Cross-multiply: } 90 \times 7 = 535 + x$$

$630 = 535 + x$ Subtract 535 from both sides.

$95 = x$

The seventh exam score was 95.

2. You can also solve missing term average problems the common-sense way.

Would you believe you've probably solved missing term average problems this way all your life without realizing what a genius you are? Suppose your dad tells you that if you average a 90 for the semester in advanced physics, he'll let you take that summer trip through Europe with your buddies that the two of you have been arguing about for months. (He figures he's safe because there's no way you're going to get such a high grade in that incredibly difficult class.) You take him at his word and begin working hard.

On the first exam, you get a 91, and you're +1 point. That is, you're one point above the ultimate score you want, a 90. On the second exam, you get an 89, which is –1. On that test, you're one point below the ultimate score you want, a 90. On the third exam, you get an 85, which is –5 — five points below your ultimate score of 90.

Are you getting the hang of this? Here's how it looks.

91 = +1

89 = –1

85 = –5

92 = +2

90 = 0

88 = –2

The +1 and –1 cancel each other out, and the +2 and –2 cancel each other out. You're left with –5, meaning you're five points in the hole. You have to make up those five points on the last exam, meaning you must get five points *above* what you want for your ultimate score. Because you want a 90, you need a 95 on the last test.

Try solving for another missing term average problem with the no-brainer method. A student takes seven exams. She gets an 88 average on all of them. Her first six scores are 89, 98, 90, 82, 88, and 87. What does she get on the seventh exam?

Average = 88

89 = +1

98 = +10

90 = +2

82 = –6

88 = 0

87 = –1

The +1 and –1 cancel. Then you have (10 + 2) = +12 and –6, for a total of +6. So this student is six points *above* what she needs for the ultimate outcome. She can afford to lose six points on the final exam, or to be six points *below* the average. That gives her an 82.

You may be given only five out of seven scores and asked for *the average of the missing two* terms. Do the same thing and then divide by 2.

Algebraic way:

Average of seven exams: 85

Scores of the first five exams: 86, 79, 82, 85, 84

Find: The average score of each of the remaining exams

$$85 = \frac{\left(86 + 79 + 82 + 85 + 84\right) + x + x}{7}$$

Cross-multiply: 595 = 416 + 2*x*

595 – 416 = 2*x*

179 = 2*x*

$\frac{179}{2} = \frac{2x}{2}$

89.5 = *x*

Common-sense way:

Average = 85

86 = +1

79 = –6

82 = –3

85 = 0

84 = –1

The +1 and –1 cancel each other out. You're left with –9 for *two* exams, or –4.5 per exam. If you're *down* four and a half points, you must *gain* those four and a half points on each of the two exams:

85 + 4.5 = 89.5

The shortcut, common-sense way is quick and easy, but don't forget to make the change at the end. That is, if you decide that you're *minus eight* points going into the final exam, you need to be *plus eight* points on that last exam to come out even. If you subtract eight points from the average rather than add them, you'll probably come up with one of the trap answers.

Working with weighted averages

In a *weighted average,* some scores count more than others.

Number of Students	Score
12	80
13	75
10	70

If you're asked to find the average score for the students in this class, you know that you can't simply add 80, 75, and 70 and divide by three because the scores weren't evenly distributed among the students. Because 12 students got an 80, multiply $12 \times 80 = 960$. Do the same with the other scores:

$13 \times 75 = 975$

$10 \times 70 = 700$

$960 + 975 + 700 = 2,635$

Divide *not by three* but by the total number of students: 35 (12 + 13 + 10)

$\frac{2635}{35} = 75.29$

You can often answer a Quantitative Comparison question on weighted averages without doing all the work, as demonstrated in the following example. (See Chapter 16 for more info about QC questions and how to answer them.)

The answer choices are

A if the quantity in Column A is greater.

B if the quantity in Column B is greater.

C if the two quantities are equal.

D if the relationship cannot be determined from the information given.

Column A		_Column B_
Clothing	_Quantity_	_Cost per Item_
Black T-shirts	5	$20
Denim shirts	8	$25
Blue jeans	20	$30

Average cost per item of clothing	$25

You can work this whole problem out by finding the cost of all the T-shirts, denim shirts, and jeans and then dividing that cost by the number of items of clothing. When you do all that work, you get 27.27 (and a headache and a sore pencil-pushing finger). Or you can use your brain and common sense: 13 items are $25 or less, and 20 items are $30. Therefore, more items are at or above $25 than below $25. So the average must be more than $25. **Remember:** Because this is a QC problem, you don't need to solve it through for the final, precise solution. You need only enough info to compare the quantities in the two columns. *Correct Answer:* A.

Percentage Panic

The mere mention of the word *percent* may strike terror in your heart. But in reality, you don't need to panic over percentages because you can easily get around them.

Ignorance is bliss: Converting percentages to decimals or fractions

Who would've imagined that ignoring percentage marks can help you figure out percentages? Here are a couple ways this trick works:

1. **Ignore the percentage's very existence. You can express a percentage as a decimal, which is a lot less intimidating, by putting a decimal point two places to the left of the percentage and dropping the % sign.**

$$35\% = .35 \qquad 83\% = .83 \qquad 50\% = .50 \qquad 33.3\% = .333 \qquad 66.6\% = .666$$

If you have a choice of working with decimals or percentages, always choose decimals.

2. **Another way to ignore a percentage is to convert it to a fraction. The word percent means *per cent*, or per hundred. Every percentage is that number over 100.**

$$50\% = {}^{50}\!/_{100} \qquad 33\% = {}^{33}\!/_{100} \qquad 75\% = {}^{75}\!/_{100}$$

If you can't ignore the percentage, remember that a percent is

$$\frac{\text{Part}}{\text{Whole}} \times 100$$

What percent *is* 45 *of* 90? Put the part, 45, over the whole, 90, as shown:

$$\frac{45}{90} = \frac{1}{2} \times 100 = \frac{100}{2} = 50\%$$

You can also solve by using the equation $\frac{is}{of} = \frac{\%}{100}$. Here's an example: 42 *is* what percent *of* 126? Put the *is*, 42, over the *of*, 126. The percentage is what you're looking for, so that becomes your variable *x*, which you place over 100.

$$\frac{42}{126} = \frac{x}{100}$$

Cross-multiply to get 4,200 = 126x, so x = .333, or 33⅓%.

Want one that's a little harder? What is 40% of 80? You may be tempted to put the *is*, 40, over the *of*, 80, and get $\frac{40}{80} = \frac{x}{100}$. However, when the problem is worded this way, you don't know the *is*. **Remember:** The question says "*What is* . . ." — that's your clue. Your equation must be $\frac{x}{80} = \frac{40}{100}$. Cross-multiply: 3,200 = 100x, so x = 32.

But hold on. There's an easier way to do it: *Of* means *times*, or multiply. Because 40% = .40, multiply .40 × 80 = 32.

Life has its ups and downs: Determining percent increase/decrease

You may see a problem asking you what percent increase or decrease occurred in the number of games a team won or the amount of commission a person earned. To find a percent increase or decrease, use this formula:

$$\text{Percent increase or decrease} = \frac{\text{Number increase or decrease}}{\text{Original whole}}$$

In basic English, to find the percent by which something has increased or decreased, you take two simple steps:

1. **Find the *number* (amount) by which the thing has increased or decreased.**

   For example, if a team won 25 games last year and 30 games this year, the number increase was 5. If a salesperson earned $10,000 last year and $8,000 this year, the number decrease was 2,000. Make that increase or decrease the numerator of your fraction.

2. **Find the original whole.**

   This figure is what you started out with before you increased or decreased. If a team won 25 games last year and 30 games this year, the original number was 25. If the salesperson earned $10,000 last year and $8,000 this year, the original number was 10,000. Make that original number your denominator.

You now have a fraction. Convert it to a decimal and multiply by 100 to make it a percentage.

In 2006, Coach Jarchow won 30 prizes at the county fair by tossing a basketball into a bushel basket. In 2007, he won 35 prizes. What was his percent increase?

(A) 100

(B) 30

(C) 16⅔

(D) 14.28

(E) .1$\overline{66}$

The number by which Coach Jarchow's prizes increased is 5 (from 30 to 35). That's the numerator. The original whole, or what he began with, is 30. That's the denominator. *Correct Answer:* Choice C.

$$\tfrac{5}{30} = \tfrac{1}{6} = 16\tfrac{2}{3}\%$$

If you picked Choice E, we fooled you. The question asks what *percent* increase there was. If you said Choice E, you thought there was a .1$\overline{66}$ percent increase. Not so. The .1$\overline{66}$ increase *as a percentage* is 16⅔%. If you selected Choice D, you fell for another trap. You put the 5 prize increase over the 35 rather than over the 30.

Two years ago, Haylie scored 22 goals while playing soccer. This year, she scored 16 goals. What was her approximate percent decrease?

(A) 72

(B) 37.5

(C) 27

(D) 16

(E) .$\overline{27}$

Find the number of the decrease: 22 – 16 = 6. Your answer (6) is the numerator. Find the original whole from which Haylie is decreasing: 22. That's the denominator: $\tfrac{6}{22} \approx .\overline{27}$, or approximately 27 percent. *Correct Answer:* Choice C.

If you picked Choice A, you put 16 over 22 instead of putting the decrease over the original whole. If you selected Choice E, you forgot the difference between .$\overline{27}$ and 27 percent. If you went for Choice B, you put the decrease of 6 over the new amount, 16, rather than over the original whole. Note how easy these traps are to fall for. Our suggestion: Write down the actual formula and then plug in the numbers. Writing down the formula may be boring, but doing so takes only a few seconds and may save you points.

Here's a tricky question that many people do in their heads (instead of writing down the formula and plugging in the numbers) and blow big time:

Carissa has three quarters. Her father gives her three more. Carissa's wealth has increased by what percent?

(A) 50

(B) 100

(C) 200

(D) 300

(E) 500

Did you fall for the trap answer, Choice C? Carissa's wealth has doubled, to be sure, but the percent increase is only 100. You can prove that with the formula. The number increase is .75 (she has three more quarters, or 75 cents), and her original whole was .75. So if you follow the formula, you get $^{75}\!/_{75}$ = 1 = 100%. *Correct Answer:* Choice B.

When you double something, you increase it by 100 percent, because you must subtract the original that you began with. When you triple something, you increase it by 200 percent, because you must subtract the original you began with. For example, if you had three dollars and you now have nine dollars, you've tripled your money but increased it by only 200 percent. Do the formula: Your number increase is 6 dollars, and your original whole was 3 dollars. So $^{6}\!/_{3}$ = 2 = 200 percent. Take a wild guess at what percent you increase when you quadruple your money? That's right, 300 percent. Just subtract the original 100 percent.

Ready, Set, Go: Number Sets

You can't escape vocabulary. Even on the math portion of the GRE, you need to know certain terms. After all, how can you solve a problem that asks you to "state your answer in integral values only" if you don't know what integral values are? Here are the number sets with which you'll be working:

- **Counting numbers:** 1, 2, 3 . . . Note that 0 is *not* a counting number.

- **Whole numbers:** 0, 1, 2, 3 . . . Note that 0 *is* a whole number.

- **Integers:** . . . –3, –2, –1, 0, 1, 2, 3 . . . When a question asks for *integral values,* it wants the answer in integers only. For example, you can't give an answer like 4.3 because that's not an integer. You need to round down to 4.

- **Rational numbers:** Rational numbers can be expressed as $^{a}\!/_{b}$, where *a* and *b* are integers.

  Examples: 1 (because 1 = $^{1}\!/_{1}$ and 1 is an integer), ½ (because 1 and 2 are integers), $^{9}\!/_{2}$ (because 9 and 2 are integers), and $^{-4}\!/_{2}$ (because –4 and 2 are integers).

Notice that every number set so far has included the previous number sets. Whole numbers include counting numbers; integers include counting numbers and whole numbers; and rationals include counting numbers, whole numbers, and integers.

✔ **Irrational numbers:** The highly technical definition here is *anything not rational*. That is, an irrational number can't be written as ⁰⁄ₒ, where *a* and *b* are integers. Numbers whose decimals don't terminate and don't repeat can't be written as a fraction and therefore are irrational.

Example: π can't be written *exactly* as 3.14, because it's nonterminating and nonrepeating.

Irrational numbers *don't* include the previous number sets. That is, irrational numbers don't include counting numbers, whole numbers, integers, or rational numbers.

✔ **Real numbers:** Briefly put, real numbers include all the preceding number sets — counting numbers, whole numbers, integers, rationals, and irrationals.

For all practical purposes, real numbers are everything you think of as numbers. When a question tells you to "express your answer in real numbers," don't sweat it. That's almost no constraint at all, because nearly everything you see is a real number.

Your imaginary friend may no longer exist, but *imaginary numbers* certainly do. However, they *aren't* on the GRE. (Did you stop reading right there, figuring that you don't even want to hear about them if they're not going to be tested? We don't blame you.) Imaginary numbers are expressed with a lowercase *i* and are studied in upper-division math classes. We don't go into them here because, once again, *they aren't tested on the GRE*. All numbers on the GRE are real numbers.

Prime Time: Prime and Composite Numbers

Prime numbers are positive integers that have exactly two positive integer factors; they can't be divided by numbers other than 1 and themselves. Examples include 2, 3, 5, 7, and 11.

Following are a few lovely tricks to prime numbers:

✔ Zero is *not* a prime number (by definition). Why? Because it's divisible by more than two factors. Zero can be divided by 1, 2, 3, and so on for infinity. Although division by 0 is undefined (and isn't tested on the GRE), you *can* divide it by other numbers. The answer, of course, is always 0: $0 \div 1 = 0$; $0 \div 2 = 0$; $0 \div 412 = 0$.

✔ One is *not* a prime number (by definition). There are no two factors of 1. It can't be divided only by 1 *and* itself. Confused? Don't worry about it. Just memorize the fact that 1 isn't a prime number.

✔ Two is the *only* even prime. People tend to think that all prime numbers are odd. Well, almost. Two is prime because it has only two factors; it can be divided only by 1 and itself.

✔ Not all odd numbers are prime. Think of 9 or 15; those numbers are odd but not prime. They have more than two factors and can be divided by more than just 1 and themselves. For example, $9 = (1 \times 9)$ *and* (3×3); $15 = (1 \times 15)$ *and* (3×5).

Composite numbers have more than two factors and can be divided by more than just 1 and themselves. Examples: 4, 6, 8, 9, 12, 14, and 15. *Note:* Composite numbers (called that because they are *composed* of more than two factors) can be even or odd.

Don't confuse *prime* and *composite* and *even* and *odd* with *positive* and *negative*. That's an easy mistake to make in the confusion of the exam. If a problem that you know should be easy is flustering you, stop and ask yourself whether you're making this common mistake.

We said that 0 and 1 aren't prime. They're also not composite. So what are they? Neither. You express this fact as, "Zero and 1 are neither prime nor composite." Perhaps you're also wondering whether 0 is positive or negative. Nope, 0 is neither positive nor negative. Why should you know this info? Here's an example of when knowing it can win you ten points (the approximate value of one correct math question):

The answer choices are

A if the quantity in Column A is greater.

B if the quantity in Column B is greater.

C if the two quantities are equal.

D if the relationship cannot be determined from the information given.

Column A	_Column B_
The number of prime numbers from 0 to 10 inclusive	The number of prime numbers from 11 to 20 inclusive

The prime numbers from 0 to 10 inclusive are 2, 3, 5, and 7. Note that 0 and 1 aren't prime. If you count either or both as prime, you miss an otherwise very easy question. In Column B, the prime numbers from 11 to 20 inclusive are 11, 13, 17, and 19. Both columns have four prime numbers. *Correct Answer:* C.

I'm All Mixed Up: Mixture Problems

A *mixture problem* is a word problem that looks much more confusing than it really is. Plan to encounter two types of mixture problems: those in which the items remain separate (when you mix peanuts and raisins, you still have peanuts and raisins, not pearains or raispeans) and those in which the two elements blend (these elements are usually chemicals, like water and alcohol). Check out the separate mixture first.

Marshall wants to mix 40 pounds of beads selling for 30 cents a pound with a quantity of sequins selling for 80 cents a pound. He wants to pay 40 cents per pound for the final mix. How many pounds of sequins should he use?

The hardest part for most test-takers is knowing where to begin. Make a chart and start with the bare essentials:

	Pounds	_Price_	_Total_
Beads			
Sequins			
Mixture			

Then fill in what the test gives you. Beads are 40 pounds at 30 cents a pound. Sequins are 80 cents per pound. You want the mixture to cost 40 cents a pound.

	Pounds	*Price*	*Total*
Beads	40	$.30	
Sequins		$.80	
Mixture		$.40	

Now comes the hard part. You don't know how many pounds of sequins you have, so that's your variable, *x*. If you start with 40 pounds of beads and add this new unknown amount of sequins, *x*, you now have (40 + *x*) pounds for the mixture. Fill in your table.

	Pounds	*Price*	*Total*
Beads	40	$.30	
Sequins	*x*	$.80	
Mixture	40 + *x*	$.40	

Then multiply across the rows to get the totals.

	Pounds	*Price*	*Total*
Beads	40	$.30	$12.00
Sequins	*x*	$.80	.80*x*
Mixture	40 + *x*	$.40	.40(40 + *x*)

Now the equation comes from adding the beads and the sequins together to get the mix (and you can even ignore the decimal points).

$$1200 + 80x = 1600 + 40x$$
$$80x - 40x = 1600 - 1200$$
$$40x = 400$$
$$x = 10$$

Careful! Keep in mind what *x* stands for. It represents the number of pounds of sequins, which is what the question asks for.

Go back and double-check by plugging this value into the equation. You already know that Marshall spent $12 on beads. If he buys 10 pounds of sequins for 80 cents, he spends $8, for a total of $20. He spends that $20 on 50 pounds: 2000 ÷ 50 = 40. How about that? It works!

Greed Is Great: Interest Problems

Interest problems are pretty problems: PRTI, to be exact. *P* = Principal, the amount of money you begin with, or the amount you invest. *R* = Rate, the interest rate you're earning on the money, expressed as a decimal. *T* = Time, the amount of time, always in years, that you leave the money in the interest-bearing account. I = Interest, the amount of interest you earn on the investment. An interest problem usually asks you how much interest someone earned on his or her investment.

The formula is *PRT = I*. Principal × Rate × Time = Interest.

Janet invested $1,000 at 5 percent annual interest for one year. How much interest did she earn?

This is the simplest type of problem. Plug the numbers into the formula.

$PRT = I$

$1,000 \times .05 \times 1 = 50$. She earned $50 interest.

The answer choices may try to trap you with variations on a decimal place, making the answers 5, 50, 500, and so on. You know that 5% = ⁵⁄₁₀₀ = .05; be careful how you multiply.

These problems aren't intentionally vicious (unlike 99 percent of the GRE, right?). You won't see something that gets crazy on interest rates, like "5 percent annual interest compounded quarterly for 3 months and 6 percent quarterly interest compounded daily," blah, blah, blah.

(Useless but fascinating trivia: In Bulgarian, the word for *thank you* is pronounced *blah-go-dah-ree-uh*. But a shortened form, like *thanks,* is simply *blah.* If your mother takes you to task for being a smart aleck and going "blah, blah, blah" when she talks, you can innocently claim that you're practicing your Bulgarian and are just thanking her for her wisdom.)

All Work and No Play: Work Problems

The formula most commonly used in a work problem is

$$\text{Work} = \frac{\text{Time put in}}{\text{Capacity}\,(\text{time to do the whole job})}$$

Find each person's contribution. The denominator is the easy part — it represents how many hours (minutes, days, weeks, and so on) it would take the person to do the whole job, working alone. The numerator is how long the person has already worked. For example, if Sarah can paint a house in six days and has been working for one day, she has done ⅙ of the work. If Evelyn can paint a house in eight days and has been working for five, she has done ⅝ of the project.

So far, so good. The difficulty comes when more than one person works at the task. You know that Sarah can paint a house by herself in six days and that Evelyn can paint a house by herself in eight days. Working together, how long will it take them to paint one house?

Find Sarah's work: $\frac{x}{6}$. Find Evelyn's work: $\frac{x}{8}$. Together, the two fractions must add up to 1 (because there's one house to paint), the entire job.

$$\frac{x}{6} + \frac{x}{8} = 1$$

Multiply by the common denominator, 48, to eliminate the fractions.

$$\frac{48x}{6} + \frac{48x}{8} = 48$$

$$8x + 6x = 48$$

$$14x = 48$$

$$x = \text{approximately } 3.43$$

It would take the two women working together about 3.43 days to paint the house.

Double-check by using your common sense. If you get an answer of 10, for example, you know you made a mistake somewhere because the two women working together should be able to do the job *more quickly* than either one working alone.

Reading between the Lines: Absolute Value

The absolute value is the magnitude of a number. So much for the official definition! The *For Dummies* definition (that is, the easy way to think about it) of *absolute value* is the positive form of a number. Absolute value is indicated by two vertical parallel lines.

Any number within those lines reads as "The absolute value of that number." For example, $|3| = 3$ reads as "The absolute value of three equals three." That seems straightforward enough, but what if the number inside the straight lines is negative? Its absolute value is still positive: $|-3| = 3$. Here's a tricky problem you're likely to see on the GRE:

$$-|-3| = -3$$

The answer may seem contrary to common sense. Isn't a negative times a negative a positive? True, but you have to work from the inside out. The absolute value of –3 is 3. Then you multiple 3 by the negative to get –3. *Correct Answer:* –3. Here's another example that's even a little harder:

$$-|-|-5|| =$$

Here's the official way to work the problem. (**Hint:** The word *official* is a clue that in a minute we're going to give you an unofficial, much easier way to solve this problem.) Work from the inside out. Say to yourself as you go along, "The absolute value of – 5 is 5. Then the negative of that is –5. But the absolute value of –5 is 5. And finally, the negative of that is –5." *Correct Answer:* –5.

Do you see the super-shortcut for the above example? You actually don't have to work the problem out at all! Anything and everything inside the absolute value signs is going to be positive. Then the one negative sign outside changes the whole problem to negative. In other words, you don't need to go through the intermediate steps. With an absolute value problem, look to see whether a negative sign is outside the first absolute value symbol. If it is, the number's negative. If it's not, the number's positive. Simple as that!

Smooth Operator: Order of Operations

When you have several operations (addition, subtraction, multiplication, division, squaring, and so on) in one problem, you must perform them in a definite order:

1. **Work with the parentheses.** Do what's inside the parentheses first.

2. **Work with the power.** Do the squaring or the cubing, whatever the exponent is.

3. **Multiply or divide.** Solve from left to right. If multiplication is to the left of division, multiply first. If division is to the left of multiplication, divide first.

4. **Add or subtract.** Solve from left to right in this case as well. If addition is to the left of subtraction, add first. If subtraction is to the left of addition, subtract first.

An easy *mnemonic* (memory) device for remembering the order of operations is *Please Excuse My Dear Aunt Sally* (PEMDAS): Parentheses, Exponents, Multiplication, Division, Addition, Subtraction.

$$10(3-5)^2 + (^{30}\!/_5)^0 =$$

First, do what's inside the parentheses: $3-5 = -2$ and $^{30}\!/_5 = 6$. Next, work with the power: $-2^2 = 4$ and $6^0 = 1$. (Did you remember that any number to the zero power equals 1?) Next, multiply: $10 \times 4 = 40$. Finally, add: $40 + 1 = 41$. *Correct Answer:* 41. Try another.

$$3 + (9-6)^2 - 5(^8\!/_2)^{-2} =$$

First, do what's inside the parentheses: $9 - 6 = 3$ and $\dfrac{8}{2} = 4$. Second, work with the powers: $3^2 = 9$ and $4^{-2} = \dfrac{1}{(4^2)} = \dfrac{1}{16}$. Multiply: $5 \times \dfrac{1}{16} = \dfrac{5}{16}$. Finally, add and subtract from left to right.

$3 + 9 = 12$. Then $12 - \dfrac{5}{16} = 11\dfrac{11}{16}$. *Correct Answer:* $11^{11}\!/_{16}$.

Measuring Up: Units of Measurement

Occasionally, you may be expected to know a unit of measurement that the test-makers deem obvious but that you've forgotten. Take a few minutes to review this brief list.

If you're an international student, you definitely need to memorize this list because you may not have grown up using some of the same units of measurement as those used in the United States (and on the GRE).

1. **Quantities**

   16 ounces = 1 pound

   2,000 pounds = 1 ton

   2 cups = 1 pint

   2 pints = 1 quart

   4 quarts = 1 gallon

You can calculate that a gallon has 16 cups, or 8 pints. To help you remember, think of borrowing a cup of sugar. Sugar is sweet, and you have a Sweet 16 birthday party. Hence, 16 sweet cups of sugar make up a gallon. It may be silly, but the best memory aids usually are.

2. Length

12 inches = 1 foot

3 feet (36 inches) = 1 yard

5,280 feet (1,760 yards) = 1 mile

Okay, so if 12 inches are in a foot, then how many square inches are there in a square foot? If you say 12, you've fallen for the trap. Why? Because $12 \times 12 = 144$ — the actual number of square inches in a square foot.

Here's how you may fall for that trap in an otherwise easy problem:

The answer choices are

A if the quantity in Column A is greater.

B if the quantity in Column B is greater.

C if the two quantities are equal.

D if the relationship cannot be determined from the information given.

Column A	_Column B_
Number of square inches in 3 square feet	36

Your first reaction is to think that the columns are equal because there are 12 inches to a foot and $12 \times 3 = 36$. However, a square foot is 12×12, which equals 144 square inches. Because 144×3 is definitely greater than 36 (don't waste any time doing the math), the answer is A. *Correct Answer:* A.

Bonus: How many cubic inches are there in a cubic foot? Not 12, and not even 144. A cubic foot is $12 \times 12 \times 12$, which equals 1,728 cubic inches.

3. Time

60 seconds = 1 minute

60 minutes = 1 hour

24 hours = 1 day

7 days = 1 week

52 weeks = 1 year

365 days = 1 year

366 days = 1 leap year

Leap year is an interesting concept in terms of math problems. It comes around every four years. The extra day, February 29, makes 366 days in the year. Why do you need to know this fact? Well, you may just see a problem like this:

Mr. Pellaton's neon sign flashes four hours a day, every day all year, for four years. If it costs him three cents a day for electricity, how much will he owe for electricity at the end of the fourth year?

You may be tempted to say that this problem is super easy — multiply 365 × 4 to find the number of days and then multiply that number by .03. Wrong-o! You forgot that extra day for leap year, and your answer is off by three cents. You *know* that the test-makers will have the wrong answer lurking among the answer choices just to trap you. **Remember:** Whenever there's a four-year period, look out for the leap year with an extra day.

What's the Point: Decimals

Here's where a calculator would be very helpful. But until the test-makers join the 21st century and let you use one, you'll have to rely on brainpower, not battery power. (By the way, did you know that students taking the SAT and ACT are now allowed to use a calculator? Times are changing.)

We won't spend much time on decimals, because you almost certainly won't spend much time on them yourself. Just remember to

✔ **Keep a wary eye on the decimal point.** Its placement is often a trap for the careless.

✔ **Go to extremes.** Determine the far-left or far-right digit and use that info to eliminate incorrect answer choices.

Adding and subtracting decimals

To add or subtract decimals accurately, line up the decimal points first. If you're rushed for time and don't want to do the whole problem, go to extremes — the far-left and far-right columns. Often, calculating the extremes alone gives you enough information to choose the right answer to a multiple-choice problem. In this case, you can look at the far right, which is the thousandths column, and know that it has to end in a 6. Suppose that your answer choices are

(A) 160.999

(B) 160.852

(C) 160.756

(D) 159.831

(E) 159.444

You know immediately that Choice C must be the correct answer.

Maybe more than one of the answer choices uses the correct digit for the far-right column. Okay, you're flexible; head for the far-left column, which here is the hundreds place. You know in this problem it has to be a 1. Suppose the answer choices are

(A) 160.756

(B) 201.706

(C) 209.045

(D) 210.006

(E) 301.786

Only Choice A has the correct far-left number.

Multiplying decimals

The biggest trap when multiplying decimals is keeping the number of decimal places correct. The number of decimal places in the product (the number you get when you multiply the terms together) must be the same as the sum of the number of decimal places in all the terms.

$$5.06 \times 3.9 =$$

$$\begin{array}{r} 5.06 \\ \times\ 3.9 \\ \hline 19.734 \end{array}$$

There are two decimal places in the first term and one in the second, for a total of three. Therefore, the final answer must have three decimal places.

The shortcut for addition and subtraction with decimals (covered in the preceding section) works in this case as well. Go to extremes. Look at the far-right and far-left terms. You know that $6 \times 9 = 54$, so the last digit in the answer has to be a 4. You can eliminate wrong answers by using that information. You know that $5 \times 3 = 15$, but you may have to carry over some other numbers to make the far-left value greater than 15 (as is the case here). At least you know that the far-left digits must be 15 *or more*. An answer choice starting with anything less than 15 can be eliminated.

Dividing decimals

To divide decimals, turn them into integers by moving the decimal point to the right the appropriate number of places for both terms — the one you're dividing and the one you're dividing by (called the *divisor*, should you happen to care).

$$4.44 \div .06 = {}^{444}\!/_{6} = 74$$

Broken Hearts, Broken Numbers: Fractions

Fractions strike fear into the hearts of most mere mortals. Fortunately, the number of fraction problems on the GRE is small — and getting smaller all the time. (We can hear your cheers and sighs of relief now.)

Adding or subtracting fractions

1. **You can add or subtract fractions only when they have the same denominator.**

$$\frac{1}{3} + \frac{4}{3} = \frac{5}{3}$$

$$\frac{3}{8} - \frac{2}{8} = \frac{1}{8}$$

2. **When fractions have the same denominator, add or subtract the numerators only.**

3. **When fractions don't have the same denominator, you must find the lowest common denominator.**

You can, of course, multiply all the denominators, but that often doesn't give you the *lowest* common denominator. Usually you end up with some humongous, overwhelming number that you'd rather not work with. Instead, use this little trick:

4. **To find the lowest common denominator, count by the highest denominator.**

   Find the lowest common denominator of 15 and 6. Sure, you can multiply $15 \times 6 = 90$, but that's not the *lowest* common denominator. Instead, count by 15's because 15 is the larger of the two. 15? No, 6 doesn't go into that. 30? Yes, both 15 and 6 go into 30. That's the *lowest* common denominator.

   Try another one: Find the lowest common denominator for 2, 4, and 5. Count by 5's: 5? No, 2 and 4 don't go into it. 10? No, 4 doesn't go into it. 15? No, 2 and 4 don't go into it. 20? Yes, all the numbers divide evenly into 20. That number is smaller than the one you get when you multiply $2 \times 4 \times 5 = 40$.

5. **In many problems, you don't even have to find the lowest common denominator. You can find any common denominator by multiplying the denominators.**

$$\frac{4}{15} + \frac{1}{6} =$$

The common denominator is $15 \times 6 = 90$. Cross-multiply: $4 \times 6 = 24$. The first fraction becomes $^{24}\!/_{90}$. Cross-multiply: $1 \times 15 = 15$. The second fraction becomes $^{15}\!/_{90}$. Now add the numerators: $24 + 15 = 39$. Put the sum over the common denominator: $^{39}\!/_{90}$. Can you reduce? Yes, by 3: $^{13}\!/_{30}$.

Follow the same process when working with variables rather than numbers.

$$\frac{a}{b} + \frac{c}{d} =$$

Find the common denominator by multiplying the two denominators: $b \times d = bd$. Cross-multiply: $a \times d = ad$. Cross-multiply: $c \times b = cb$. Put the sum of the results of the cross-multiplication over the common denominator: $\dfrac{(ad + cb)}{bd}$.

Multiplying fractions

Multiplying fractions is easy. Just do it. Multiply horizontally, starting with the numerators and then moving to the denominators.

$$\frac{3}{4} \times \frac{2}{5} = \frac{(3 \times 2)}{(4 \times 5)} = \frac{6}{20} = \frac{3}{10}$$

Always check whether you can cancel before you begin working to avoid having to deal with big, awkward numbers and to avoid having to reduce at the end. In the preceding example, you can cancel the 4 and the 2, leaving you with

$$\frac{3}{{}_2\cancel{4}} \times \frac{\cancel{2}^1}{5} = \frac{(3 \times 1)}{(2 \times 5)} = \frac{3}{10}$$

You get to the right solution either way. Canceling in advance just makes the numbers smaller and easier to work with.

Dividing fractions

To divide by a fraction, *invert* it (turn it upside down) and multiply.

$$\frac{1}{3} \div \frac{2}{5} = \frac{1}{3} \times \frac{5}{2} = \frac{5}{6}$$

Playing with mixed numbers

A *mixed number* is a whole number with a fraction tagging along behind it, like $2\frac{1}{3}$, $4\frac{2}{5}$, or $9\frac{1}{2}$. Multiply the whole number by the denominator and add that to the numerator. Then put the sum over the denominator.

$$2\frac{1}{3} = (2 \times 3) + 1 = 7 \rightarrow \frac{7}{3}$$

$$4\frac{2}{5} = (4 \times 5) + 2 = 22 \rightarrow \frac{22}{5}$$

$$9\frac{1}{2} = (9 \times 2) + 1 = 19 \rightarrow \frac{19}{2}$$

The Stats Don't Lie: Statistics

Don't panic; statistics are tested on the GRE only in the most rudimentary way. If you can master three basic concepts, you can solve any statistics problem on this exam. Those concepts are median, mode, and range.

The only trap you're likely to see in the statistics questions is in the answer choices. The questions themselves are quite straightforward, but the answer choices may assume that some people don't know one term from another. For example, one answer choice to a median question may in fact be the *mean* (the average). One answer choice to a range question may be the mode. To keep from falling for this trap, mentally note the word in the question that tells you what you're looking for.

Median

Simply put, the *median* is the middle number when all the terms are arranged in order. Think of the median strip, which is the middle of the road. Median = middle. Be sure to arrange the numbers in order (increasing or decreasing, it makes no difference) before you find the median.

Find the median of –3, 18, –4, ½, 11.

(A) –3

(B) 18

(C) –4

(D) ½

(E) 11

Put the numbers in order: –4, –3, ½, 11, 18. The one in the middle, ½, is the median. It's as simple as that. *Correct Answer:* Choice D.

Note: If the list has an even number of terms, put them in order and find the middle two. Then find the average of those two terms.

Find the median of 5, 0, –3, –5, 1, 2, 8, 6.

(A) 0

(B) 1

(C) 1.5

(D) 2

(E) 5

Put the numbers in order: –5, –3, 0, 1, 2, 5, 6, 8. The middle two terms are 1 and 2. Find the average of those two numbers and get 1.5. That's it. *Correct Answer:* Choice C.

Don't confuse median (middle) with mean. A mean is simply the average.

Mode

The *mode* is the most frequent number. Remember the *mo* part! *Mo*de is the *mo*st used term. We suggest you put the numbers in order again. The one that shows up the most often is the mode.

Find the mode of 11, 18, 29, 17, 18, –4, 0, 19, 0, 11, 18.

(A) 11

(B) 17

(C) 18

(D) 19

(E) 29

There are three 18's but no more than two of any other number. *Correct Answer:* Choice C.

Range

The *range* is the distance from the greatest to the smallest. In other words, take the biggest term and subtract the smallest term. Your answer is the range.

Find the range of the numbers 11, 18, 29, 17, 18, –4, 0, 19, 0, 11, 18.

(A) 33

(B) 29

(C) 19

(D) 0

(E) –4

Ah, did this one getcha? True, 33 isn't one of the numbers in the set. But to find the range, you must subtract the smallest number from the largest: 29 – –4 = 29 + 4 = 33. *Correct Answer:* Choice A.

A Picture Is Worth a Thousand Words: Graphs

You may encounter one or two graphs on the GRE. When you have a graph, all the questions following it are kept together. In other words, you won't have a graph with a question, then a question on something else, then a second graph question. Even the GRE isn't that cruel! Four basic types of graphs show up frequently:

- ✔ **Circle or pie graph:** The circle represents 100 percent. The key to this graph is noting of what total the percentages are a part of. Below the graph, you may be told that in 2001, 5,000 students graduated with Ph.D.s. If a 25-percent segment on the circle graph is labeled "Ph.D.s in history," you know that the number of history Ph.D.s is 25 percent of 5,000, or 1,250.

- ✔ **Two axes line graph:** A typical line graph has a bottom axis and a side axis. You plot a point or read a point from the two axes. This is probably the simplest type of graph you'll come across.

- ✔ **Three axes line graph:** This type of graph, with its left side axis, bottom axis, and right side axis, is rare. The left side axis may represent, for example, the number of crates of a product, whereas the right side axis may represent the percentage that those crates are of the whole shipment. You read the points on a three axes graph the same as you do on a two axes graph — by paying special attention that you answer what the question is asking you. If the question asks you for the number of crates, read the left side. If the question asks you for the percentage of crates, read the right side.

- ✔ **Bar graph:** A bar graph has vertical or horizontal bars that may represent actual numbers or percentages. If the bar goes all the way from one side of the graph to the other, it represents 100 percent.

Some questions use two graphs in one problem. Following is such an example.

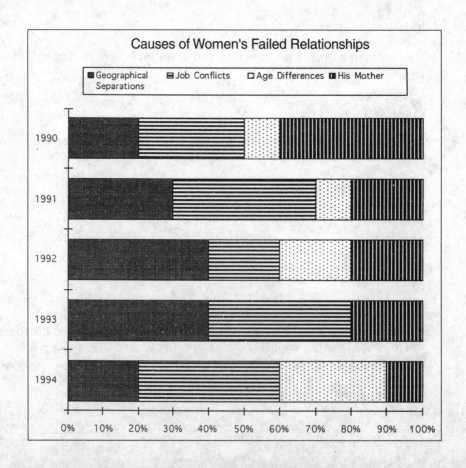

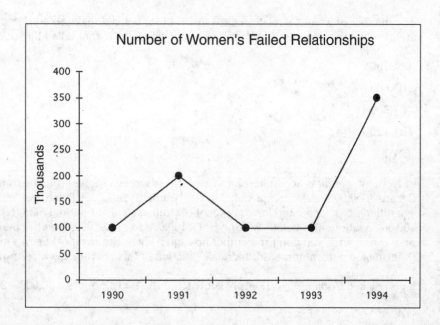

The two graphs here must be read in conjunction. The first graph is a bar graph that goes from 0 to 100 percent. Read the graph by *subtracting* to find the appropriate percentage. For example, in 1990, the Job Conflicts category (as a cause of failed relationships) began at 20 and rose to 50, a difference of 30 percent. If you say that Job Conflicts rose 50 percent, you're falling for a trap. In 1993, the His Mother category rose from 80 to 100, meaning mothers-in-law caused 20 percent of failed relationships.

The second graph gives you the actual number of failed relationships in thousands. Be sure to look at the labels of the axes. For example, in 1990, 100,000 relationships failed, not 100. Use the graphs together to find out the number of relationships caused to fail by a particular event or situation. For example, in 1991, 200,000 relationships failed. Also in 1991, age differences (from 70 to 80, or 10 percent) caused 10 percent of these failed relationships. Multiply 10 percent or .10 × 200,000 = 20,000 relationships.

Ready to try some practice questions? Usually, three to five questions follow a graph, but we're going easy on you here and just providing two.

How many relationships did women have from 1990 to 1994 inclusive?

(A) 850

(B) 8,500

(C) 85,000

(D) 850,000

(E) It cannot be determined from the information given.

Did we getcha? The title of the graph says it all: The Causes of Women's *Failed* Relationships. You have no way to determine how many relationships worked. *Correct Answer:* Choice E.

The number of women's relationships in 1994 that failed due to job conflicts was what percent greater than the number of women's relationships in 1992 that failed due to age differences?

(A) 700

(B) 600

(C) 500

(D) 120

(E) 7

In 1994, job conflicts accounted for 40 percent of women's failed relationships (from 20 to 60). Because 350,000 relationships failed in 1994, multiply .40 × 350,000 to get 140,000. In 1992, age differences accounted for 20 percent of women's failed relationships (60 to 80). In 1992, 100,000 relationships failed. Multiply .20 × 100,000 to get 20,000. Find the percent change between them. If you don't remember how, go back to the earlier "Life has its ups and downs: Determining percent increase/decrease" section of this chapter. *Correct Answer:* Choice B.

If you picked Choice D, you simply subtracted the two amounts: 140,000 – 20,000 = 120,000.

Math Concepts You Absolutely MUST Know

If you were told that the world would end in two hours, what would you do? Order a pizza? Go surfing? Play hoops with friends? Life has its priorities. If someone were to inform you that your math study time for the GRE was up in two hours, what would your priorities be? Here are our suggestions (although pizza doesn't sound half bad).

Angles

Understand the various types of angles: acute, obtuse, right, and straight. Also, make sure you know how to identify exterior angles and how to solve for the sum of the interior angles of any polygon.

The sum of the interior angles is $S = 180(n - 2)$, where n is the number of sides in the polygon.

Circles

Be able to find circumference, area, sectors, and arcs of circles, as well as the degree measures of central and inscribed angles. For a refresher on formulas, check out the following:

- **Circumference:** $C = 2\pi r$
- **Area:** $A = \pi r^2$
- **Length of an arc in a sector:** Find the ratio of the number of degrees in the sector to 360°. Then multiply this fraction times the circumference of the whole circle.
- **Area of the sector:** Find the ratio of the number of degrees in the sector to 360°. Then multiply this fraction times the area of the whole circle.

Central angles are equal to the arc; inscribed angles are equal to half the arc.

Common Pythagorean ratios

Keep in mind that in a right triangle, the sides may be in the following ratios:

$3:4:5$ $s:s:\sqrt{2}$ (or $\frac{s}{\sqrt{2}}:\frac{s}{\sqrt{2}}:s$)

$5:12:13$ $s:s\sqrt{3}:2s$

$7:24:25$

Exponents

Understand how to add, subtract, multiply, and divide like bases. Also, remember that

✔ A number or variable to the zero power equals 1.

✔ A number or variable to a negative power is the *reciprocal* (upside-down version) of that number or variable.

For example, simplify $(2x)^3(-3x)^2 + 2x^5$. This is really just an order of operations problem with variables. First, take care of all the exponents: $(8x^3)(9x^2) + 2x^5$. Now multiply: $72x^5 + 2x^5$. Finally, add to get $74x^5$.

A negative exponent takes the *positive reciprocal*, nothing else: $x^{-5} = \dfrac{1}{x^5}$. Notice that the variable moved into the denominator, and the exponent became positive.

FOIL method of algebra

Use the FOIL method: *First, Outer, Inner, Last* to multiply algebraic equations. For example, say you're asked to multiply $(x - 6)(x + 2)$:

FIRST: $x \times x = x^2$

OUTER: $x \times 2 = 2x$

INNER: $-6 \times x = -6x$

LAST: $-6 \times 2 = -12$

The product is the sum of these terms: $x^2 + 2x - 6x - 12 = x^2 - 4x - 12$.

Graphing

Be able to find a point on a graph given its (x,y) coordinates. Remember that the point of origin is $(0,0)$. If you connect all the points where x and y are the same, such as $(4,4)$ or $(-3, -3)$, you get a line that forms a 45-degree angle.

Linear algebraic equations

Isolate the variables. That is, get the variables on one side of the equal sign and the nonvariables on the other side (remembering to change from a positive to a negative or vice versa when crossing over the equal sign). Add like terms. Then divide both sides by what's next to each variable.

For example, solve the equation: $4x - 3(x + 2) = 6(x - 3)$. First, distribute: $4x - 3x - 6 = 6x - 18$. Next, combine like terms: $x - 6 = 6x - 18$. Now get the variable onto the same side of the equation: $x - 6x - 6 = -18$ or $-5x - 6 = -18$. Now, isolate the variable: $-5x = -18 + 6$ or $-5x = -12$; $x = \frac{12}{5}$. Voilà!

Ratios

Remember that the possible total is a multiple of the sum of the numbers in the ratio. A ratio is written as $\frac{of}{to}$ or of:to.

For example, say a recipe calls for 1 cup of milk and 3 cups of flour. The ratio of milk to flour is 1:3. That means 1 cup + 3 cups = 4 cups of stuff in your recipe. If you needed to make three times the recipe, you'd use 3 cups of milk and 9 cups of flour, which is conveniently 12 cups of stuff in the recipe (exactly 4 — the old total — times 3).

Square roots

Know how to multiply and divide like radicals and how to simplify radicals. For example, simplify $\sqrt{20} \times \sqrt{2}$. First, simplify any roots: $\sqrt{20} = \sqrt{(4 \times 5)} = 2\sqrt{5}$. Now multiply: $2\sqrt{5} \times \sqrt{2} = 2\sqrt{10}$.

Symbolism

Remember that the GRE tests two basic types of symbolism:

- **Plugging the numbers into the expression:** For example, if $f(x) = x^3 - 6x + 2$, then to find $f(2)$, replace x in the expression with 2: $(2)^3 - 6(2) + 2 = 8 - 12 + 2 = -2$.

- **Talking through the symbolism explanation in English:** If you're asked to translate the expression "The sum of two consecutive even integers is 26," what would you do? Look at what you're being asked to write one piece at a time. Consecutive even integers are in a row, such as 44, 46, and 48. One number is always two greater than the one before it. If x is the first even integer, then $x + 2$ is the next consecutive even integer. Finding their sum means to add them: $x + x + 2$. The fact that their sum is 26 is easy to translate: $x + x + 2 = 26$.

Part IV

Your Number's Up:
Math Questions

"Careful Sundance, this one's been locked up studying for the GRE a1111 week, and he's gotten pretty mean."

In this part . . .

There are two types of people in the world: those who've never met an equation they didn't like . . . and those who wish they'd never met an equation at all. The following math chapters and practice questions can be a lot of fun.

In these chapters, you learn all sorts of good tricks. Sure, we also sneak in some Real Math (stuff like formulas and rules), but we focus on the tricks and traps you're likely to see on the GRE, including tips for sidestepping them. But please note: GRE math has no relation to the Real World. Just review it, ace the Math section, and be done with it.

The Math section features two types of problems: Quantitative Comparisons and Problem Solving questions. You get the unexpected pleasure of using your brain, your whole brain, and nothing but your brain to solve these problems. In other words, you can't use a calculator. You may not bring in your own calculator, and the computer you use won't have any calculator functions available. The proctor will provide you with scratch paper (again, you may not bring your own) that you can use to jot down calculations — or gnaw and rip up if you get totally frustrated!

Chapter 16

The Incomparable Quantitative Comparisons

In This Chapter
▶ Finding the elusive QC answer choices
▶ Knowing how to approach a QC problem
▶ Recognizing and running from built-in traps
▶ Putting it all together so you can work smarter, not harder

Question: What do quicksand and quantitative comparisons have in common?

Answer: They can both suck you in and pull you down before you realize what's happening.

The Quantitative Comparison (QC) section of the GRE consists of 14 or so questions — and a zillion or more traps. QCs rarely require power math, but they do require paranoia (to recognize the traps) and finesse (to avoid the traps). Hmmm . . . Paranoia & Finesse. Sounds like a law firm, doesn't it?

Where Did All the Answers Go? The QC Format

A QC question lists a quantity in Column A and another quantity in Column B. The quantities can be numbers, variables, equations, words, figures, compromising photos of you at the last fraternity or office holiday party — anything. Your job is to compare the quantity in Column A to the quantity in Column B. (Hence the title "Quantitative Comparisons." We bet some rocket scientist got big bucks for thinking that one up!)

No answer choices are given below the quantities in QC questions. Instead, you're to compare the quantities and

- Choose A if the quantity in Column A is greater than the quantity in Column B.
- Choose B if the quantity in Column B is greater than the quantity in Column A.
- Choose C if the quantity in Column A is equal to the quantity in Column B.
- Choose D if not enough information is provided for you to determine the relationship between the quantities.

Got all that? Just choose A if A is bigger, B if B is bigger, C if they're the same (with C standing for *same* if you spell poorly), and D if you can't tell (as in D for *d'oh!*).

As Easy as π: Approaching QC Questions

The hardest part of answering a QC question is knowing where to begin. You can save considerable time — and frustration — if you develop good habits now that carry over to the exam later. Follow this simple three-step approach:

1. Solve for the quantity in Column A.

You may solve an equation, talk through a word problem, or do nothing but look at what's given. Here are some examples of what you may see in Column A:

Column A

$$x^2$$

40% of 340

The number of miles hiked by Ken, who hikes at 3 mph for 6½ hours

2. Solve for the quantity in Column B.

Again, "solve" can mean solving an equation, talking through a word problem, or just looking at the column, as you can see in the following examples:

Column B

$$x^3$$

340% of 40

18

3. Compare the two columns.

Sounds simple enough, right? Wait until you see some of the traps the GRE powers-that-be can build into the QCs.

Gotchas and Other Groaners: Tips, Traps, and Tricks

QCs have so many tricks and traps that we give you a separate section for each one, with a few examples to illustrate how easily you can fall for the traps.

Keep in mind that the following sections feature tips, not rules. A *tip* is a pointer that works most of the time, but not always. Never shut off your own brain in favor of a tip. The purpose of a tip is just to make you think twice before falling for a trap.

Remembering that equal appearances can be deceiving

If Column A and Column B appear to be equal at first glance, don't fall for it — a trap is almost always involved. Check out the following examples:

Column A	*Column B*
π	3.14

Your gut reaction may be to choose C because both columns are equal. After all, wasn't it drilled into your head in school that 3.14 equals π? (If you've been out of school for quite a while, you may be very pleased with yourself for remembering the numerical value of π. Put the self-congratulations on hold; you've just fallen for a trap.) The value of π is only *approximately* 3.14. For convenience, your teachers and math books rounded π to two decimal places: 3.14. Actually, however, π is larger than that and continues as a nonrepeating, nonterminating decimal: 3.141592. . . . Thus, A is the right choice. *Correct Answer:* A.

Column A	*Column B*
.0062 × 3600	6200 × .3600

You probably checked that the number of digits and decimal places are the same and chose C. But the answer is B. When you multiply them out, Column A equals 22.32, and Column B equals 2,232. *Big* difference. The moral of the story? If your first reaction is that the problem is a no-brainer — that the answer is obviously, clearly, undoubtedly C — slap yourself upside the head and work through the problem. *Correct Answer:* B.

Keeping an eye out for scale

If a figure in a QC problem isn't drawn to scale, the answer is often D. How can you tell? Look for the words "***Note:*** Figure not drawn to scale" underneath the picture. This message is a warning buzzer alerting you to the presence of a built-in trap. If a figure isn't drawn to scale, you can't rely on it. Because you can't just eyeball it to figure things out, you need solid information such as the lengths of lines or the measures of angles. If those details aren't provided, you often can't determine the relationship between the columns and must choose D.

Column A   Column B

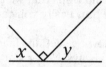

Note: Figure not drawn to scale.

x	y

Sure, *x* and *y* each appear to be 45 degrees. Go ahead and choose C. You'll blow the GRE, never get into grad school, and end up walking some rich woman's poodles for a living, lamenting, "If only I'd noticed that the figure wasn't drawn to scale!"

Because the figure isn't drawn to scale, you can't use it to estimate. You can't look at the figure and deduce that *x* and *y* are equal. Yes, *x* and *y* add up to 90 degrees. That's because angles along a straight line add up to 180 degrees, and you already have a right angle: 180 – 90 = 90. But you *don't* know how much of the 90 is *x* and how much is *y*. Are they 45 and 45? 60 and 30? 89 and 1? The figure isn't to scale, so any of those values may be correct. Because you don't have enough information to compare the quantities, go with D. *Correct Answer:* D.

Column A   Column B

Note: Figure not drawn to scale.

2x	y

If you fell for this one, you can kiss your 800 goodbye. This QC question is an example of a classic D. Yes, yes — the figure appears to be an isosceles right triangle. You know that the two *x*'s are equal and that the angles in a triangle add up to 180 degrees. But no one said that Angle *y* is 90 degrees. What's that you say? It *looks* like 90 degrees? Tooooo bad. You can't look at the figure if it's not drawn to scale. As far as you know, Angle *y* may be 89 degrees or 91 degrees or all sorts of other possibilities. Maybe *x* = 40, so 2*x* = 80 and *y* = 100. Maybe *y* = 60, so 2*x* = 120 and *y* = 60. What? That can't be, because it's obvious that this isn't an equilateral triangle with all angles equal? *Remember:* Nothing is obvious; you can't use the figure if it's not drawn to scale. Because anything is possible, choose D. *Correct Answer:* D.

"Not drawn to scale" problems have fallen out of favor with the GRE lately. In our opinion, these problems were just too easy for students to get right, so the GRE naturally took them off the test. Don't be surprised if you don't see a "not drawn to scale" problem — but be prepared just in case you do. (You'll definitely see some on the practice exams, because we want you to be prepared for every possibility.)

Testing your artistic abilities — or not

If the answer to a QC question *de*pends on how you draw the figure, choose D. Approximately one-third of GRE math is geometry, and many of the QC geometry problems are word problems that give no figures or diagrams. These questions often demand that you draw the figure yourself. In that case, the answer may *de*pend on how you draw the figure.

Column A	**Column B**
Area of a decagon	Area of a pentagon

The trap answer is A. True, a decagon has ten sides and a pentagon has five sides, and true, 10 > 5, even in new math. The correct answer, however, *de*pends on how you draw the figures and how long each side is. You could very well draw the shapes three different ways:

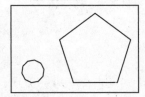 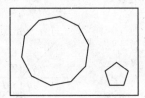 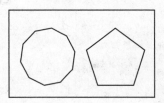

If everything *deeeeee*-pends on the *deeeeee*-rawing, choose D. *Correct Answer:* D.

Column A	**Column B**

A skating rink is 5 miles from a yogurt shop
and 6 miles from a restaurant.

Distance from the yogurt shop to the restaurant	1 mile

Did you fall for the trap answer, C? The correct answer is D. Two tips come into play here:

   ✔ **If the columns look equal, the question is usually a trap.**

   ✔ **If the answer *de*pends on how you draw the figure, choose D.**

Here are a couple ways of drawing the figure:

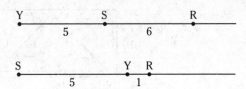

Avoiding distraction from a pretty picture

If a picture is drawn for you, the answer is rarely D. This tip is the flip side of the preceding one. The GRE is rather wishy-washy about figures. The directions say something like this: "Questions have figures that are drawn as accurately as possible, but you should use mathematics, not estimation or measurement based on the figure, to answer the questions." Huh? What does all that mean? It means that the figures really are pretty much drawn to scale, but that the GRE folks don't want you just looking at a figure to get the answer; they want you to calculate and do things the hard, "official" way.

Our advice? Don't worry about scale. As far as you're concerned, the figures are to scale unless a note specifically says otherwise. Your measurements would have to be incredibly precise for the lack of exact scale to mess you up. The answer, therefore, is rarely D when a figure is given.

Column A	_Column B_

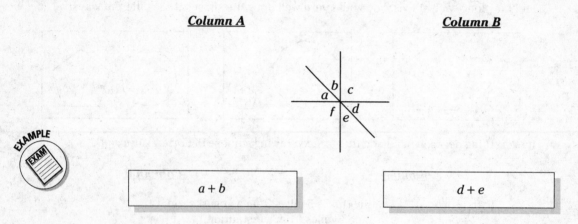

$a + b$	$d + e$

Angle _a_ is a vertical angle to Angle _d,_ meaning that they're opposite and of equal measure. Angle _b_ is a vertical angle to Angle _e,_ meaning that they're opposite and of equal measure. Because each part of Column A is equal to its counterpart in Column B, both columns are equal. _Correct Answer:_ C.

At first glance, you may be tempted to choose D for this problem because no numbers are given. True, you can't solve for the exact measurement of $a + b$, or the exact measurement of $d + e$, but the question doesn't expect you to. The QC section of the GRE isn't about problem solving; it's about quantitative comparisons — all you need to do is compare the quantities. You can compare them here (and see that they're equal), so you know D is definitely wrong.

Column A	_Column B_

10

20

Number of square units in the area of the triangle	100

Fight the temptation to choose D automatically just because you don't have numbers for the lengths of the sides of the triangle. You know that the figure is drawn to scale, so you can probably compare the quantities.

The formula for the area of a triangle is ½ *base* × *height*. What's the base? You don't know, but you *do* know that it's less than the base of the rectangle because the sides of the triangle don't extend all the way to the sides of the rectangle. Just call it *less than 20*. How much is the height? You don't know that either, but you do know that it's less than 10 because the top and bottom of the triangle don't touch the top and bottom of the rectangle. Call it *less than 10*. Multiply *less than 10* × *less than 20* to get *less than 200*. Half of *less than 200* is *less than 100*. Because *less than 100* is smaller than 100, choose B. *Correct Answer:* B.

Canceling out identical quantities

Think of canceling quantities that are identical in both columns as clearing the decks or simplifying the picture so you can more easily compare the two columns. After all, a QC problem is like a balance: If something is the same on one side as on the other, it doesn't affect the balance — you can ignore it. Be careful that you cancel only *identical* terms though. For example, you can't use –5 to cancel 5.

Column A	**Column B**
$x^2 - 21$	$x^2 - 35$

Cancel the x^2 in both columns. Copy the problem onto your scratch paper, just so you can have the joy of scratching out the identical quantities. You're now left with –21 and –35. Caution! Remember that a *negative* 21 is greater than a *negative* 35. *Correct Answer:* A.

Column A	**Column B**
$(a+b)^2$	$(a-b)^2$

You can't cancel out a and b on both sides and say that the columns are equal. The expression $(a + b)^2$ is *not* the same as $(a - b)^2$. You should memorize these two expressions (they're covered in detail in Chapter 14):

$$(a + b)^2 = a^2 + 2ab + b^2 \qquad\qquad (a - b)^2 = a^2 - 2ab + b^2$$

Now you can cancel identical terms: Slash off the a^2 and the b^2 from both columns. You're left with $+2ab$ in Column A and $-2ab$ in Column B. Because both a and b are greater than 2, you don't need to worry about negatives or fractions. *Correct Answer:* A.

In the preceding problem, you don't need to do any pencil pushing if you reason the answer out. Because a is greater than b and both a and b are positive numbers (greater than 2), you know that the sum $(a + b)$ must be greater than the difference $(a - b)$. Also, squaring a larger (positive) number gives you more than squaring a smaller number, so you can deduce that Column A is bigger without doing any paperwork.

Weighing the columns

Pretend the QC problem is a balance when comparing each part of Column A to its counterpart in Column B. If both parts of Column A are greater, or "heavier," than both parts of Column B, A is greater.

Column A	Column B
$\dfrac{17}{21} + \dfrac{47}{80}$	$\dfrac{19}{81} + \dfrac{23}{97}$

Don't even *think* about reaching for your pencil to work this problem through. Compare each part of Column A to its counterpart in Column B. Which is greater: $\frac{17}{21}$ or $\frac{19}{81}$? Reason that 17 is more than half of 21, whereas 19 is much less than half of 81. The same is true for the second pair of numbers. You know that 47 is more than half of 80; in contrast, 23 is less than half of 97. Because both parts of Column A are greater than both parts of Column B, A is the answer. No muss, no fuss. *Correct Answer:* A.

Of course, some spoilsport always wants to know what happens if one part of Column A is greater than its counterpart in Column B, but the other part of Column A is less than its counterpart in Column B. That scenario just doesn't happen. If it did, you'd miss the entire point of the question, which is to recognize and use the test-makers' hidden trick so you can work smarter, not revert to a basic arithmetic, pull-out-your-pencil-type problem. If lightning strikes and that problem does arise, well, you have no choice but to lift a finger. *Which* finger you lift is up to you.

Plugging in the Sacred Six

Here's the best tip you're likely to get outside a racetrack: Whenever you have variables, plug in the Sacred Six — 1, 2, 0, –1, –2, and ½, specifically in that order. These numbers cover most of the contingencies: positive, negative, zero, odd, even, fraction, and 1, which has special properties. Memorize these numbers and throw them into a problem whenever possible. *Note:* This tip works even if an equation contains more than one variable.

Column A	Column B
x^2	x^4

The trap answer is B. Everyone says that, *of course,* a number to the fourth power is greater than the same number squared. (A variable must have the same value in Column A as in Column B *within any one problem.* That is, if x is 5 in Column A, it's also 5 in Column B. Always. No exceptions.)

Ah, but whenever you hear yourself saying "of course," you know that you're headed for a trap. Play the "what if" game: What if $x = 1$? Then the two columns are alike, and C prevails. What if $x = 2$? Then Column A = 4 and Column B = 16, and the answer is B. Therefore, the answer can be C or B, depending on what you plug in. If an answer *de*pends on what you plug in, choose D. *Correct Answer:* D.

You don't always have to go through all the Sacred Six numbers. As soon as you find that you get two different answers, you can stop. If plugging in 1 and 2 gives you the same answer, go on to 0, –1, –2, and ½, plugging in as many as necessary. You'll be pleasantly surprised, however, to find out how often 1 and 2 alone get the job done.

Column A	Column B

$$x \neq 0$$

Column A	Column B
$\frac{1}{x}$	$\frac{x}{1}$

Again, B is the trap answer. Most people think that Column A comes out to be a fraction of less than 1. It may . . . or it may not. And who's to say that x is more than 1 in the first place? Play the "what if" game again.

What if $x = 1$? Then the columns are equal, and C is correct. What if $x = 2$? Then Column B is greater. The answer *de*pends on what you plug in, so choose D. *Correct Answer:* D.

On the real exam, you'd stop here, but for now, plug in a few more numbers to see what else can happen. You can't plug in 0 because the problem tells you that x isn't equal to 0 (division by 0 is undefined). What if $x = -1$? Then Column A is -1 and Column B is -1; they're equal. What if $x = -2$? Then Column A $= -\frac{1}{2}$ and Column B $= -2$; now A is bigger. You've seen all the possibilities at this point: A can be bigger, B can be bigger, or the two columns can be the same. We haven't even gotten into fractions yet. And if it's all the same to you, we won't.

Throwing down a hundred

If a question deals with dollars or percentages, plug in 100 to make it a nice round number. (Hey, we're all about making your life easier.)

Column A	Column B

A book bag costs x dollars.

Column A	Column B
Cost of the book bag on sale at 60% off	$.6x$

If you make the book bag cost $100, you can easily determine that 60 percent of 100 is 60; subtract $100 - 60$, and you get 40. In Column B, $.6(100) = 60$. The answer is B. This type of problem is easy to miss because of carelessness. Many people choose C automatically. (Of course, if you read the earlier "Remembering that equal appearances can be deceiving" section, you'd know that *if the columns look equal, it's probably a trap.* For a greater chance of QC-problem-solving success, slow down, plug in 100, and work out the problem. *Correct Answer:* B.

Column A	Column B
One year's interest on x dollars at 6% annual interest	$12

Gotcha! We threw this one in to remind you that this chapter features *tips*, not rules, and that you should never sacrifice common sense in favor of tips. Sure, if you plug in 100 for x dollars, you know that the interest is $6 and B is the answer. But what if $x = \$1,000,000$? Then Column A is significantly larger. Here, the correct answer *de*pends on which value you plug in for x. Although plugging in 100 often works, that tactic isn't infallible. Think! *Correct Answer:* D.

When pigs fly . . .

Question: Can you ever plug in all the Sacred Six and still fall for a QC trap?

Answer: Yeah, you can (although that's unlikely). Here's an example:

Column A	_Column B_
$x \neq 0$	
$\frac{1}{x}$	3

Now you play the "what if" game. What if $x = 1$? Then Column B is larger. What if $x = 2$? Then Column B is larger. Because x isn't equal to 0 (division by 0 is undefined), you skip to the next number in the Sacred Six. What if $x = -1$? Column B is still larger. What if $x = -2$?

Yes, yes, Column B is still larger. Finally, what if $x = \frac{1}{2}$? Then Column A = 2 (to divide by a fraction, invert and multiply) and Column B is still larger. Now, 99 percent of the Thinking World would choose B at this point and feel very confident. And 99 percent of the Thinking World would go straight down the tubes. The answer, in fact, is D. What if $x = \frac{1}{3}$? Then Column A = 3, and the two columns are equal — which means the answer is C. If the answer could be B and could also be C, the answer _de_pends and therefore is D.

A problem in which the Sacred Six don't do the job for you is incredibly rare, but it can happen. Sorry about that, but of course, plugging in the Sacred Six is a _tip,_ not a rule. It's not perfect. Close, though. . . .

Inserting variety when working with multiple variables

Plug in consecutive terms first and then nonconsecutive terms. If you need to plug in numbers for two or three variables, first plug in the numbers all in a row: 1, 2, and 3. Then try plugging in numbers that aren't in a row: 1, 5, and 7. Sometimes the spacing between the numbers makes a difference.

Column A	_Column B_
$a < b < c$	
$\dfrac{a + c}{2}$	b

The normal response is to plug in consecutive numbers: 1, 2, and 3. If you do that, Column A is $1 + 3$, or 4, divided by $2 = 2$. In Column B, b is 2. The columns are equal — a bright red warning flag. **Remember:** Equal-looking columns are often a trap, so you should double-check your work.

Plug in some nonconsecutive numbers: 1, 5, and 7. Now Column A is $1 + 7 = 8$, divided by $2 = 4$. In Column B, b is 5. Now the answer is B. If the answer _de_pends on which values you plug in for the variables, choose D. _Correct Answer:_ D.

Column A	_Column B_
$x > y > z$	
$y + z$	x

The trap answer is C. The right answer is D, because the answer _de_pends on which numbers you plug in. If you plug in 3, 2, and 1, $y + z = 2 + 1 = 3$. Because $x = 3$, the columns are equal. But when you plug in nonconsecutive numbers, 100, 2, and 1, now $y + z = 2 + 1 = 3$. But $x = 100$; Column B is larger. The answer can be C or B, _de_pending on what you plug in. Choose D. _Correct Answer:_ D.

Familiarity Breeds Content(ment): A Review

Before going on to the practice questions in the following chapter, review the approach and tips described here.

Approach

1. **Solve for the quantity in Column A.**

2. **Solve for the quantity in Column B.**

3. **Compare the two quantities.**

4. **Choose A if the quantity in Column A is greater than the quantity in Column B.**

   Choose B if the quantity in Column B is greater than the quantity in Column A.

   Choose C if the quantity in Column A is equal to the quantity in Column B.

   Choose D if you don't have enough information to determine the relationship between the quantities.

Tips

- If the columns look equal, the question is usually a trap.

- If a figure isn't drawn to scale, the answer is often D.

- If the answer *de*pends on how you draw the figure, choose D.

- If a picture is drawn to scale, the answer is rarely D.

- Cancel quantities that are identical in both columns.

- Compare each part of Column A to its counterpart in Column B.

- When plugging in numbers, use the Sacred Six — 1, 2, 0, –1, –2, and ½, in that order.

- Plug in 100 for dollars and percentages.

- Plug in consecutive terms first and then nonconsecutive terms when you have two or more variables.

Chapter 17

Putting It All Together: QC Practice Questions

. . . .

*I*f you're waiting until someone makes a movie about this stuff, forget it. The info on Quantitative Comparisons in the preceding chapter is all she wrote (so to speak). If you didn't read it carefully, please go back and do so now — before you humiliate yourself on this QC section trial run.

All done? Good. Now, check your ego at the door, or it may get trashed on this exam. We've written a dozen problems that incorporate the meanest, cruelest, and stupidest traps you're likely to see on the real GRE. How many are you going to fall for?

The answer choices are

A if the quantity in Column A is greater.

B if the quantity in Column B is greater.

C if the two quantities are equal.

D if the relationship cannot be determined from the information given.

1.

Column A	_Column B_
$10\left[(4\times3)^2+5^0\right]$	1440

This question tests two concepts: the order of operations and the zero exponent. Always do what's inside the parentheses first: $4 \times 3 = 12$; $12^2 = 144$. Then do what's inside the brackets: $5^0 = 1$. Any number to the zero power equals 1. Add: $144 + 1 = 145$. Then multiply by what's outside the brackets: $10 \times 145 = 1,450$. *Correct Answer:* A.

If you chose C, you thought that 5^0 was 0, giving you $144 + 0 = 144$; $144 \times 10 = 1,440$. Look out for the zero exponent; it appears often in tricky questions. Also, always double-check all of your C answers. We've found more QC traps in which people choose C than all the other traps combined.

2.

Column A	_Column B_

A cubic box has a total surface area of 600 square units.

Number of cubic units in the volume of the box	1,000

The total surface area of a cube is the sum of the areas of all surfaces. A cube has six surfaces: $600 \div 6 = 100$. Each surface of the cube, which is a square, has an area of 100. That means each edge is 10 because the area of a square is *side* × *side*. The volume of a cube is $edge^3$. In this case, that's $10 \times 10 \times 10 = 1,000$. *Correct Answer:* C.

Many of the geometry problems ask you to go forward and backward. You're given a volume and asked to find a total surface area, or vice versa. You may be given a circumference and asked to find a sector, or vice versa. Be comfortable enough with the geometry formulas to work problems inside out, upside down, and any which way. If you don't know how to find a volume and a total surface area, return to the thrilling pages of Chapter 13.

3.

Column A	**Column B**
$\sqrt{66+85}$	12

First, add the numbers under the square root sign: $66 + 85 = 151$. Then take the square root of that. Stop! Don't have a panic attack right here. No, you aren't allowed to use a calculator. That's the bad news. The good news is that you don't have to. You don't need to get an exact answer for a QC problem; you just have to compare the quantities in the columns.

Look for a perfect square close to 151. How about 144, which is 12^2, or 169, which is 13^2? Because 151 is between 144 and 169, the square root of it must be between 12 and 13. You couldn't care less exactly what it is. (That's right — don't bother finding the exact square root!) As long as it's more than 12, Column A is larger. *Correct Answer:* A.

4.

Column A	**Column B**
$.10 \times 10 \times 100$	1

You needn't have withdrawal pains from your calculator because of this one. Solving it is truly much easier than it looks. Multiply $.10 \times 10$ to get 1. You know that $1 \times 100 = 100$, which is certainly greater than 1. That's all you have to do. If you chose C, you got careless and were swayed by the hypnotic power of the columns. Don't let the Cs *mesmerize* (hypnotize) you; double-check them any time you encounter them. *Correct Answer:* A.

5.

Column A	**Column B**

On a road trip, Kimberly drove 600 miles and used 45 gallons of gas.
Her friend Whitney drove half as far and used 30 gallons of gas.

Miles per gallon of Kimberly's car	Miles per gallon of Whitney's car

This problem requires basic arithmetic. To find the mileage, divide the number of miles driven by the gallons used: $600 \div 45$ compared to $300 \div 30$. *Correct Answer:* A.

Before you begin making pencil scratches, look at both columns. Often you don't need to work through the actual arithmetic. You know that $300 \div 30$ is 10; you can do that in your head. Is $600 \div 45$ more than 10, equal to 10, or less than 10? It's more than 10, because $600 \div 60$ would be 10. Stop right there. You don't have to work the problem through to the bitter end; just compare the quantities. We want you to be able not only to get all the QC questions correct but also to get them correct quickly.

6.

Column A	Column B
$18y + 18x$	$18y - 18x$

You didn't fall for the cheesy and *egregious* (heinous, truly terrible) trap built into this very simple question, did you? If so, consider yourself totally humiliated because you forgot the tip presented in Chapter 16 about crossing off quantities that are identical in both columns. Cancel the $18y$. You're now left with $+18x$ compared to $-18x$. Although common sense tells you that $18x$ is greater, common sense should take a flying leap because there's nothing common about QC questions. Play the "what if" game: What if $x = 1$? Then A is greater. What if $x = 2$? Then A is still greater. Ah, but what if $x = 0$? Then the columns are equal. If the answer *de*pends on what you plug in, choose D. *Correct Answer:* D.

The more variables you have, the greater the likelihood that the answer is D because those variables could, well, vary. Whenever you have to plug a number in for a variable, use the Sacred Six we cover in Chapter 16. (If you skipped Chapter 16 and went right to the practice problems, you missed some good stuff. Here's your second chance.) Plug in 1, 2, 0, –1, –2, and ½, in that order. You don't usually need to plug them *all* in. As soon as you get two different possibilities, you know the answer *de*pends on what you plug in, and you choose D.

7.

Column A	Column B

$$ab = -40$$

Column A	Column B
$(a+b)^2$	$(a-b)^2$

Did you memorize the expanded forms of these two expressions — $(a + b)^2 = a^2 + 2ab + b^2$ and $(a - b)^2 = a^2 - 2ab + b^2$? (If you don't know how we got 'em, flip back to Chapter 14 for a refresher on the FOIL method.) Great! Now cancel the quantities that are identical in both columns (just like we showed you how to do in Chapter 16) by slashing off a^2 and b^2. You're left with $+2ab$, which would be -80, compared to $-2ab$, which would be $+80$ (because a negative times a negative is a positive). *Correct Answer:* B.

If you chose A, you got careless with your negative. Keeping the signs straight is one of the most important safeguards you can take in any algebra problem. Write the problem on your scratch paper just to be sure you avoid this type of careless mistake (which is far easier to make when you're working a problem through in your mind).

8.

Column A	Column B

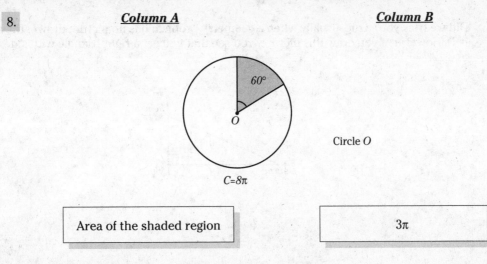

Circle O

$C = 8\pi$

Column A	Column B
Area of the shaded region	3π

A shaded portion of a circle is called a *sector*. Its area is a fraction of the area of the circle. To find the area of a sector, first find the area of the circle. The formula for the area of a circle is $\pi \times radius^2$. You must work backward from the circumference to find the radius. The circumference of a circle is $2\pi \times radius$. Therefore $C = 8\pi$, so $2\pi r = 8\pi$, or $r = 4$. Area $= \pi r^2$, or 16π.

Next, you know that the degrees in a circle total 360. The shaded portion has a 60-degree angle, making it $\frac{1}{6}$ ($\frac{60}{360}$) of the circle. Multiply the fraction by the area: $\frac{1}{6} \times 16\pi = \frac{16}{6}\pi$, or $\frac{8}{3}\pi$, which is less than 3π. *Correct Answer:* B.

Chapter 13 has a good explanation of everything to do with circles, including sectors. Circles, in our not-so-humble opinion, are among the easiest of the geometry problems to get correct, so consider circle-related problems total gimmies.

9.
Column A	**Column B**
$^{47}/_{299} + {}^{18}/_{101}$	$^{17}/_{31} + {}^{7}/_{13}$

Did you see the shortcut? That's right — you aren't expected to do common denominators and go through all the garbage math. If you're facing a QC problem, there's usually a trick. Use our tip: Compare each element of Column A to its counterpart in Column B.

In this case, compare $^{47}/_{299}$ to $^{17}/_{31}$. Because 47 out of 299 is less than half, and 17 out of 31 is more than half, Column B is larger. Next, compare the remaining two quantities. Because 18 out of 101 is less than half, and 7 out of 13 is more than half, Column B is larger here as well. Thus, both parts of Column B are greater than both parts of Column A. *Correct Answer:* B.

No, the test-makers will not, repeat, will *not* give you a problem of this sort in which one quantity is larger in Column A but the other quantity is larger in Column B. Doing so would defeat the point that this question is asking. Believe it or not, the test-makers don't get a fiendish glee out of watching you do a lot of pencil pushing. They're trying to see whether you're smart enough to *avoid* doing the work.

10.
Column A	**Column B**

Michelle and Mike begin walking and go 5 miles due north.
Their friend Devrae begins at the same point and goes 12 miles due west.

Shortest distance from Michelle to Devrae	13 miles

Did we trick you? True, usually when a geometry problem has no picture drawn, the answer is D. However, if you draw this picture, you see that you get a right triangle with sides of 5 and 12.

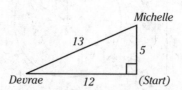

You can use the Pythagorean theorem of $a^2 + b^2 = c^2$ and find that $5^2 + 12^2 = 25 + 144 = 169$; $169 = c^2$; $c = 13$. Or you can be grateful you weren't too ***parsimonious*** (cheap) to plunk down some dough for this book and remember from Chapter 13 that one of the Pythagorean triples is 5:12:13. That is, in a right triangle (which is created if one person goes due north and the other person goes due west), if one side is 5 and the other side is 12, the hypotenuse must be 13. You don't have to do the work at all. *Correct Answer:* C.

Did you have trouble figuring out the square root of 169? Then you need to go memorize square roots and perfect squares. In the meantime, you can always work backward from the Column B quantity: $13 \times 13 =$ (son of a gun!) 169.

Once again we say unto you: Don't panic, especially over square roots. We've never seen a GRE question that depended on your ability to find an exact square root. We *have* seen a ***plethora*** (an abundance), indeed a ***superfluity*** (an excessive number), of problems that can be answered by knowing the basic Pythagorean triples, which just so happen to be given and explained in Chapter 13.

11.

Column A	*Column B*
The greatest prime factor of 1,210	The greatest prime factor of 12,100

A prime factor is a *prime number,* a number that can be divided only by itself and 1. The prime numbers are 2, 3, 5, 7, 11, and so on. (Notice that 0 and 1 aren't prime numbers.) To factor down a number ending in 0, divide by 10. For Column A, that gives you 121×10. Theoretically you've memorized your perfect squares and know that $121 = 11 \times 11$. For Column B, dividing by 10 gives you $1,210 \times 10$. Divide by 10 again to get $121 \times 10 \times 10$. Because 10 factors down into 2 and 5, the greatest prime factor of both columns is 11. *Correct Answer:* C.

12.

Column A	*Column B*
$9x^2 - 4x = 69$; $3x^2 - 10x = -3$	
$x^2 + x$	15

This problem is straightforward algebra. Traps are rarely found in algebra problems and are usually pretty basic when they are. For this example, write the two expressions vertically and either add or subtract to make the *numerical coefficients* (the numbers before the x^2 and the x) the same.

$9x^2 - 4x = 69$

$3x^2 - 10x = -3$

If you add the two equations, you get $12x^2 - 14x = 66$, not the same numerical coefficient. Because the numerical coefficients aren't the same, no variable "drops out" or can be canceled. On to Plan B. If adding the equations doesn't work, subtract the second equation, which means changing the signs on all the numbers.

$9x^2 - 4x = 69$

$-3x^2 + 10x = 3$

You get $6x^2 + 6x = 72$. Divide both sides through by 6 to get $x^2 + x = 12$. *Correct Answer:* B.

Chapter 18

Real Math at Last: Problem Solving

In This Chapter
▶ Developing a plan of attack for Problem Solving questions
▶ Sidestepping snares and avoiding built-in traps

Problem Solving is a rather ritzy name for regular math problems. A Problem Solving question, amazingly enough, actually expects you to solve a problem. These question types are different from the Quantitative Comparison questions (covered in Chapter 16), in which you often don't need to solve the problem through to the bitter end — you just compare the quantities. (Who thinks of these catchy names anyway? How much do they get paid, and where can we apply for the job?)

Strategic Planning: The Attack Strategy

Are you an Algebra Ace? A Mathematics Master? A Geometry Guru? Us neither. Isn't it lucky that you don't have to be one of these enlightened individuals to do well on the Problem Solving questions? To improve your chances of acing the material, try to understand and apply the strategies we present in this chapter.

We realize you may not have taken math classes in a long, long time. Maybe you're a senior in college, and because you tested out of math while you were still in high school, you never took any math at all in college. Perhaps you're returning to school after spending several years working or having a family or traveling or pursuing the idle and decadent lifestyle of the independently wealthy. Whatever the cause, you may be so rusty in math that your pencil creaks when you pick it up. We realize that you aren't going to get every single math question correct on the GRE, and you should realize that you don't have to.

The following steps can help you maximize your points with a minimum of time and bother:

1. **Read each problem through carefully and jot down on your scratch paper what the question is asking for.**

People who are really math-phobic often miss this crucial point. Predicting or anticipating what a question is asking for — without taking note of what it *really* wants — is all too easy. Always give each question what it wants. If a question asks for a circumference, circle or jot down the word *circumference* and don't solve for an area. If a question wants you to find the number of hours already worked rather than the total number of hours a job would take, be sure that you supply the correct figure.

Of course, of course, *of course,* the answer choices feature trap answers; this fact goes without saying on the GRE. If a question asks for the perimeter, you can bet your bottom dollar that the area will also be one of the answers — it's a trap for people who don't read the question carefully. Just because the answer you came up with is staring you in the face doesn't mean that it's the correct answer. Sure, it might be . . . or it might also be a trap. Before you press the Confirm button on your computer, go back and look at the information: Are you answering the right question?

2. **Preview every set of answer choices; look to see how precise your answer must be and how careful you must be on the decimal points.**

   If the answer choices are 4, 5, 6, 7, and 8, you probably have to solve the problem to the bitter end, calculating rather than estimating. This type of problem may take a long time. However, if the answer choices are .05, .5, 5, 50, and 500, you know that the digit is definitely going to be a 5 and that you have to keep your decimal point straight. You may be able to use common sense on this type of problem and estimate the answer without working the problem out.

3. **Solve each problem forward and backward.**

   Work out a problem and get an answer; then plug that answer back into the problem to guarantee it makes sense. If you found the average of 4, 6, 7, 9, and 10 to be 36, you can look at the answer and reason that you made a mistake somewhere, because the average can't be bigger than the biggest number. (Did you see the mistake? If you got 36, you found the sum of the terms but forgot to divide by the number of terms. Interim answers of this sort are common trap answer choices on the GRE.)

Three Common-Sense Suggestions for Problem Solving

Problem Solving questions are much more straightforward than the Quantitative Comparison (QC) problems we cover in Chapter 16. There aren't as many traps, but you can learn a few good, fairly common-sense techniques that can speed up your work or help you avoid careless mistakes.

Eliminate illogical (read: stupid) answer choices

You know how some teachers always reassure students by saying, "Oh, there's no such thing as a stupid question or answer; just try!" Wrong. Stupid answers *do* exist. If you're asked for the temperature of milk and one of the answer choices is –200° Fahrenheit, it's unlikely that milk would be that cold. In reality, it'd freeze and no longer be a liquid! If you're asked for the age of a person and one answer is 217, we want to know what kind of vitamins that person has been taking! When you preview the answers, dump the ones that seem to make no sense.

Don't choose a "close enough" answer

Suppose you do a ton of calculations and get the answer 36. One of the answer choices is 38. Don't shrug and say, "Ahh, close enough; I must've made a mistake somewhere." You sure did, and you're about to make a second mistake by being lazy and choosing an answer that's "close enough." Close counts only in horseshoes (which you may want to bring to the exam for luck, come to think of it) and hand grenades (which may be what you feel has hit you when you see some of these math questions).

Don't let us scare you *too* much about the Math section. The GRE does not, repeat does *not*, test trigonometry or calculus. It tests basic arithmetic, algebra, and geometry. Even if you haven't had those subjects in years, you can cover enough ground in a quick math review to do well.

Give your pencil a workout

Before the GRE starts, you'll receive scratch paper so you can scribble to your heart's content. (And no, you can't use your own. The proctor supplies the scratch paper and is usually more than happy to give you as much as you want, a few sheets at a time that is.) As you'll see when you go through the sample questions and practice exams, writing down formulas and plugging numbers into them, or drawing pictures and putting numbers on the pictures, is an excellent way to avoid careless errors and to clarify and organize your thoughts. Don't think you're wasting time by using your pencil; you may actually be saving time by avoiding confusion.

I'm Sure I Know You from Somewhere: A Quick Review

Before you go on to the practice questions in Chapter 19, review the approach and the tricks necessary to score Problem Solving success.

Approach

Although a GRE Problem Solving question is a basic multiple-choice math question that's similar to what you've encountered on exams all your life, following these common-sense steps can help you answer one more quickly and with fewer errors:

1. **Read each problem through carefully and jot down what the question is asking for.**

2. **Preview every set of answer choices.**

3. **Solve each problem forward and backward (plugging in the multiple-choice answers).**

Tricks

The test-makers know all the traps test-takers can fall for, and they delight in building those traps into the questions. Just because the answer you came up with is one of the answer choices in front of you doesn't mean that your answer is correct. Keep the following tricks in mind as you go through the Problem Solving questions:

✔ Eliminate illogical (read: stupid) answer choices.

✔ Don't choose a "close enough" answer.

✔ Plug in numbers, write down formulas, and draw pictures. Give your pencil a workout.

Chapter 19

A Chance to Show Off: Problem Solving Practice Questions

. . . .

So you think you understand everything from the math-review chapters? Well, we're calling your bluff. Prove you're for real by acing these practice questions.

1. At a park, the ratio of softball players to volleyball players is 3:4. If the total number of softball and volleyball players is 63, how many more volleyball players than softball players are in the park?

   (A) 3

   (B) 4

   (C) 6

   (D) 9

   (E) 12

The total of a ratio is a multiple of the sum of the numbers in that ratio. In simple English, that means you add the numbers in the ratio: 3 + 4 = 7. Think of 7 as the number of athletes in one clique or one batch. In 63, there are 9 cliques or batches, because ⁶³⁄₇ = 9. If there are 9 batches of 3 softball players, that's 27. If there are 9 batches of 4 volleyball players, that's 36. 36 − 27 = 9. *Correct Answer:* Choice D.

Ratios should be among the easiest of questions to answer correctly. Chapter 14 has a very easy explanation of how to get through these problems without even lifting your pencil.

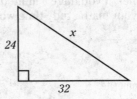

2. What is the length of Side *x* in the figure above?

   (A) 48

   (B) 40

   (C) 35

   (D) 32

   (E) 30

Because the longest side of any right triangle is always the *hypotenuse* (the side opposite the right, or 90-degree, angle), you know that answers less than or equal to 32 are wrong. Eliminate Choices D and E.

You can solve this problem the long and boring way — by using the Pythagorean theorem to find that $a^2 + b^2 = c^2$. That means you have to square 24, square 32, and then find the square root of whatever humongous number results. (Don't ask us what it is; we're not about to do all that hard work.) At this stage, you should be reminding yourself that there should be an easier way. And there is!

The sides of right triangles are in specific proportions or ratios, called the *Pythagorean triples*. If you haven't memorized 'em yet, go back to Chapter 13 and do so right now. You'll save yourself a lot of work (and earn a lot of points) if you memorize these special triples. The one that works here is the most common triple used on the test: 3:4:5. Each side is a multiple of those terms. The first side is 3×8, or 24. The next side is 4×8, or 32. That means the last side must be 5×8, or 40. Brain overload avoided. *Correct Answer:* Choice B.

3. Given a regular hexagon of side 5, what is the sum of the interior angles?

(A) 900

(B) 720

(C) 540

(D) 360

(E) 180

The term *regular* simply means that all sides and all angles are equal. For example, an equilateral triangle and a square are both regular figures. The interior angles of a figure are found with the formula $(n-2)180$, where n stands for the number of sides of the figure. Because a hexagon has six sides (think of the x in *six* and the x in *hex* to help you to remember this one), your formula is $(6-2)180 = (4 \times 180) = 720$. *Correct Answer:* Choice B.

If you picked Choice C, you fell for the trap. You let the 5, which is the *length* of the side, be the number of sides. The two numbers are totally different: six sides, each measuring 5 units. Only the number of sides is important here.

Chapter 13 provides a very good analysis of how to find the interior (and exterior) angles of any figure. Because geometry problems are the easiest to get right after you've learned the formulas, we suggest that, if you have a limited amount of time to work on this material, you spend the majority of your math study time working on geometry.

4.

> $\boxed{x}$ = x^2 if x is prime.
>
> $\boxed{x}$ = $(x+1)^2$ if x is composite.

Solve for $\boxed{3}$ + $\boxed{4}$.

(A) 41

(B) 34

(C) 25

(D) 23

(E) 7

This one's a classic symbolism problem. Talk your way through it, substituting the number in the circle for the x in the directions. First, you have ③. Because 3 is a *prime number* (which has no positive integer factors other than 1 and itself), you use the first line of the directions. Square 3 to get 9. Next you have ④. Because 4 is a *composite number* (meaning it has factors other than just 1 and itself), you use the second line of directions. Add 1 to the 4 first and then square the sum: $1 + 4 = 5$; $5^2 = 25$. Now add the two answers: $9 + 25 = 34$. *Correct Answer:* Choice B.

Did you fall for one of the trap answers? If you added 1 to both terms and squared them, you got Choice A. If you didn't add 1 to either term and instead squared them alone, you got Choice C. We want you to avoid a false sense of security. The mere fact that the answer you came up with is among the answer choices doesn't mean it's the correct answer (although if it's not there, it's definitely the wrong one).

5. Given that $a \neq 0$, solve for $\dfrac{a^2 a a^3}{a^4}$.

   (A) $a^{3/2}$

   (B) a^1

   (C) a^2

   (D) a^3

   (E) a^9

This is a relatively simple problem, after you know how to work with bases and exponents. When you multiply like bases, you add the exponents. Keeping in mind that a by itself is a^1, you get $a^{(2+1+3)} = a^6$. When dividing like bases, subtract the exponents like this: $a^{(6-4)} = a^2$. The answer isn't $a^{3/2}$; even the GRE folks wouldn't put an answer that nasty on the exam. Well, allow us to *renege* (take back) that statement. They *would* put an answer that nasty on the test; the answer just wouldn't be correct. *Correct Answer:* Choice C.

If you selected Choice B, you forgot that a is the same as a^1. You thought it was a^0 and added $a^{(2+0+3)}$ to get a^5. But any number to the zero power is 1 — not that number itself.

Yes, you guessed it: There's an explanation in the math review (Chapter 14 if you want the specifics) of working with bases and exponents. We suggest you go back and study it now.

6. $a - 3b + c = 15$; $6a - 2b + 6c = 23$. $b =$

   (A) $^{11}\!/_{15}$

   (B) 1

   (C) $^{15}\!/_{11}$

   (D) $^{-60}\!/_{11}$

   (E) $^{-67}\!/_{16}$

To find b, you must make the a and c variables drop out. That means you need to subtract one equation from the other until you're left only with b. Multiply the first equation by 6 so that you have $6a - 18b + 6c = 90$. Then subtract the second equation from that. The result looks like this:

$$6a - 18b + 6c = 90$$
$$-(6a - 2b + 6c = 23)$$

When you subtract, you change the signs on the second term. That means you have $6a - 6a$; the a's drop out. You have $-18b + 2b = -16b$. You have $6c - 6c$; the c's drop out. All you have now is $-16b = 67$. Divide both sides through by the -16: $b = {}^{-67}\!/_{16}$. *Correct Answer:* Choice E.

Part V
Getting into Analysis: Analytical Writing

The 5th Wave   By Rich Tennant

"Okay—now that the paramedic is here with the defibrillator and smelling salts, prepare to open your test booklets..."

In this part . . .

The GRE features two essay questions: One is Present Your Perspective on an Issue; the second is Analyze an Argument. Your creativity and erudition can shine on the perspective essay because the test-makers want to know what you think, what your take on the issue is. The second essay, alas, isn't as kind to your free-spirited side. With the analysis essay, the GRE essay gurus give you an issue and an argument and simply expect you to determine how well or poorly the topic is argued. They don't want you to provide your opinion of the issue at hand.

Chapter 20

Analytical Writing

. . . .

In This Chapter

▶ Reviewing the two types of essays on the GRE

▶ Knowing how to score with graders — and send them away screaming

▶ Picking up pointers for crafting stellar essays, paragraph by paragraph

. . . .

The best part about the Analytical Writing section is that you get it over with first. The GRE features two essays: a 45-minute essay called Present Your Perspective on an Issue and a 30-minute essay called Analyze an Argument.

 Different schools evaluate your performance on the Analytical Writing section differently. Some schools place little importance on it; some consider it critical. What's more, different graduate programs within the same school often prioritize this section quite differently. Before you pull your hair out over this portion of the GRE, investigate the policies of the schools or programs to which you're applying.

 The computer program used for the essay portion of the GRE is specially written just for this test. It has NO spell checker or grammar checker; you're responsible for your own mistakes. The program, thank goodness, does have a cut-and-paste function, so if you need to, you can swap parts of your essay around.

Your Opinion Counts: Present Your Perspective on an Issue

In the Present Your Perspective on an Issue portion, the GRE test-makers give you an issue and ask you to introduce and then explain your views on that issue. Fortunately for you, you always get two issues to choose from. So make it easy on yourself and pick the one you know the most about. The format goes a little something like this:

 Topic 1

"Criticism is the weakest tool an educator can use; praise is the strongest tool."

Topic 2

"Real wisdom can only be learned through living."

Directions: Write an essay on either topic in which you take a perspective on one of the quotes above. In developing your essay, use relevant reasons and statements that support your position while considering ways in which the statement may or may not hold true.

How do you get started? If your writer's block is as big as an Egyptian pyramid, you're welcome to use the following organized plan of attack. (*Note:* Much more detailed coverage of the steps to take when writing the essays comes later in this chapter. The following material is just an overview to get you going.)

- Begin by considering the issue or opinion: What exactly is the *point* that the statement makes? (In the preceding example of Topic 1, the point is that praise is a better teaching tool than criticism.)

- Specifically state your point of view on the opinion or issue: Do you agree or disagree? Also, do you think that the author has gone too far or not far enough?

- Support your point of view with examples from personal or professional experiences, readings, or other general background knowledge that you possess: What have you seen, done, or heard about that formed your opinion?

Full of Sound and Fury: Analyze an Argument

The second essay portion is called Analyze an Argument and consists of a paragraph with a specific conclusion or argument. Your job is to analyze that argument, and you don't get multiple arguments to choose from.

Directions: Discuss how well-reasoned you find this argument.

> "Many considerations point to the conclusion that Flint's restaurant should be changed from a youth-oriented, family-style restaurant to a Western-style saloon serving alcoholic beverages and featuring country bands. First, few families live in the area surrounding the restaurant; most have gone farther out into the suburbs. Second, Flint owns and operates two other saloons that have liquor licenses, making him experienced in the field. And finally, alcohol has a higher profit margin than food."

Discuss how compelling you find this argument. Analyze the reasoning presented, paying special attention to the evidence that supports it. Explain your analysis of the argument, addressing details that would make the argument more convincing or evidence that, in fact, weakens the conclusion.

Your opinion on the issue counts for zilch here; no one cares. Don't confuse the two writing samples. With the Analyze an Argument essay, you're not asked to express a personal preference (should Flint's change from a family restaurant to a saloon?). The fine men and women responsible for the GRE want you to analyze the author's argument. The only opinion you should give is whether you find the author's arguments valid and sound. Proceed by doing the following:

- Begin by stating the assumptions the author of the statement makes and analyzing whether you consider those assumptions sound or unsound.

- Identify evidence in the author's argument that strengthens or weakens his or her position.

- Provide outside counterexamples or supporting information to strengthen or weaken your analysis of the author's argument.

Half a Dozen Is Better than None: Scoring

For each essay, the GRE graders give you a score from 0 to 6. The final score on your score report is an average of two scores from separate graders. Zero is the lowest possible score. Almost the only way to receive a score that low is to not write on the assigned topic. (We know someone who wrote, "While pollution was important, our generation has that under control. What is really of concern to us is the economy, which I will address." Guess what her score was?) A score of 6 is considered outstanding. It demonstrates your grasp of writing with focus, developing a position on an issue, and identifying strengths and weaknesses of an argument.

Hunting for the next Hemingway: What evaluators look for

Apart from offering the evaluators huge bribes to score big, you need to take care of business by paying attention to the following advice. (If you're a GRE evaluator and you're reading this book, we were just kidding about the whole bribe thing . . . unless, of course — no, forget it. Really.)

✔ **Be obvious.** Make it clear to the evaluator what your opinion is on the issue or whether you think the argument is sound or unsound.

The evaluators hate nothing more than not knowing where you stand. Although good writers address both sides of an argument and anticipate objections and counterexamples, the evaluator must clearly know what you think. Students often fall for a common trap by being so politically correct or fair-minded that they fail to take and support a position. For the Present Your Perspective on an Issue essay, expressing an opinion that's different from that of the mainstream is perfectly okay (as long as you can write a strong essay explaining yourself). For the Analyze an Argument essay, if you think that the argument is weak and unsubstantiated, don't hesitate to say so.

Be careful to remember that the person grading your essay has opinions too. Being waaay too controversial may put you at risk for being judged too harshly. If you can back up your opinions, do so, but remember not to get too heated.

✔ **Make sure that your content is logical.** The evaluators want to be certain that your supporting statements are reasonable and feasible. For example, if you state that capital punishment is useless as a deterrent against crime, you need to cite instances in which people were executed and then explain that crime rates went up anyway. Don't give a wholly emotional argument such as, "Too many people are upset when there is an execution, and the other prisoners don't like it." Also, don't attack a person rather than an argument. Something like "The proponent of this plan of action is most likely a racist; he is certainly narrow-minded and not open to new situations" isn't a proper analysis. Go after the logic and reasoning of the argument itself, not the person making the argument.

Again, remember that the person reading your essay may be on the opposite side of the argument from the side you choose. If you say anyone supporting the argument is racist and narrow-minded, the grader may take that personally!

✔ **Clearly organize your essay.** Ding! Ding! Ding! You've hit upon probably the most important feature of an essay. The points must flow logically from one to another. As you're writing, stop every few minutes to reread what you've written. Writing without organizing is what we call diarrhea of the pen (or in this case, diarrhea of the keyboard). You can't just write down your thoughts as they come into your head.

Your exam computer has either a cut-and-paste or edit function — make use of it.

Grading: A foreign language with subtitles

The people who review your essays are known by many different names — graders, readers, evaluators — and they in turn have different names for essay grades. Here are the titles they bestow on your works (with the corresponding point totals in parentheses).

✔ Outstanding (6)

✔ Strong (5)

✔ Adequate (4)

✔ Limited (3)

✔ Seriously flawed (2)

✔ Fundamentally deficient (1)

✔ No essay (0)

✔ **Use proper diction, grammar, usage, and spelling.** The Analytical Writing section of the GRE isn't a test of grammar, spelling, and so on. Assessing your thinking and analytical skills — your critical reasoning — is the point of all this. But the graders are only human. (Interesting tidbit: The GMAT features two very similar essays. Those essays are actually graded by a computer, not by humans! However, your GRE essays are graded by two humans, at least for the time being.) Evaluators note and probably can't help being influenced by (at least subconsciously) any mistakes you make. Even the best analysis is hurt by numerous misspellings and grammar mistakes.

Providing pointless information: What drives evaluators crazy

A pointless paper is one that gets zero points. So far, the only ways to get a zero have been not to write an essay at all or to write an essay that's totally off subject (addressing the economy, for example, when the topic is pollution). But you can do several things, such as the following, to end up with next to nothing:

✔ **Avoid taking a stand.** Although arguing both sides of an issue or discussing strengths and weaknesses is good, you must — we repeat *must* — make your opinion or conclusion clear. Remember that no one answer is right or wrong. You can be against moms, apple pies, and puppies and still receive an outstanding score. Taking a stand and supporting your stand are the important factors.

✔ **Peregrinate and meander.** Sound like spices found in hot sauce, don't they? Well, your stomach will feel like you just drank some hot sauce when you get your essay scores if you let your thoughts wander around the page as you write. We have three words for you: Organization, organization, organization! Think of this suggestion as the GRE version of the real estate axiom location, location, location! Put your thoughts in logical order. The philosophy "Tell 'em what you're going to tell 'em, tell 'em, and then tell 'em what you told 'em" works well here. Don't put your conclusion in the middle paragraph and then remember a few more points to add at the end. Follow your (mental) outline.

✔ **Improperly use sesquipedalianism.** *Sesqui* means one and a half; for example, a sesquicentennial celebration is a 150-year anniversary. *Ped* means foot. ***Sesquipedalianism*** is using foot-and-a-half-long words . . . in other words, putting your foot in your mouth. You aren't paid by the word; you aren't credited by the syllable. Don't outsmart yourself by using big words. You may misuse a word or simply look idiotic, pompous, and pretentious — not the impression you want to give the evaluators.

✔ **Use off-color language, slang, or inappropriate humor.** You say you're the Seinfeld of your crowd? Well, there's no accounting for taste. The joke that absolutely cracked up your friends at the coffee shop doesn't necessarily appeal to the evaluators. Scatological humor (anything dealing with bodily functions and bathrooms) is definitely out. Even if a joke is pure and wholesome, it may drop like a lead balloon and annoy the evaluators. Play it safe: Be as dull and boring as the exam itself.

Presenting Your Perspective in a Well-Wrapped Package

Had enough generalities? Okay, now we get down to specifics. The following sections present a boilerplate or standard format you can use to practice writing a good Present Your Perspective on an Issue essay.

Paragraph one

Use your first sentence to address the issue specifically. For example, if the point is whether capital punishment does or does not serve as a deterrent to crime, your topic sentence may be, "Capital punishment succeeds in its stated purpose of deterring crime." In your topic sentence, make your perspective on the issue obvious.

The most egregious mistake you can make is to fail to present your perspective on the issue.

In your second sentence, show that you recognize the presence of two sides to the issue and that you, in fact, anticipate and address objections to your point of view while crushing them under the weight of your brilliant logic and reasoning. Here's a good second sentence: "Although capital punishment may have, in specific instances, failed to deter people from committing crimes, I argue that these instances are infrequent and insignificant." The rest of your first paragraph fleshes out these first lines. You may want to present how you came to this opinion by using personal examples: Did you work in a prison or do volunteer work with troubled youth? Have you taken classes in social welfare or law enforcement? Have you known someone who took a wrong turn in life and became a criminal?

One of the major, major, MAJOR points the evaluators consider is organization. A paragraph, by definition, is centered on one point — you should state and then support one point per paragraph. Don't take a scattered approach, introducing one point after another after another but not backing up any one of them. (To see an example of this flawed approach, look at the essay that scored a 2/1 in Chapter 21.)

First impressions count. A superstrong first sentence can cover a multitude of weaknesses later in the paper. If the evaluator is impressed by your opening gambit, he or she is probably going to score your paper higher than if you start off slowly and warm up. Ever hear of the halo effect in psychology? Roughly stated, it means that the person who thinks highly of you in one area transfers that high opinion of you over to other areas; your halo surrounds everything you do. Take the time to write a great first sentence or two, you little angel.

Paragraph two

Your second paragraph introduces a specific point that supports your argument. For example, the first sentence of your second paragraph may be, "In states such as Texas that have carried out the death penalty, violent crime has dropped significantly." See how we used a specific state in our argument? Good writing is specific, not vague like, "States with no death penalties have higher violent crime rates than states with death penalties." Oh yeah, says who?

You don't need to be 100-percent correct in your statements. You can fudge a little bit as long as what you're saying sounds feasible. The evaluator isn't going to head to the newspaper archives to find out exactly how many executions took place in each state last year.

The next sentences in the second paragraph support the topic sentence. Give more information on how the violent crime rate has dropped in Texas: Are murders down? Are rapes down? Are armed robberies down? Define your terms: What do you mean by violent crime? On what do you base your statements? Did you read this information, learn it in a class, or discover it in the course of doing your job? Again, remember that all the info in this paragraph should be on the same topic; don't introduce something new in the middle of the paragraph. Ideas should be grouped or clustered.

International students, here's your chance to shine. The evaluators, who are understandably bored by reading a thousand similar essays from American students, are intrigued if you discuss a problem from a foreign perspective. Talk, for instance, about how capital punishment has or hasn't worked in your own country.

Using strong transitions can greatly contribute to the organization and coherence of your essay. Don't just jump abruptly from one topic to another. Use transitioning statements. You may want to have a list of handy phrases in mind that you can draw upon as needed while writing your essay. Here are a few gems you can include on your list:

- Closely related to this idea is . . .
- Conversely . . .
- On the other hand . . .
- Similarly . . .

Paragraphs three and four

The third and fourth paragraphs give yet more supporting examples. You may say something like, "According to articles written by psychologists, interviews with criminals have consistently shown that the criminals did, in fact, stop to consider the consequences of their actions prior to committing the crimes and took precautions not to let their crimes develop to extremes, such as murder. In these instances, the criminals were deterred by the threat of capital punishment." List places in which you have read (or feasibly may have read, if you aren't being entirely truthful) such statements.

The middle of your essay often has more filler than the beginning and end. We're not suggesting that you add a bushel of babble just to fill up space, but if you know that your essay is heading toward only being about ten lines long, you have to flesh out your argument somewhere. The middle paragraphs are the place to bulk up your paper. Using quotations (even if somewhat made up, which you can ascribe to paraphrasing) can add quite a bit of information without sounding too much like filler. For example, you may want to say, "In an interview on a television news show, an expert criminologist said something roughly along these lines: 'Deterrence. . . .'" Be sure, however, to expand on what the expert said by giving your opinion of her opinion. Don't simply quote a bunch of people; the point of the essay is to present *your* perspective on an issue. The people you quote simply support your own perspective.

Paragraphs five and six

The next few paragraphs can either add additional points supporting your perspective or introduce new points that address the opposite perspective. Example: "There have been instances in which capital punishment did not serve as a deterrent. In medieval England, criminals were hanged, yet their hangings served as occasions for other criminals to work the crowds, committing even more crimes." Develop this topic a little further with one or two sentences.

If possible, turn the opposition around, showing that although the counterargument has some validity, it isn't as strong of a point of view as the one you're arguing. Example: "Today's executions are not social gatherings but closely monitored, private affairs that are reported on but not shown. Would-be criminals hear about the consequences and perhaps let their imaginations torment them with ideas of what those final few moments must have been like for the condemned. One's own imagination can perhaps be the most effective deterrent of all."

Paragraph seven

This paragraph pulls everything together. Don't merely rehash your point, saying something vague like, "Therefore, based on these arguments, it is my opinion that capital punishment works well in civilized societies." Instead, "Tell 'em what you told 'em." Continuing with the preceding example, we'd use this statement as our concluding sentence, "Therefore, although capital punishment occasionally fails to deter criminal behavior, statistical and empirical evidence found in dropping crime rates and in interviews with the criminals themselves demonstrates that capital punishment is an effective deterrent."

Time's up

Question: How long does this writing sample have to be?

Answer: To some extent, the length of the essay depends on your typing speed. In general, we suggest a minimum of six paragraphs with at least four sentences each. If you're a quick thinker and an even quicker typist, you may come up with an essay of six to eight paragraphs. If your essay is any longer than that, you're probably just inserting a lot of extraneous filler.

Although your sentences shouldn't be long enough for you to ramble and lose direction, don't rely only on short, declarative sentences. Don't let your essay read like, "I think capital punishment is effective. Studies have shown it can be a deterrent. There are many psychologists who agree." Vary your sentence structure. Make some sentences much longer and more complicated; make others short and distinct. While discussing an essay with a score of 6, one evaluator called the sentences "varied and complex."

You have 45 minutes for your first essay and 30 minutes for your second. That's actually quite a bit of time — especially if you've practiced writing these analytical samples previously. The more homework you do and the more essays you write in advance, the more comfortable you get with your organization and ability to write within the time constraints.

Analyzing an Argument in Six Paragraphs

Ever see one of those carpets with footsteps on it that dance instructors use to show novices the steps necessary to dance like Fred Astaire? Think of the following sections as steps on a carpet that can lead you to a good Analyze an Argument essay.

Paragraph one

The first paragraph states your analysis of the argument — whether you're in extreme agreement or disagreement. Like a good debater, your argument essay isn't necessarily your personal opinion. In the Analyze an Argument essay, you analyze, as the name implies, the strengths or weaknesses of the given argument.

Suppose the passage argues that putting a 25-cent tax on every bottle and can will provide an incentive for consumers to recycle bottles and cans and thus cut down on waste. Here's a good opening line: "This author's statement that a tax on bottles and cans will cut down on their waste is unsupported by evidence and is illogical given current recycling parameters set by the government and consumer behavior."

Continue the first paragraph by telling why, in your opinion, the argument is incorrect. Perhaps the author gives no facts or statistics to buttress his argument but appears to base it on unsound assumptions. Maybe the author argues from a personal point of view and doesn't address the broader concerns. Or perhaps the author assumes an ideal state that society hasn't yet reached.

We suggest that you have a grab bag of several refutations ready before you even get to the exam. The preceding examples are good; you can always attack a writer's source of facts or personal biases (although, as mentioned earlier in this chapter, you don't want to attack the writer himself). Think of several tactics that you use to shoot down an argument when you debate with friends (writing is easier if you use what comes naturally) and have them handy.

Paragraphs two, three, and four

Your second, third, and fourth paragraphs address each assumption that you believe the author makes. If the author assumes that a financial incentive is more important than any other type of incentive, say so and then either support or refute that assumption. If the author makes the assumption that people won't do what's right unless a law tells them to do so, state that assumption and then argue for or against it.

Paragraph five

In the fifth paragraph, provide possible counterexamples, flaws in the author's reasoning. If the author says that a tax of 25 cents per can and bottle would double the recycling rate, cite a situation in which increased taxes on bottles and cans haven't led to a significant increase in recycling. If the author states that people want to do the right thing but need a financial incentive, refute that argument by saying that a tax would have to be so large as to be prohibitive.

Even if you believe the author's argument is fundamentally sound and you support it, you should still be able to show the GRE evaluator that you can recognize that others may think flaws exist in the argument. Try something like this: "Although some people who hear this proposal may think that it is flawed due to the difficulty of passing any law, it is, in fact, feasible to have such laws passed on a smaller, more local scale. . . ."

Don't fall into your own trap. If you argue that the writer's assumption is based on personal logic, unsupported by facts, be sure that your refutation isn't based on personal logic, unsupported by facts. The last thing you need to do is point out the author's weakness and then make the reader chuckle as he marks you down for having the exact same weakness.

Paragraph six

In the final paragraph, give your conclusions. Once again, say whether the author makes a valid point or is just wasting everyone's time and briefly reiterate your reasons for thinking so.

If you can't think of a different way to write the material in the last paragraph so it's different than the first paragraph, skip the last paragraph. You don't want to parrot the first paragraph entirely. Instead, you want to summarize your writing, which doesn't involve repeating what you said earlier. Either put a new, neatly packaged slant on the material, or eliminate this paragraph entirely.

Time's up

Question: How long should an Analyze an Argument essay be?

Answer: You have less time for this essay (30 minutes) than for the other essay (45 minutes). Therefore, you'll probably write a little less in this section. Because you go more in depth analyzing the argument, each paragraph may be longer than those in the Present Your Perspective on an Issue essay, resulting in fewer paragraphs.

Keep in mind that everything you read in this chapter about length is simply a suggested format. No one length is right or wrong (although too short can definitely be a problem). We give you these pointers as guidelines you can use when practicing your essay writing. After a few practice essays, you'll know your comfort zone — the length of the passage you can write in the allotted time without going crazy.

And speaking of practice essays, go on to Chapter 21 and get ready to try a few on your own. Please write these essays using a word-processing program on a computer, because that's what you use to write them on the test day. Don't grab some lined paper and bang these essays out when you're in the library one afternoon. Sit down at your computer, type the essays (just like you have to do on the real test), and be sure to time yourself. For most people, the writing itself isn't that difficult; the hard part is coming up with a decent essay in just 30 minutes. After you finish, ask a friend to read the grading criteria in Chapter 21, evaluate each essay on a scale of 1 to 6 (you can't get a zero because you've actually written something), and discuss his or her reasoning with you.

Chapter 21

Do You Have the Write Stuff? Analytical Writing Practice Questions

*W*e promised you in the Introduction to this book that each lecture, including the practice question chapters, would take you about two hours. Going through the material in Chapter 20 should have taken you less than an hour. Use your remaining time to write two essays: your Present Your Perspective on an Issue essay and your Analyze an Argument essay.

Set your timer for 45 minutes for the perspective essay and 30 minutes for the analysis essay, but if you can't finish an essay, go ahead and ignore the time constraint — just this once. Finish your writing. After you finish, check out how long you took to complete the task. If you took 35 minutes for the 30-minute passage, you should be able to speed up your writing enough to cover that extra bit of inspiration that ate up 5 additional minutes. However, if you took 40 or 50 minutes for the 30-minute essay, you have to decide how you're going to cut your time down. Here are a few suggestions:

- ✔ **Cut out a few of the middle paragraphs.** Your most important points should be in the beginning and end of your essay. (Tell 'em what you're going to tell 'em, tell 'em, and then tell 'em what you told 'em.) Although you must provide some support for your thesis, you can present your supporting arguments in one or two paragraphs rather than three or four.

- ✔ **Limit the length of your paragraphs.** Many writers end up saying the same thing over and over. They keep making the same important point — they just say it slightly differently each time. Here's an example from one of our own students: "Community service instead of jail time serves no purpose because the criminals learn no lesson from their service. The people who commit the crimes don't take community service time seriously. There is nothing learned by the criminals who have to serve only community service time." Although the writer obviously has a point, she makes it three times — once would've been enough.

- ✔ **Have a boilerplate format and several refutations or support statements in your mind before you get to the test.** Coming up with some astonishingly creative piece of writing that blows away the evaluators would be nice, but creativity isn't as easy to come by as you may think. Besides, in the Analyze an Argument essay, your creativity is irrelevant because the graders are judging your analytical abilities. The Analytical Writing section as a whole tests your ability to reason well and to express your thoughts cogently and clearly. If you can come up with some basic support statements at home, you'll be pleasantly surprised at how well they work into an essay. For example, we almost always put in something about financial repercussions. Everything has financial repercussions. We also write about individual rights versus the power of the government; we can find something to say about that issue for nearly every topic. If timing is a problem, have a few stock phrases in mind that you can adapt to your essay as needed.

Ready? Computer fired up and cursor blinking at you? Fingers limber? Then set your timer and go!

Present Your Perspective on an Issue

Directions: Present your perspective on one of the two following issues using relevant reasons and examples to support your views. You have 45 minutes.

Topic 1

"Because society is always changing, laws should always change to reflect the times as well. In addition, laws should be open to interpretation based on the facts of each individual circumstance."

Topic 2

"School uniforms would decrease the violence in schools and increase the potential for learning."

Answer explanations

Following are three sample answers to the first topic. An evaluator would probably give these three essays a 6/5, a 4/3, and a 2/1, respectively.

Sample answer one: Score 6 (outstanding) or 5 (strong)

My French grandmother was fond of saying, "Plus ça change, plus c'est la même chose," which roughly means that the more something seems to change, the more it actually remains the same. This saying is appropriate when considering the laws of our nation. By changing or updating laws and statutes, by being flexible in their interpretation, we fundamentally remain the same: We continue to be fair and just, as the creators of the laws intended. In law, considering the spirit of the law is often necessary before creating the letter of the law.

A prime example of the necessity for flexibility is the Three Strikes Law in California. This law is paraphrased as "Three strikes, you're out!" by police officials and other law-enforcement personnel who have supported it whole-heartedly. The law states that a person who previously has been convicted of two crimes will be sent to prison for life when convicted of a third crime. Newspapers are fond of reporting stories of a transient who receives a life sentence for stealing a candy bar from a gas station, or a young man who goes to prison for life for smoking a marijuana joint in public. Although one may argue there are, in fact, incorrigible criminals, ones who will continue to commit crime after crime despite all legal deterrents, common sense would dictate that spending twenty, thirty, or even fifty years in prison is not a suitable punishment for stealing a 59-cent bag of chips.

Some laws have never changed, yet they are rarely enforced. Every time a new law goes into effect, news reporters present human-interest stories about unusual laws that have officially never been repealed. There is the example of "It's illegal to walk on the sidewalks of Philadelphia carrying goldfish," or "It is a crime to sing to your horses in the hearing of others." Every state and every county has a number of these laws that newspapers and television stations trot out occasionally for the amusement of the audiences on slow news days.

And what should we make of the so-called "Blue Laws," laws that attempt to mandate morality? In certain counties, it's illegal to sell or purchase alcoholic beverages on Sunday. In the county in Indiana where I grew up, it was against the law to dance on Sundays. Of course, no one ever enforced that statute; it was simply a curiosity. The question is raised, therefore, do we need to enact new laws, rescind the old ones, or practice a policy of benign neglect, simply not enforcing those laws we consider unnecessary? And if we neglect certain laws, who gets to choose which laws are enforced and which are ignored? By being more flexible in the passage and creation of the laws, we are able to avoid this dilemma.

Many years ago, England had two court systems: The courts of law (which is why lawyers are called "attorneys at law") and the courts of equity. The courts of equity attempted to "make known the King's conscience," showing mercy and treating cases equitably even when such treatment was against the law. Both courts were merged years ago but leave a legacy of flexibility and moral justice in their interpretation of the law. A legal system that cannot change with the times *will* not survive, and a legal system that will not treat cases fairly and justly *should* not survive.

Reader comments on the 6/5 essay

This essay presents an excellent answer to the question. The writer uses interesting, intriguing comments (such as the opening with the grandmother's French saying); strong, evocative vocabulary (such as "incorrigible" and "trot out"); and a good variety of sentence structures. (The use of the occasional question was particularly effective.)

The writer's opinion is clear from the start and is supported by well-reasoned and thoroughly developed examples. The three examples are separated, yet they flow together well via the use of good transitions. The ending is perhaps a bit dramatic, but leaves no doubt as to the author's opinion.

Sample answer two: Score 4 (adequate) or 3 (limited)

Laws must change when Society changes. This is true for all types of laws, the major laws and the minor laws. This is true for all types of Societies, the so called First World, and the so-called Third World. This is true for all types of situations, from the serious to the silly to the macabre.

An example of when a law must change is the death penalty. Many years ago, condemned prisoners were executed routinely. Such executions became major events, almost parties, with the public making an excursion to watch the hanging. The irony, of course, is that the huge crowds at the execution attracted additional criminals who then committed more crimes (theft, pickpocketing, assault) and perpetated the cycle. Today, while there are less executions, they have become media events. We don't attend the executions in person, but we live through them vicariously, watching them on tv. When Timothy McVee, the Oklahoma City bomber, was given a lethal injection, the tv stations carried a minute-by-minute report. The amount of money and time and energy that was put into this could have been better spent elsewhere.

A second reason laws must be flexible is in time of war or social upheaval. Take, for example, the 1960's. The United States had a sea change during that decade. Many more things were acceptable socially then than had ever been before, and the laws had to change to reflect that fact. The possession of certain drugs became much less serious than it had been before. People weren't sentenced to twenty years for *using* drugs, just for *pushing* them. Today even more liberal attitudes towards drugs enable people to use them legally, as in the case of glaucoma or AIDS patients who smoke pot.

Traffic laws are a less serious, but still good, example of when laws should change. The speed limit in downtown New York must obviously be less than that in the outskirts of Podunk, Idaho (my apologies to the Podunkians!). Many people in Wyoming and other sparsely-populated Western states fought against having a federally-mandated speed limit of 55 on the freeways, argueing that in their areas, 65 or even 75 would be more logical. This is an example of the need for a change to meet the needs of a local community or Society. The same is true for the age at which youngsters can get a license, as they are more mature earlier now than before.

In conclusion, laws are not static because people are not static. We change from decade to decade, and from locale to locale. While it is important to adhere to the Declaration of Independence's statement that "all men are created equal," and thus should have equal rights, not all times are created equal, and thus should not have equal laws.

Reader comments on the 4/3 essay

This is a generally acceptable response. The writer presents an unequivocal answer to the question and uses some good vocabulary ("macabre," "vicariously"). In addition, the length is good, with three well-organized examples.

The essay does have weaknesses that prevent it from receiving a higher score. There are mistakes in grammar ("less" instead of "fewer," "so-called" once with a hyphen and once without) and spelling ("perpetated," "argueing,"), as well as instances of inappropriate humor ("my apologies to the Podunkians!"). In addition, some concepts were introduced without being fully developed, such as the final sentence in the traffic paragraph.

Sample answer three: Score 2 (seriously flawed) or 1 (fundamentally deficient)

"Because Society is always changing, laws should always change to reflect the times as well." This is a very true statement. Nothing ever remains exacly the same, and things change all the time. Isn't it logical to think that the laws should change as people and other situations change? My example the American society. We are much more ethnical diverse than we were a generation or two ago, and our laws have guaranteed this diversity. Old laws said that, for example, African-American people were not allowed in certain clubs or given certain jobs and this of course was wrong. Now there are laws to show how Society has changed and accepted this variety of people. Maybe someday there will be laws needed to protect White people who can't get jobs neither.

"In addition, laws should be open to interpretation based on the facts of each individual circumstance." This also is true. What about car accidents? If a person has an honest accident and hits and kills someone because he just lost control, that's a lot different than if he has been drunk and lost control that way and killed someone. It's not fair to send someone to prison for life because he had one horrible minute, but maybe it is fair to send someone to prison for life because he made the choice to drink and drive, the wrong choice.

In conclusion, I agree totally with both parts of the statement above. People need to realize that our Society changes and because laws are meant to protect Society, those laws must also change, too.

Reader comments on the 2/1 essay

The writer presents a clear response to the question, both at the beginning and the end of the essay. The writer, however, simply repeats the issue and makes a general statement of agreement.

Although a few examples are given to support the writer's opinion, the organization of the essay isn't developed well. The writer makes the comment that, "Now there are laws to show how Society has changed. . . ." The quality of the essay would be improved were the writer to add more examples and explain each example more fully. The closing statement in the second paragraph appears to introduce a new topic, which isn't fully covered.

Poor spelling ("exacly") and grammar ("much more ethnical diverse") hurt the response as well. Although the writer's opinion is still understandable, these errors contribute to the low score.

Analyze an Argument

Directions: Discuss how well-reasoned you find this argument. You have 30 minutes to write your analysis.

> The following appeared in an in-house memo sent from a marketing director to the editorial department of a television news station.

> "Our research shows that when the news director comes on screen at the end of the newscast to present his perspective on an issue, many viewers switch stations or turn off the television entirely. Besides losing viewers, which lowers our ability to charge top dollar for advertising spots, we are wasting extra time that we could be filling with more ads. In addition, people tell us that they feel editorials are best read in the newspaper, not heard on television. Therefore, we recommend stopping all editorials at the ends of newscasts."

Answer explanations

Following are three sample answers. An evaluator would probably give these three essays a 6/5, a 4/3, and a 2/1, respectively.

Sample answer one: Score 6 (outstanding) or 5 (strong)

The marketing director concludes that the news station should stop all editorials because viewership decreases when the news director presents his perspective on an issue at the end of the newscast. The memo argues that when people don't watch the end of the newscast, the station loses advertising revenue.

The conclusion is based on a number of questionable assumptions. First, the director recommends that the station stop all editorials at the end of newscasts because people are turning off what is currently offered. By proposing that the station eliminate *all* editorials, the memo assumes that viewers would not watch any kind of editorial. It could be that viewers simply don't like the news director or are turned off by the "perspective on an issue" format.

Second, the director claims that the time devoted to the current editorial could be sold to advertisers. He assumes, then, that people who turn off the television or switch stations when the news director comes on will not do so when an advertisement comes on in the editorial's place. If viewers stop watching the station when they know the news is over, they will probably do the same when commercials come on instead of the editorial. When advertisers find out that people are not watching their commercials, they will pay the station less.

Third, the director notes that people tell the station's marketing team that editorials are best read in the newspaper, not heard on television. As with any survey, this finding assumes that the people who are saying these things are representative of the larger population. In other words, the marketing department assumes that these "people" are representative of the station's viewers. The memo is vague about the identity of these people. Perhaps they are not viewers at all and, therefore, cannot be used to represent the television viewing audience. The director also fails to mention how numerous these people are and does not include any information about how many people may have expressed the opposite opinion to the marketing team. An analogous situation: Just because some people support a political candidate does not mean that others don't prefer somebody else. In addition, the people who said that editorials are best read in the newspaper could have been people who are more oriented towards reading and writing. There is a good chance that these people wrote letters to the station. If station employees had called viewers during the newscast, they may have received many responses claiming that editorials are better to watch on TV than read.

Finally, that director bases his argument on making money for the news station. This proposal assumes that the purpose of a news station is to make money. The editorials may not generate as much advertising revenue as other television presentations would, but the editorials are better to include if one assumes that the purpose of a news station is to inform viewers and stimulate their thinking.

To improve the argument, the news director needs to address the above issues. He needs evidence that shows that viewers would turn off any kind of editorial at the end of the newscast. He also needs to demonstrate that viewers would watch advertisements after the presentation of news. He should also clarify how the marketing team received the comments about editorials in newspapers. Ideally, the director should show that such comments were generated by a scientific survey of people who actually watch the news station. The director should also articulate that the primary aim of the news station is to attract viewers and generate revenue.

Reader comments on the 6/5 essay

This very strong response presents a coherent, well-organized, direct analysis that introduces and fully develops the various points. It identifies four central issues that weaken or even undermine the argument, and it supports each point with evidence before summarizing in a brief conclusion. The language, grammar, spelling, and general writing skills also contribute to the excellence of this essay.

Sample answer two: Score 4 (adequate) or 3 (limited)

This editorial is relatively well-reasoned, although flawed in some aspects. The primary weakness, in my opinion, is found at the beginning, where the memo states, "Our research has shown. . . ." without specifying what that research is. Did someone poll viewers who regularly watched the show? Did someone send out a questionaire which was returned only by a small percentage of people, some of whom did not regularly watch the news? How were the questions phrased by the researcher (as we all know, a question can easily beg the answer, be skewed so as to direct the response in the direction the questioner wants it to go). A good editorial will state the basis for the conclusions it makes.

The argument has inspecificity. Nowhere does the editorial say why the viewers switch stations. Maybe they don't like that particular news director. The station can experiment by having the editorials read by others on the staff, by reporters, or even by the public at large. There are some stations where I live that do that, have local people at the end of the newscasts tell their opinions. Many of my friends, at least, tune in to watch what their peers have to say.

Is the purpose of the last few minutes of a newscast to sell ads? Maybe, if there were no editorial, there would be an extra two minutes of news reporting, not of advertisements. There are already so many ads in a newscast as it is; more would possibly alienate the viewers even more than the editorial does. Also, I believe there is an FCC mandate as to how many minutes per hour or half hour can be commercials, at least in prime time. If the station didn't have the editorial, but ran commericials, they may acceed this limit.

Reader comments on the 4/3 essay

This response is adequate. The organization is acceptable, although it would be improved by the use of transitional phrases. The writer appears to have a basic understanding of the argument but doesn't fully develop his comments except in a personal vein. A few basic spelling errors ("acceed," "questionaire") also detract from the paper. Finally, the lack of a coherent conclusion shifts this paper from a possible 5 to a 4 or 3.

Sample answer three: Score 2 (seriously flawed) or 1 (fundamentally deficient)

The reasoning in this arguement is not well-reasoned. The writer didn't convince me of their point at all. He doesn't talk about the possibility of moving the editorial, maybe putting the perspective at the beginning of the newscast, when people are probly more interested than at the end when they've already heard everything they tuned in for. He doesn't say anything about maybe having the editorials paid for by an advertisement. He doesn't cover the possibility of the fact that the government considers some editorials public service anouncements. He doesn't go into enough detail to make a good case on anything.

If I was the memo-writer, I would also talk about how the editorials maybe appeal to a more educated, higher-class (to use a politically incorrect term) audience, one that maybe spends more money on the products. Like some sitcoms appeals to a different audience (some to older viewers or white viewers, some to younger more hip maybe black viewers) the newscast can appeal to more educated viewers with the editorials.

Reader comments on the 2/1 essay

This essay is seriously hurt by the lack of organization. Ideas are introduced but not fully developed before new ideas are added. No one argument or theme is developed. There are many errors in grammar (pronoun agreement, saying "The writer" and "their" and "If I was") and spelling ("arguement," "probly," "anouncements"), and the essay demonstrates a lack of variety in its sentence structure.

The writer shows little ability to analyze the argument and gives no support for the points made. Instead, the writer presents a personal opinion, giving his own views rather than analyzing and evaluating the points made by the author of the memo.

Part VI
It All Comes Down to This: Full-Length Practice GREs

The 5th Wave   By Rich Tennant

REAL LIFE APPLICATION OF CORRECT ANTONYM IDENTIFICATION

"Let's see-your listed salad dressings are 'Vinaigrette', 'Creamy Garlic', and 'Hydrochloric Acid'. Hmm, I think I'll go with the 'Hydrochloric Acid'."

In this part . . .

Just when you think your brain can't be stuffed with one more factoid, relief is at hand. You finally get to download some of the information you've been inputting for this test. Trust us, you'll feel better once you let it all out.

This unit has two Verbal and Math exams that are as close to the actual GRE as we can get without having briefcase-bearing barristers pounding on our doors. We take these tests seriously, and you should, too. Do them under actual test conditions, sitting in a quiet room and timing yourself. Open books are definitely out (sorry!). We have spies everywhere; we'll know if you cheat on these tests. You'll hear a knocking at your door one foggy night . . .

After you've done your duty on these practice exams, you'll have a good time going through the answer explanations, which are nowhere as dry and stuffy as the exams themselves.

Chapter 22

How to Ruin a Perfectly Good Day, Part I: Practice Exam 1

● ●

*Y*ou're now ready to take a sample GRE. Like the actual GRE, the following exam consists of one 30-minute Verbal section, one 45-minute Math section, one 30-minute essay, and one 45-minute essay. The actual GRE may also include one additional Verbal or Math section, which doesn't count toward your GRE score. (The test won't include an extra Analytical Writing essay.) Because this section won't be identified as a test that isn't scored, you must give every section your best effort. You may also get an extra section that will be identified as experimental, meaning that it won't affect your score. Here, we don't include an experimental section because we don't want to put you through any more anguish and agony than absolutely necessary. You're welcome.

You're familiar with the question formats by now, so you shouldn't need to read the instructions for each specific question type when you take the actual GRE. Nevertheless, take as much time as you need to go through the computer tutorial, which precedes the timed part of the exam. Don't start the test until you're comfortable with how to scroll down passages, graphs, and figures; mark an answer; and turn the clock off and on. The tutorial covers these topics, along with some other basic information. Even if you're extremely comfortable with using the computer to take the GRE, use the tutorial time to block the outside world from your mind and focus on the task ahead of you.

Please take this practice test under normal exam conditions and approach it as if it were the real GRE. This is serious stuff here!

1. **Work when you won't be interrupted (even though you'd probably welcome any distractions).**

2. **Use scratch paper that's free of any prepared notes.**

   On the actual GRE, you'll receive blank scratch paper before your test begins. You'll have a little time before the clock starts to jot down a few notes and formulas and a series of columns of numbers or letters that you may want to use to help you eliminate answer choices, but you may not whip out a ready-made version of such test-taking aids.

3. **Turn on the clock at the beginning of each test section and be very careful on the first five questions. Remember that these earlier questions contribute more to your score than do the later questions.**

4. **Guess and move on if a question is truly impossible for you.**

   You don't have the option of skipping the question and coming back to it. The computer won't let you move on until you mark and confirm an answer.

5. **Make sure that you get to the end of the test section (30th question for Verbal and 28th question for Math).**

   If you have to, make wild guesses to reach the end before time expires. Unanswered questions will hurt your score more than incorrect answers will.

6. **If you get to the last question before time expires, you can either answer it right away and finish your test early or relax for a while and mark your answer shortly before time expires.**

   You can't use the time to go back and check your work, so do the former if you feel pumped up and you're on a roll. Give yourself the breather if you feel bombarded by the test.

7. **Don't leave your desk while the clock is running on any section.**

8. **You'll be given a one-minute break after the first section and the option to take a ten-minute break after the second section.**

   Try to simulate these conditions when you take this practice test.

After completing this entire practice test, check your answers with the answer key at the end of this chapter. Use Chapter 23 to go through the answer explanations to *all* the questions, not just the ones you miss. There's a plethora of worthwhile information in the answer explanations — material that provides a good review of everything you went over in the previous chapters. We even toss in a few good jokes to keep you somewhat sane.

Answer Sheet

Begin with Number 1 for each new section. If any sections have fewer than 50 questions, leave the extra spaces blank.

Verbal Section

1. (A) (B) (C) (D) (E)	26. (A) (B) (C) (D) (E)
2. (A) (B) (C) (D) (E)	27. (A) (B) (C) (D) (E)
3. (A) (B) (C) (D) (E)	28. (A) (B) (C) (D) (E)
4. (A) (B) (C) (D) (E)	29. (A) (B) (C) (D) (E)
5. (A) (B) (C) (D) (E)	30. (A) (B) (C) (D) (E)
6. (A) (B) (C) (D) (E)	31. (A) (B) (C) (D) (E)
7. (A) (B) (C) (D) (E)	32. (A) (B) (C) (D) (E)
8. (A) (B) (C) (D) (E)	33. (A) (B) (C) (D) (E)
9. (A) (B) (C) (D) (E)	34. (A) (B) (C) (D) (E)
10. (A) (B) (C) (D) (E)	35. (A) (B) (C) (D) (E)
11. (A) (B) (C) (D) (E)	36. (A) (B) (C) (D) (E)
12. (A) (B) (C) (D) (E)	37. (A) (B) (C) (D) (E)
13. (A) (B) (C) (D) (E)	38. (A) (B) (C) (D) (E)
14. (A) (B) (C) (D) (E)	39. (A) (B) (C) (D) (E)
15. (A) (B) (C) (D) (E)	40. (A) (B) (C) (D) (E)
16. (A) (B) (C) (D) (E)	41. (A) (B) (C) (D) (E)
17. (A) (B) (C) (D) (E)	42. (A) (B) (C) (D) (E)
18. (A) (B) (C) (D) (E)	43. (A) (B) (C) (D) (E)
19. (A) (B) (C) (D) (E)	44. (A) (B) (C) (D) (E)
20. (A) (B) (C) (D) (E)	45. (A) (B) (C) (D) (E)
21. (A) (B) (C) (D) (E)	46. (A) (B) (C) (D) (E)
22. (A) (B) (C) (D) (E)	47. (A) (B) (C) (D) (E)
23. (A) (B) (C) (D) (E)	48. (A) (B) (C) (D) (E)
24. (A) (B) (C) (D) (E)	49. (A) (B) (C) (D) (E)
25. (A) (B) (C) (D) (E)	50. (A) (B) (C) (D) (E)

Math Section

1. (A) (B) (C) (D) (E) 26. (A) (B) (C) (D) (E)
2. (A) (B) (C) (D) (E) 27. (A) (B) (C) (D) (E)
3. (A) (B) (C) (D) (E) 28. (A) (B) (C) (D) (E)
4. (A) (B) (C) (D) (E) 29. (A) (B) (C) (D) (E)
5. (A) (B) (C) (D) (E) 30. (A) (B) (C) (D) (E)
6. (A) (B) (C) (D) (E) 31. (A) (B) (C) (D) (E)
7. (A) (B) (C) (D) (E) 32. (A) (B) (C) (D) (E)
8. (A) (B) (C) (D) (E) 33. (A) (B) (C) (D) (E)
9. (A) (B) (C) (D) (E) 34. (A) (B) (C) (D) (E)
10. (A) (B) (C) (D) (E) 35. (A) (B) (C) (D) (E)
11. (A) (B) (C) (D) (E) 36. (A) (B) (C) (D) (E)
12. (A) (B) (C) (D) (E) 37. (A) (B) (C) (D) (E)
13. (A) (B) (C) (D) (E) 38. (A) (B) (C) (D) (E)
14. (A) (B) (C) (D) (E) 39. (A) (B) (C) (D) (E)
15. (A) (B) (C) (D) (E) 40. (A) (B) (C) (D) (E)
16. (A) (B) (C) (D) (E) 41. (A) (B) (C) (D) (E)
17. (A) (B) (C) (D) (E) 42. (A) (B) (C) (D) (E)
18. (A) (B) (C) (D) (E) 43. (A) (B) (C) (D) (E)
19. (A) (B) (C) (D) (E) 44. (A) (B) (C) (D) (E)
20. (A) (B) (C) (D) (E) 45. (A) (B) (C) (D) (E)
21. (A) (B) (C) (D) (E) 46. (A) (B) (C) (D) (E)
22. (A) (B) (C) (D) (E) 47. (A) (B) (C) (D) (E)
23. (A) (B) (C) (D) (E) 48. (A) (B) (C) (D) (E)
24. (A) (B) (C) (D) (E) 49. (A) (B) (C) (D) (E)
25. (A) (B) (C) (D) (E) 50. (A) (B) (C) (D) (E)

Analytical Writing: Present Your Perspective on an Issue

Time: 45 minutes

One essay

Directions: Present and explain your view on one of the following issues. Although there is no one right or wrong response to either issue, be sure to consider various points of view as you explain the reasons behind your own perspective.

Topic 1

"Complete disclosure of facts by a country's leaders is not always in the best interest of the public."

Topic 2

"The right to bear arms is not the direct cause of the level of violence in a country."

Choose a topic and justify your position by using examples from your personal or professional experience, reading, or general observation.

Go on to next page

Go on to next page

Go on to next page

Go on to next page

Analytical Writing: Analyze an Argument

Time: 30 minutes

One essay

Directions: Critique the following argument. Identify evidence that will strengthen or weaken the argument, point out assumptions underlying the argument, and offer counterexamples to the argument.

The following appeared in a memo sent by an outside efficiency expert hired by a firm to evaluate employee performance.

"In the six months that I have been watching the employees, their productivity has increased by over 12 percent. Therefore, my recommendation is that the employees either be watched by, or think that they are watched by, an outside evaluator at all times from this point on."

Discuss the merits of the previous argument. Analyze the evidence used as well as the general reasoning. Present points that would strengthen the argument or make it more compelling.

Go on to next page

Go on to next page

Go on to next page

Go on to next page

Verbal Section

Time: 30 minutes

30 questions

Choose the best answer to each question. Blacken the corresponding oval on the answer grid.

Directions: Choose the answer choice most nearly opposite in meaning to the question word.

1. SAGACIOUS

   (A) isolated

   (B) erudite

   (C) ignorant

   (D) ludicrous

   (E) short

2. INEPT

   (A) profane

   (B) skilled

   (C) prolific

   (D) thrifty

   (E) indigenous

Directions: Each of the following questions features a pair of words or phrases in capital letters, followed by five pairs of words or phrases in lowercase letters. Choose the lowercase pair that most closely expresses the same relationship as that of the uppercase pair.

3. SWAGGER : ARROGANCE ::

   (A) swindle : veracity

   (B) renege : consistency

   (C) orchestrate : harmony

   (D) wheedle : certitude

   (E) stagger : imbalance

4. SHEAF : PAPERS ::

   (A) discourse : arguments

   (B) collection : items

   (C) cygnet : swans

   (D) quiver : arrows

   (E) quarter : dimes

Go on to next page

Directions: Each of the following sentences has two blanks indicating that words or phrases are omitted. Choose the answer that best completes the sentence.

5. The earliest models of bicycles, - - - - in the late 1700s, were called "walking" bicycles as the only way to - - - - the vehicle was to use the feet to push both rider and bicycle forward.

   (A) constructed . . . propel

   (B) introduced . . . stop

   (C) advocated . . . move

   (D) implemented . . . steer

   (E) built . . . develop

6. Reluctant to - - - - the man as the complete fraud she suspected him to be, Jill chose to attack the weaker points of his theory, - - - - them one by one.

   (A) denounce . . . debunking

   (B) ridicule . . . proving

   (C) castigate . . . applauding

   (D) expose . . . strengthening

   (E) recommend . . . disseminating

Directions: Each passage is followed by questions pertaining to that passage. Read the passage and answer the questions based on information stated or implied in that passage.

Line   The Canyon Pintado Historic District in northwest Colorado was occupied by numerous prehistoric peoples for as long as 11,000 years, including the Fremont culture that left behind
(05) rock-art sites. Fremont rock art has recurring motifs that link it to other cultures in that time period. Strange humanlike figures with broad shoulders, no legs, and horned headdresses are similar to the Barrier Canyon style of southwest-
(10) ern Utah. Figures with shields or shieldlike bodies are like Fremont figures from the San Rafael region of Southern Utah.

Some figures have large, trapezoidal-shaped bodies, sticklike legs, trapezoidal heads, and in many cases, are adorned with necklaces. Another (15) motif of the Fremont culture is the mountain sheep, with graceful curvilinear horns. Designs such as concentric circles, snakelike lines, hands, corn plants, and rows of dots are also often found in Fremont art. A unique figure in Douglas Creek is (20) Kokopelli, the humpbacked flute player of Anasazi mythology. His presence indicates some kind of tie with the more advanced culture of the Four Corners area.

7. The author mentions the connection to the culture of the Four Corners area to

   (A) challenge the claim that the Fremont culture was the most advanced of its time.

   (B) refute the assertion that Fremont rock art merely copied art from other cultures.

   (C) suggest that the mimicking of art from other cultures may indicate contact between the cultures.

   (D) prove the relationship between art and the level of civilization.

   (E) ridicule the suggestion that there is a connection between artistic images and warfare success.

8. The passage supplies information for answering which of the following questions?

   (A) What significance is there to the lack of legs on the humanlike figures?

   (B) What was the purpose of the rock art?

   (C) Were curved lines absent in Fremont rock art?

   (D) How much of the artwork was sacred and how much was secular?

   (E) What other cultures besides those in the Four Corners influenced Fremont rock art?

Go on to next page

Line   The war that many people commonly refer to as the Civil War has had many appellations throughout history. While the war was being fought, the South labeled it the "War Between the
(05) States." Sundry Southerners used the term "The Second American Revolutionary War," emphasizing their belief that they were attempting to secede from what they considered a tyrannical federal government.
(10)   One primary etiology of the Civil War may have been the 1820 Missouri Compromise. The compromise admitted Missouri into the Union as a slave state, while accepting Maine as a free state. The compromise also banned slavery in all
(15) western territories. However, it wasn't until 1860 when Abraham Lincoln, who was known to be against slavery, was elected President that South Carolina withdrew from the Union. At that time, the president was James Buchanan, who did not
(20) fight against the secession. By 1860, six more states had withdrawn, banding together to form the Confederate States of America, which eventually was comprised of 11 states. Their president was Jefferson Davis; the Confederacy's capital,
(25) which originally was Montgomery, Alabama, moved to Richmond, Virginia.
   The first battle of the Civil War was fought at Bull Run in Virginia. Schoolchildren today are still told how the local people treated the battle as if
(30) it were a social event, taking picnic baskets and sitting on top of the hill to watch the fighting. The Federal troops lost the battle and had to retreat. Later, there was a Second Battle of Bull Run, which the Union lost as well.
(35)   General Ulysses S. Grant, later president of the United States, gained fame as a great Civil War strategist. When he captured Vicksburg, Mississippi, he made it possible for the Union to control all the Mississippi River, a critical point
(40) given that goods were often shipped along that river. The Union, therefore, was able to prevent materials from reaching the Confederate troops, a situation which many historians considered essential to the quick termination of the war.
(45) Grant had the honor of receiving the surrender of the South from General Robert Lee at Appomattox Courthouse, near Richmond, Virginia, on April 9, 1865. It was only five days later that President Lincoln was assassinated.
(50)   The Civil War was the first war to have photographers, leaving to posterity the real evidence of the battles. This war also was more industrialized than many other wars, employing railroads, iron ships, and submarines.

9. All of the following were discussed in the passage EXCEPT

(A) the causes of the Civil War.

(B) the South after the Civil War.

(C) the various names of the Civil War.

(D) great generals of the Civil War.

(E) strategies that won the Civil War.

10. The author would best strengthen his point in the first paragraph by doing which of the following?

(A) Supplying alternate names that the Northerners called the Civil War.

(B) Explaining the ambiguity of the term "Civil" War.

(C) Listing reasons the South wanted to secede from the Union.

(D) Discussing the actions the North had taken that the South considered tyrannical.

(E) Refuting the common misconception that slavery issues caused the Civil War.

11. By stating, "It was only five days later that President Lincoln was assassinated," the author implies that

(A) Southern troops fighting the war had made their way to the capital seeking revenge on Lincoln.

(B) The president was improperly protected because the guards believed that when the war had ended, there was little threat to Lincoln.

(C) The course of history, especially the reconstruction of the country and rehabilitation of the former slaves, would have been greatly altered had Lincoln lived to serve out his term.

(D) There may have been a connection between the end of the war and the assassination.

(E) The former Confederate government wanted a chance to place its people in positions of power.

Go on to next page

12. Which of the following statements would most logically follow the last sentence of the passage?

    (A) The photographs proved that the Civil War was the bloodiest war ever fought on American soil.

    (B) The new technology, especially submarines, gave the North an advantage in the War that the less industrialized South did not possess.

    (C) Many of the photographs are kept in the Smithsonian Museum in Washington, D.C.

    (D) People not fighting directly in the war were, for the first time, able to comprehend the reality of the war.

    (E) The railroad technology developed during this time led eventually to the expansion of the West.

Directions: Choose the answer choice most nearly opposite in meaning to the question word.

---

13. INTRANSIGENT

    (A) tawdry

    (B) vulnerable

    (C) flexible

    (D) querulous

    (E) precocious

14. EXTROVERTED

    (A) bombastic

    (B) unnecessary

    (C) shy

    (D) stationary

    (E) ubiquitous

Directions: Each of the following questions features a pair of words or phrases in capital letters, followed by five pairs of words or phrases in lowercase letters. Choose the lowercase pair that most closely expresses the same relationship as that of the uppercase pair.

---

15. HARDY : STRONG ::

    (A) puny : grandiose

    (B) unruly : disorganized

    (C) stubborn : flexible

    (D) dubious : ineligible

    (E) lucid : clouded

16. VACILLATE : INDECISIVE ::

    (A) select : certain

    (B) hesitate : steadfast

    (C) repress : straightforward

    (D) affect : candid

    (E) contemplate : incurious

Directions: Each of the following sentences has one or two blanks indicating that words or phrases are omitted. Choose the answer that best completes the sentence.

---

17. To criticize a new employee for working slowly may actually be - - - -, as the employee becomes so flustered that he slows down even further in an attempt to concentrate on his task.

    (A) counterproductive

    (B) praiseworthy

    (C) worthwhile

    (D) essential

    (E) reasonable

18. Solar power is - - - - by its - - - - as a way to protect the environment, increase energy independence, reduce electricity bills, and protect against blackouts and accidents within the energy grid.

    (A) derided . . . supporters

    (B) denounced . . . champions

    (C) touted . . . advocates

    (D) lampooned . . . beneficiaries

    (E) lauded . . . detractors

Go on to next page

Directions: Choose the answer choice most nearly opposite in meaning to the question word.

19. PROGNOSTICATE

    (A) recall

    (B) exasperate

    (C) curtail

    (D) abhor

    (E) confiscate

20. CRYPTIC

    (A) destructive

    (B) craven

    (C) picayune

    (D) multifaceted

    (E) frank

21. ABSTAIN

    (A) sneer

    (B) participate

    (C) approximate

    (D) meander

    (E) infuriate

Directions: Each of the following questions features a pair of words or phrases in capital letters, followed by five pairs of words or phrases in lowercase letters. Choose the lowercase pair that most closely expresses the same relationship as that of the uppercase pair.

22. STAPLE : ATTACH ::

    (A) button : sew

    (B) carpet : impede

    (C) water : dehydrate

    (D) incision : open

    (E) petition : review

23. SKULL : BRAIN ::

    (A) cuticle : toe

    (B) blanket : bed

    (C) cover : book

    (D) trinket : shelf

    (E) armor : body

Directions: Each of the following sentences has one or two blanks indicating that words or phrases are omitted. Choose the answer that best completes the sentence.

24. It is unfortunate that Heather's first day on the job was filled with so many mistakes that her supervisor felt - - - - his original recommendation not to hire her.

    (A) justified in

    (B) discontented with

    (C) objective about

    (D) vituperative regarding

    (E) innovative in

25. Unable to complete the project yet - - - - to admit defeat, Liz worked at the task until she was lucky enough to find a solution that nearly - - - - the difficulty.

    (A) proposing . . . destroyed

    (B) unwilling . . . resolved

    (C) reluctant . . . worsened

    (D) eager . . . doubled

    (E) determined . . . reduced

Go on to next page

Directions: Each passage is followed by questions pertaining to that passage. Read the passage and answer the questions based on information stated or implied in that passage.

Line   Studies have shown that certain components of the immune system behave abnormally in people with chronic fatigue syndrome. Chemicals called interleukin-2 and gamma interferon, which
(05) the body produces during its battle against cancer and infectious agents, may not be made in normal amounts. There is evidence that a low-grade battle is being waged by the immune system of CFS patients, given the slight increase
(10) in the number of white cells that usually accumulate in the blood when people are fighting off an infection. Natural killer cells, though, that also help the body in this battle are found in slightly reduced numbers. It's important to note that clin-
(15) ical depression has the identical small reduction in natural killer cell activity. In addition, some depressed patients produce higher amounts of antibodies to certain viruses. There may be more of a connection between depression, the immune
(20) system, and chronic fatigue syndrome than is realized even now, which introduces the somewhat controversial aspect of the syndrome — its neuropsychological features.

26. Which of the following does the author mention to support his theory that the immune system may be affected by chronic fatigue syndrome?

(A) Clinical depression may be more physical than psychological.

(B) Interleukin-2 and gamma interferon are not produced in normal amounts.

(C) Antibody levels are higher in depressed people than in nondepressed people.

(D) White-cell levels in people with neuro-psychological problems tend to decrease.

(E) Natural killer cells reduce the number of white blood cells.

27. When the body battles cancer,

(A) it produces chemicals like gamma interferon.

(B) it turns against its own immune system.

(C) it stimulates the condition known as clinical depression.

(D) it reduces the number of antibodies available to battle viruses.

(E) it develops abnormal lesions around the area of the cancer.

Directions: Choose the answer choice most nearly opposite in meaning to the question word.

28. ILLICIT

(A) expedient

(B) insufficient

(C) legal

(D) affable

(E) coarse

29. IRRITATE

(A) badger

(B) soothe

(C) pressure

(D) scratch

(E) dry

Directions: Each of the following questions features a pair of words or phrases in capital letters, followed by five pairs of words or phrases in lowercase letters. Choose the lowercase pair that most closely expresses the same relationship as that of the upper-case pair.

30. JITTERBUG : DANCE ::

(A) page : book

(B) drawer : dresser

(C) clatter : sound

(D) sliver : slab

(E) mortgage : house

Math Section

Time: 45 minutes

28 questions

Notes:

All numbers used in this exam are real numbers.

All figures lie in a plane.

Angle measures are positive; points and angles are in the position shown.

The answer choices are

A if the quantity in Column A is greater.

B if the quantity in Column B is greater.

C if the two quantities are equal.

D if the relationship cannot be determined from the information given.

Column A	Column B

1. *a* is an integer greater than zero

$(\frac{1}{2}a)^2$	$\frac{1}{2}a^2$

2. $= (3x)^2 - \frac{1}{3}x$

3. $0 > a > b > c$

$a - c$	$a + b$

4.

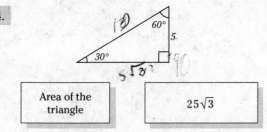

Area of the triangle	$25\sqrt{3}$

Column A	Column B

5. $16a + 5b = 37;\ 3b - 8a = -21$

$a + b$	2

6. | Area of a rectangle of perimeter 20 | Area of a triangle of perimeter 20 |
|---|---|

7. $a \neq 0, 1$

a^2	1

8. $3a + 5b = 12;\ 3b + 5a = 28$

$3(a + b)$	15

9. A right cylinder of volume 200π cubic units has a height of 8.

Circumference of the base	10

Go on to next page

10.   **_Column A_**   **_Column B_**

$2^{25} - 2^{24}$ 2^{23}

11.   A sequence repeats as shown:
$-5, 0, 5, -5, 0, 5, -5, 0, 5.$

Sum of 250th and 251st terms   5

12. $x < 1 < y; x^2 > y^2$

$(x+y)^2$ $x^2 + y^2$

13. $a + b + c = 47; a + b - 2c = 14$

$a + b$ 33

14.   Bob traveled 40 percent of the distance of his trip alone, went another 20 miles with Anthony, and then finished the last half of the trip alone. How many miles long was the trip?

(A) 240

(B) 200

(C) 160

(D) 100

(E) 50

15.   Square _RSTU_ has a perimeter of 48. If A, B, C, and D are the midpoints of their respective sides, what is the perimeter of Square _ABCD?_

(A) 32

(B) $24\sqrt{2}$

(C) 24

(D) $12\sqrt{3}$

(E) $12\sqrt{2}$

16.   Gigi and Neville, working together at the same rate, can mow the estate's lawn in 12 hours. Working alone, what fraction of the lawn can Gigi mow in three hours?

(A) $\frac{1}{24}$

(B) $\frac{1}{12}$

(C) $\frac{1}{8}$

(D) $\frac{1}{4}$

(E) $\frac{1}{3}$

The answer choices are

A if the quantity in Column A is greater.

B if the quantity in Column B is greater.

C if the two quantities are equal.

D if the relationship cannot be determined from the information given.

Column A   **_Column B_**

8

17.   Number of square units in the shaded portion of the square   20

Go on to next page

Use the following graphs to answer questions 18–20.

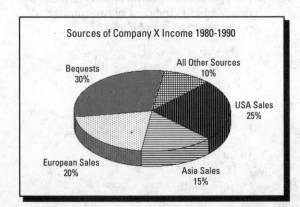

Sources of Company X Income 1980-1990

All Other Sources 10%

Bequests 30%

USA Sales 25%

European Sales 20%

Asia Sales 15%

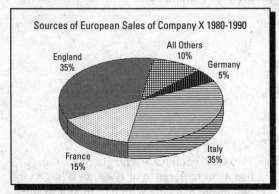

Sources of European Sales of Company X 1980-1990

All Others 10%

England 35%

Germany 5%

France 15%

Italy 35%

18. If Company X received $50,000 in bequests from 1980 through 1990, how much money did it receive from sales to France?

   (A) $16,666

   (B) $3,333

   (C) $5,000

   (D) $333

   (E) $250

19. From the information given, the 1980 sales to England were what percent of the sales to Italy?

   (A) 100

   (B) 50

   (C) 35

   (D) 25

   (E) It cannot be determined.

20. From the information given, if sales to Italy accounted for $1 million more than sales to France, how much income came from U.S. sales?

   (A) $200,000

   (B) $6,250,000

   (C) $5 million

   (D) $25 million

   (E) It cannot be determined.

21. If $x \neq -1$ or 0 and $y = \frac{1}{x}$, then $\frac{1}{(x+1)} + \frac{1}{(y+1)} =$

   (A) 1

   (B) 3

   (C) x

   (D) $x + 1$

   (E) $\frac{(x+1)}{(x+2)}$.

22. If a is six greater than b, and the sum of a and b is -18, then $b^2 =$

   (A) 144

   (B) 36

   (C) 16

   (D) 4

   (E) 0

Go on to next page

Questions 23 and 24 refer to the following graphs.

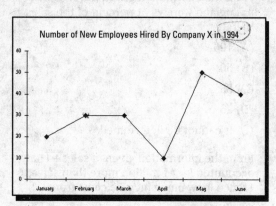

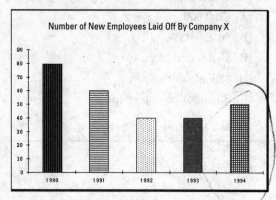

23. If new employees hired in May 1994 were ⅕ of the total employees, new employees laid off in 1994 would be what percent of the total employees in the company?

   (A) 60

   (B) 50

   (C) 33⅓

   (D) 24

   (E) 20

24. In 1995, the increase in the percentage of new employees laid off over that of the previous year was the same as the increase in the percentage of new employees hired between January and February of 1994. How many new employees were laid off in 1995?

   (A) 10

   (B) 20

   (C) 50

   (D) 60

   (E) 75

25. If ten plums cost a cents and six apples cost b cents, what is the cost of two plums and two apples in terms of a and b?

   (A) $\dfrac{3a+5b}{15}$

   (B) $3a + 5b$

   (C) $15ab$

   (D) $5a+\dfrac{3b}{15}$

   (E) $\dfrac{1}{15ab}$

26. If $x \neq 4$, solve for $\dfrac{\sqrt{x}+2}{\sqrt{x}-2}$

   (A) -1

   (B) $\dfrac{x+4}{x-4}$

   (C) $-\sqrt{x}-1$

   (D) $\sqrt{x}+4$

   (E) $\dfrac{x+4\sqrt{x}+4}{x-4}$

27. Two cans each have a height of 10. Can A has a circumference of 10π. Can B has a circumference of 20π. Which of the following represents the ratio of the volume of Can A to the volume of Can B?

   (A) 1:10

   (B) 1:8

   (C) 1:4

   (D) 1:2

   (E) 1:1

28. A plane flies from Los Angeles to New York at 600 miles per hour and returns along the same route at 400 miles per hour. What is the average (arithmetic mean) flying speed for the entire route?

   (A) 460 mph

   (B) 480 mph

   (C) 500 mph

   (D) 540 mph

   (E) It cannot be determined from the information given.

Answer Key for Practice Exam 1

Verbal Section

1. C
2. B
3. E
4. B
5. A
6. A
7. C
8. C
9. B
10. A
11. D
12. B
13. C
14. C
15. B
16. A
17. A
18. C
19. A
20. E
21. B
22. D
23. E
24. A
25. B
26. B
27. A
28. C
29. B
30. C

Math Section

1. B
2. A
3. A
4. B
5. C
6. D
7. D
8. C
9. A
10. A
11. B
12. B
13. A
14. B
15. B
16. C
17. B
18. C
19. E
20. B
21. A
22. A
23. E
24. E
25. A
26. E
27. C
28. B

Chapter 23

Practice Exam 1: Answers and Explanations

Verbal Section

1. **C.** *Sagacious* means wise. If you have more degrees than a thermometer, then you're sagacious. Always try to think of the question word in another, more common form. For example, you probably know that a sage is a wise person. So what's the opposite of a wise person? An ignorant one. Tada! If you selected Choice B, you fell for the trap: You picked a synonym rather than an antonym. *Erudite* means educated, scholarly. Choice E may have trapped you, had you confused sagacious with a *saga* — a long tale.

2. **B.** *Inept* means bungling or foolish. An inept person makes a mess of anything he attempts. The prefix *in-* means not, so an inept person isn't adept. In other words, he's not skillful. Choice C, *prolific,* means abundant, or producing much. An inept person is only prolific at creating chaos. Choice E, *indigenous,* means native to. Long-legged blondes are indigenous to California beaches.

3. **E.** To *swagger* is to walk with arrogance or to strut your stuff. Remember all those bad war movies you watched on Saturday afternoons back in the good old days when all your time wasn't spent studying for this exam? The evil commandant often had a short stick tucked under his arm. That little piece of hardware was called a swagger stick, because it was a symbol of the officer's authority and *arrogance* (conceit). To *stagger* is to teeter, to walk with difficulty, or to have trouble maintaining your balance. (Don't confuse *swagger* with *stagger.* You swagger off the football field when you score the winning touchdown. You stagger out of the locker room after drinking too much champagne while celebrating your winning touchdown.)

   To *swindle* is to cheat. *Veracity* is truthfulness (*ver* means truth; *-ity* makes the word a noun). You don't cheat someone with truthfulness — you cheat someone with dishonesty.

   Here's a special tip to all you international students: If a word in English is difficult, try pronouncing it with the accent of your native language. You may find that the word pronounced in your native accent sounds like a word in your own language that's similar in meaning. For example, *verdad* in Spanish means truth. Knowing that fact, you may be able to make a connection with *veracity.*

   To *renege* is to go back on your word or to not be consistent at all. (If you tell your friends that you'll split your lottery winnings with them, and then a miracle happens and you actually do win ten gazillion dollars, would you *renege* on your promise? That all depends on your *veracity* in making the statement in the first place.)

   To *orchestrate* is to arrange to achieve a maximum effect. For example, a good hostess orchestrates a dinner party by arranging the seating and the entertainment to give the maximum amount of pleasure to her guests. If you fell for this answer, hang your head in shame. The connection between orchestra and harmony is just a little too hokey, don't you think? One of our goals is to get you thinking the GRE way (don't worry, the condition isn't permanent) so that you can recognize cheap tricks like this one.

And finally, to *wheedle* is to beg or flatter. It has nothing to do with *certitude,* which is just what it looks like (certainty, confidence, or assurance). Someone sure of himself or herself probably wouldn't have to beg or wheedle.

4. **B.** A *sheaf* is a collection or bundle of papers. (You may have heard the lyric "Bringing in the sheaves," which refers to harvesting sheaves, or bundles, of wheat.) A *collection* is a bundle of items. A *discourse* is conversation. A *cygnet* is a baby swan. A *quiver* contains arrows. A *quarter* isn't a collection of dimes. *Bonus trivia:* A quarter has exactly 119 grooves on its circumference. A dime has 118. You can thank us when you win the pot at a trivia night someday.

5. **A.** The second blank is the key to this question. If the feet were used to push both rider and bicycle forward, the vehicle wasn't being stopped, developed, or steered. Only Choices A and C work. Choice C doesn't fit the first blank. *Advocated* means defended or supported a cause. You may advocate the abolishment of all GRE testing.

6. **A.** You can predict the types of words you need to fill in the blanks. Jill was reluctant to show the man to be a fraud, so she attacked or put down or criticized the weaker points of his theory. To *denounce* is to criticize, to speak harshly of. To *debunk* is to disprove. (The root *de* means down from, away from, to put down). The first words in Choices B, C, and D fit well; the second words don't. To *castigate* is to criticize or punish. (For you men who are crossing your legs, relax. *Castigate* doesn't mean *castrate,* although both are certainly punishing!) In Choice E, to *disseminate* is to spread, to disburse.

7. **C.** First, use the verbs to help eliminate wrong answers. Passages are rarely negative and don't ridicule anything (Choice E). This very factual passage doesn't *refute* (deny or disprove) anything, which eliminates Choice B. A strong word like *prove* (Choice D) is rarely correct (and how much can be proven in one paragraph, anyway?). Just by examining the verbs, you can narrow your answers to two, giving you a 50-50 shot at the right one.

On the GRE, you must answer before the computer permits you to go to the next question. Sometimes a 50-50 shot is a real gift.

Choice A is tempting — except that the author never makes the claim that the Fremont culture was the most advanced, so how can that claim be challenged? Choice C fits: recurring motifs between cultures may indicate connections between those cultures.

8. **C.** Choice A sounds like something that would be interesting to know (hmmm . . . just why *didn't* the figures have a leg to stand on?), but the passage doesn't supply the answer. Choice B is the trap. Logically, you'd think that a passage about rock art would discuss the purpose of the art, but this very short passage doesn't provide that detail.

You may be tempted to throw out Choice C after reading that sheep were depicted with curvilinear lines and that circles were a frequent motif — info that serves to answer the question in Choice C with a definitive no. The important thing to remember here is that the question simply asks *which* question can be answered — whether the answer is "yes" or "no" makes no difference.

Choice D is completely irrelevant; nothing was said about religion. Choice E may have tempted you because the author did mention a possible connection between the Fremont artists and people of the Four Corners area, but you shouldn't take the info further. Nothing was said about people from other cultures beyond those of the Four Corners area.

9. **B.** A negatively phrased question, such as "all of the following are true EXCEPT" or "which of the following is NOT true," is often a time waster. You may need to go back to the passage again and again and again, eliminating answers one by one until you have only one left. If time is short for you, this type of question is a good one to guess on quickly. In the passage, nothing was mentioned about the South after the Civil War.

10. **A.** The key to this question is to identify the purpose of the first paragraph. The main idea of the first paragraph was to discuss the names of the Civil War. The material listed names that the South called the War; supplying names used by the North as well would strengthen the point.

11. **D.** When something is implied, it's stated indirectly, meaning that the author may not be making a very strong point. Choose a wishy-washy, "possibly" or "maybe" style of answer. The other choices go too far. Nothing was said about Southern troops going to the capital, about the protection of Lincoln (or threats made against him), or about a conspiracy by the Confederate government. Choice C is a logical answer, and it may be true, but the statement in the passage doesn't imply it.

Just because a statement is true doesn't mean it's a correct answer.

12. **B.** The theme of the paragraph is the new technology. The rest of the paragraph would probably discuss the impact of that technology on the war. Choices A, C, and D, dealing with photography, are too specific. Choice E may be true but probably isn't the point of the passage. Industrialization in general and its effect on the war are the important parts, not the photography or railroads per se.

13. **C.** Use your roots to help you define the question word. *In-* usually means not. *Trans* means change, as in transferring from one place to another. An *intransigent* person doesn't change. He or she is stubborn and not flexible. Choice A, *tawdry,* means tacky, gaudy, or cheap. ***Bonus trivia:*** Do you know the origin of the word tawdry? It's a corruption of *St. Audrey's lace,* referring to a lace collar worn by a holy woman and copied in a cheaper form by the common people. *Querulous* means complaining and peevish. (Note that it doesn't mean quarreling — although certainly enough complaining may lead to a quarrel.) *Precocious* means advanced for one's age.

14. **C.** *Extroverted* means outgoing. The opposite is *shy. Bombastic* means big talking or grandiloquent. *Ubiquitous* means everywhere at once. After you learn these words, you'll be surprised how ubiquitous they are. You'll start to see these words in advertisements, editorials, and even love letters — well, maybe not in every love letter, but probably in those from your more bombastic companions!

Fun Fact: You won't see this word on the GRE, but *ubiety* is a great word to use with your friends — especially the bombastic ones who think their vocabularies are superior to yours. Although *ubiquitous* means everywhere at once, *ubiety* means having the property of being in one particular place at one particular time. For example, the planets have ubiety. If you're so wedded to routine that your friends can set their clocks by you, you have ubiety.

15. **B.** *Hardy* means strong. You'd get this question right even if you didn't know the words, assumed that they were synonyms, and made the *is* sentence: "Hardy is strong." (When you were young, did you ever read the adventure-book series about the Hardy boys? That name expressed the type of young men the main characters were.) *Unruly* means unable to be ruled, uncontrollable. A group of elementary school kids is unruly when a substitute teacher tries to take over the class. Roots can help you define Choices D and E. *Dubious* means doubtful: *dub* means doubt; *-ous* means full of. *Lucid* means clear: *luc* means light or clear. Unless someone has a lucid explanation of why he wants to borrow your car, it's dubious you'll let him take it.

16. **A.** This was a difficult question. If you don't know what vacillate means, assume the words are synonyms and make the *is* sentence: "To vacillate is to be indecisive." In fact, that's correct. To *vacillate* is to waver, to show indecision. You vacillate over whether to take the GRE or the GMAT.

You can also get this question correct by process of elimination. In Choice A, *select* is to choose, which means you're certain, not uncertain. To *hesitate,* Choice B, is to be uncertain, wavering, or vacillating — just the opposite of *steadfast* (holding steady, holding fast). To *repress* is to hold back, to *not* be straightforward. To *contemplate* is to be thinking about something or to be curious, not incurious. All three of these answers have the same relationship — they're antonyms — so all three must be wrong. You may know Choice D, *affect,* in another form, affected or affectatious, meaning pretentious, artificial, or doing something just for show. *Candid,* which means open and sincere, is just the opposite.

17. **A.** The gist of the sentence is that criticizing the employee for working slowly makes him work even more slowly. The action, therefore, hurts rather than helps the situation and is *counterproductive*, meaning having a different result or consequence than what was intended. For example, staying up late studying the night before the GRE may actually be counterproductive; you'll be so tired that you may do worse on the exam than you would've had you studied less and slept more.

Try to predict whether the word that you'll place in the blank should be a "good" or positive word or a "bad" or negative word. You know that if the employee gets flustered and slows down, something bad has happened. Looking for a negative word allows you to eliminate Choices B, C, D, and E.

18. **C.** Given all the good stuff the sentence says about solar power, you can logically assume that both blanks will be filled with positive words. Go through the answer choices and eliminate any with a negative word. So basically you can eliminate Choices A (*deride* means to put down), B (*denounce* means to put down), and E (*detractors* are people who put something down or criticize). Note that all these words with the root *de* mean to put down, to criticize (if you don't know your roots yet, be sure to go back and review them, along with prefixes and suffixes, in Chapters 4 and 8). Choice D may have been tempting, but to *lampoon* is to ridicule or slander (think of *National Lampoon,* the magazine and the movies). By process of elimination, Choice C is correct. To *tout* is to praise highly: We tout memorizing roots, prefixes, and suffixes. To *advocate* is to support or champion (the prefix *ad-* means toward; if you advocate something, you go toward it, you like it). A *beneficiary* benefits or gets something good (*ben-* means good). To *laud* is to praise (think of applaud).

19. **A.** This question rewards you for knowing your roots. *Gnos* means knowledge. One of the three meanings of *pro* is before. The suffix *-ate* means to make. To *prognosticate* is "to make knowledge before," or to predict. We prognosticate that your score on this exam will be excellent. To *recall* is to remember, as in, "I recall that once upon a time I didn't know what prognosticate meant." To *exasperate* is to annoy. To *curtail* is to shorten. (Think of this word as "to cut the tail off," which makes something shorter.) To *abhor* is to hate. (The prefix *ab-* means away from; when you abhor or hate something, you stay away from it.) Choice E is the trap. Did you think that *con* in confiscate is the opposite of *pro* in prognosticate? Sorry, not this time. To *confiscate* is to take, like when a teacher confiscates a child's bubble gum in school.

20. **E.** *Cryptic* means hidden, mysterious, or baffling. (*Crypt* means hidden.) The opposite is *frank,* meaning open, straightforward, and concealing nothing. *Craven* in Choice B means cowardly. Choice C, *picayune* (yes, that's how you spell the word that's pronounced *pick-a-yune*) means small, trivial, or petty. *Multifaceted* means complex, having a variety of features or parts. Most relationships are multifaceted and fall apart because of a spat over some picayune point.

21. **B.** To *abstain* is to refrain or hold back (*ab-* means away from). You may abstain from voting in the student elections if you don't like any of the candidates. The opposite is to participate. Choice D, *meander,* is to wander aimlessly, to ramble. To *infuriate* is to annoy greatly, to make furious. A good public speaker abstains from meandering too much because rambling can infuriate the audience.

22. **D.** The purpose of a staple is to attach something; the purpose of an *incision* (a cut) is to open something. A surgeon makes an incision to get into your chest, for example.

If you picked Choice A, you fell for a trap. Although a button is sewn on, the purpose of a button isn't to sew. Don't fall for a trap answer by looking at the meanings of the words. The fact that buttons and staples both attach items isn't relevant here. You need to look at the relationships between the words, not their meanings.

The purpose of a carpet isn't to *impede,* which is to hold back or hinder. If you want to go roller skating, then roller skating across a carpet would impede your progress. However, impeding progress isn't a carpet's primary function. The purpose of water is to *hydrate* (moisten something), not to *dehydrate* (dry something out). The purpose of a petition is to suggest or demand that something happen, not to review what happened. If you create a petition against the GRE, your purpose is to suggest that the exam be abolished from polite society, not to review the status of the exam.

23. **E.** This question should've been relatively easy. Make the sentence: A *skull* protects the brain; *armor* protects the body. A *cuticle* is part of a toe, but it doesn't offer much protection when you drop a GRE book on your foot. A blanket covers, but doesn't protect, a bed. A cover of a book affords some protection, but not much. A *trinket* goes on a shelf.

Speaking of what's inside your skull, here's some bonus brain trivia: How old are you right now? If you're over 20, we've got some bad news. You're heading downhill from the nose up. The brain reaches its maximum weight — about three pounds — at age 20. Over the next 60 years, the brain loses about 3 ounces as billions of its nerve cells die. The brain begins to lose cells at a rate of 50,000 per day by the age of 30.

24. **A.** If the supervisor was afraid to hire the worker who *bungled* (messed up) badly on her first day, it appears the supervisor's fears were well-founded or justified.

In Choice C, *objective* means neutral or unbiased — just the opposite of what the supervisor was. Choice D, *vituperative,* means violently abusive. And *innovative* means new and original. A vituperative person may come up with some innovative *epithets* (names, titles) to call the object of his *wrath* (anger).

25. **B.** The only excuse for missing a question such as this one is laziness or carelessness. So many of the Sentence Completion questions test very hard vocabulary that when you get to one like this with very easy vocabulary, you should take your time and go through each answer choice carefully to ensure you find the correct one.

To resolve a difficulty is to solve the problem. If Liz kept working, she was unwilling to abandon the project. Only Choices B and C work for the first blank; the second word in Choice C is just the opposite of what the sentence intends to say.

26. **B.** The first two sentences of the passage tell you that " . . . certain components of the immune system behave abnormally in people with chronic fatigue syndrome" and " . . . interleukin-2 and gamma interferon . . . may not be made in normal amounts." This one is a simple detail or fact question.

Choice C is a trap answer. The author does in fact say that antibody levels are higher in depressed people; however, he doesn't make that statement to support the theory that the immune system may be affected by chronic fatigue syndrome. Just because a statement is true doesn't mean that it's the correct answer. Always be sure to address what a question is asking.

Questions usually go in order through the passage — especially science passages (which require you to find specific facts rather than make inferences). Because this is the first question, go back to the first sentence or two.

27. **A.** This is a very simple detail or fact question. The passage tells you that the body produces chemicals such as interleukin-2 and gamma interferon during its battle against cancer.

As you've probably noticed by now, the questions on science passages are often easier than the questions on other types of passages. Even if the science passages themselves are boring or difficult to understand, the questions relating to them are usually quite straightforward. Frequently, you just need to skim for a specific fact or detail.

28. **C.** *Illicit* means illegal. The opposite is legal. *Affable* means friendly. (We like to think of *affable* as "af-friend-able.")

29. **B.** To *irritate* is to annoy. The opposite is to soothe. Choice A, *badger,* is to harass, bother, or annoy. Occasionally, the answer choices feature a word that's a synonym to the question word. Choosing this answer is easy, because uppermost in your mind is the definition. "Badger, hmmm. That means to annoy or to irritate. Oh, there it is!" Keep in mind that the name of the game is *antonyms,* not synonyms.

30. **C.** A *jitterbug* is a type of dance; a *clatter* is a type of sound. A *page* is a part of a book, not a type of book. A *drawer* is a part of a dresser, not a type of dresser. A *sliver* is a small part of a slab. A *mortgage* is usually necessary to buy a house, but it isn't a type of house.

Math Section

1. **B.** Plug in numbers. Suppose that $a = 1$. Then Column A is $\frac{1}{2} \times 1$, which is $\frac{1}{2}$, and then $(\frac{1}{2})^2$, which is $\frac{1}{4}$. Column B requires you to square the 1 first, which is simply 1, and then multiply by $\frac{1}{2}$ to get $\frac{1}{2}$. So far, Column B is bigger. Try a different number. Suppose that $a = 2$. Then Column A is $\frac{1}{2}$ of 2, which is 1. You know that $1^2 = 1$. Column B is $\frac{1}{2}$ of 4 (because $2^2 = 4$) and guess what — Column B is still greater. No matter what you plug in, Column B is larger.

With this type of problem, you should always plug in more than one number. Otherwise you'll never know whether the answer depends on what you plug in. Do you remember the Sacred Six you need to plug in for variables? They are 1, 2, 0, –1, –2, and $\frac{1}{2}$. Usually, just plugging in 1 and 2 gets the job done. Turn back to Chapter 16 for more info.

2. **A.** Ah, if you chose C, you got careless.

Whenever you see a seemingly obvious C answer, double- and triple-check it. More traps lie in the C answers than in most of the rest of the answers. If your first instinct is to choose C, you're probably just making some nasty test-maker's day by falling for her trap.

First, you have to say to yourself in English what the symbols mean. Say, "I have something in a triangle. First, I multiply that something by 3. Then I square that answer. Then I take a third of that something. Then I subtract the second from the first." In other words, substitute the number in the triangle for the x in the equation. For Column A, you have 3×-3, which is –9. Then $-9^2 = 81$. Next, $\frac{1}{3}$ of –3 = –1. Finally, $81 - (-1)$ means $81 + 1 = 82$. For Column B, you have $3 \times 3 = 9$. Then $9^2 = 81$. Next, $\frac{1}{3}$ of 3 =1. Finally, $81 - 1 = 80$. You must keep your negatives and positives straight.

Whenever a problem has a negative variable, double-check your signs. You can easily make a careless mistake with them.

3. **A.** You have absolutely no excuse for missing this problem, even if you did get a brain cramp when you first looked at it. Remember our tip from Chapter 16: Cancel quantities that are identical in both columns. Slash off the a in both columns so that you're left with $-c$ and $+b$. Because c is negative, a negative c is a double negative, which is actually a positive. In Column B, b remains negative (because a positive times a negative is negative). Because any positive is greater than any negative, Column A is larger.

Did you look at all the variables and choose D, thinking the answer depended on what you plugged in? That's a very good first reaction, but be sure to do the actual plugging in. Say that the numbers are –1, –2, and –3. (Be careful not to get messed up and put –3, –2, –1. With negatives, everything is backward: –1 is greater than –2.)

Column A is $-1 - (-3) = -1 + 3 = 2$. Column B is $-1 + (-2) = -3$. Please, please be careful not to overuse and abuse our tips. They're glorious and will help you if you treat them with respect. When you use one, make a commitment to it and always work it through to the end. If you decide that the answer is going to depend on what you plug in, *actually plug in the numbers* and work the problem through.

Usually, Choice D is valid in three instances. Think D when you encounter a QC geometry problem without a picture. Think D when a picture specifically says that it isn't drawn to scale (something that's very rare on the GRE). And think D when you've *actually* plugged in different values for variables, *actually* done the work, and *actually* gotten different answers.

4. **B.** If you chose D, you fell for the trap. You probably looked at the question, saw that only one side was given, and figured that you didn't have enough info to answer the question. Wrong. You should've reminded yourself of this tip — when a figure is given, the answer is rarely D. (This is the flip of the tip that when a QC geometry problem gives words but no pictures, the answer is usually D.)

Do you remember your Pythagorean triples? We cover these threesomes in Chapter 13. For many right triangles, the sides have a special ratio. For a 30:60:90 triangle, that ratio is $side : side\sqrt{3} : 2side$. The side opposite the 30-degree angle is the shortest side — the 5 in this case.

The side opposite the 60-degree angle is the next shortest side, the "$side\sqrt{3}$" side. With this question, that's $5\sqrt{3}$. Although you don't need to know this fact to find the area of the triangle, the *hypotenuse* (the side opposite the 90-degree angle) is the longest side — the "$2side$" side. Here, it's 10.

The area of a triangle is ½ *base* × *height.* The base is $5\sqrt{3}$; the height is 5. Therefore, the area is $\frac{1}{2} \times 5\sqrt{3} \times 5 = \frac{25}{2}\sqrt{3}$. Don't bother finding the exact number; it's certainly less than $25\sqrt{3}$. If you chose C, you did *allllllll* that work and, because you forgot the very last step, you missed the stupid question anyway.

How can you prevent making a careless mistake like forgetting to multiply by ½ in this problem? Simple. Immediately write down the formula for the problem on the scratch paper. Writing the formula may seem childish or like extra work, but it only takes a gigasecond and can prevent careless errors. When you see the formula, you can more easily plug the numbers into it and work it through.

5. **C.** It's amazing how many QC questions that require you to actually do the work and solve the problem turn out to have C answers. We're not saying that you should choose C as soon as you start shoving the pencil around, but the more calculations a question requires, the more often the answer seems to be C. (That's the flip of the tip in Chapter 16 that if the quantities appear to be equal at first glance, without doing any work, a trap is probably lurking.) Here, set up the equations vertically:

$$16a + 5b = 37$$
$$-8a + 3b = -21$$

You want to either add or subtract to get the same *numerical coefficient* (the number that goes in front of the variable) for the *a* and the *b*. When you add the equations here (notice how we've moved the *a* to the front of the second equation to make the variables add up neatly?), you get $8a + 8b = 16$. Divide both sides by 8 to get $a + b = 2$.

You don't have to go through the whole mess of substitution. And because you don't have to do it, we're not even going to show you how!

6. **D.** When a QC geometry problem doesn't include a figure, the answer is often D because it *de*pends on how the figure is drawn. A rectangle of perimeter 20 can have, for example, sides of 1 and 9 and 1 and 9, making the area 9. Or it can have sides of 6 and 4 and 6 and 4, making the area 24. (The area of a rectangle is *length* × *width.*) A triangle of perimeter 20 can have sides of 4, 7, and 9, or a **plethora** (abundance) of other combinations. And because you don't know whether the triangle is a right triangle, you have no idea what the height is. That height could be a leg of the triangle, be inside the triangle, or be outside the triangle. There isn't enough information to compare the quantities.

7. **D.** If you chose A, you fell right for our cunningly devised trap (okay, so it was a cheap trick). Don't forget that a negative squared is a positive. If *a* is –2, for example, then $-2^2 = 4$, and Column A is larger. And what if *a* is a fraction? If $a = \frac{1}{2}$, then $\left(\frac{1}{2}\right)^2 = \frac{1}{4}$, and B is bigger. If the answer could be A or B, it *de*pends on what you plug in — pick D.

Remember the Sacred Six that we asked you to get into the habit of plugging in? These numbers are 1, 2, 0, –1, –2, and ½. You don't need to plug in 0 or 1 this time, but you do need to plug in the fraction. You should chant this phrase to yourself as if it were a mantra: "Positive, negative, zero, fraction. Positive, negative, zero, fraction." Got it?

8. **C.** Line the equations up vertically and either add or subtract them to get the same numerical coefficients (the numbers before the variables). In this case, you add.

$$3a + 5b = 12$$
$$\underline{5a + 3b = 28}$$
$$8a + 8b = 40$$

Now divide both sides of the equation by 8 to get $a + b = 5$. Finally, $3 \times 5 = 15$.

9. **A.** The volume of any figure is *area of the base* × *height*. Because the base of a cylinder is a circle, the volume of a cylinder is $\pi\,radius^2 \times height$. Divide the volume, 200π, by the height, 8, to find that the area of the base is 25π. Because the base is a circle of area = $\pi\,radius^2$, the radius is 5. But don't choose B; you're not finished yet.

The circumference of a circle is $2\pi\,radius$, which here is 10π. If you chose C, you fell for the trap. You forgot your π! The circumference of 10π is actually $10 \times$ approximately 3.14, which is more than 10 (don't bother to figure it out exactly). The moral of the story: Keep your eye on the π.

If your first thought when you look at a QC problem is that the columns are equal, think again. Usually — not always — you have to do actual calculations to get a C.

Typically, when a QC geometry problem is all words and no pictures, the answer is D because the comparison *de*pends on what the picture looks like. This is an exception to that tip. We included it here just to keep you from using the tips automatically rather than actually thinking problems through.

10. **A.** Why would we give you a problem like this without allowing you access to your calculator? Well, you have two choices (and no, murder and mayhem aren't among them). You can make a quick guess at the answer to this problem and pretty much blow it off entirely. Or you can be very smart and realize that if a principle is valid with a large number, it's usually valid with a small number. In other words, instead of 2^{25} or 2^{24}, make it 2^5 or 2^4. You can quickly figure 2^5 as $2 \times 2 \times 2 \times 2 \times 2 = 32$. Then 2^4 is 16, and $32 - 16 = 16$. Therefore, $2^5 - 2^4$ is 2^4, just as $2^{25} - 2^{24}$ is 2^{24}, which is definitely bigger than 2^{23}.

11. **B.** There are three terms in the sequence, and every third term is 5. Divide 250 by 3 to get 83 with a remainder of 1. That means that the 249th number is 5 (because 249 divides evenly by 3), the 250th number is –5, and the 251st number is 0. Add –5 + 0 = –5.

The people who devise the GRE put questions like this one on it to get you to waste your time. Oh sure, you could've counted on your fingers up to the 250th term, but who has that sort of time? Find the closest number that divides by 3 and then work from there.

Did you choose D for this problem? If so, you probably confused "It *de*pends" with "Don't have a clue — duuuh!" A D answer doesn't mean *you* don't know how to do the problem but rather that no one could do the problem with the **paucity** (lack) of information presented. In other words, don't take the question personally. Just because you can't do a problem yourself doesn't indicate it's undoable, or worthy of a D answer.

12. **B.** Did you fall for trap answer A? It's wrong because $(x + y)^2 = (x + y)(x + y) = x^2 + 2xy + y^2$. Column A has $2xy$, which Column B doesn't have. Don't jump on A in this case just because you see that Column A has something extra. You know that y is positive because $y > 1$, but for x^2 to be greater than y^2 when $x < y$, x must be negative. With a negative x and a positive y, $2xy$ will be negative, making Column A with the extra $2xy$ less than Column B.

Don't like algebra? Try a simpler way to do this problem: Plug in numbers. You need to be absolutely sure that the numbers you plug in fit the constraints given by the centered information. For example, you can't say $x = 1$ because the problem states $x < 1$. Why don't you try $x = 0$ and $y = 2$? Wait, wait: Those numbers don't work with the second equation. 0^2 is definitely not larger than 2^2. Try some different numbers. How about $x = -1$ and $y = 2$? No, -1^2 isn't larger than 2^2. Try –3 for x and 2 for y. Ah, that works: -3^2, which is 9, is in fact larger than 2^2, which is 4. (Note that this "plug 'n' chug" technique, although easy, can be tricky and time-consuming.) Now plug these values into the question: $(-3 + 2)^2 = -1^2 = 1$. Column B: $-3^2 + 2^2 = 9 + 4 = 13$. Column B is correct. BUT you need to plug in again, just to be sure. Try –4 and 3: $(-4 + 3)^2 = 1^2 = 1$, so $-4^2 + 3^2 = 16 + 9 = 25$. Column B is still greater.

13. **A.** Line up the equations vertically and subtract so that *a* and *b* fall out.

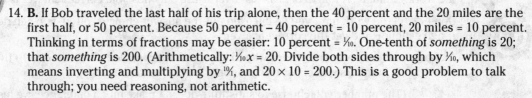

$$a + b + c = 47$$
$$\underline{-\left(a + b - 2c = 14\right)}$$
$$0 + 0 + 3c = 33$$

Don't forget that you're subtracting a negative. A negative negative is a positive, so "minus minus 2*c*" is +2*c*. Clean up the new equation to get 3*c* = 33, so *c* must be 11. Plug that into the first equation to get *a* + *b* + 11 = 47, so *a* + *b* must be equal to 36. Because 36 is sitting in column A, A is the lucky winner!

If you chose C, you probably got confused on the negative signs and said –(–2*c*) = *c*, then *c* = 33.

14. **B.** If Bob traveled the last half of his trip alone, then the 40 percent and the 20 miles are the first half, or 50 percent. Because 50 percent – 40 percent = 10 percent, 20 miles = 10 percent. Thinking in terms of fractions may be easier: 10 percent = ¹⁄₁₀. One-tenth of *something* is 20; that *something* is 200. (Arithmetically: ¹⁄₁₀*x* = 20. Divide both sides through by ¹⁄₁₀, which means inverting and multiplying by ¹⁰⁄₁, and 20 × 10 = 200.) This is a good problem to talk through; you need reasoning, not arithmetic.

15. **B.** The four sides of a square are equal, such that one side of Square *RSTU* is 12. If the points are midpoints, each one divides the large square's sides into two parts, with each part consisting of 6 units. Connecting these midpoints gives you four isosceles right triangles (*RAD*, *SAB*, *TCB*, and *UDC*). The ratios of the sides of an isosceles right triangle are $side : side : side\sqrt{2}$.

That means the hypotenuse of Triangle *RAD*, for example, is $6\sqrt{2}$. These hypotenuses are the sides of Square *ABCD*. Add the four sides to get $24\sqrt{2}$, Choice B.

If you chose A, you said that four "root 2's" equaled 8 and added 24 + 8 = 32. You can't add square roots like that.

16. **C.** The key to this problem is knowing that Gigi and Neville work at the same rate. If they finish the lawn in 12 hours, each did ½ of the job in 12 hours. Therefore, Gigi working alone would've taken 24 hours to finish the lawn. Because 3 hours is ⅛ of 24 hours, she could've done ⅛ of the job in that time.

17. **B.** Think of a shaded area as a leftover: It's what's left over after you've subtracted the unshaded area from the figure as a whole. Because Column A tells you that the figure is a square, you find its area by multiplying *side* × *side*: 8 × 8 = 64. The diameter of the circle is the same as the length of the square, 8. The radius of a circle is half the diameter, or 4. The area of a circle is $\pi\, radius^2$, or 16π. Find the shaded area by subtracting 64 – 16π.

Don't, we repeat, don't bother figuring out how much 16π is. You know that π is slightly larger than 3.14, but we wouldn't even make it that complicated. Just say that π is bigger than 3. Multiply 16 × 3 to get 48. Subtract 64 – 48 to get 16. The actual area will be even smaller than that because you'll be subtracting some number larger than 48 (whatever you get when you multiply 3.14 × 16, which we aren't about to do, and neither should you). Because 16 is smaller than 20, and the "real" answer will be even smaller than 16, Column B is bigger.

If you can't recall how to do shaded areas, flip to Chapter 13, where we provide a simple three-step approach.

18. **C.** Bequests account for 30 percent of total income. *Hint:* Ignore the zeros; just let the equation be 50 = .3*x*. Divide both sides through by .3 to get *x* (total income) = 166.67. European sales were 20 percent of total income, or 166.67 × .20 = 33.3. Sales to France were 15 percent of that figure: .15 × 33.3 = 5.

Estimate wildly. The answer choices are so far apart that you can get away with murder here. Say that bequests are about a third of the total, making the total 15. Then European sales are 20 percent, or a fifth of the total (which is 3). Then French sales are 15 percent of that, or .45. The only answer even remotely close to that is Choice C. If this question really slows you down, just guess.

19. **E.** Read the titles on the graphs: They show income and sales from 1980 through 1990. You can't figure out sales in one particular year. If you picked Choice A, you fell for the trap. And shame on you for being so **credulous** (gullible). You should've been more paranoid than that. **Remember:** If something looks too good to be true, it probably is.

20. **B.** Good problem. If you got this question right, **kudos** and **accolades** and **encomium** (praises) to you. This question takes a lot of backtracking.

Sales to Italy are 20 percent more than sales to France (35 percent – 15 percent), meaning that 20 percent = 1 million, or $\frac{1}{5}$ = 1 million. Thus, 100 percent = 5 million. But this is 100 percent of the second graph, which is still only 20 percent of the first graph. In other words, the total 5 million in the second graph is 20 percent, or $\frac{1}{5}$, of the first graph. Therefore, the total of the first graph is 25 million. (Are you totally confused yet? Just keep reading.) U.S. sales are 25 percent, or $\frac{1}{4}$, of that: $.25 \times \$25$ million is — hey, stop right there! Don't actually do all the work. Estimate. A fourth of 25 is just over 6; the only possible correct answer is Choice B.

Don't do all the work until you've checked out the answer choices; often, you can do just a rough estimate and get the correct answer.

21. **A.** There's an easy way and a hard way to approach this problem. We'll start with the easy way: Plug in numbers and substitute numbers for the variables.

Let $x = 3$. (The number you choose to substitute doesn't make much difference; we just chose 3 because it's small and easy to deal with. We didn't want to use 1 because of the fractions: $\frac{1}{1}$ doesn't help much.) If $x = 3$, then $y = \frac{1}{3}$.

Now plug these numbers into the entire equation:

$$\frac{1}{(x+1)} + \frac{1}{(y+1)} = \frac{1}{(3+1)} + \frac{1}{(\frac{1}{3}+1)} = \frac{1}{4} + \frac{1}{(\frac{4}{3})} = \frac{1}{4} + \frac{3}{4} = 1$$

Although Choice A is correct, in this case you MUST go through the final step of checking every answer option. Here, Choice B is obviously wrong. Choice C, $x = 3$, is wrong (remember, you're looking for a final answer of 1). In Choice D, $3 + 1 = 4$. Choice E is $^{(3+1)}/_{(3+2)} = \frac{4}{5}$. Why bother with this last step of checking every answer? Depending on what number you plug in, more than one answer could work. In that case, you'd have to change your numbers and try again.

If you're a more abstract thinker and prefer to use basic algebra, think of this one as a substitution problem. Substitute $y = \frac{1}{x}$ for the y in the expression $\frac{1}{(y+1)}$:

$$\frac{1}{(x+1)} + \frac{1}{(\frac{1}{x}+1)}$$

To get rid of that ugly second part of the expression, multiply $\frac{1}{(\frac{1}{x}+1)}$ by $\frac{x}{x}$ (and don't forget to distribute):

$$\frac{1}{(x+1)} + \frac{1}{(\frac{1}{x}+1)} \times \frac{x}{x} = \frac{1}{(x+1)} + \frac{x}{(1+x)}$$

Now you have a common denominator (remember that $x + 1$ is the same as $1 + x$), so add the fractions:

$$^{(1+x)}/_{(x+1)} = 1 \text{ (Choice A)}$$

22. **A.** Set up the equations: $a - b = 6$ (because a is six greater than b, the difference between them is 6) and $a + b = -18$. Line them up vertically, and add.

$$a - b = 6$$
$$\underline{a + b = -18}$$
$$2a = -12$$
$$a = -6$$
$$-6 + b = -18$$
$$b = -12$$
$$-12^2 = 144$$

The key to this problem is lining up the equations vertically and then adding them so that one variable (the *b* in this case) drops out. Solve for the other variable and then substitute that number back into one of the equations.

23. **E.** This relatively simple problem takes two steps. Fifty new employees were hired in May: 50 = 20 percent, or ⅕ of the total number of employees (250). If there were 250 employees and 50 of them were laid off, then ⅕ (back to that same number!) were laid off.

    Did you see the shortcut in this problem? The 50 in the top graph is the same as the 50 in the bottom graph. Therefore, whatever percent you have for the top graph is the same as the percent for the bottom graph. You don't need to go through all that work.

24. **E.** First, figure out the percent increase in new hires between January and February. Twenty new employees were hired in January, and 30 were hired in February. To find a percent increase or decrease, you use the formula: *number increase or decrease divided by original whole* (the number you began with). Here, that's ¹⁰⁄₂₀ = ½ = 50 percent.

    The number of employees laid off in 1994, according to the bottom graph, was 50. The number laid off in 1995 was 50 percent greater. Fifty percent of 50 is ½ of 50, or 25. Add 50 + 25 = 75.

    Did you fall for Choice D? The increase in new hires between January and February was 10, but that doesn't mean that the number of layoffs in 1995 was 10 higher than the number in 1994. You must figure the *percentage*.

25. **A.** If 10 plums cost *a* cents, then each plum costs ¹⁄₁₀*a* and 2 plums cost ²⁄₁₀, or ⅕*a*. If 6 apples cost *b* cents, then each apple costs ⅙*b* cents, and 2 apples cost ²⁄₆*b*, or ⅓*b* cents. Now use 15 as a common denominator for 5 and 3. Convert: ⅕*a* = ³⁄₁₅*a*, and ⅓*b* = ⁵⁄₁₅*b*.

    This pretty confusing problem assumes you have some sort of sick fetish for fractions. Fortunately, you can work out the problem without stooping so low as to deal with those nasty little things. The easy way to solve this problem is to substitute numbers for the variables. Let *a* = 10, such that each plum costs 1 cent and two plums cost 2 cents. Let *b* = 6, such that each apple costs 1 cent and 2 apples cost 2 cents. Then the total is 4 cents. Plug the same values into the answer choices to see which one comes out to be 4. In *a*, you have 3(10) + 5(6) = 60 divided by 15 = 4.

    You must check all the answer choices when you plug in your own numbers. Did you get as far as Choice E? If you did, you got 4 there as well (¹⁄₁₅ × 10 × 6 = ¹⁄₁₅ × 60 = 4). What now? If you get more than one correct answer based on the terms you plug in, plug in different terms and try again.

    Suppose that this time *a* = 20 and *b* = 6. Now the cost of each plum is 2 cents, making the cost of two of them 4 cents. The cost of the apples remains the same. Two plums (4 cents) plus 2 apples (2 cents) = 6 cents. The new answer you're looking for is 6.

    Don't bother going through all the answer choices again. You've already narrowed the field down to A or E; try just those two.

    Now Choice A is (60 + 30) ÷ 15 = 90 ÷ 15 = 6. It works. Choice E is ¹⁄₁₅ × 20 × 6 = ⅕ × 120, which doesn't equal 6. Throw Choice E away; Choice A is correct.

    We were incredibly kind with this problem by making Choice A the correct answer. Less magnificent human beings would've switched Choices A and E. Then, if you didn't bother plugging in your answers for every single answer option and stopped at Choice A, you'd fall for the trap.

26. **E.** Does this problem make you think of Egyptian hieroglyphics? Join the crowd. Instead of just saying, "That's history, babe!" and guessing at this problem, make it easy to work through by *plugging in numbers*. Choose a number with an easy square root. Make *x* = 9 (because $\sqrt{9} = 3$). Now, solve the question:

$$\left(\sqrt{9}+2\right) \div \left(\sqrt{9}-2\right) = (3+2) \div (3-2) = \frac{5}{1} = 5$$

Keep in mind that 5 is the answer to the problem. It isn't the value of *x*. Jot the 5 down to the side, draw a circle around it, put arrows pointing to it, or do whatever it takes to remind yourself that the answer you want is 5. Now go through each answer choice and see which one comes out to be 5. Only Choice E works:

$$\left(9 + 4\sqrt{9} + 4\right) \div 9 - 4\left(9 + 4 \times 3 + 4\right) \div 5 = \left(9 + 12 + 4\right) \div 5 = 25/5 = 5$$

Be very, very careful not to put 3 in for *x* in the problem. Remember *x* = 9 — the square root of *x* = 3. We suggest you make a chart to the side, simply writing down *x* = 9 and ANSWER = 5.

When you plug in numbers, go through every single answer choice, *soporific* (sleep-inducing) though that may be. If you were to start with Choice E, for example, and make a careless mistake, you'd find that Choices D, C, and B don't work either . . . and probably choose Choice A by process of elimination. If you take just a second to work out Choice A, you'll see that it too is wrong, alerting you to the fact that you made a careless mistake somewhere.

For you algebra addicts who can't live without your fix, simplify the denominator by multiplying each side through by $\left(\sqrt{x}+2\right)$.

$$\frac{\sqrt{x} + 2}{\sqrt{x} - 2} \times \frac{\sqrt{x} + 2}{\sqrt{x} + 2}$$

The numerator is $\left(\sqrt{x}+2\right)\left(\sqrt{x}+2\right)$. Use FOIL (First, Outer, Inner, Last) to multiply these terms: $\sqrt{x} \times \sqrt{x} = x$. Then $\sqrt{x} \times 2 = 2\sqrt{x}$. Next, $2 \times \sqrt{x} = 2\sqrt{x}$. Finally, $2 \times 2 = 4$. Add: $x + 4\sqrt{x} + 4$.

The denominator is $\left(\sqrt{x}-2\right) \times \left(\sqrt{x}+2\right)$. Use FOIL again to multiply these terms: $\sqrt{x} \times \sqrt{x} = x$. Then $\sqrt{x} \times 2 = 2\sqrt{x}$. Next, $\sqrt{x} \times -2 = -2\sqrt{x}$. Finally, $2 \times 2 = 4$.

The $2\sqrt{x}$ and $-2\sqrt{x}$ cancel each other out, leaving you with $x - 4$.

If you took our advice in Chapter 14 and memorized some basic FOIL problems, you knew immediately that $(a + b)(a + b) = a^2 + 2ab + b^2$ (just substitute *x* for the *a* and 2 for the *b*). You knew that $(a + b)(a - b) = a^2 - b^2$ (substitute the *x* for the *a* and the 2 for the *b*). If you haven't memorized these handy pieces of FOIL, go back to Chapter 14 and do so now.

27. **C.** The volume of any right prism is *(area of base) × height*. The base of a cylinder is a circle. Because the area of a circle is πr^2, the volume of a cylinder is $\pi r^2 h$.

The circumference of a circle is $2\pi r$. Therefore, the radius of Can A = 5; the radius of Can B = 10. The volume of Can A = $5^2 \pi \times 10 = 250\pi$. The volume of Can B = $10^2 \pi \times 10 = 1{,}000\pi$. Finally, $250\pi : 1{,}000\pi = 1:4$.

You may — *or may not* — be given the necessary formulas to solve this type of question. Don't take any chances: Memorize the geometry formulas.

28. **B.** If you selected Choice C, our work here has been in vain. To find an average, you add up the terms and then divide by the number of terms. But this is a Time-Rate-Distance problem, and the terms here aren't simply 600 and 400. You have to find the length of time spent flying at 600 mph *and* the length of time spent flying at 400 mph and then add *those* numbers and divide.

If you think logically about this problem, you know the answer can't be Choice C, but if you don't want to spend time working it out, you can eliminate a few more answers. You know that the plane must go more time at the slower rate and less time at the faster rate. That means the average is going to be less than half of the "average" 500 mph. Immediately narrow your answers down to Choices A and B. If you're in a hurry, guess and go.

You probably wanted to make a simple Time-Rate-Distance chart for this problem, right? Good thinking . . . but that tactic doesn't work here. To make a chart of that sort, you must have at least two of the three variables. For example, if you know rate and distance, you can find time. But here, you have only one variable — rate. You can't solve for time and distance. What do you do now? Find a ratio.

Use a common multiple of 12 (actually, 1,200) miles. In 2 hours, the plane traveling at 600 mph will go 1,200 miles. In 3 hours, the plane traveling at 400 miles will go 1,200 miles. To find the average, add 600 twice and 400 three times . . . then divide by 5 (three hours there plus two hours back again), not by 2. The math looks like this: 600 + 600 + 400 + 400 + 400 = 2,400; $\frac{2,400}{5} = 480$.

Did the words "arithmetic mean" confuse you? They're put there to prevent any lawsuits over confusion of terms. The "average" can mean different things to different people; the "arithmetic mean" is the precise term. The short story? Don't worry about info in parentheses — it's usually there to cover fundamental anatomical regions in case of litigation. You can ignore it.

Analytical Writing Sections

Give your essays to someone to read and evaluate for you. Refer that helpful person to Chapter 20 for scoring guidelines.

Chapter 24

How to Ruin a Perfectly Good Day, Part II: Practice Exam 2

• •

Are you bloody but unbowed and ready to have another go at it? The following exam consists of four sections — one 30-minute Verbal section, one 45-minute Math section, one 30-minute essay, and one 45-minute essay. (You were kind enough to laugh at our jokes; we're kind enough to leave out the unscored section.) You're familiar (okay, practically *intimate*) with the question formats by now.

Please take this practice test under normal exam conditions and approach it as if it were the real GRE. This is serious stuff here!

1. **Work when you won't be interrupted (even though you'd probably welcome any distractions).**

2. **Use scratch paper that's free of any prepared notes.**

    On the actual GRE, you'll receive blank scratch paper before your test begins. You'll have a little time before the clock starts to jot down a few notes and formulas and a series of columns of numbers or letters that you may want to use to help you eliminate answer choices, but you may not whip out a ready-made version of such test-taking aids.

3. **Turn on the clock at the beginning of each test section and be very careful on the first five questions. Remember that these earlier questions contribute more to your score than do the later questions.**

4. **Guess and move on if a question is truly impossible for you.**

    You don't have the option of skipping the question and coming back to it. The computer won't let you move on until you mark and confirm an answer.

5. **Make sure that you get to the end of the test section (30th question for Verbal and 28th question for Math).**

    If you have to, make wild guesses to reach the end before time expires. Unanswered questions will hurt your score more than incorrect answers will.

6. **If you get to the last question before time expires, you can either answer it right away and finish your test early or relax for a while and mark your answer shortly before time expires.**

    You can't use the time to go back and check your work, so do the former if you feel pumped up and you're on a roll. Give yourself the breather if you feel bombarded by the test.

7. **Don't leave your computer while the clock is running on any section.**

8. **You'll be given a one-minute break after the first section and the option to take a ten-minute break after the second section.**

Try to simulate these conditions when you take this practice test.

After you finish, check your answers with the answer key. Take a few minutes to go over the answer explanations to *all* the questions, not just the ones you miss. This is your last chance to pick up one more nugget of knowledge — the final bit of information that could put you over the top.

Answer Sheet

Begin with Number 1 for each new section. If any sections have fewer than 50 questions, leave the extra spaces blank.

Verbal Section

1. Ⓐ Ⓑ Ⓒ Ⓓ Ⓔ   26. Ⓐ Ⓑ Ⓒ Ⓓ Ⓔ
2. Ⓐ Ⓑ Ⓒ Ⓓ Ⓔ   27. Ⓐ Ⓑ Ⓒ Ⓓ Ⓔ
3. Ⓐ Ⓑ Ⓒ Ⓓ Ⓔ   28. Ⓐ Ⓑ Ⓒ Ⓓ Ⓔ
4. Ⓐ Ⓑ Ⓒ Ⓓ Ⓔ   29. Ⓐ Ⓑ Ⓒ Ⓓ Ⓔ
5. Ⓐ Ⓑ Ⓒ Ⓓ Ⓔ   30. Ⓐ Ⓑ Ⓒ Ⓓ Ⓔ
6. Ⓐ Ⓑ Ⓒ Ⓓ Ⓔ   31. Ⓐ Ⓑ Ⓒ Ⓓ Ⓔ
7. Ⓐ Ⓑ Ⓒ Ⓓ Ⓔ   32. Ⓐ Ⓑ Ⓒ Ⓓ Ⓔ
8. Ⓐ Ⓑ Ⓒ Ⓓ Ⓔ   33. Ⓐ Ⓑ Ⓒ Ⓓ Ⓔ
9. Ⓐ Ⓑ Ⓒ Ⓓ Ⓔ   34. Ⓐ Ⓑ Ⓒ Ⓓ Ⓔ
10. Ⓐ Ⓑ Ⓒ Ⓓ Ⓔ   35. Ⓐ Ⓑ Ⓒ Ⓓ Ⓔ
11. Ⓐ Ⓑ Ⓒ Ⓓ Ⓔ   36. Ⓐ Ⓑ Ⓒ Ⓓ Ⓔ
12. Ⓐ Ⓑ Ⓒ Ⓓ Ⓔ   37. Ⓐ Ⓑ Ⓒ Ⓓ Ⓔ
13. Ⓐ Ⓑ Ⓒ Ⓓ Ⓔ   38. Ⓐ Ⓑ Ⓒ Ⓓ Ⓔ
14. Ⓐ Ⓑ Ⓒ Ⓓ Ⓔ   39. Ⓐ Ⓑ Ⓒ Ⓓ Ⓔ
15. Ⓐ Ⓑ Ⓒ Ⓓ Ⓔ   40. Ⓐ Ⓑ Ⓒ Ⓓ Ⓔ
16. Ⓐ Ⓑ Ⓒ Ⓓ Ⓔ   41. Ⓐ Ⓑ Ⓒ Ⓓ Ⓔ
17. Ⓐ Ⓑ Ⓒ Ⓓ Ⓔ   42. Ⓐ Ⓑ Ⓒ Ⓓ Ⓔ
18. Ⓐ Ⓑ Ⓒ Ⓓ Ⓔ   43. Ⓐ Ⓑ Ⓒ Ⓓ Ⓔ
19. Ⓐ Ⓑ Ⓒ Ⓓ Ⓔ   44. Ⓐ Ⓑ Ⓒ Ⓓ Ⓔ
20. Ⓐ Ⓑ Ⓒ Ⓓ Ⓔ   45. Ⓐ Ⓑ Ⓒ Ⓓ Ⓔ
21. Ⓐ Ⓑ Ⓒ Ⓓ Ⓔ   46. Ⓐ Ⓑ Ⓒ Ⓓ Ⓔ
22. Ⓐ Ⓑ Ⓒ Ⓓ Ⓔ   47. Ⓐ Ⓑ Ⓒ Ⓓ Ⓔ
23. Ⓐ Ⓑ Ⓒ Ⓓ Ⓔ   48. Ⓐ Ⓑ Ⓒ Ⓓ Ⓔ
24. Ⓐ Ⓑ Ⓒ Ⓓ Ⓔ   49. Ⓐ Ⓑ Ⓒ Ⓓ Ⓔ
25. Ⓐ Ⓑ Ⓒ Ⓓ Ⓔ   50. Ⓐ Ⓑ Ⓒ Ⓓ Ⓔ

Math Section

1. (A) (B) (C) (D) (E)
2. (A) (B) (C) (D) (E)
3. (A) (B) (C) (D) (E)
4. (A) (B) (C) (D) (E)
5. (A) (B) (C) (D) (E)
6. (A) (B) (C) (D) (E)
7. (A) (B) (C) (D) (E)
8. (A) (B) (C) (D) (E)
9. (A) (B) (C) (D) (E)
10. (A) (B) (C) (D) (E)
11. (A) (B) (C) (D) (E)
12. (A) (B) (C) (D) (E)
13. (A) (B) (C) (D) (E)
14. (A) (B) (C) (D) (E)
15. (A) (B) (C) (D) (E)
16. (A) (B) (C) (D) (E)
17. (A) (B) (C) (D) (E)
18. (A) (B) (C) (D) (E)
19. (A) (B) (C) (D) (E)
20. (A) (B) (C) (D) (E)
21. (A) (B) (C) (D) (E)
22. (A) (B) (C) (D) (E)
23. (A) (B) (C) (D) (E)
24. (A) (B) (C) (D) (E)
25. (A) (B) (C) (D) (E)

26. (A) (B) (C) (D) (E)
27. (A) (B) (C) (D) (E)
28. (A) (B) (C) (D) (E)
29. (A) (B) (C) (D) (E)
30. (A) (B) (C) (D) (E)
31. (A) (B) (C) (D) (E)
32. (A) (B) (C) (D) (E)
33. (A) (B) (C) (D) (E)
34. (A) (B) (C) (D) (E)
35. (A) (B) (C) (D) (E)
36. (A) (B) (C) (D) (E)
37. (A) (B) (C) (D) (E)
38. (A) (B) (C) (D) (E)
39. (A) (B) (C) (D) (E)
40. (A) (B) (C) (D) (E)
41. (A) (B) (C) (D) (E)
42. (A) (B) (C) (D) (E)
43. (A) (B) (C) (D) (E)
44. (A) (B) (C) (D) (E)
45. (A) (B) (C) (D) (E)
46. (A) (B) (C) (D) (E)
47. (A) (B) (C) (D) (E)
48. (A) (B) (C) (D) (E)
49. (A) (B) (C) (D) (E)
50. (A) (B) (C) (D) (E)

Analytical Writing: Present Your Perspective on an Issue

Time: 45 minutes

One essay

Directions: Present and explain your view on one of the following issues. Although there is no one right or wrong response to the issue, be sure to consider various points of view as you explain the reasons behind your own perspective.

Topic 1

"Television and videos are going to leave a more lasting and valid perception of our society to future generations than is literature."

Topic 2

"Gas-alternative means of transportation will eventually replace gas-powered transportation."

Choose a topic and justify your position by using examples from your personal or professional experience, reading, or general observation.

Go on to next page

Go on to next page

Go on to next page

Go on to next page

Go on to next page

Go on to next page

Analytical Writing: Analyze an Argument

Time: 30 minutes

One essay

Directions: Critique the following argument. Identify evidence that will strengthen or weaken the argument, point out assumptions underlying the argument, and offer counterexamples to the argument.

The following appeared in a letter to the editor of the Flint Herald newspaper.

"School board elections are coming up in a few months. Voters should vote for Martinez Westwood for school board member, rather than for the incumbent, Harris Black, because the current school board is doing a poor job. In the past two years since the current board was elected, the dropout rate has increased by 30 percent, voters did not approve the necessary tax increase to raise teacher salaries, and the morale of both educators and students is down. By electing Martinez Westwood, these problems will be resolved quickly and correctly."

Discuss the merits of the previous argument. Analyze the evidence used as well as the general reasoning. Present points that would strengthen the argument or make it more compelling.

Go on to next page

Go on to next page

Go on to next page

Go on to next page

Go on to next page

Go on to next page

Verbal Section

Time: 30 minutes

30 questions

Choose the best answer to each question. Blacken the corresponding oval on the answer grid.

Directions: Choose the answer choice most nearly opposite in meaning to the question word.

1. LUCID

    (A) turbid

    (B) vivacious

    (C) minuscule

    (D) domineering

    (E) spicy

Directions: Each of the following questions features a pair of words or phrases in capital letters, followed by five pairs of words or phrases in lowercase letters. Choose the lowercase pair that most closely expresses the same relationship as that of the uppercase pair.

2. TONSORIAL : HAIR ::

    (A) professorial : job

    (B) medical : disease

    (C) stentorian : throat

    (D) sartorial : apparel

    (E) canine : teeth

3. CHATTER : MONKEYS ::

    (A) pride : lions

    (B) fawn : deer

    (C) snake : viper

    (D) low : cattle

    (E) pelt : fox

Directions: The following sentence has one blank indicating that a word is omitted. Choose the answer that best completes the sentence.

4. Although often - - - -, James Michael realized the importance of proceeding slowly with his task and deliberately forced himself to examine all the options available to him before making the decision on the best way to proceed.

    (A) impetuous

    (B) pensive

    (C) uncouth

    (D) dilatory

    (E) unenthusiastic

Directions: Choose the answer choice most nearly opposite in meaning to the question word.

5. INDIGENOUS

    (A) foreign

    (B) amiable

    (C) satisfactory

    (D) lustrous

    (E) pallid

6. HACKNEYED

    (A) belligerent

    (B) mercenary

    (C) flexible

    (D) fresh

    (E) passive

Go on to next page

Directions: Questions 7 and 8 pertain to the following passage. Read the passage and answer the questions based on information stated or implied in the passage.

Line   Community property is a legal concept that is growing in popularity in the United States. A few years ago, only the western states had community property laws, and few people east of
(05) the Mississippi had ever heard the expression "community property." Now several states have adopted or modified laws regarding community property.

Both wife and husband jointly own commu-
(10) nity property. Generally, the property that a spouse owned before the marriage is known as separate or specific property. It remains the property of the original possessor in case of a separation or divorce. Community property is anything
(15) gained by the joint effort of the spouses.

Gifts specifically bestowed upon only one party, or legacies to only one spouse, are separate property. However, courts often determine that a donor had the intention to give the gift to
(20) both parties, even though his words or papers may have indicated otherwise. Community property goes to the surviving partner in case of the death of one spouse. Only that half of the property owned by the testator can be willed away.

7. In which of the following instances would a gift to one party become community property?

  I. When the court determines the intent of the donor was to make a gift to the couple.

  II. When the property is real (land) rather than personal (possessions).

  III. When the court determines that the intent to give the gift was formed by the donor prior to the party's marriage.

    (A) I only

    (B) II only

    (C) I and III only

    (D) II and III only

    (E) I, II, and III

8. You may infer that the author would most likely agree with which of the following?

    (A) Community property is the fairest settlement concept for marital property.

    (B) Community property laws currently discriminate against the working spouse in favor of the homemaker spouse.

    (C) Community property laws will probably continue to increase in number throughout the United States.

    (D) Community property laws will be expanded to include all property acquired during the marriage, regardless of its source.

    (E) All inheritances received by one party during the marriage are in theory, if not in fact, community property.

Directions: Choose the answer choice most nearly opposite in meaning to the question word.

9. HAPLESS

    (A) saturnine

    (B) fortunate

    (C) cacophonous

    (D) mordant

    (E) ambiguous

10. BURGEON

    (A) garble

    (B) purchase

    (C) aggravate

    (D) wither

    (E) dominate

Go on to next page

Directions: Questions 11–14 pertain to the following passage. Read the passage and answer the questions based on information stated or implied in the passage.

Line A key study has shown that the organic matter content of a soil can be altered to a depth of 10 cm or more by intense campfire heat. As much as 90 percent of the original organic matter (05) may be oxidized in the top 1.3 cm of soil. In the surface 10 cm, the loss of organic matter may reach 50 percent if the soil is dry and the temperature exceeds 250°C. The loss of organic matter reduces soil fertility and water-holding capacity (10) and renders the soil more susceptible to compaction and erosion.

Sandy soils attain higher temperatures and retain heat longer than clay soils under similar fuel, moisture, and weather conditions. From this (15) standpoint, it is desirable to locate campgrounds in an area with loam or clay-loam soil. Sandy soils are less susceptible to compaction damage, however, and are more desirable for campgrounds from this standpoint.

(20) A water-repellent layer can be created in a soil by the heat from the campfire. This condition was noted only in sandy soils where the temperature remained below 350°C during the campfire burn. Campfires often produce temperatures above this (25) level. By comparison, forest fires are a shorter-duration event, and soil temperatures produced are more likely to create water repellency-inducing conditions. The greater extent of forest fires makes them a more serious threat than campfires in (30) terms of causing soil-water repellency.

If the soil remained moist for the duration of the campfire, the increased heat capacity of the soil and heat of water vaporization kept the soil temperature below 100°C. At this temperature, (35) little loss of organic matter occurred, and no water repellency was created. For areas where the soil remains very moist, campfires probably have little effect on the soil properties.

Studies show that softwood fuels burn faster (40) and produce less heat flow into the soil than do hardwood fuels under the same conditions. Elm and mesquite were the hottest burning and longest lasting fuels tested. In areas where some choice of fuels is available, the use of softwood (45) fuels should be encouraged in an effort to minimize the effect of campfires on soil properties.

By restricting the fire site to the same area, the effects of campfires on the soil in a campground can be lessened, even if permanent concrete (50) fireplaces are not installed. In this manner,

any harmful effects are restricted to a minimum area. If campfires are allowed to be located at random by the user, the harmful effects tend to be spread over a larger part of the campground. The placement of a stone fire ring in the chosen (55) location is one way to accomplish the objective.

These data support the decision to install permanent fireplaces in many areas and to restrict the use of campfires elsewhere in the park. This eliminates the harmful effects of camp- (60) fires on the soil and allows the campground to be located on sandy soil with low compactibility and good drainage.

11. It can be inferred from the passage that campfire users generally

(A) evaluate the amount of soil damage that can result before they build a campfire.

(B) are concerned with the possibility that their campfire can cause a forest fire.

(C) have no regard for the biological consequences that result from their campfires.

(D) consider many areas of a campground to be suitable for a campfire.

(E) favor sandy soil over clay-loam soil as a campfire site.

12. The main idea of this passage is that

(A) excessive campfires will eventually make it impossible to grow crops.

(B) soil temperature affects soil fertility.

(C) only certain woods allow for high-quality campfires.

(D) soils must be able to absorb water to sustain organic matter.

(E) steps can be taken to minimize soil damage from campfires.

13. Long-lasting campfires are more likely than short-lived ones to

(A) create water repellency–inducing conditions.

(B) maintain soil fertility.

(C) occur with softwood fuels.

(D) restrict damage to the top 1.3 cm of soil.

(E) produce higher soil temperatures.

Go on to next page

14. It can be inferred from the passage that the author would be most likely to agree with which of the following?

    (A) Campfires should be banned as destructive to campground soil.

    (B) Organic matter decreases soil erosion.

    (C) Clay-loam soil is preferable to sandy soil for campsites.

    (D) The longer the duration of the fire, the higher the resistant soil temperatures.

    (E) Campfires will not burn in areas with moist soil.

Directions: Choose the answer choice most nearly opposite in meaning to the question word.

15. EQUIVOCAL

    (A) shy

    (B) direct

    (C) vapid

    (D) incongruous

    (E) obtuse

16. SANGUINE

    (A) supple

    (B) stygian

    (C) doting

    (D) morose

    (E) voracious

17. ABJURE

    (A) tamper

    (B) placate

    (C) exacerbate

    (D) advocate

    (E) extirpate

Directions: The following sentences have one or more blanks indicating that words are omitted. Choose the answer that best completes the sentence.

18. Although he lacked the - - - - that he would like to have in the field, Dr. Dickstein felt confident enough of his premise to continue arguing - - - - against the physician, whom he considered to be a dangerous quack and a charlatan.

    (A) fidelity . . . exhaustively

    (B) grace . . . indifferently

    (C) skill . . . lackadaisically

    (D) expertise . . . vehemently

    (E) ability . . . tentatively

19. The feeling that one is being watched is not always mere paranoia; indeed, the - - - - and random viewing of citizens by some governmental bureaus is quite probably more - - - - than is commonly known.

    (A) intermittent . . . widespread

    (B) haphazard . . . ironhanded

    (C) arbitrary . . . fly-by-night

    (D) flagrant . . . surreptitious

    (E) unauthorized . . . banal

Directions: Each of the following questions features a pair of words or phrases in capital letters, followed by five pairs of words or phrases in lowercase letters. Choose the lowercase pair that most closely expresses the same relationship as that of the uppercase pair.

20. ANTHEM : SONG ::

    (A) picture : portfolio

    (B) score : instrument

    (C) bellow : whisper

    (D) prologue : epilogue

    (E) panegyric : speech

Go on to next page

21. HEIRLOOM : ANCESTOR ::

    (A) red herring : magician

    (B) bequest : testator

    (C) instrument : musician

    (D) rules : renegade

    (E) throne : usurper

22. INCITE : STIFLE ::

    (A) exorcise : remove

    (B) stymie : confuse

    (C) begrudge : deny

    (D) abscond : return

    (E) verify : prove

Directions: The following sentences have one or more blanks indicating that words are omitted. Choose the answer that best completes the sentence.

23. At the ---- of his career, Ken basks in the kudos and ---- of judges and audiences alike.

    (A) apogee . . . plaudits

    (B) lapse . . . reproofs

    (C) apex . . . fecklessness

    (D) genesis . . . effrontery

    (E) nascency . . . perjury

24. Purchasing lengthy, often incomprehensible ---- for the sole purpose of displaying them in one's bookcase has been labeled by some ---- as "intellectual vanity."

    (A) collages . . . pundits

    (B) maxims . . . writers

    (C) brochures . . . sages

    (D) scores . . . teachers

    (E) tomes . . . wags

Directions: Each of the following questions features a pair of words or phrases in capital letters, followed by five pairs of words or phrases in lowercase letters. Choose the lowercase pair that most closely expresses the same relationship as that of the uppercase pair.

25. THIN : EMACIATED ::

    (A) happy : ecstatic

    (B) reclusive : solitary

    (C) sentimental : apathetic

    (D) relevant : immaterial

    (E) fickle : constant

26. ANGRY : INCENSED ::

    (A) noticeable : flamboyant

    (B) obdurate : stubborn

    (C) ancient : outmoded

    (D) melodious : euphonious

    (E) calm : pacific

Directions: Questions 27–29 pertain to the following passage. Read the passage and answer the questions based on information stated or implied in the passage.

In many ways, a Cherokee woman in the time of the "Wild West" had more power within her social group than did a European woman. It was through the mother of the family that membership in clans and general kinship were determined. A Cherokee (the name comes from a Creek Indian word "Chelokee" meaning "people of a different speech;" however, today many Cherokee prefer to be called Tsalagi from their own name for the Cherokee Nation, Tsalagihi Ayili) woman was not forced to marry someone whom her family had chosen in advance for her, as was the practice in European families. Instead, the Cherokee woman had the right to choose her own mate. That mate then had the job to build a house for the woman, which was considered the woman's property. If the woman already had a house of her own, the man would go live there. Should the man be unable or unwilling to build a house, the couple would live with the woman's parents.

Line

(05)

(10)

(15)

(20)

Go on to next page

A Cherokee house was wattle and daub. Often described as looking like an upside-down basket, it was a simple circular frame with inter-woven branches. The house was plastered with
(25) mud and sunken into the ground. Although many people do not associate log cabins with Native Americans, these dwellings became common among the Cherokee later in their history. They also built large council houses to keep the sacred
(30) fire, which was never allowed to go out.

Divorce was very simple. The woman would place her husband's possessions outside of the house, which was considered sufficient notice to free both the woman and the man to remarry.
(35) The woman kept the house her husband built for her. It was accepted for a woman to have one husband after another. Adultery in the marriage, therefore, was relatively uncommon.

Any children born to the couple were consid-
(40) ered the woman's as well. The father had very few child-rearing responsibilities; instead, the mother and her brothers took charge of the chil-dren, showing them the tribal ways. The woman also controlled how many children would sur-
(45) vive. She had the legal right to destroy any chil-dren who were not born healthy or give away any children she felt were beyond the number she was capable of feeding and caring for. The father had no such right.
(50) Rights for women were just one aspect of the Cherokee civilization. During the early 1800s, the Cherokee developed a formal written constitu-tion. Cherokees had their own courts and schools, considered by some to be of a higher
(55) standard than those of their White counterparts. Even today, the Cherokee level of education and living standard ranks among the highest of all Native American tribes.

27. The passage serves primarily to

  (A) ridicule the idea that Cherokee women were less advanced than White women.

  (B) compare and contrast the educational systems of Cherokees and Whites.

  (C) praise the advances that Cherokees made in the face of White resistance.

  (D) inform the reader of the rights of Cherokee women.

  (E) refute the theory that Cherokee women were less capable of fighting than were Cherokee men.

28. Which of the following questions is NOT answered in the passage?

  (A) When did the Cherokee nation begin following a written constitution?

  (B) What do the Cherokee people call themselves?

  (C) How is a Cherokee house constructed?

  (D) Who educated Cherokee children?

  (E) How did a Cherokee woman choose a mate?

29. The author's strategy in this passage is best described as

  (A) presenting a chronological history of events.

  (B) presenting and then refuting a theory.

  (C) proposing a theory and then anticipat-ing a countertheory.

  (D) stating an idea and then giving support-ing examples.

  (E) refuting a controversial idea.

Directions: The following sentence has one or more blanks indicating that words are omitted. Choose the answer that best com-pletes the sentence.

30. Experts - - - - that dog carvings and statues found in such - - - - places as Egypt, Mexico, and China were of the dachshund, whose German name means badger hound.

  (A) conjecture . . . ancient

  (B) hypothesize . . . disparate

  (C) refute . . . similar

  (D) insist . . . geographic

  (E) deny . . . inauspicious

Math Section

Time: 45 Minutes

28 questions

Notes:

All numbers used in this exam are real numbers.

All figures lie in a plane.

Angle measures are positive; points and angles are in the position shown.

The answer choices are

A if the quantity in Column A is greater.

B if the quantity in Column B is greater.

C if the two quantities are equal.

D if the relationship cannot be determined from the information given.

Column A	**Column B**
1. In Debittown, the roller rink is 10 kilometers from the school, which is 3 kilometers from the coffee shop.	
Distance from the roller rink to the coffee shop	13 kilometers

2. $a = \frac{2}{3}b;\ b = \frac{3}{4}c$

Fraction that a is of c	$\frac{1}{3}$

3.

$x^{-y}y^{-x}$	1

4.

$a^{10} \times a^5 \times \frac{1}{a^3}$	a^{12}

5.

Area of Circle O = 36π

Length of Arc *NP*	36π

6. | **Column A** | **Column B** |
|---|---|
| $-2 \le x < 0$ | |
| Greatest possible value of | 0 |

7. $a * b * c = 3a + 4b - \frac{1}{2}c$

$3 * 6 * 12$	27

8. The test scores of a group of five students are 72, 70, 68, 75, and 80.

The median test score	73

9.

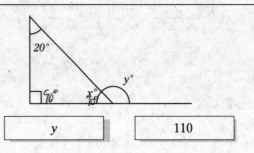

y	110

Go on to next page

10.   **_Column A_**   **_Column B_**

| 300% of 30 | 60% of 15 |

11. $a \times b = c$

| c | b |

12.

| 20 percent of 120 | 120 percent of 20 |

13.

| The number of days in four years | The number of years in forty decades |

14.

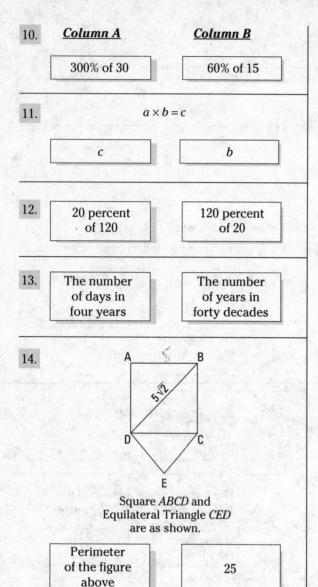

Square *ABCD* and
Equilateral Triangle *CED*
are as shown.

| Perimeter of the figure above | 25 |

15   The average scores of students on a final exam are as shown on the following chart.

Student	Average Score
Dustin	75
Kristiana	82
Leoni	79
Tim	91
Deidre	93

What is the positive difference between the mean and the median of their scores?

(A) 84

(B) 82

(C) 12

(D) 5

(E) 2

16.   An equilateral polygon (not shown) has a total interior angle measure of 1,260. If one side of the figure is 6, what is the perimeter of the figure?

(A) 60

(B) 54

(C) 42

(D) 9

(E) 7

Go on to next page

Questions 17–18 are based on the following graph.

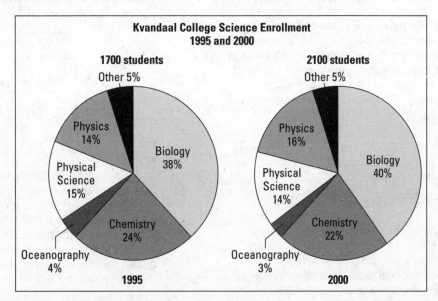

17. To the nearest whole percent, the 2000 biology enrollment was what percent greater than the 1995 biology enrollment?

    (A) 2

    (B) 5

    (C) 8

    (D) 24

    (E) 30

18. A switch from physics to chemistry of how many students in 2000 would have produced a physics to chemistry ratio equal to that of 1995?

    (A) 22

    (B) 42

    (C) 44

    (D) 84

    (E) 114

19. A number of friends are at a party. At 11 p.m., ¼ of the friends leave. At midnight, ⅓ of the remaining friends leave. At 1 a.m., as many people leave as left at 11 p.m. Exactly 30 people remain. How many people were at the party to begin with?

    (A) 60

    (B) 90

    (C) 120

    (D) 160

    (E) 180

20. $\dfrac{6a^{10}b^5c^7}{3a^5b^9c^7}$

    (A) $2a^2b^4c$

    (B) $\dfrac{2a^2b^4}{c}$

    (C) $\dfrac{2a^5b^4}{c}$

    (D) $2a^5b^4$

    (E) $\dfrac{2a^5}{b^4}$

21. A box of candy contains three types of candy: 20 creams, 15 chews, and 12 nuts. Each time LaVonne reaches into the box, she pulls out a piece of candy, takes a bite out of it, and throws it away. She pulls out a cream, a nut, a chew, a nut, a cream, and a chew. What is the probability that on the next reach, she will pull out a nut?

    (A) $^{15}/_{47}$

    (B) $^{13}/_{41}$

    (C) $^{10}/_{41}$

    (D) $^{13}/_{15}$

    (E) $^{11}/_{15}$

Go on to next page

22. Barb, Jim, Angie, Mike, Laura, Carissa, and Sara enter a tournament. Each contestant must compete once against every other contestant, one match at a time, in each of the following five activities: hot-air balloon race, golf, mile run, one-on-one basketball, and a talent competition. How many matches will be played in the tournament?

(A) 125

(B) 105

(C) 50

(D) 42

(E) 21

23. One hundred job applicants show up in response to a classified ad. If 60% of the applicants are female and if 75% of the female applicants are willing to relocate if the job demands it, how many people are not willing to relocate?

(A) 60

(B) 55

(C) 45

(D) 15

(E) It cannot be determined from the information given.

24. If Line Segment XY (not shown) goes from $(-2, 6)$ to $(4, 6)$, what are the coordinates of the midpoint of XY?

(A) $(-1,6)$

(B) $(0,0)$

(C) $(1,6)$

(D) $(3,0)$

(E) $(3,6)$

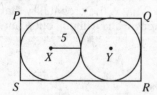

25. Area of Circle X = Area of Circle Y

What is the area of Rectangle $PQRS$?

(A) 200

(B) 180

(C) 150

(D) 100

(E) 25

26.

| $\widehat{x} = x + x^2$ for all prime numbers. |
| $\widehat{x} = x^2 - x$ for all composite numbers. |

$\widehat{4} + \widehat{5} =$

(A) 50

(B) 42

(C) 40

(D) 20

(E) 19

27. At a warehouse store, eight cans of frozen concentrated orange juice cost d dollars. If each can makes m milliliters of orange juice when mixed with three cans of water, what will be the total cost, in dollars, to make 400 milliliters of orange juice if one can of water costs c cents?

(A) $3200md + 96c$

(B) $\dfrac{(md+3c)}{400}$

(C) $\dfrac{(d+3c)}{50m}$

(D) $\dfrac{(8d+96c)}{m}$

(E) $\dfrac{(50d+12c)}{m}$

28. Circle B is perfectly inscribed in Semicircle A (not shown). If the area of Circle A is 16π, what is the circumference of Circle B?

(A) 16π

(B) 12π

(C) 8π

(D) 4π

(E) 2π

Answer Key for Practice Exam 2

Verbal Section

1. A
2. D
3. D
4. A
5. A
6. D
7. A
8. C
9. B
10. D
11. D
12. E
13. E
14. B
15. B
16. D
17. D
18. D
19. A
20. E
21. B
22. D
23. A
24. E
25. A
26. A
27. D
28. E
29. D
30. B

Math Section

1. D
2. A
3. D
4. C
5. B
6. B
7. C
8. B
9. C
10. A
11. D
12. C
13. A
14. C
15. E
16. B
17. E
18. B
19. C
20. E
21. C
22. B
23. E
24. C
25. A
26. B
27. E
28. D

Chapter 25

Practice Exam 2: Answers and Explanations

Verbal Section

1. **A.** You probably got this question right by the process of elimination. *Lucid* means clear (*luc* means light or clear). A lucid explanation *elucidates,* or makes clear, the material. *Turbid* means thick, cloudy, dense. When you stir up waters that are muddy, they become turbid. If you put ice cubes into a glass of *ouzo* (a Greek liqueur), the liquid becomes turbid. *Vivacious* means lively, full of life (*vi* means life; *-ous* means full of). *Minuscule* means very small.

   Don't confuse *turbid* with *turgid*. *Turgid* means swollen or distended. A corpse floating in turbid waters after a few days would become turgid. (Where else but in *The GRE Test For Dummies,* 6th Edition, can you read answer explanations that manage to work in both Greek liqueurs and floating corpses?)

2. **D.** *Tonsorial* means pertaining to hair. No one really expects you to know this word. Instead, assume that unknown words are synonyms and make your sentence, "Tonsorial is hair." Then you can probably narrow the answers down to the two words you don't know (stentorian and sartorial) and make a quick guess. (If we're underestimating your genius and your vocabulary, we abjectly apologize.) *Sartorial* means pertaining to clothing or apparel. If you want to get your money's worth out of this book, tell your mother that she's looking sartorially resplendent when she asks how she looks in her new outfit. And to be sure that she gets the message, bellow your praise in a *stentorian* (loud) voice. In Homer's poetry, Stentor is a character who "has the voice of 50 men." In other words, he's a loudmouth.

   Professorial doesn't mean pertaining to a job. That word would be *professional,* pertaining to a profession or job. *Professorial* means like a professor. In Choice B, *medical* means pertaining to medicine, not pertaining to a disease. Choice C may have made you pause for a moment. Yes, we have canine teeth, but *canine* actually means pertaining to a dog, not pertaining to teeth. Our canine teeth are called that because they're pointed like dogs' teeth.

3. **D.** Unless you're a cowboy or cowgirl, you probably answered this question by the process of elimination. *Chatter* is the sound that monkeys make. *Low* is the sound that cattle make. A *pride* is a group of lions. A *fawn* is a baby deer. A *viper* is a type of snake. A *pelt* is the skin of a fox.

    If you think the GRE is a beastly exam, you're right. Analogy questions sometimes require you to know the terms for the young of animals, groups of animals, or where animals live; therefore, we'd advise you to learn the terms. Use flashcards. Label one "young animals" and write on it such terms as *kit, joey,* and *cygnet.* Label a second card "habitats" and write words such as *den, corral,* and *sty.* Label a third card "groups of animals" and write down *pride, pod,* and *flock.* Roots, prefixes, and suffixes can't help you define these types of words, so a few minutes of memorization can really pay off.

4. **A.** The "although" alerts you to the fact that you want a word meaning the opposite of "proceeding slowly." Because an *unenthusiastic* individual probably *would* proceed slowly (how fast do *you* go when you approach a task unenthusiastically?), eliminate it. Scratch off *pensive,* which means thoughtful or meditative. A pensive person would naturally slow down and examine all aspects of a situation. Eliminate *dilatory,* or slow, as well. A slow individual wouldn't have to *force* himself to slow down. Congrats! You've just narrowed your possible answers down to two. *Uncouth* means unsophisticated or ill-mannered; it has no connection to the sentence. *Impetuous* means hasty, rash, precipitate. An impetuous person would usually rush into things and would have to force himself to slow down and examine the situation more carefully.

5. **A.** *Indigenous* means native to. Monsters are indigenous to the space under a child's bed. Something not native to an area is *foreign* to it. *Amiable* means friendly (**Hint:** Think of *ami,* which is *friend* in French, or *amigo,* which is *friend* in Spanish). *Lustrous* means shiny (*lus* means light or clear). *Pallid* means pale.

6. **D.** *Hackneyed* means made trite by overuse. A phrase like "Have a happy day!" is hackneyed. Most slang becomes hackneyed after a few months. Choice A, *belligerent,* means warlike, ready to fight (*belli* means war or fight). *Mercenary* means greedy, done for money.

7. **A.** The passage states that a court may deem a gift community property if the donor's intent was to give it to both parties, even if the donor didn't state so specifically. Because Statement I is correct, eliminate Choices B and D. Statement II is wrong; it brings in the distinction between real and personal property, which wasn't covered in the passage. (For those of you who've gone through *acrimonious* — bitter — divorces and are all too familiar with the concept of community property, shelf your knowledge while answering these questions. Answer them based only on the information stated or implied by the passage.) Statement III is also wrong but very tricky. Nothing in the passage states that the time of the intent to make the gift is important, only the intent of the donor. If you picked Choice C, you read too much into the question.

8. **C.** The author mentions early in the passage that there used to be just a few community-property states, but that the number has been steadily increasing. From this fact, you may infer that this increase will continue.

   Choice A is definitely a judgment call. Who's to say whether the community property concept is fair, not fair, the fairest, or the least fair? Passages (unless they're editorial or opinion types, which are infrequently included on the GRE) rarely give personal opinions or push one person's theories or philosophies. Choice B is well outside the scope of this passage; nothing is mentioned about homemakers. Choice D goes overboard. Just because the author believes there will be more community-property states doesn't mean states will turn *all* possessions into community property.

   As advised in Chapter 10, be wishy-washy with your answers, not dramatic. Eliminate any answer choices with strong words, such as *all, every, never,* and *none.* Choice E has the same problem: It features the excessive word *all.*

9. **B.** *Hapless* means without luck, unlucky (*hap* means luck; a mishap is bad luck; *haphazard* means depending on luck or chance). Choice A, *saturnine,* means gloomy or morose. Choice C, *cacophonous,* means bad sounding or raucous (*caco* means bad; *phon* means sound; *-ous* means full of). Choice D, *mordant,* means sarcastic or caustic. Choice E, *ambiguous,* means uncertain, able to be interpreted in two or more ways (*ambi* means both; *-ous* means full of. Ambiguous is "full of both," unclear). An ambiguous response is often the best answer to a no-win question such as, "Does this outfit make me look fatter than before?"

10. **D.** To *burgeon* is to blossom and grow. The opposite is to *wither.* To *garble* is to distort or jumble. A student may garble her words and mispronounce this question as "surgeon" or even (our favorite) "sturgeon." Pretty hard to find the opposite of sturgeon, wouldn't you say? (To whom do you complain when you get a bad batch of caviar? The sturgeon general!)

11. **D.** The last two paragraphs of the passage urge measures to restrict campfire location. The author claims that without such measures, campfires will be built just about everywhere and that soil damage will be widespread. You can thus infer that campfire users, when left to their own devices, will build a campfire just about anywhere, which leads to Choice D as the answer. Because the opposite of Choice A appears to be true, eliminate this option. Choice B is plausible, but the author doesn't mention a connection between campfire users and forest fires. Forest fires are covered briefly in the third paragraph in relation to water repellency, but Choice C goes overboard. The passage doesn't provide any detail to indicate whether campfire users favor a certain type of soil, eliminating Choice E. The scientific findings described in the second paragraph point to an advantage of one type or the other, but you can't tell whether the campfire users actually consider this evidence.

12. **E.** This passage contains a lot of dry detail about how campfires damage soil and its ability to support life, and the author uses these details to recommend a certain action. Choice E fits perfectly with the author's concern that campfires damage soil and her desire to minimize this damage. Choice A is too extreme. Choices B and D are true statements, but they're just two of several factors mentioned by the author.

    Just because a statement is true doesn't mean it's the correct answer; in a main idea question, all five choices may in fact be true. Choice C is also a detail but is wrong, primarily because the author is concerned that certain woods will lead to soil damage, not with how well the woods will work with the campfire per se.

13. **E.** Common sense suggests that Choice E is the right answer — a notion that's confirmed by the third paragraph, which mentions that short-lived forest fires are more likely than campfires to create water repellency–inducing conditions (knocking out Choice A). This information implies that campfires last longer. Combine this reasoning with the explicit mention that campfires typically exceed 350 degrees, and you've got your answer. Choice C is directly contradicted by the fourth paragraph. Choices B and D don't make sense. The passage often mentions that heat flow into the soil damages it. A long-lasting campfire produces more heat flow than a short-lived one.

Although you certainly don't need to have any background knowledge to answer Reading Comprehension questions (all the necessary info is given or implied in the passage), don't hesitate to use your common sense, especially with biological and physical science passages. Common sense is a good place to start, but do be sure to check your "obvious" answer with the facts given in the passage.

14. **B.** The last sentence of the first paragraph states that the loss of organic matter reduces water-holding capacity and renders the soil more susceptible to erosion. Note that this question basically requires you to truly understand the whole passage. If you didn't read the passage carefully and instead skimmed for specific answers to specific questions, this question would've been a good one to guess at.

15. **B.** *Equivocal* means misleading, ambiguous, uncertain. When you ask your parents whether they'll buy you a fire-engine-red Ferrari should you finish your Ph.D., their "We'll see" is an equivocal response.

You may be more familiar with this word in its negative sense, *unequivocal,* which means absolutely direct, certain, no doubt about it. When you ask your parents to let you use your college fund to backpack around the world, their response will be an unequivocal "NO!"

Vapid means lifeless, dull, boring. It can also mean literally tasteless, as in vapid soda that has gone flat. (Vapid is akin to the word *vappa,* which means stale wine.) *Incongruous* means inconsistent, or not in agreement. You know that congruent angles in geometry are equal; incongruent angles aren't equal. *Obtuse* can mean blunt, or it can mean dull metaphorically, as in slow to understand. An obtuse boyfriend buys his girlfriend a new car battery for her birthday, even though she has been leaving jewelry store ads in his room, backpack, and car.

16. **D.** *Sanguine* means cheerful, optimistic, and confident. Don't confuse sanguine with *sanguinary,* meaning bloodthirsty. The opposite is *morose,* which means gloomy or sullen. Choice A, *supple,* means flexible, lithe. Choice E, *voracious,* means greedy, ravenous. Are you voracious for yet more vocabulary, or has this section sated you?

17. **D.** To *abjure* is to give up (*ab-* means away from; when you abjure your rights, you go away from them, you give them up). To *advocate* (*ad-* means toward) is to support, be in favor of. After you've aced the GRE, you'll abjure studying this material and advocate making it into confetti to celebrate your excellent score. To *tamper* is to interfere or meddle with. As an April Fool's joke, you may tamper with the bathroom scale so that your sorority sister thinks she's ten pounds heavier than she is. To *placate* (*plac* means peace or calm) is to mollify, appease, pacify, or stop from being angry. To placate your friend who's furious about your April Fool's joke, you turn the scale back ten pounds to make her think she's thinner than she is. To *exacerbate* is to aggravate, to make more intense, to irritate. Your second prank just exacerbated the situation, making it worse. To *extirpate* is to destroy or remove (*ex* means out of or away from), to abolish. Your more mature friends extirpate the bathroom scale, tossing it into the trash to avoid any more crises.

18. **D.** Focus on the second blank. If Dr. Dickstein felt that the man against whom he was arguing was dangerous, he'd argue pretty strongly against him. Eliminate Choice B (*indifferently* means not caring one way or the other), Choice C (*lackadaisically* means in a mellow, laid-back, nonenergetic way), and Choice E (*tentatively* means hesitantly or uncertainly). The second word in Choice A is possible; *exhaustively* means thoroughly. (It doesn't mean the same thing as exhausted, although an exhaustive search of the house for your missing car keys may leave you exhausted.) The first word, however, doesn't fit. *Fidelity* means faithfulness, as in fidelity among a loving couple (or the fidelity exhibited by Fido the faithful companion). That leaves Choice D. *Vehemently* means powerfully, strongly felt.

Do you know the words *charlatan* and *quack* in the question? A *charlatan* or a *quack* is a fraud or nonexpert. A GRE tutor who says you'll get a 1600 if you stand naked in the light of the full moon and bury a toad in your backyard is a charlatan.

19. **A.** Vocabulary is the key to this sentence. You probably could predict relatively easily what types of words go in the blanks; the trouble is finding the words with those definitions. Start with the second blank. Say: The practice is probably more *common* than realized. *Widespread* means common, spread about everywhere. *Ironhanded* means severe, strong. Ever hear the expression "rules with an iron fist"? Such a ruler is ironhanded.

Here's a word to the wise for international students: Throughout this book, we use clichés and expressions common to English, like "rules with an iron fist" (and "word to the wise"). If you don't understand these expressions or aren't comfortable with them, get someone to explain them to you. Many vocabulary words on this exam are parts of *aphorisms* (sayings) or *adages* (sayings). We suggest that you pull out an index card and write the cliché or saying on the card along with an explanation of how it's used and what words are related to it (such as ironhanded).

Fly-by-night is another cliché. It means temporary, not permanent. It came from the idea that a less-than-honest company would pack up in the middle of the night and leave town, taking its customers' money with it. It would, in effect, fly away in the middle of the night. Hence the cliché: fly-by-night. *Surreptitious* means secretive, concealed. *Banal* means dull or stale from overuse. A cliché is banal.

Here's the vocabulary for the first blanks. *Intermittent* means off and on, not constant. Don't confuse this word with *interminable,* which means endless, or seemingly endless. A lecture can be interminable; a good lecturer uses jokes intermittently to try to keep the listeners' attention. *Haphazard* means nonsystematic, unplanned. *Arbitrary* means dependent on individual discretion and not fixed by law. You make an arbitrary choice when you buy a grab bag.

20. **E.** An *anthem* is a song, usually one of praise. A *panegyric* is a speech (or a piece of writing), usually one of praise. ***Bonus trivia:*** Did you know that Sir Walter Scott wrote the words to the American presidential anthem, "Hail to the Chief"?

Choice B is a trap. A trap answer often has the same general meaning (in this case, music, score, anthem, song) as the question. Remember to create and use a sentence that expresses the relationship between the words. An anthem is a type of song; a *score* isn't a type of instrument. A *bellow* is the opposite of a whisper. A *prologue* (*pro* meaning before, *log* meaning speech) comes before the main speech and is the opposite of the *epilogue,* which comes at the end.

21. **B.** This is a hard question because so many of the answer choices are similar. The best sentence is that an *heirloom* is something left to you by an ancestor. A *bequest* (a gift to an heir) is left to you by a *testator* (one who makes the last will and testament). Although a magician may incorporate a *red herring* (something that tries to mislead or trick) into his act, he doesn't leave you one. Although a musician uses an instrument, he doesn't leave you one. A *renegade* is a person who breaks the rules, a rebel. He leaves you with nothing. A *usurper* is one who takes without authority or right. He takes the throne; he doesn't leave it to you.

22. **D.** To *incite* is to stir up or rouse something, as in inciting a riot. To *stifle* is to hold back, suppress, or inhibit. With the help of this book, you'll be unable to stifle your cheers when you see your excellent GRE scores. The relationship is opposites. To *abscond* is to run away quickly — the opposite of to return.

Knowing your roots and prefixes can help you here: *ab-* means away from. Choice A, to *exorcise* is to take away (*ex* means out of, away from). To *stymie* is to confuse or bewilder. To *begrudge* is to give with reluctance, as in begrudging a friend a bite of your favorite dessert. To *verify* (*ver* means truth) is to prove true.

23. **A.** Start with the second blank. If Ken is *basking* in something, he's enjoying it immensely, so it must be good. You could deduce the same thing by knowing that *kudos* means praise, glory, fame. The second word that goes with *kudos and . . .* must be positive as well. *Plaudits* are praises. An *apogee* is the zenith, the highest point. Winning one night on *Jeopardy!* was the apogee of our friend (don't ask what happened the next night; it was her career *nadir,* or low point).

Choice B, a *lapse,* is a pause or break. She had a brain cell lapse the second night on *Jeopardy!* and was full of self-reproof. *Reproofs* are criticisms or condemnations. (To reprove doesn't mean to prove again; it means to criticize or condemn. People often misdefine this word.) In Choice C, an *apex* is the top point, the zenith, the apogee. This word works for the first blank, but the second blank lets you down. *Fecklessness* is feebleness, irresponsibility. In Choice D, the *genesis* of something is the beginning. *Effrontery* is audacity, shameless boldness. And finally, Choice E, *nascency,* is birth, the process of being brought into existence. *Perjury* is false testimony, lying under oath.

24. **E.** A *tome* is a lengthy, ponderous, scholarly book. The word usually refers to the type of heavy book that could serve as a foundation stone in a skyscraper. A *wag* is a wit, a clever person. A *collage* is a collection of images, like a photo collage. You don't think of a collage as lengthy or incomprehensible. A *pundit* is a learned person; a *sage* is an intelligent person.

25. **A.** Someone very, very thin is *emaciated*. Someone very, very happy is *ecstatic*. Choice B is backward. *Solitary* means reclusive, but *reclusive* (a recluse is a hermit) has the connotation of being very, very solitary, essentially not wanting anything to do with the world. Choice C is antonyms; someone *sentimental* is full of feeling (*senti* means feeling); someone *apathetic* has no feeling (*a-* means not or without; *path* means feeling). Choice D is antonyms. *Immaterial* (*im-* means not) is equal to irrelevant — learning most languages (especially Spanish and French) can help you with the GRE, but learning sign language is immaterial. Choice E is also antonyms. A *fickle* person isn't constant.

When three answers all have the same relationship, all three must be wrong. Therefore, even if you don't know what emaciated means, you can eliminate Choices C, D, and E and assume that emaciated is a synonym, not an antonym, of thin.

26. **A.** The relationship is from lesser degree to greater degree. First, you're angry, and then you become *incensed,* which means furious, or burning mad (think of burning incense). Choice A also moves from a lesser to a greater degree. Something may be *noticeable,* like a new hair-cut. However, when you dye your hair neon green, the hairdo turns from noticeable to *flam-boyant,* very noticeable or showy.

    The words in Choice B are a pair of synonyms: *obdurate* means stubborn. You can remember this definition by pairing obdurate with a more familiar *ob-* word, *obstinate* (also meaning stubborn). *Outmoded* means out of fashion. Something ancient may or may not be out of fashion; as the song says, "Everything old is new again." In Choice D, *melodious* and *euphonious* are synonyms. You can figure out *euphonious* with roots, prefixes, and suffixes: *eu-* means good; *phon* means sound; *-ous* means full of. Something *euphonious* is melodius, or full of good sound. Choice E also lets you use your roots: *pac* means calm.

27. **D.** Because the primary purpose or main idea question is so common in Reading Comprehension passages, always read them with an eye toward identifying those points. Although this passage grows more general at the end, it's primarily about the rights of Cherokee women.

28. **E.** A negatively phrased question, such as "Which is NOT true" or "All of the following are true EXCEPT" is often very difficult or tricky, or just plain time-consuming. Good test-takers often just guess and go, guessing quickly on this type of question and going on to the next one. Here, although the passage says the Cherokee woman has the right to choose her own mate, the procedure for this decision isn't covered anywhere.

29. **D.** The best way to answer this question is through the process of elimination. There's no *chronology* (timeline) of events (Choice A). Nor is there any *refutation* (disproving) of a theory (Choice B) or counterexample to a theory (Choice C). There's also no proof or dis-proof of a controversial theory (Choice E). All the author does is state his idea and then give examples to support what he's said.

30. **B.** The key to this question is the second blank. The countries of Egypt, Mexico, and China are neither similar nor *inauspicious* (unfavorable). They are geographic, but that word makes no sense in the context of the sentence. The countries are ancient, but they still exist, making Choice A illogical. *Disparate,* meaning distinct or different, makes sense. The first word in Choice A, *conjecture,* is another way of saying *hypothesize,* which is the first word in Choice B.

Math Section

1. **D.** Please tell us you didn't fall for this trap. Did you pick up your pencil and start to draw a picture of the roller rink, the school, and the coffee shop? As soon as you have to draw a picture for a QC problem, you should be thinking D. Why? Because the answer *de*pends on how you draw the picture. If you put the roller rink, the school, and the coffee shop all in a straight line in that order, then the coffee shop and the skating rink are in fact 13 kilometers apart. But (and this is a big but, because whenever you see a C answer, you should be para-noid and double-check it) what if you put the coffee shop 3 kilometers to the other side of the school, between it and the rink? Then the distance from the rink to the coffee shop is only 7 kilometers, making the answer B. If the answer changes *de*pending on how you draw the figure, choose D.

    Problems that require you to find a distance between places or people often have D answers because the distance *de*pends on the sequence those places or people are in. When you see a "line 'em up" problem, think D.

2. **A.** Are you, like most people, a fraction-phobe? Then avoid fractions altogether and simply plug in numbers. Work backward and plug in a number for *c* that will be divisible by both 4 and 3. Try 12. If *c* = 12, then *b* = ¾ × 12 = 9. If *b* = 9, then *a* = ⅔ × 9, or 6. Now ⁶⁄ = ⁶⁄₁₂, or ½.

Because ½ is greater than ⅓, A is the answer. Although this tactic works no matter what number you plug in for *c*, why not make life easy and plug in a nice, round number? If you plug in something like 10, then *b* = ¾ × 10 or ³⁰⁄₄ and that's a pain in the *fundament* (that portion of your body upon which you're sitting right this very moment).

Doing this problem "the real way" isn't hard, if that's your preferred approach. You just need to know that *of* means × and multiply the whole shebang: ⅔ of ¾ of *c* = ⅔ × ¾ × *c* = ⁶⁄₁₂ × *c* = ½ × *c*. It comes out the same.

3. **D.** If you chose C, you fell for the trap. You can't simply multiply the exponents of two unlike bases. For example, if you were to multiply 5^{-2} (which is $\frac{1}{5^2}$, or $\frac{1}{25}$) × 2^{-5} (which is $\frac{1}{2^5}$, or $\frac{1}{32}$), the answer wouldn't be 1. The answer depends on the values of *x* and *y*: Are they positive? Negative? Fractions? With this many possibilities, the answer is D.

The more variables you have, the better your chances of getting a D answer. Don't immediately choose D when you see a lot of *x* and *y* variables, but do entertain the possibility that the answer will *de*pend on the numbers you plug in.

Will the end of the QCs have several D answers like this? Not necessarily. However, because questions go from easier to harder, and because the hard or tricky questions often have D answers, don't be surprised if you have what seems like a disproportionate number of D answers at the end of the exam.

4. **C.** To multiply like bases, add the exponents. One over a^3 is the same as *a* to the negative third power. Add: $a^{10} \times a^5 \times a^{-3}$ = *a* to the (10 + 5 − 3) = a^{12}.

Did you choose D because you don't know what *a* is? The value of *a* here, although unknown and unknowable given the information you have, is irrelevant: $a^{12} = a^{12}$, no matter what the value of *a* is. This question is very similar to Question 10. If both questions *befuddled* (confused) you, return to Chapter 14.

5. **B.** This problem is rather lengthy *unless* you see the shortcut. Here's the long way first: An *arc* is a fraction of the circumference of the circle. The circumference is 2π*radius*. Because the area of a circle is π*radius*², the radius here is 6. The circumference, therefore, is 12π. The arc is the same fraction of the circle that the central angle is of 360. Here, put ⁴⁵⁄₃₆₀ and reduce it to ⅛. That means the arc is ⅛ of the circumference of the circle, and ⅛ of 36π is certainly less than 36π.

Ready for the shortcut? You can cut off the last step entirely, but you still must break down the area to find the radius and then work back up to find the circumference. (You should be so comfortable with formulas that you can do this step without even breathing hard.) You can see by looking at the figure that the arc isn't the entire circumference, but instead only a part of it. That means that the arc is less than 36π, and B is larger. You don't need to — and certainly don't want to — find the exact measure of the arc.

If you're getting brain cramps, go back to the circles section of Chapter 13 and look for the arc info.

6. **B.** When a negative is cubed, it remains a negative. For example, $-2^3 = -2 \times -2 \times -2 = -8$. Therefore, whatever Column A is, it's negative. Stop right there and don't strain your brain any further.

As you go through the QC questions, keep reminding yourself that the name of the game is Quantitative Comparisons, not Problem Solving. More times than not, you don't need to solve the problem. You just have to work until you see which column is going to be greater, and then you stop. The actual solution is irrelevant and unnecessary. Every second that you save by *not* working on the QCs is another second that you can use on the regular multiple-choice problems where you *do* need to do all that drudge work.

7. **C.** This is a symbolism problem that looks more intimidating and difficult than it actually is. Substitute the numbers for the variables in the explanation. Use the numbers in the same order as the variables. That is, 3 is in the first position and *a* is in the first position, so

substitute a 3 for an *a*. Because 6 is in the second position and *b* is in the second position, go ahead and substitute a 6 for a *b*. Likewise, with 12 in the third position and *c* in the third position, you should substitute a 12 for a *c*. That gives you $3(3) + 4(6) - \frac{1}{2}(12) = 9 + 24 - 6 = 27$.

The more calculations you do, the less surprised you should be when the answer turns out to be C. Of course, we don't mean that as soon as you find yourself doing a lot of pencil pushing, you should give up and choose C, hoping for the best. We simply mean that if you do no work and you just think the columns are equal, you've probably fallen for a trap. To get a correct C answer, you frequently have to perform the actual calculations to prove that the columns are equal.

8. **B.** If you chose C, you fell for the trap. The *mean* (average) of the scores is 73, but the median is 72. A *median* is the middle term when all terms are arranged in order: 68, 70, 72, 75, 80.

To remember a median, think of the median strip when you're driving down the road: It's in the middle. If you're rusty on the three Ms, mean (average), median (middle term), and *mode* (most repeated term), check out the miscellaneous math review in Chapter 15.

9. **C.** You can approach this QC problem in two ways. The sum of the angles in any triangle is 180 degrees. Because you know two angles are 90 degrees (the box indicates a right, or 90-degree, angle) and 20 degrees, for a sum of 110 degrees, you know the remaining angle must be 70 degrees (180 – 110 = 70). That angle and the *y* angle are along a straight line, which means they're supplementary and add up to 180 degrees. Subtract 70 from 180, and you get 110.

That's one way to solve this problem, but here's an even easier one. The exterior angle is equal to the sum of the two remote interior angles. In simple speech, that means an angle outside the triangle is the same as the sum of the two angles away from it inside the triangle. In this problem, Angle *y* = 90 + 20 = 110.

Most geometry problems simply require you to know the properties of angles and figures. We can't emphasize enough the importance of memorizing everything you can wrestle your brain cells around in geometry. Learn the rules until you can mutter them in your sleep, and they'll return to you in your hour of need.

10. **A.** This QC problem is easy if you convert the percentages to decimals (all right-thinking people despise percentages) and remember that *of* means ×. Column A, therefore, is 3.0 (300 percent is the same as 3, or 3.0) × 30 = 90. Column B is .60 × 15 = 9.

Did you fall for the trap and choose C? Don't be **disheartened** (sad); it happens to the best of us. You were thinking of only the numerals and forgetting your decimal places. You could've avoided all this grief by using your brain rather than your yellow #2. You know quickly that 300 percent of 30 is more than 30. You know just as quickly that 60 percent of 15 is less than 15. Because more than 30 is greater than less than 15, Column A is greater. Whenever possible, try to talk the problem through instead of solving it precisely. No one really cares what the answer is.

11. **D.** If you chose A, you fell for the trap. What if *a* = 1 and *b* = 1? Then *c* = 1, and the columns are equal. What if *a* = 2 and *b* = 2? Then *c* = 4, and A is the answer. If the answer *de*pends on what you plug in, choose D.

12. **C.** Please tell us you didn't actually work out this problem. You know that the word *of* means times, or to multiply. If you were to do this problem as a decimal, you'd have .20 × 120 and 1.20 × 20. Because the number of decimal places is the same, the solution is the same as well.

This type of QC problem is very common. However, don't get complacent, see this sort of question, and immediately choose C. What if Column A said 0.20 percent rather than 20 percent? That would make the multiplication .0020 × 120, a very different answer indeed. Keep a wary eye on the decimal point.

13. **A.** You didn't actually work this problem out either, did you? Part of what the QC questions test is your knowledge of when to pick up your pencil and when just to guesstimate. This one is a definite guesstimate. With 365 days per year (366 in a leap year), Column A would

be $365 \times 3 + 366$. Don't actually work it out. Column B is 40×10, because a decade has ten years. You can see at a glance that Column A is much larger.

Although the leap year isn't a trap in this particular problem, often a question can getcha if you forget about it. For example, if a question asks you how much money Mark makes if he earns $200 a day every single day for four years, your answer will be $200 off unless you remember that one of those years has 366 days, not 365.

If you didn't grow up in the United States, you may be accustomed to different units of measurement, such as metric units rather than standard units. Take a few minutes to go back to the units-of-measurement portion of Chapter 15 and make sure that you know, for example, how many inches are in a foot and how many pounds are in a ton.

14. **C.** A diagonal divides a square into two 45:45:90 triangles. The ratio of the sides of a 45:45:90 triangle are $s : s : s\sqrt{2}$ (this concept is explained in the Chapter 13 review). If the diagonal, or *hypotenuse*, is $5\sqrt{2}$, each side of the square is 5. If the bottom of the square (Side *DC*) is 5, then each side of the triangle (which you're told is equilateral) is also 5. Add up all the sides to get 25.

If you got a number greater than 25, you probably added Side *DC* twice, or you added Side *AC*. **Remember:** The perimeter is the *outside* of the figures.

15. **E.** This question is as much vocabulary as it is math. A *mean* is the average of numbers: Add the numbers together (420) and divide by the number of numbers ($420 \div 5 = 84$). A *median* is the middle number when the numbers are put in order.

If you picked Choice D, you fell for the trap of thinking that 79 was the median because it's the "middle number." You must put the numbers in numerical order first: 75, 79, 82, 91, 93. Now you can see that 82 is the median. Subtract the median from the mean: $84 - 82 = 2$. **Bonus:** As long as we're talking vocabulary, do you know what the mode is? A *mode* is the most repeated term — the one that shows up the most. For example, if the numbers were 2, 3, 2, 4, 5, the mode would be 2.

16. **B.** The formula (given in Chapter 13, in case you forgot it) for the interior angle measure of a polygon is $(n - 2)180$, where n stands for the number of sides. In other words, take the number of sides, subtract 2, and multiply by 180. (Why? There are two fewer triangles in any polygon than sides. For example, a square, which has 4 sides, can make 2 triangles. A hexagon, which has 6 sides, can make 4 triangles, and so on. Each triangle has 180 degrees.) Therefore, your equation here is: $(n - 2)180 = 1,260$; $180n - 360 = 1,260$; $180n = 1,620$; $n = 9$.

If you selected Choice D, you didn't answer what the question's asking. It wants the perimeter of the figure if each side measures 6. Finish the problem: $9 \times 6 = 54$. If you went with Choice E, you got the $(n - 2)$, and if you picked Choice C, you multiplied 7 by 6, rather than 9 by 6.

17. **E.** If you simply subtracted $40 - 38$ and got Choice A, you fell for the trap. Very few questions on the GRE are that simple. Chapter 15 gives you a way to find an increase or decrease in percent by creating a fraction. The *numerator* (top) is the change in the number, and the *denominator* (bottom) is the starting number — what you began with.

Did you simply say the difference between 38 and 40 is 2, and ⅖₈ is about 5%? If so, you fell for the trap: Choice B. You did the math correctly, but missed the whole point of having two graphs. You still have work to do.

The greater amount is 40% of 2,100 minus 38% of 1,700. Note that the numbers at the bottom of each graph, which represent the totals, are different. Now do the work (remembering that *of* means *times*): 40% of $2,100 = .40 \times 2,100 = 840$, and 38% of $1,700 = .38 \times 1,700 = 646$. The increase, therefore, isn't merely from 38 to 40, but from 646 to 840, or 194. Divide 194 by 646 (the starting number) to get approximately .30, which equals 30% (Choice E).

18. **B.** The fastest way to solve this problem is to realize that 2000 physics enrollment must drop from 16% to 14% while chemistry enrollment must rise from 22% to 24% to produce the 1995 ratio of 14% to 24%. You'll get the right answer if you move 2% of the total number of students in the year 2000 from physics to chemistry: 2% of 2,100 = .02 × 2,100 = 42 (Choice B).

    Choice D is a tempting answer because there's a 6% difference between physics and chemistry for 2000 and a 10% difference for 1995. Although this difference in percentages is 4%, you don't want to take 4% of 2,100 (which is 84) because taking 2% from physics and giving 2% to chemistry will produce the required 4% change.

    Confused? Think of this problem another way: If you have $100 and we have $100, and we give you $5, how much more money do you have than us? The answer isn't $5, but $10. You have $5 more ($105), whereas we have $5 less ($95) for a difference of $10.

    Some mathletes may figure that in 1995, 238 students took physics (14% of 1,700) while 408 students took chemistry (24% of 1,700). This difference is 170 students, but don't just try to make the chemistry total for 2000 exceed the 2000 physics total by 170. Choices A and C could each, by various irrelevant methods of calculation (don't worry, we won't make you suffer through them), produce a difference of 170. But you must remember that a ratio involves a difference that's related to division, not subtraction.

    Choice E would produce the required 24 to 14 ratio if 114 additional students changed from being enrolled in no class to being enrolled in chemistry. The question, however, requires you to move students from physics to chemistry.

19. **C.** Figure out the fraction of people who left. First, ¼ of the people left. That means ¾ remain. Then ⅓ of the remaining people leave: ⅓ of ¾ = ⅓ × ¾ = ³⁄₁₂ = ¼. At 1 a.m., another ¼ of the people leave.

    Be sure not to say ¼ of the *remaining* people leave. If as many people leave at 1 a.m. as left at 11 p.m., then ¼ of the original number left. Add all the fractions: ¼ + ¼ + ¼ = ¾. If ¾ of the people have left, then only ¼ remain. The new equation is: $30 = \frac{1}{4}T$ (*T* standing for total). Divide both sides through by ¼, which is the same as multiplying by ⁴⁄₁ (the inverted form of the fraction), to get 30 × 4 = 120.

20. **E.** If you picked Choice A, you fell for a trap. (Getting sick and tired of reading that expression? Don't fall for so many traps, and you won't have to.) Dividing like bases means subtracting the exponents. For a^{10} divided by a^5, subtract: 10 − 5 = 5. Divide 6 by 3 and get 2. You know that the first two factors are $2a^5$, so you can narrow the possible answers down to Choices C, D, and E.

    Because b^5 divided by b^9 is b^{-4}, or $\frac{1}{b^4}$, that result eliminates Choices C and D; you can stop now.

    Just for fun, though, we'll finish this calculation: c^7 divided by c^7 is 1. Any number divided by itself is 1. (Or you could think of it as being 7 − 7 = 0; any number to the 0 power is 1.) The answer 1 doesn't change in the multiplication; ignore it.

    Choices A and B are traps for people who tried 10 ÷ 5 = 2 instead of subtracting exponents. Choices C and D are traps for people who forgot that a negative exponent is in the denominator, not the numerator — 2^{-3} really is $\frac{1}{2^3}$. If you forgot this rule, return to the oh-so-thrilling Chapter 14.

21. **C.** You can find the probability by using this formula:

    $$\frac{\text{\# of possible desired outcomes}}{\text{\# of total possible outcomes}}$$

    The first step is to find the denominator. How many candies will be left after LaVonne has chomped into the others? She starts with 47 candies (20 + 15 + 12). You know that she throws some of them away. You can eliminate Choice A immediately, because the denominator must be less than 47.

LaVonne throws away a cream (down to 46), a nut (down to 45), a chew (down to 44), a nut (down to 43), a cream (down to 42), and a chew (down to 41). The denominator for the probability of the next candy that she pulls out will be 41 because she'll have some chance out of 41 of pulling out a nut. That narrows the possible answers down to Choices B and C.

As a shortcut, subtract 6 (the number of candies that she already pulled out) from 47 (the number of candies that originally were in the box). We solved the problem the long way to show you where the 41 really comes from.

Now find the numerator. LaVonne starts out with 12 nuts, pulls out one (down to 11), and then pulls out another (down to 10). The probability that her next candy will be a nut is $^{10}/_{41}$. (This type of problem is explained in the probability section of Chapter 14.)

22. **B.** Take this one step at a time. If you're Barb, you need to take on 6 people in a hot-air balloon race. Because each of the 7 contestants has to race 6 other people, it's tempting to say that 42 hot-air balloon races (7×6) will take place: the trap, Choice D. The problem with this thinking is that it counts each match twice. Barb's race against Jim is the same as Jim's race against Barb. So although each contestant has 6 races, the total number of hot-air balloon races is 7×6 (42) divided by 2, or 21 (watch out for Choice E; it's also a trap). The last step is to multiply 21×5 to account for all the different activities. There are 21 matches in each activity and 5 activities: $21 \times 5 = 105$.

23. **E.** If you picked Choice B, C, or D, you fell for a trap. If there are 100 applicants and 60% are female, there are 60 females . . . and 40 males. You can figure out that 75%, or 45, of the females will relocate and 15 won't relocate, but what about the males? The question asks for the number of people who aren't willing to relocate. If you selected Choice B, you just assumed that all the men won't relocate, when in fact, you have no information whatsoever about what the men will or won't do. ***Note:*** "It cannot be determined" answers are rare on the GRE, but if you see one, consider carefully whether there's a trap in the problem.

24. **C.** Line Segment *XY* must be a horizontal line parallel to the *x*-axis because the *y* coordinate doesn't change. If the line segment goes from –2 to +4, it's 6 units long. The midway point would be 3 units long. Start at –2 and count: From –2 to –1 is one unit. From –1 to 0 is two units total. From 0 to 1 is 3 units total.

If you said Choice E, you fell for the trap. Yes, you're moving three units to the right, but you're moving *from* –2. You go only from –2 to 1, not to 3.

25. **A.** This problem is easier than it looks. If two circles have the same area, they have the same radius because the area of a circle is π*radius*^{2}. The radius of Circle *Y* is 5 as well. The diameters of the two circles are 10 each, because the diameter of a circle is twice its radius. Therefore, the length of the rectangle is 20, and the width is 10.

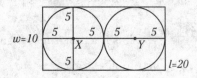

The area of a rectangle is *length* × *width*: $20 \times 10 = 200$.

26. **B.** Understand what the explanation means. (The explanation is made up for this particular problem. "Circle" operations don't exist in the real world — only in the little universe of the GRE. Lucky you.) The explanation says that you have a number in the circle. If that number in the circle is a *prime number* (meaning that it can be divided only by itself and 1), you add the number in the circle to the square of the number in the circle.

If the number in the circle is a *composite number* (one that can be divided by something other than just 1 and itself), you square that number and subtract the number in the circle from the square.

Ugh. You may have to repeat those instructions to yourself a few times. In reality, you're really just substituting the number in the circle for the x in the appropriate equation.

Because 4 is composite, you use the second line of the explanation. Square 4: $4^2 = 16$. Subtract from that the number in the circle: $16 - 4 = 12$. Because 5 is prime, you add it to its square: $5 + 25 = 30$. Add the two results: $12 + 30 = 42$.

This problem has all sorts of trap answers. If you used the first line $(x + x^2)$ for both terms, you got 50. If you used the second line $(x^2 - x)$ for both terms, you got 32. If you confused prime and composite numbers by using the composite rule for 5 and the prime rule for 4, you got 40.

27. **E.** Did you get a brain cramp just reading the problem? If you're totally confused, you may want to guess quickly on this advertisement for aspirin and get on to something better. After all, a good test-taker knows which problems are worth investing time in — and which ones aren't.

When dealing with variables, we suggest you plug in numbers. In this case, try:

$d = 16$ so that 8 cans of juice cost $16, meaning each can costs $2.

$m = 800$ so that each can makes 800 milliliters.

$c = 2$ so that each can of water costs 2 cents.

Take this problem one step at a time. One can of juice costs $2. One can of water costs 2 cents. You need to add three cans of water, or 6 cents' worth of water. Your grand total is now $2.06.

This $2.06 is the cost for 800 milliliters. The problem asks for the cost of 400 milliliters; divide by 2 to get $1.03, the cost for 400 milliliters. (Why didn't we let $m = 400$? Sometimes when dealing with 1, several of the answer choices come out correct, and you need to substitute new numbers anyway. We like using a 2 in these longer, harder problems.)

Next, plug $d = 16$, $m = 800$, and $c = 2$ into each choice and eliminate those that don't yield 1.03 dollars:

(A) $3{,}200(800)(16) + 96(2)$. You can tell without doing all the work that this answer will be much too large.

(B) $\dfrac{[(800)(16) + 3(2)]}{400} = \dfrac{12{,}806}{400}$. This one is also certainly more than 1.03.

(C) $\dfrac{[16 + 3(2)]}{50(800)} = \dfrac{22}{40{,}000}$. This number is going to be a fraction.

(D) $\dfrac{[8(16) + 96(2)]}{800} = \dfrac{320}{800}$. This fraction is less than 1. The answer had better be

Choice E, or we're in trouble.

When you get to this point, where you've decided the answer absolutely has to be Choice E, still go ahead and solve Choice E. Why? What if you've made a careless mistake in one of the earlier answers (something easy to do with all these numbers)? When Choice E doesn't come out right, you'll realize you bungled somewhere, leading you to go back and check your work.

(E) $\dfrac{50(16) + 12(2)}{800} = \dfrac{824}{800} = 1.03$ At last!

If you're an algebra whiz, you may find it easier to do the straightforward algebra, so the following instructions are for you.

Write down the units to make sure that you're left with dollars. For the cans of orange juice:

$$\left(\frac{d \text{ dollars}}{8 \text{ cans}}\right) \times \left(\frac{1 \text{ can}}{m \text{ milliliters}}\right) = \frac{d \text{ dollars}}{8m \text{ milliliters}} \left(\text{the cans cancel}\right)$$

Because you want 400 milliliters, multiply as follows:

$$\left(\frac{d \text{ dollars}}{8m \text{ milliliters}}\right) \times 400 \text{ milliliters} = \frac{50d \text{ dollars}}{m} \text{ (The milliliters cancel.)}$$

Now it's time for the water, remembering that you must convert the cents to dollars:

$$\left(\frac{3c \text{ cents}}{\text{can}}\right) \times \left(\frac{1 \text{ dollar}}{100 \text{ cents}}\right) = \frac{3c/100 \text{ dollars}}{\text{can}} \left(\text{the cents cancel}\right)$$

Work in the milliliters:

$$\left(\frac{3c/100 \text{ dollars}}{\text{can}}\right) \times \left(\frac{1 \text{ can}}{m \text{ milliliters}}\right) = \frac{3c/100m \text{ dollars}}{\text{milliliters}} \left(\text{cans cancel}\right)$$

As with the juice, multiply by 400:

$$\frac{3c \text{ dollars}}{\text{milliliters}} \times 400 \text{ milliliters} = \frac{12c}{m \text{ dollars}} \text{ (The milliliters cancel.)}$$

You now have $50\%_m$ for the cost of the juice and $12\%_m$ for the cost of the water, so add to get $\frac{(50d + 12c)}{m \text{ dollars}}$ (Choice E).

28. **D.** Draw yourself a diagram as shown:

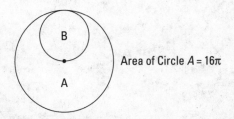

Area of Circle $A = 16\pi$

The area of a circle is πr^2, which means that $16\pi = \pi r^2$; $r^2 = 16$; $r = 4$. If the radius of Circle A is 4, the diameter of Circle B is 4. The circumference of a circle is $2\pi r$, or πd. The circumference of Circle B is 4π.

Analytical Writing Sections

Give your essays to someone to read and evaluate for you. Refer that helpful person to Chapter 20 for scoring guidelines.

Part VII
The Part of Tens

The 5th Wave   By Rich Tennant

"I hate the synonyms part of this test.
I always get stumped, stymied,
and puzzled."

In this part . . .

What would any *For Dummies* title be without the famous Part of Tens? This unit is your reward for surviving the previous chapters. These final few chapters require no brainpower. You don't have to work through math problems, you don't have to memorize new vocabulary, and actually, you don't have to stimulate your synapses at all. These chapters are just for fun, but they do provide invaluable information. Read on.

Chapter 26

Ten False Rumors about the GRE

In This Chapter

▶ Debunking common score-related myths

▶ Setting you straight about what the GRE does and doesn't test

*Y*ou've heard 'em — the horror stories about the GRE. Rumors abound, growing wilder with each telling: "You have to know calculus!" (Absolutely not true.) "It's an open-book test this year!" (You wish!)

As test-prep tutors, we get calls all the time from students trying to check out the latest scuttlebutt. Here are ten stories (from most common to least common) that make the rounds every year — they're as dependable as oversleeping the morning of your most important final.

Missing the First Few Questions Gives You an Easier Test and a Better Score

Right and wrong. The first five questions do indeed determine the difficulty level of the whole exam. For all practical purposes, you start off with a score of 500 — right in the middle of the score range (your score can go from 200 to 800).

If you get the first question right, you get about +100 and have a 600-level exam going. If you miss the first question, you get about –100 and have a 400-level exam going. The second question is worth about 70 points. If you get it right and you got the first question right, the computer thinks you're smart enough to be working at a 670+ level, and you take a nice hard test. If you miss both the second and first questions, you're working down in the 300s. You'll get an easy test, but you have almost no way to bring your score back up into the 600s.

The moral of the story is: The first few questions are that "first impression" the computer gets about you. You never have a second chance to make a good first impression.

The GRE Has a Passing Score

You can't pass or fail the GRE, but a particular graduate school may have a cutoff score that you must obtain in order to be considered for admission. This score is often based on your grade-point average (GPA). A school may decree, for example, that if your GPA is in the 3.0 to 3.5 range, you can get an 1100 (combined Verbal and Math score). But if your GPA is in the 2.5 to 3.0 range, your overall GRE score must be at least a 1200.

Find out what the acceptable GRE score range is at each of the schools you're considering.

Your Score Won't Improve if You Keep Retaking the GRE

Although having your score jump hundreds of points is uncommon, it has happened. Your improvement depends on the reason your score was low in the first place and on how much you study before retaking the exam.

If your score was low because you didn't understand the format of the exam (for example, you looked at a Quantitative Comparison question and wondered where the answer choices were), you can certainly improve that score by taking a few practice exams and becoming more comfortable with the question styles.

If your score was low because you fell for all the traps set in the GRE, you can improve your score by going through these materials, figuring out how to recognize those traps, and studying the tips and tricks for avoiding 'em. However, it's unrealistic for a slow reader to think that a few weeks of study is going to double her reading speed, or for someone who doesn't understand algebra at all to think he can get a year's worth of algebra instruction in an afternoon. You do need *some* basics under your belt.

The study time you put into preparing for the second exam is also important. If you take the exam, receive your scores, register for another exam, and then begin studying again just a few days before the second exam, you may as well forget it. Although experience helps, your score won't soar simply because you've done this before. You have to study for the second test — or else you'll repeat the mistakes of the first.

You Can't Study for the GRE

Why would we be writing this book if that were so? Studying can be done in two ways, each advantageous in its own right:

- ✔ **The last-minute cram:** In a few weeks, you review the types of questions, the approach to each question, and the tricks and traps involved in the questions. (Guess what? This method is what you work on throughout this book.)

- ✔ **The long-range study program:** From your freshman year in college on, you learn vocabulary and work on math questions. Obviously, if you have a year or two to put into studying, you should get a dynamite score. Most people, however, benefit greatly from even a few weeks or months of intense study.

Your GRE Score Will Be about the Same as Your High School SAT Score

Are you the same person you were in high school? No. You've matured, acquired better study habits, and suddenly come to the shocking realization that no one is going to spoon-feed you anymore. You may not have studied much for the SAT, figuring that you could always get into *some* college, somewhere, no matter what your score. You were probably right. But getting into graduate school isn't as easy.

There aren't as many graduate programs as undergraduate programs, which makes for cutthroat competition. Because you realize this fact of life, you now study harder and smarter. Besides, your vocabulary almost certainly has improved significantly after four years of college, and vocabulary is usually the most difficult element of the exam.

The GRE Tests IQ

Nope, the GRE doesn't test IQ. It supposedly tests your ability to do well in graduate school, but some cynics say that all the GRE tests is your ability to take the GRE. Getting into a debate over that point is rather futile; you're stuck with taking the GRE and worrying about it just wastes brainpower you can use for other activities. But be reassured that the GRE isn't an IQ test. You can figure out how to improve your GRE score with all sorts of tips, tricks, and techniques — that's *much* harder to do on IQ tests.

Ever hear of MENSA, the national high-IQ society? Although the GRE isn't actually a measure of IQ, if you do well on the GRE, you can sometimes get automatic membership in MENSA (something that looks great on résumés and impresses the socks off a date's parents). Call your local MENSA chapter to find out what the qualifying score is. Hey, you put the effort into getting the score. Why not scarf up all the benefits from it that you can?

You Must Pass Certain Classes to Take the GRE

Although taking classes like advanced logic or linguistics is useful, few people take those courses today. If you're reading this book as a freshman or sophomore and have the option of taking logic classes, excellent. Doing so will help you with the analytical-ability portion of the GRE. But you certainly don't *have* to take a class like that to do well on the GRE. (Whew! Who has room for that type of class in an already overcrowded curriculum anyway?)

As far as math goes, the GRE tests basic algebra, geometry, and arithmetic. A year of algebra and a year of geometry are sufficient. In short, the GRE has no prerequisites.

You Can Take the GRE on Your Own Computer at Home

Oh sure, suuuuuuure. You can take the test at home — with your computer, your dictionary, your reference books, and your cousin Morty the Math Genius all standing by, ready to help you! We'd even be glad to come by and stand at your shoulder, pointing out all the traps.

Sorry. You can't take the GRE anywhere but at a recognized testing center.

You Can Bring Your Own Laptop to the Testing Center

Wouldn't bringing your laptop be nice? You could load all sorts of programs into it, such as math formulas and algorithms or pages and pages of vocabulary. Taking the GRE would be a snap in that case.

Unfortunately, the GRE people are way ahead of you on this one. Not only do you have to take the exam at a special testing center but you also have to take it on the center's computers. The only thing you supply is the brainpower.

Computer Geniuses Have an Unfair Advantage on the GRE

Computer geniuses have an unfair advantage over everyone in this high-tech age, so why should the GRE be any different? Now that that's out of our system, it's reality-check time. Sure, students who are very comfortable with a computer may have a little advantage because they have one less stress factor going into the test, but the advantage ends there. The computer skills required for taking the GRE are so minimal that they're almost irrelevant.

Chapter 27

Ten Stupid Ways to Mess Up Your GRE

•••

In This Chapter

▶ Competing with the clock or your best bud

▶ Worrying about what you can't control

•••

Throughout this book, you discover techniques for doing your best on the GRE. We're sorry to say, however, that there are just as many techniques for messing up big time on this test. Take a few minutes to read through them now to see what crazy things people do to totally blow the exam. By being aware of these catastrophes, you may just prevent them from happening to you.

Cheating

Cheating on the GRE is a loser's game — it's just plain stupid. Apart from the legal, moral, and ethical questions, it's simply not practical: You can't predict what types of vocabulary words will show up in the questions. What are you going to do, copy a dictionary on the palm of your hand? All the math formulas you need can't fit on the bottom of your shoe. Copying everything that you *think* you may need would take more time than just buckling down and learning the material. Besides, the GRE tries very hard to test critical-reasoning skills, not just rote memorization.

The test never asks a question as straightforward as, "How many degrees are there in a triangle?" GRE questions require thinking and reasoning, not just copying down a formula. Short of having a brain transplant, cheating is impractical (as well as dumb!).

Losing Concentration

When you're in the middle of an excruciatingly boring Reading Comprehension passage, the worst move you can make is to let your mind drift off to a more pleasant time (last night's date, last weekend's soccer game, the time you stole your rival school's mascot and set it on the john in the dean's private bathroom). Although *visualization* (picturing yourself doing something relaxing or fun) is a good stress-reduction technique, it stinks when it comes to helping your GRE score.

Even if you have to pinch yourself to keep from falling asleep or flaking out, stay focused. The GRE is just a few hours of your life. You've had horrible blind dates that lasted longer than that, and you managed to survive them. This too shall pass.

Not Taking Advantage of the Breaks

You're offered a short break (in either one- or ten-minute increments) between sections (Verbal, Math, and Analytical Writing). If you don't take those breaks between the sections, you'll be sitting still for hours. We often see students pass on the breaks, especially the first one, wanting to get this whole ordeal over with as soon as possible.

Although we sympathize with the desire, we strongly, strongly suggest that you take all the breaks that are offered. Even just standing up, swinging your arms, and grumbling a little bit will make you feel better. A minute may not seem like enough time to relax, but trust us, it is. Use it.

Obsessing about the Previous Sections

Think of the GRE as three separate lifetimes. You're reborn twice and get two more chances to do it right. Every time the computer prompts you to go to a new section, you receive a fresh start. You have one Verbal section, one Math section, and one Analytical Writing section. (We cover the breakdown in much more detail in Chapter 1.)

The computer is inexorable. You can't go back to a previous section if you suddenly recall a vocabulary word that eluded you (such as *inexorable* in the previous sentence!) Nor can you double-check your arithmetic on a math question. Forget one section as soon as you enter the next. You can't even go back to a previous question in the same section, let alone an entirely different section.

Think of each section of the GRE as you would a new boyfriend or girlfriend in your life: Out with the old and in with the new.

Panicking over Time

Every section of the GRE has a specified time limit. The on-screen clock (which you do have the option of turning off, in case it's driving you crazy) displays the time you have remaining. Relax. Thanks to Chapter 1, you know going into the test exactly how many questions are in each section and, therefore, how many minutes you have per question. It's not as if this is some big mystery.

Rushing through the Confirm Step

After you answer a question, the computer gives you a second chance. Your screen offers you a Confirm button that you must click before your answer becomes permanent. Life has few second chances, so take advantage of this one. Sure, you may feel rushed (everyone does), but take those few extra seconds.

Keep reminding yourself that the exam isn't like a paper-and-pencil test, in which you can come back at the end and double-check for careless mistakes. You make a choice, confirm that choice, and that's all she wrote. Take the few extra seconds before clicking the Confirm button.

Scheduling the Test at the Same Time as Your Best Friend

Depending on the size and availability of the test center, you and your buddy may be able to take the test at the same time. Big mistake. It's only human to try to compare your progress with your friend's. Unfortunately, you and your friend won't get the exact same exam. Your questions will be different. If you see your buddy zooming through the material with a big smile on his face, you may depress yourself unnecessarily.

Think of the GRE as a journey you take with an electronic machine. The relationship is between you and the computer. You may enjoy the company of your friend, but the GRE is one place where the buddy system just doesn't work.

Stressing Out over Your Computer Skills (Or Lack Thereof)

The GRE, in and of itself, is stressful enough. The last thing you need to do is add more anxiety to the whole nerve-racking experience of taking the test by worrying about your computer expertise. Can you type, even a little bit, in a one-finger style? If so, you've mastered all the computer skills that the GRE requires of you.

Before you begin taking the test, you complete a very brief tutorial (no, the time spent on this tutorial doesn't count as actual testing time) that refreshes your computer abilities. You also have the Help key available to you at all times during the actual test.

Trying to Keep Track of the Question Breakdown

Keeping track of your own (mental, emotional, and psychological) breakdown is a good idea. Keeping track of the question breakdown is not. By "the question breakdown," we mean the number of each type of question you've answered.

You know that in the Verbal portion, for example, you have questions in four formats: Antonyms, Analogies, Sentence Completions, and Reading Comprehension. These questions can be in any order. In other words, don't say to yourself, "Well, I've finished three Sentence Completion questions. I know it's time for Reading Comprehension." The computer makes those decisions — not you.

Worrying about which type of question comes next is the high-tech equivalent of flipping forward to see how many pages you have left to read of a novel. All you do is waste your time, not shorten the number of pages.

Worrying about the Hard Problems

The GRE contains some incredibly hard problems. If you get the first few questions on the exam correct, the computer assumes that you're a genius and confidently offers you real mind-bogglers later on. If you miss the first few questions, the computer takes it easy on you and gives you a kinder, gentler exam (and, alas, a lower, wimpier score).

Suppose you ace the first few questions and then get some superhard questions. Of course, you have to answer them because the computer doesn't let you go on until you punch in an answer. But if the question is just way, way beyond you, make a quick guess (emphasis on quick!), go on, and don't fret.

Ridiculously few students achieve total 800s every year. If you get into the 700s, or even the 600s, you're in a superelite club of only a few of the thousands of students who take the GRE annually. Just accept the fact that you can't be sure of your answer on some of the questions and learn to live with your imperfections.

Chapter 28

Ten Relaxation Techniques to Try before and during the GRE

. . . .

In This Chapter

▶ Practicing physical stress relievers

▶ Figuring out how to calm down your mind

. . . .

Most people have butterflies dancing in their stomachs before the GRE. The key to combating this stress is to use relaxation techniques that keep your mind on your test and not on your tummy.

Breathe Deeply

The value of breathing deeply is grossly underrated. Take a deep breath until your belly expands, hold it for a few counts, and then expel the air through your nose. (Be careful not to blow out anything but air, especially if your boyfriend or girlfriend is sitting next to you.)

Try not to take short, shallow breaths, which could cause you to become even more anxious by depriving your body of oxygen. Try breathing in and out deeply while reciting something in your mind, such as your favorite line from a movie or a silly rhyme.

Rotate Your Head

Work the kinks out of your neck by trying to see behind your head. Move your head as far as possible to the right until you feel a tug on the skin on the left side of your neck. Then move your head all the way to the left until you feel a tug on the skin on the right. Return your head back to center and then move it straight back, as if you're looking at the ceiling, and then down, as if looking at your feet. You'll be surprised how much tension drains out of you if you do these moves a few times.

Be careful to perform this exercise with your eyes closed and make what you're doing obvious. You don't want a suspicious proctor to think you're craning your neck to look at someone else's computer screen.

Rotate Your Scalp

Put your open hand palm-down on your scalp. Move your hand in small circles. Feel your scalp rotate. Lift your hand and put it down somewhere else on your scalp. Repeat the circular motions. Hey, guess what? You're giving yourself a very relaxing scalp massage!

Cross and Roll Your Eyes

Cross your eyes and then look down as far as you can into your lower eyelids. Look to the right, then up into your eyelids, and then to the left. After you repeat this sequence a few times, your eyes will feel refreshed. Oh yeah, and look down at your desk as you do this move so people don't think you're even stranger than they already know you are.

Cup Your Eyes

Cup your hands, fingers together. Put them over your closed eyes, blocking out all the light. You're now in a world of velvety-smooth darkness, which is very soothing. Try not to let your hands actually touch your eyes. (If you see stars or flashes of light, your hands are pushing down on your eyes.)

Hunch and Roll Your Shoulders

While breathing in, scrunch up your shoulders as if you're trying to touch them to your ears. Then roll them back and down, breathing out. Arch your back, sitting up superstraight, as if a string is attached to the top of your head and is being pulled toward the ceiling. Then slump and round out your lower back, pushing it out toward the back of your chair. These exercises relax your upper and lower back and are especially useful if you develop a kink in your spine.

Shake Out Your Hands

You probably shake your hands out automatically when you need to get rid of writer's cramp. Go ahead and do it more consciously and more frequently. Put your hands down at your sides, hanging them below your chair seat, and shake them vigorously. Imagine all the tension and stress going out through your fingers and dropping onto the floor.

Extend and Push Out Your Legs

While you're sitting at your desk, straighten your legs out in front of you and think of pushing something away with your heels. Point your toes back toward your knees. You'll feel a stretch on the backs of your legs. Hold for a count of three and then relax.

Curtail Negative Thoughts

Any time you start panicking or thinking negative thoughts, make a conscious effort to say to yourself, *"Stop!"* Don't dwell on anything negative. Instead, switch over to a positive track.

Suppose you catch yourself thinking, "Why didn't I study this math more? I saw that formula a hundred times but can't remember it now!" Change the script to, "I got most of this math right. If I let my subconscious work on that formula, maybe I'll get it, too. No sense in worrying now. Overall, I think I'm doing great."

Visualize before the Test or during a Break

You don't want to visualize *during* the test because that just causes you to waste time and lose concentration. Before the exam, however, or at a break, practice visualization in this manner:

- ✔ Close your eyes and imagine yourself in the exam room, seeing questions you know the answers to and cheerfully punching the Confirm button.
- ✔ Picture yourself leaving the exam room, dancing in the parking lot because you got your unofficial score right off the computer, and eagerly rushing home to begin your mailbox vigil for the official good news.
- ✔ Imagine the acceptance letter you get from the graduate school of your dreams.
- ✔ Picture yourself driving a fire-engine-red Ferrari ten years from now, telling the *TIME* magazine reporter in the passenger seat that your success started with your excellent GRE scores.

The goal of this exercise is to associate the GRE with good feelings.

Index

• A •

a- prefix, 34
aberrant, 88
abeyance, 88
abhor, 248
abjure, 50, 292
abscond, 293
absolute value, 156
abstain, 248
abstemious, 88
acrid, 88
acrimonious, 290
activity, 21
acumen, 88
acute angle, 105
adage, 292
adding radicals, 139
admonition, 88
adulation, 40
advocate, 248, 292
advocated, 246
affable, 249
affect, 247
affluent, 72
agitated, 69
agoraphobic, 38
algebra
  bases, 127–130
  exponents, 127–130
  factoring, 138
  FOIL method, 137–138
  probability, 140–142
  radicals, 139–140
  ratios, 130–132
  solving for x, 136
  symbolism, 132–135
alias, 39
altercation, 37
amalgamate, 88
ambiguous, 290
ambu, 64
ameliorate, 88
amiable, 290
an- prefix, 34
analogous, 82
Analogy questions
  approaching, 30–31
  eliminating answers, 36
  format of, 29–30
  practice questions, 37–43
  review, 36
  tips for
    determining parts of speech, 31–32
    identifying common relationships, 33
    prefixes, 34
    roots, 33
    salient features of words, 32
    suffixes, 35
    verb/infinitive conversion, 31
    working backward, 33
Analytical Writing score, 11–13
Analytical Writing section
  Analyze an Argument portion
    overview, 200
    paragraph by paragraph, 205–207
  number of correct answers needed for, 13
  practice questions
    Analyze an Argument portion, 213–215
    overview, 209
    Present Your Perspective on an Issue portion, 210–213
  Present Your Perspective on an Issue portion
    overview, 199–200
    paragraph by paragraph, 203–205
    review, 205
  scores
    pointless information, 202–203
    what evaluators look for, 201–202
Analyze an Argument portion
  overview, 200
  paragraph by paragraph, 205–207
  practice questions, 213–215
  review, 207
andro, 64
angles, 105–108, 166
ante- prefix, 34
antepenultimate, 66
anthem, 293
anthro, 64
anticipating questions, 22
antonym, 38
Antonym questions
  approaching, 48
  format of, 47
  practice questions, 53–57
  review, 51
  strategy for, 49

Antonym questions *(continued)*
  tips
    connotation cards, 50
    ignoring synonyms, 49
    misreading, 50
    prefixes, 49–50
    roots, 49–50
    suffixes, 49–50
apathetic, 293
apex, 293
aphorism, 292
apogee, 293
arbitrary, 292
arbitrator, 40
arc, 124–125, 166
area
  of circle, 122, 166
  of parallelogram, 115
  of rectangle, 114
  of rhombus, 114
  of sector, 166, 186
  of squares, 114
  of trapezoid, 115
  of triangle, 111, 177
armor, 249
arrogance, 245
articulate, 69
artificial study aid (drugs), 22
ascetic, 88
assiduous, 88
astute, 88
-ate suffix, 35
attenuate, 42
attitude, 22
attitude questions, 77–79
audacious, 88
austere, 88
author perspective, 76
author questions, 80
authorization voucher, 18
aver, 88
averages
  missing term average problems, 145–147
  overview, 144–145
  weighted, 147–148

• B •

backward answers, 37
badger, 249
banal, 88, 292
bar graph, 164
barnacle, 31
base, 127–130, 195

basking, 293
befriend, 56
befuddled, 295
begrudge, 293
beguiling, 42
belli, 64
bellicose, 42
belligerent, 290
bellow, 293
bellu, 64
ben- prefix, 34
benefactor, 42
beneficiary, 248
bequest, 293
bespoke, 9
best title questions, 79–80
biological passage, 74–75, 78
blank questions, 12, 18
blatant, 88
bluestocking, 42
bolster, 88
bombastic, 88, 247
bon- prefix, 34
bowdlerize, 84
boycott, 84
breaks, 310
breathing technique, 313
bubbles, 27
bubbly, 49
bungling, 3, 249
burgeon, 88, 290

• C •

caco- prefix, 34
cacophony, 39, 88, 290
cadging, 49
calculator, 19
canceling score, 11
candid, 247
canine, 289
cantankerous, 47
carping, 70
castigate, 246
cause and effect relationship, 33
center, circle, 121
central angle, 123
certitude, 246
chaos, 70
characteristic relationship, 33
charismatic, 43
charlatan, 292
charts, mixture problem, 153–154
chatter, 289

chatterbox, 42
cheating, 309
checklist, 18
chicanery, 41–42, 88
chord, 121–122
chronology, 294
circle graph, 164
circles, 120–126, 166
circumference, 122, 166, 186
clatter, 249
claustrophobia, 38
clock, 26, 310
coda, 89
cognizant, 89
collage, 293
collection, 246
colloquial, 89
commensurate, 71
complementary angle, 106
composite numbers, 134–135, 152–153, 195
compromise, 41
computer
    skills, 308, 311
    using personal, 307–308
computerized GRE
    on-screen icons, 26–27
    rules, 26
    selecting answers, 27
    tutorials, 25–26
condign, 56
confidence building strategies, 22–23
Confirm Answer icon, 27, 310
confirm step, 310
confiscate, 248
conjecture, 294
conjunctions, 60
connotation card, 50
consecutive probabilities, multiplication of,
    141–142
consecutive terms, 180
consternation, 89
contemplate, 247
contentious, 89
contrite, 89
contumacious, 89
convoluted, 62
coordinate geometry, 120
corresponding angles, 107
counterexamples, 206
counterproductive, 248
counting number, 151
cow, 38
craven, 89, 248
creativity, 209
cred, 64

credulous, 54
cryptic, 248
cube
    total surface area of, 119
    volume of, 118
curtail, 69, 248
cuticle, 249
cygnet, 246
cylinder
    total surface area of, 119
    volume of, 118

• D •

dashiki, 32
de, 64
dearth of, 72
debacle, 21
debunk, 246
decagon, 116–117
decimals
    adding, 159
    converting percentages to, 149
    dividing, 159–160
    multiplying, 160
    subtracting, 159
decorum, 89
degree measure of arc, 125
dehydrate, 248
deleterious, 89
delineate, 89
denominator, 140
denounce, 246, 248
deride, 89, 248
derision, 89
derogate, 42
descriptive sentence, 30
desiccate, 41
desultorily, 72
desultory, 89
detail questions, 80
detractors, 248
detritus, 30
diameter, 121–122
diatribe, 89
diction, 202
didactic, 89
diesel, 84
dilatory, 89, 290
DIRT formula, 143–168
disconcert, 89
discourse, 246
disheartened, 296
disparaging, 39, 99

disparate, 294
dissembling, 20, 89
disseminate, 246
dissolution, 89
distance, 143–144
divest, 89
dividing radicals, 139–140
divisor, 160
divulge, 71, 89
docile, 32
dogmatic, 83
dour, 55
draconian, 84
drawer, 249
drugs, 22
dubious, 89, 247
dupe, 40, 89
duplicity, 40, 71
dynamic, 39

• **E** •

eating, 21
ebullient, 64, 79, 89
ecstatic, 293
edges, cube, 118
effervescent, 49, 54
efficacious, 72
efficacy, 89
effrontery, 71, 89, 293
-efy suffix, 35
egregious, 71, 185
egress, 89
elegy, 39, 89
elicit, 89
elucidate, 289
emaciated, 42, 293
embellish, 89
empirical, 101
emulate, 89
enervate, 20, 89
engender, 89
enigma, 64
enigmatic, 64
ennui, 89
ephemeral, 89
epilogue, 293
epithet, 42, 249
eponym, 84
equal appearance, 173
equanimity, 89
equating section, 13
equiangular triangle, 108
equilateral triangle, 108

equivocal, 89, 291
eradicate, 90
eructation, 39
erudite, 42, 90, 245
erudition, 3
eschew, 90
esoteric, 90
etiquette, 61
-ette suffix, 35
eu- prefix, 34
euphonious, 294
ex, 64
exacerbate, 56, 69, 90, 99, 292
exasperate, 248
exception questions, 80–81
exculpate, 41, 90
exercise, 21
exhaustively, 292
exigency, 90
Exit Section icon, 27
exonerate, 41
exorcise, 293
expatiate, 90
experimental section, 13
exponent, 127–130, 167, 195
exterior angle, 108–109, 194
extirpate, 90, 292
extroverted, 247
eye relaxation technique, 314

• **F** •

facetious, 90
fact questions, 80
factoring, 138
fallacious, 90
fanaticism, 40
fatuous, 90
fawn, 289
fecklessness, 293
fees, GRE, 19
ferret out, 71
fervor, 90
fickle, 293
fidelity, 292
first sentence, 203
flamboyant, 294
flashcards, 35, 50, 87, 289
fledgling, 90
fly-by-night, 292
FOIL method, 137–138, 167
foment, 90
foreign, 290
forestall, 90

fractions
  adding, 160–161
  converting percentages to, 149
  dividing, 162
  mixed numbers, 162
  multiplying, 161
  probabilities and, 140–141
  subtracting, 160–161
frank, 248
froward, 50
frugal, 90
fulminate, 90
function, 135
fundament, 295

• G •

gainsay, 90
garble, 290
garrulous, 90
genesis, 293
geometry problems
  angles, 105–108
  circles, 120–126
  coordinate geometry, 120
  polygons, 116–117
  quadrilaterals, 114–116
  total surface area, 119
  triangles
    area of, 111
    overview, 108–109
    perimeter of, 111
    Pythagorean theorem, 112–113
    similar figures, 110–111
  volume, 118
germane, 90
gnos, 65
goad, 90
grammar, 202
grandiloquent, 90
graphs, 164–166, 167
GRE
  breakdown, 10–11
  computerized
    on-screen icons, 26–27
    rules, 26
    selecting answers, 27
    tutorials, 25–26
  false rumors about
    bringing personal laptop, 308
    computer geniuses, 308
    high school SAT score, 306–307
    IQ, 306–307
    missing first few questions, 305

passing certain classes to take test, 307
    passing score, 305
    retaking test, 306
    studying for test, 306
    taking test on personal computer at home, 307
  intermissions, 14–15
  overview, 9
  repeating, 20–21
  scores
    guessing, 12
    median, 12
    number of correct answers needed for, 12–13
    ranges, 11–12
  unscored (experimental or equating) section, 13–14
GRE Information and Registration Bulletin, 9
greater to lesser relationship, 33
greg, 65
gregarious, 90
grouse, 70
guessing, 12, 49
guileless, 90
gullible, 90
gyn, 65

• H •

hackneyed, 290
halcyon, 90
hand relaxation technique, 314
haphazard, 72, 290, 292
hapless, 290
harangue, 90
harbinger, 90
hardy, 247
hasty, 72
head relaxation technique, 313
health
  activity, 21
  artificial study aids (drugs), 22
  eating, 21
  relaxation, 21–22
heedlessly, 72
height, triangle, 111
heirloom, 293
Help icon, 27
heptagon, 116–117
heresy, 90
heretic, 42
hesitate, 247
hexagon, 116–117
histrionic, 56
homogeneous, 90
humanities passage, 76, 78

humor, 203
hydrate, 248
hydrophobia, 38
hyperbole, 90
hypotenuse, 112, 194
hypothesize, 294

• *I* •

iconoclast, 90
icons
  on-screen, 26–27
  used in book, 5
identical quantities, 177
-ify suffix, 35
ignominious, 90
illicit, 249
-illo suffix, 35
im- prefix, 34
imaginary number, 152
imbecile, 43
immaterial, 293
immense, 72
immutable, 53
impartial, 72
impecunious, 90
impede, 90, 248
imperious, 90
imperturbable, 90
impervious, 91
impetuous, 290
implacable, 39
implicit, 91
importune, 91
impugn, 91
in- prefix, 34
inadvertently, 91
inane, 91
inauspicious, 294
incensed, 69, 294
inchoate, 91
incision, 248
incite, 293
incongruous, 291
indifferently, 292
indigenous, 245, 290
indolence, 64, 91
ineffable, 91
inept, 3, 245
inert, 91
inexorable, 91
infinitive/verb conversion, 31
infuriate, 248
innocuous, 39, 91

innovative, 249
inscribed angle, 123
insolvent, 72
insouciant, 91
integer, 151
interest problems, 154–155
interior angle, 109, 194
interminable, 292
intermissions, 14–15
intermittent, 292
international students, 14, 204
intransigent, 247
intrepid, 91
inure, 91
invidious, 91
IQ, 307
irascible, 55, 91
ironhanded, 292
ironic, 70
irrational number, 152
irritate, 249
isosceles triangle, 108
-ist suffix, 35
itinerant, 91
-ity suffix, 35
-ize suffix, 35

• *J* •

jitterbug, 249

• *K* •

kudos, 293

• *L* •

lackadaisically, 292
laconic, 91
lampoon, 70, 248
lapse, 293
latent, 91
laud, 56, 70, 248
laudable, 91
learning disabilities, 19
leg relaxation technique, 314
length measurements, 158
length of arc, 125, 166
licentious, 91
line graph, 164
linear algebraic equations, 167–168

line-referenced questions, 81–82
lix, 65
loc, 65
location relationship, 33
log, 65
logical content, essay, 201
long-range study program, 306
loq, 65
loquacious, 47, 54, 91
losing concentration, 309
low, 289
lowest common denominator, 161
luc, 65
lucid, 91, 247, 289
lugubrious, 64
lum, 65
lus, 65
lustrous, 290

• *M* •

magnanimity, 91
main idea questions, 79–80
mal- prefix, 34
malingerer, 42, 91
malleable, 91
math problems
  absolute value, 156
  algebra
    bases, 127–130
    exponents, 127–130
    factoring, 138
    FOIL method, 137–138
    probability, 140–142
    radicals, 139–140
    ratios, 130–132
    solving for x, 136
    symbolism, 132–135
  angles, 166
  averages
    missing term problems, 145–147
    overview, 144–145
    weighted, 147–148
  circles, 166
  decimals, 159–160
  DIRT formula, 143–168
  exponents, 167
  FOIL method, 167
  fractions
    adding, 160–161
    dividing, 162
    mixed numbers, 162
    multiplying, 161
    subtracting, 160–161
  geometry
    angles, 105–108
    circles, 120–126
    coordinate geometry, 120
    polygons, 116–117
    quadrilaterals, 114–116
    total surface area, 119
    triangles, 108–113
    volume, 118
  graphs, 164–166, 167
  interest problems, 154–155
  linear algebraic equations, 167–168
  mixture problems, 153–154
  number sets, 151–152
  order of operations, 157
  percentage
    converting to decimals or fractions, 149
    increase/decrease, 149–151
    overview, 148
  prime and composite numbers, 152–153
  Pythagorean theorem, 167
  ratios, 168
  square roots, 168
  statistics, 162–163
  symbolism, 168
  units of measurement, 157–159
  work problems, 155–156
Math score, 11–13
Math section, 13
Math subtest, 10, 14
mausoleum, 84
maverick, 84, 91
meander, 248
measurement, units of, 157–159
medical, 289
member to group relationship, 33
memory aids, 18, 157
mendacious, 55, 91
mendicant, 55
MENSA, 307
mercenary, 290
merriment, 38
mesmerizing, 99, 184
meta, 65
metamorphosis, 91
meticulous, 72, 91
minuscule, 289
misanthrope, 91
miser, 42
misnomer, 37, 73
missing questions, 305
missing term average problems, 145–147
mistakes, 20
mitigate, 56, 91
mixture problems, 153–154

mnemonic, 157
Moby Dick, 67
modicum, 91
mollify, 91
morbidity, 70
mordant, 91, 290
moribund, 55
morose, 91, 292
morph, 65
mortgage, 249
multifaceted, 248
multiplying radicals, 139–140
mundane, 71, 91
music, 87–88
mut, 65

• N •

nadir, 293
narcissist, 43
nascency, 293
ne- prefix, 34
nefarious, 92
negate, 92
negative numbers, 177
negative questions, 80–81
negative-attitude words, 78
neophyte, 92
neutral attitude (tone), 78
Next icon, 27
nibble, 39
nicotine, 84
nonagon, 116–117
nonconsecutive terms, 180
not drawn to scale problems, 173–174
noxious, 57
number sets, 151–152
numerator, 141
numerical coefficient, 129–130, 187
nutrition, 21

• O •

obdurate, 92, 294
obfuscate, 92
objective, 78, 249
obsequious, 43, 92
obsessing, 310
obstinate, 294
obtuse, 291
obtuse angle, 106
obviate, 69, 92
octagon, 116–117
odious, 92

officious, 92
on-screen icon, 26–27
onus, 92
opaque, 54
opposites relationship, 33
opprobrium, 92
orchestrate, 245
order of operations, 157
organization, essay, 201–203
oscillate, 92
ostentation, 92
-ous suffix, 35
outmoded, 294
overall score, 14

• P •

pac, 65
painstaking, 72
palliate, 56
pallid, 290
palpable, 92
panegyric, 293
panicking, 310
paragon, 92
paragraphs, length of, 209
parallelogram, 115
parentheses, 129
parsimonious, 92, 187
part to whole relationship, 33
partisan, 92
parts of speech, 31–32
path, 65
pathos, 92
paucity, 66, 92
peccadillo, 39
pecuniary, 72
pedant, 42
pelt, 289
PEMDAS (Please Excuse My Dear Aunt Sally), 157
penchant, 92
penny-pincher, 42
pensive, 290
pentagon, 116–117
penurious, 72, 92
percentage
    converting to decimals or fractions, 149
    increase/decrease, 149–151
    overview, 148
peremptory, 32
perennial, 92
perfidy, 38, 92
perimeter of triangle, 111
perjury, 293
permeable, 92

pernicious, 92
perspective, 23
perturb, 41
pervasive, 92
phlegmatic, 39, 55, 92
phon, 65
photo ID, 18
physical disabilities, 19
physical science passage, 74–75, 78
picayune, 248
pie graph, 164
pious, 92
plac, 65
placate, 92, 292
placid, 69
platitude, 92
plaudits, 293
Please Excuse My Dear Aunt Sally (PEMDAS), 157
plethora, 3, 33, 92, 187
point of origin, 120
polygons, 116–117
porous, 92
portend, 92
poseur, 32
position relationship, 33
positive attitude, 22, 78
positive reciprocal, 167
post- prefix, 34
practice exam 1
    Analytical Writing section
        Analyze an Argument portion, 228–232
        Present Your Perspective on an Issue portion, 223–227
    answer key, 243
    answer sheet, 221–222
    answers and explanations
        Analytical Writing section, 257
        Math section, 250–257
        Verbal section, 245–249
    Math section, 239–242
    overview, 219–220
    Verbal section, 233–238
practice exam 2
    Analytical Writing section
        Analyze an Argument portion, 270–276
        Present Your Perspective on an Issue portion, 263–269
    answer key, 287
    answer sheet, 261–262
    answers and explanations
        Analytical Writing section, 301
        Math section, 294–301
        Verbal section, 289–294
    Math section, 283–286
    overview, 259–260
    Verbal section, 277–282

practice questions
    analogies, 37–43
    Analytical Writing section
        Analyze an Argument portion, 213–215
        overview, 209
        Present Your Perspective on an Issue portion, 210–213
    antonyms, 53–57
    Problem Solving questions, 193–195
    Quantitative Comparison questions, 183–187
    Reading Comprehension questions, 97–102
    sentence completions, 69–72
pragmatic, 92
precarious, 92
precipitate, 72, 92
precocious, 92, 247
prefixes
    analogies, 34
    antonyms, 49–50
    sentence completions, 64–66
prescience, 92
Present Your Perspective on an Issue portion
    overview, 199–200
    paragraph by paragraph, 203–205
    practice questions
        answer explanations, 210
        sample answers, 210–213
    review, 205
prevaricate, 93
pride, 289
prime numbers, 134–135, 152–153, 187, 195
pro, 65
probability, 140–142
Problem Solving questions
    approaching, 189–190
    practice questions, 193–195
    review, 191
    tips, 190–191
proclivity, 93
prodigious, 93
prodigy, 42
professorial, 289
profound, 93
prognosticate, 71, 248
prohibited items, 19
proliferate, 41, 93
prolific, 245
prologue, 293
propensity, 93
prophet, 40
prudence, 93
puerile, 93
pug, 66
pugilist, 42
pugnacious, 93
puissant, 57

pulchritudinous, 49
pundit, 293
pungent, 93
purpose or function relationship, 33
pusillanimous, 93
pyromaniac, 39
Pythagorean theorem, 112–113, 167, 187, 194

• Q •

QC (Quantitative Comparison) questions
  approaching, 172
  format of, 171
  practice questions, 183–187
  review, 181
  tips
    artistic abilities, 175
    avoiding distraction, 176–177
    columns, 177–178
    equal appearances, 173
    identical quantities, 177
    multiple variables, 180
    plugging in one hundred, 179
    sacred six, 178–179
    scale, 173–174
quack, 292
quadrilateral
  overview, 114–115
  shaded-area problems, 115–116
  strange, 115
quagmire, 49
qualm, 93
Quantitative Comparison questions. *See* QC
  questions
Quantitative subtest, 10, 14
quantities, measurements of, 157
quarter, 246
querulous, 247
questions, breakdown, 11, 311
quibble, 93
quiescence, 93
quisling, 84
Quit Test icon, 27
quitting, 26
quiver, 246
quixotic, 93, 100

• R •

radicals, 139–140
radius, 121
rash, 72
rate, 143–144

rational number, 151–152
ratios, 110, 112–113, 130–132, 168, 193
Reading Comprehension questions
  passages
    biological and physical science passages,
      74–75
    humanities passages, 76
    social sciences passages, 75–76
  practice questions, 97–102
  recognizing, 73–74
  review, 84–85
  traps, tips and tricks
    avoiding drama, 83–84
    avoiding negativity, 83
    key words, 83
  types of
    attitude or tone, 77–79
    detail or fact, 80
    extending author's reasoning, 82–83
    main idea or best title, 79–80
    negative or exception, 80–81
    Roman numeral, 81
    text-referenced, 81–82
  vocabulary
    memorizing most common words, 88–96
    studying, 87–88
Reading Comprehension section, 14
real number, 152
recall, 248
recant, 93
reciprocal, 128, 167
recluse, 42
reclusive, 293
recondite, 93
rectangle, 114
rectangular solid
  total surface area of, 119
  volumes of, 118
recuperate, 53
red herring, 293
redress, 93
reflex angle, 107
refulgent, 56
refutation, 206, 294
refute, 70, 246
regular hexagon, 194
regular polygon, 116–117
relaxation techniques
  breathing, 313
  eyes, 314
  hands, 314
  head, 313
  importance of, 21–22
  legs, 314
  negative thoughts, 315

scalp, 314
  shoulders, 314
  visualization, 315
renegade, 293
renege, 195, 245
repress, 247
reprobate, 93
reproof, 37, 293
repudiate, 93
rescind, 93
reservoir, 33
resilience, 70
respite, 93
retaking GRE, 20–21, 306
reticent, 71, 93
retrospection, 40
reverent, 93
rhetoric, 93
rhombus, 114
right angle, 106
Roman numeral questions, 81
Romance languages, 14
roots
  analogies, 33
  antonyms, 49–50
  sentence completions, 64–66
roots, prefixes, and suffixes (RPS), 49, 63
rout, 93
rubble, 30
ruminate, 93
rushing, 310
rustic, 57
ruth, 40
ruthless, 40

• *S* •

Sacred Six, 178–180
saga, 245
sagacious, 93, 245
sagacity, 3
sage, 293
salacious, 57, 93
salubrious, 55, 93
sanction, 41, 93
sanguinary, 62, 292
sanguine, 93, 292
sartorial, 289
SAT score, 306–307
satiate, 93
saturnine, 290
savor, 93
saxophone, 84
scale, 173–174

scalene triangle, 109
scalp relaxation technique, 314
scanty, 72
scatological humor, 203
scheduling test, 9, 311
scien, 66
scores
  Analytical Writing section
    pointless information, 202–203
    what evaluators look for, 201–202
  essay, 202
  guessing, 12
  median, 12
  number of correct answers needed for
    Analytical Writing, 13
    Math, 13
    overview, 12
    Verbal, 13
  passing, 305
  previous, 21
  ranges, 11–12
scratch paper, 18–19, 189, 191
screech, 37
scrolling, 26
secrete, 93
sections
  breakdown by, 10
  number of correct answers needed, 13
  unscored, 13–14
sector, 125–126, 166, 186
sedulous, 93
seethe, 93
select, 247
selecting answers, 27
seminal, 93
Sentence Completion questions
  practice questions, 69–72
  prefixes, 64–66
  recognizing, 59
  review, 66
  roots, 64–66
  suffixes, 64–66
  tips
    connections count, 62
    dissection, 62–63
    guessing, 63–64
  when unsure about
    inserting answer choices, 61
    predicting words to fit blanks, 60–61
    reading entire sentence, 60
sentence length, 205
sentimental, 293
serendipitous, 55
serpentine, 55
sesquipedalianism, 64, 202

shaded-area problems, 115–116
shard, 94
sheaf, 246
shirk, 94
shoddy, 94
shoulders relaxation technique, 314
shrapnel, 84
silhouette, 84
similar figures, 110–111
simony, 84
sinuous, 94
skeptic, 94
skeptical, 54
skimming text, 73
skittish, 94
skull, 249
slander, 94
slang, 203
sliver, 249
sloth, 94
snacks, 15
social sciences passage, 75–76, 78
solecism, 70
solicitous, 94
solitary, 293
solving for x, 136
som, 66
son, 66
songs, 87–88
sonorous, 94
sop, 66
soporific, 94
specious, 94
spelling, 50, 202
spendthrift, 94
spurious, 94
square, 114
square roots, 168
stagger, 245
statistics
    median, 162–163
    mode, 163
    range, 163
steadfast, 247
stentorian, 94, 289
stifle, 293
stigma, 94
stint, 94
stipulate, 94
stoicism, 71
stolid, 94
straight angle, 106
striated, 94
strut, 94
stymie, 293

subterfuge, 94
subtracting radical, 139
suffixes
    analogies, 35
    antonyms, 49–50
    sentence completions, 64–66
summation, 70
supercilious, 64, 94
superfluity, 187
superfluous, 94
supersede, 94
supine, 94
supplant, 50
supple, 292
Supplement for Test Takers with Disabilities
        brochure, 19
supplementary angle, 106
suppress, 69
surreptitious, 292
swagger, 245
swiftly, 72
swindle, 41, 245
sycophant, 42
symbolism, 132–135, 168, 194–195
synonym relationship, 33
synonyms, 49

• T •

tacit, 94
taciturn, 42, 47, 71, 94
tamper, 292
tangential, 94
tantamount, 94
tawdry, 94, 247
temerity, 94
tempestuous, 94
tenacious, 94
tenuous, 94
tepid, 55, 94
test aids, 19
testator, 293
testing center, 18
text-referenced questions, 81–82
thrall, 94
three axes line graph, 164
thwart, 94
time, DIRT formula, 143–144
Time icon, 26, 27
timing
    measurements, 158
    requirements, 3
    tips, 17–18

titillate, 95
toady, 42
tome, 293
tone questions, 77–79
tonsorial, 289
topic sentence, 79, 203
torpid, 95
tortuous, 95
total surface area (TSA), 119
tout, 248
tractable, 95
transgression, 39, 95
transitioning statements, 204
transmute, 95
transparent, 95
transpire, 95
transversal, 107
trapezoid, 115
trepidation, 95
triangle
  area of, 111
  interior angles of, 117
  overview, 108–109
  perimeter of, 111
  Pythagorean theorem, 112–113
  similar figures, 110–111
trinket, 249
truculence, 95
TSA (total surface area), 119
tumultuous, 40
turbid, 289
turgid, 289
tutelage, 95
tutorial, 25–26, 311
two axes line graph, 164
tyro, 95

• U •

ubiquitous, 95, 247
umbrage, 95
unanswered questions, 12, 18
unassuaged, 95
uncouth, 95, 290
undermine, 95
unequivocal, 291
unerringly, 95
unfazed, 69
ungainly, 95
unison, 95
units of measurement, 157–159
unruly, 95, 247
unscored section, 13–14
untenable, 95

upbraid, 95
usurper, 293

• V •

vacillate, 95, 247
vacuum, 33
vagabond, 95
vainglory, 95
valorous, 95
vantage, 95
vapid, 95, 291
variegated, 95
vehement, 95, 292
venerate, 95
veracious, 95
veracity, 245
Verbal section, 13
verbiage, 95
verb/infinitive conversion, 31
verbose, 95
verify, 293
vertical angles, 107
vestigial, 72
viable, 55
vicissitude, 95
viper, 289
visage, 69
viscous, 95
visualization relaxation technique, 309, 315
vital, 55
vituperative, 95, 249
vivacious, 289
vocabulary
  grouping, 48
  and international students, 14
  memorizing most common words, 88–96
  from *Moby Dick*, 67
  studying, 87–88
vociferous, 96
volatile, 96
volume, 111, 118
voracious, 292
votary, 32

• W •

wag, 293
waltz, 37
warranted, 96
wary, 96
weighted average, 147–148
welter, 96

wheedle, 246
whimsical, 96
whole number, 151
whorl, 96
widespread, 292
wince, 38
winsome, 96
wither, 290
word problems, 14
work problems, 155–156
wrath, 249
wreak, 96
writhe, 96

x-axis, 120

y-axis, 120
yore, 96

• Z •

zealot, 96
zealous, 40
zeitgeist, 96

Notes

Notes

angles less than 90° — acute

2 angles that = 90° = complementary

angle greater than 90° = obtuse

180° angle = straight angle

2 angles = 180° = supplementary

angle greater than 180° less than 360° = reflex

Median — middle # when sequence is
 arranged in order

Mode — most used number

Range — distance from greatest to smallest

Notes

Notes

BUSINESS, CAREERS & PERSONAL FINANCE

Accounting For Dummies, 4th Edition*
978-0-470-24600-9

Bookkeeping Workbook For Dummies†
978-0-470-16983-4

Commodities For Dummies
978-0-470-04928-0

Doing Business in China For Dummies
978-0-470-04929-7

E-Mail Marketing For Dummies
978-0-470-19087-6

Job Interviews For Dummies, 3rd Edition*†
978-0-470-17748-8

Personal Finance Workbook For Dummies*†
978-0-470-09933-9

Real Estate License Exams For Dummies
978-0-7645-7623-2

Six Sigma For Dummies
978-0-7645-6798-8

Small Business Kit For Dummies, 2nd Edition*†
978-0-7645-5984-6

Telephone Sales For Dummies
978-0-470-16836-3

BUSINESS PRODUCTIVITY & MICROSOFT OFFICE

Access 2007 For Dummies
978-0-470-03649-5

Excel 2007 For Dummies
978-0-470-03737-9

Office 2007 For Dummies
978-0-470-00923-9

Outlook 2007 For Dummies
978-0-470-03830-7

PowerPoint 2007 For Dummies
978-0-470-04059-1

Project 2007 For Dummies
978-0-470-03651-8

QuickBooks 2008 For Dummies
978-0-470-18470-7

Quicken 2008 For Dummies
978-0-470-17473-9

Salesforce.com For Dummies, 2nd Edition
978-0-470-04893-1

Word 2007 For Dummies
978-0-470-03658-7

EDUCATION, HISTORY, REFERENCE & TEST PREPARATION

African American History For Dummies
978-0-7645-5469-8

Algebra For Dummies
978-0-7645-5325-7

Algebra Workbook For Dummies
978-0-7645-8467-1

Art History For Dummies
978-0-470-09910-0

ASVAB For Dummies, 2nd Edition
978-0-470-10671-6

British Military History For Dummies
978-0-470-03213-8

Calculus For Dummies
978-0-7645-2498-1

Canadian History For Dummies, 2nd Edition
978-0-470-83656-9

Geometry Workbook For Dummies
978-0-471-79940-5

The SAT I For Dummies, 6th Edition
978-0-7645-7193-0

Series 7 Exam For Dummies
978-0-470-09932-2

World History For Dummies
978-0-7645-5242-7

FOOD, GARDEN, HOBBIES & HOME

Bridge For Dummies, 2nd Edition
978-0-471-92426-5

Coin Collecting For Dummies, 2nd Edition
978-0-470-22275-1

Cooking Basics For Dummies, 3rd Edition
978-0-7645-7206-7

Drawing For Dummies
978-0-7645-5476-6

Etiquette For Dummies, 2nd Edition
978-0-470-10672-3

Gardening Basics For Dummies*†
978-0-470-03749-2

Knitting Patterns For Dummies
978-0-470-04556-5

Living Gluten-Free For Dummies†
978-0-471-77383-2

Painting Do-It-Yourself For Dummies
978-0-470-17533-0

HEALTH, SELF HELP, PARENTING & PETS

Anger Management For Dummies
978-0-470-03715-7

Anxiety & Depression Workbook For Dummies
978-0-7645-9793-0

Dieting For Dummies, 2nd Edition
978-0-7645-4149-0

Dog Training For Dummies, 2nd Edition
978-0-7645-8418-3

Horseback Riding For Dummies
978-0-470-09719-9

Infertility For Dummies†
978-0-470-11518-3

Meditation For Dummies with CD-ROM, 2nd Edition
978-0-471-77774-8

Post-Traumatic Stress Disorder For Dummies
978-0-470-04922-8

Puppies For Dummies, 2nd Edition
978-0-470-03717-1

Thyroid For Dummies, 2nd Edition†
978-0-471-78755-6

Type 1 Diabetes For Dummies*†
978-0-470-17811-9

* Separate Canadian edition also available
† Separate U.K. edition also available

Available wherever books are sold. For more information or to order direct: U.S. customers visit www.dummies.com or call 1-877-762-2974.
U.K. customers visit www.wileyeurope.com or call (0)1243 843291. Canadian customers visit www.wiley.ca or call 1-800-567-4797.

INTERNET & DIGITAL MEDIA

AdWords For Dummies
978-0-470-15252-2

Blogging For Dummies, 2nd Edition
978-0-470-23017-6

**Digital Photography All-in-One
Desk Reference For Dummies, 3rd Edition**
978-0-470-03743-0

Digital Photography For Dummies, 5th Edition
978-0-7645-9802-9

**Digital SLR Cameras & Photography
For Dummies, 2nd Edition**
978-0-470-14927-0

**eBay Business All-in-One Desk Reference
For Dummies**
978-0-7645-8438-1

eBay For Dummies, 5th Edition*
978-0-470-04529-9

eBay Listings That Sell For Dummies
978-0-471-78912-3

Facebook For Dummies
978-0-470-26273-3

The Internet For Dummies, 11th Edition
978-0-470-12174-0

Investing Online For Dummies, 5th Edition
978-0-7645-8456-5

iPod & iTunes For Dummies, 5th Edition
978-0-470-17474-6

MySpace For Dummies
978-0-470-09529-4

Podcasting For Dummies
978-0-471-74898-4

**Search Engine Optimization
For Dummies, 2nd Edition**
978-0-471-97998-2

Second Life For Dummies
978-0-470-18025-9

**Starting an eBay Business For Dummies,
3rd Edition†**
978-0-470-14924-9

GRAPHICS, DESIGN & WEB DEVELOPMENT

**Adobe Creative Suite 3 Design Premium
All-in-One Desk Reference For Dummies**
978-0-470-11724-8

**Adobe Web Suite CS3 All-in-One Desk
Reference For Dummies**
978-0-470-12099-6

AutoCAD 2008 For Dummies
978-0-470-11650-0

**Building a Web Site For Dummies,
3rd Edition**
978-0-470-14928-7

**Creating Web Pages All-in-One Desk
Reference For Dummies, 3rd Edition**
978-0-470-09629-1

**Creating Web Pages For Dummies,
8th Edition**
978-0-470-08030-6

Dreamweaver CS3 For Dummies
978-0-470-11490-2

Flash CS3 For Dummies
978-0-470-12100-9

Google SketchUp For Dummies
978-0-470-13744-4

InDesign CS3 For Dummies
978-0-470-11865-8

**Photoshop CS3 All-in-One
Desk Reference For Dummies**
978-0-470-11195-6

Photoshop CS3 For Dummies
978-0-470-11193-2

Photoshop Elements 5 For Dummies
978-0-470-09810-3

SolidWorks For Dummies
978-0-7645-9555-4

Visio 2007 For Dummies
978-0-470-08983-5

Web Design For Dummies, 2nd Edition
978-0-471-78117-2

Web Sites Do-It-Yourself For Dummies
978-0-470-16903-2

Web Stores Do-It-Yourself For Dummies
978-0-470-17443-2

LANGUAGES, RELIGION & SPIRITUALITY

Arabic For Dummies
978-0-471-77270-5

Chinese For Dummies, Audio Set
978-0-470-12766-7

French For Dummies
978-0-7645-5193-2

German For Dummies
978-0-7645-5195-6

Hebrew For Dummies
978-0-7645-5489-6

Ingles Para Dummies
978-0-7645-5427-8

Italian For Dummies, Audio Set
978-0-470-09586-7

Italian Verbs For Dummies
978-0-471-77389-4

Japanese For Dummies
978-0-7645-5429-2

Latin For Dummies
978-0-7645-5431-5

Portuguese For Dummies
978-0-471-78738-9

Russian For Dummies
978-0-471-78001-4

Spanish Phrases For Dummies
978-0-7645-7204-3

Spanish For Dummies
978-0-7645-5194-9

Spanish For Dummies, Audio Set
978-0-470-09585-0

The Bible For Dummies
978-0-7645-5296-0

Catholicism For Dummies
978-0-7645-5391-2

The Historical Jesus For Dummies
978-0-470-16785-4

Islam For Dummies
978-0-7645-5503-9

**Spirituality For Dummies,
2nd Edition**
978-0-470-19142-2

NETWORKING AND PROGRAMMING

ASP.NET 3.5 For Dummies
978-0-470-19592-5

C# 2008 For Dummies
978-0-470-19109-5

Hacking For Dummies, 2nd Edition
978-0-470-05235-8

Home Networking For Dummies, 4th Edition
978-0-470-11806-1

Java For Dummies, 4th Edition
978-0-470-08716-9

**Microsoft® SQL Server™ 2008 All-in-One
Desk Reference For Dummies**
978-0-470-17954-3

**Networking All-in-One Desk Reference
For Dummies, 2nd Edition**
978-0-7645-9939-2

**Networking For Dummies,
8th Edition**
978-0-470-05620-2

SharePoint 2007 For Dummies
978-0-470-09941-4

**Wireless Home Networking
For Dummies, 2nd Edition**
978-0-471-74940-0

OPERATING SYSTEMS & COMPUTER BASICS

iMac For Dummies, 5th Edition
978-0-7645-8458-9

Laptops For Dummies, 2nd Edition
978-0-470-05432-1

Linux For Dummies, 8th Edition
978-0-470-11649-4

MacBook For Dummies
978-0-470-04859-7

Mac OS X Leopard All-in-One Desk Reference For Dummies
978-0-470-05434-5

Mac OS X Leopard For Dummies
978-0-470-05433-8

Macs For Dummies, 9th Edition
978-0-470-04849-8

PCs For Dummies, 11th Edition
978-0-470-13728-4

Windows® Home Server For Dummies
978-0-470-18592-6

Windows Server 2008 For Dummies
978-0-470-18043-3

Windows Vista All-in-One Desk Reference For Dummies
978-0-471-74941-7

Windows Vista For Dummies
978-0-471-75421-3

Windows Vista Security For Dummies
978-0-470-11805-4

SPORTS, FITNESS & MUSIC

Coaching Hockey For Dummies
978-0-470-83685-9

Coaching Soccer For Dummies
978-0-471-77381-8

Fitness For Dummies, 3rd Edition
978-0-7645-7851-9

Football For Dummies, 3rd Edition
978-0-470-12536-6

GarageBand For Dummies
978-0-7645-7323-1

Golf For Dummies, 3rd Edition
978-0-471-76871-5

Guitar For Dummies, 2nd Edition
978-0-7645-9904-0

Home Recording For Musicians For Dummies, 2nd Edition
978-0-7645-8884-6

iPod & iTunes For Dummies, 5th Edition
978-0-470-17474-6

Music Theory For Dummies
978-0-7645-7838-0

Stretching For Dummies
978-0-470-06741-3

Get smart @ dummies.com®

- **Find a full list of Dummies titles**
- **Look into loads of FREE on-site articles**
- **Sign up for FREE eTips e-mailed to you weekly**
- **See what other products carry the Dummies name**
- **Shop directly from the Dummies bookstore**
- **Enter to win new prizes every month!**

* Separate Canadian edition also available
† Separate U.K. edition also available

Available wherever books are sold. For more information or to order direct: U.S. customers visit www.dummies.com or call 1-877-762-2974.
U.K. customers visit www.wileyeurope.com or call (0) 1243 843291. Canadian customers visit www.wiley.ca or call 1-800-567-4797.

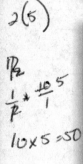